The Global Translator's Handbook

The Global Translator's Handbook

Morry Sofer

TAYLOR TRADE PUBLISHING

Lanham • New York • Boulder • Toronto • Plymouth, UK

Published by Taylor Trade Publishing
An imprint of The Rowman & Littlefield Publishing Group, Inc.
4501 Forbes Boulevard, Suite 200, Lanham, Maryland 20706
www.rowman.com

10 Thornbury Road, Plymouth PL6 7PP, United Kingdom

Distributed by National Book Network

British Library Cataloguing in Publication Information Available

Library of Congress Cataloging-in-Publication Data
Sofer, Morry.
  The global translator's handbook / Morry Sofer.
    p. cm.
  Includes bibliographical references and index.
  ISBN 978-1-58979-759-8 (pbk. : alk. paper) — ISBN 978-1-58979-760-4 (electronic)
  1. Translating and interpreting—Handbooks, manuals, etc.   2. Translating and interpreting—Vocational guidance.   3. Translating services.   4. Machine translating.
I. Title.
  P306.2.S667 2013
  418'.02—dc23

                                                                    2012027715

♾™ The paper used in this publication meets the minimum requirements of American National Standard for Information Sciences—Permanence of Paper for Printed Library Materials, ANSI/NISO Z39.48-1992.

Printed in the United States of America

Contents

CONTENTS

CONTENTS

Acknowledgments

The first seven editions of this book attest to its continued popularity among translators everywhere. Translators-to-be as well as well-established and highly regarded translators all over the world have used and praised this book. To all of them, my heartfelt thanks. Without them, there would be no seventh revised edition.

I have not attempted to cite in the text all the authorities and sources consulted in the preparation of this handbook because of space limitations. Literally hundreds of people have been consulted, and all of them deserve my sincere thanks. A particular word of thanks to all those who sent us comments on the previous editions, helping us update and improve each subsequent edition.

I would like to thank the staff of Schreiber Translations Inc. for all the help, especially Irina Knizhnik, who advised me on Russian, Japanese, and Chinese dictionaries; Margaret Flynn, who helped edit the second revised edition; Henri-Axel Carlander for helping me update the chapter on translators and the latest digital technology; and particularly Marla Schulman, without whose support I would still be laboring on this project. Also, my heartfelt thanks to Dan Poynter, the patron saint of independent publishers, without whose wise and practical words this book and this publisher would still be in the realm of dreams.

Over the years, I have had the great privilege of working with some truly phenomenal translators. I will mention three. The first is the late George Kent, originally from Ajo, Arizona. With no linguistic background, George successfully cracked the codes of all European languages, and he could translate all of them with equal ease. The second is Gerald Geiger, originally from Austria, who can still tackle any subject in German or in any Romance language with a speed that is unmatched among translators. He served the Allies well in World War II, helped liberate Dachau, and was awarded the Legion of Honor medal by the French. The third is Irinia Knizhnik, originally from Ukraine, whose linguistic prowess stretches from Far East to Slavic and other languages, and whose English when she arrived in the United States was better than most of us. Do they still make them like this?

Finally, a word of thanks to the hundreds of colleagues, past and present, from whom I learned everything I know about translation, one of the most fascinating activities I have ever had the privilege to pursue.

M.S.

Warning-Disclaimer

This book is designed to provide information in regard to the subject matter covered. It is sold with the understanding that the publisher and author are not engaged in rendering legal, accounting, or other professional services. If legal or other expert assistance is required, the services of a competent professional should be sought.

It is not the purpose of this handbook to reprint all the information that is otherwise available to the author and/or publisher, but to complement, amplify, and supplement other texts. You are urged to read all the available material, learn as much as possible about translation, and tailor the information to your individual needs. For more information, see the many references in the appendices.

Translation is not a get-rich-quick scheme. Anyone who decides to pursue translation, either as a freelancer or as a full-time career, must be prepared to invest a great deal of time and effort, with a view to making it a long-term, preferably a lifelong pursuit. Not everyone who knows more than one language is ipso facto a potential translator. But many are, and they stand to benefit from it.

Every effort has been made to make this handbook as complete and as accurate as possible. However, there *may be* mistakes both typographical and in content. Therefore, this text should be used only as a general guide and not as the ultimate source of translation and/or interpretation information. Furthermore, this handbook contains information on translation current only up to the printing date.

The purpose of this handbook is to inform and to help. The author and the publisher shall have neither liability nor responsibility to any person or entity with respect to any loss or damage caused, or alleged to be caused, directly or indirectly by the information contained in this book.

If you do not wish to be bound by the above, you may return this book to the publisher for a full refund.

Welcome!

Some have asked, who is Morry Sofer? It is my pen name, and it is time I took off the mask and ended my anonymity. Morry is my nickname, and Sofer is the Hebrew translation of my family name. My real name is Mordecai Schreiber. I am now retired from the publishing and the translation business, and I operate under my real name.

I would like to welcome you to *The Global Translator's Handbook*, which is in effect the eighth edition of the original handbook (ninth, if you count the progenitor of this book, namely, the *Guide for Translators*). This edition, in keeping with what has happened every two to three years in the past, is fully updated to serve the needs of translators everywhere.

When you begin to use this book, you become part of a worldwide community of linguists who for the most part labor away from the limelight, yet perform a function without which our world would be deaf and dumb. For years, translation for me was a hobby, a literary passion, and a sideline. I never dreamed of making a living as a translator. In 1979, as Israel and Egypt were getting ready to sign a peace treaty, I was invited by the U.S. Department of State as a private citizen to compare the English and the Hebrew versions of the treaty. Without seeing the Hebrew version, I translated the English into Hebrew. Lo and behold, my translation, with the exception of a word or two, was identical to the official Hebrew version. The deputy director of the language division was so pleased with me he began to send me regular assignments. It was then that for the first time I realized one could make a living as a freelance translator. I had turned forty, and I had modest expectations of making a somewhat respectable income as a linguist. Soon I began to gain the confidence of language contracting officers throughout the government system, and also in the private and public sectors. Within three years I had organized a large network of translators in a growing number of languages, and today the company I started, Schreiber Translations Inc. (STI), is one of the largest in the United States.

Quite frankly, I would have been content to remain a solo translator and be able to support my family, especially since my wife had a successful career in health care and we were able to send our children to good schools. But apparently translation really liked me, and I really liked it, and so we did quite well together. So I welcome you to share my experience through the pages of this book, and I want to make you aware of the fact that translation does offer some good financial opportunities and a great deal of job satisfaction. The key, I suspect, will always be doing the best job you can and gaining the trust and approval of your clients.

Happy translating,
Mordecai Schreiber

Introduction

When you stop and think about it, everything in life is translation. We translate our feelings into actions. When we put anything into words, we translate our thoughts. Every physical action is a translation from one state to another. Translating from one language into another is only the most obvious form of an activity that is perhaps the most common of all human activities. This may be the reason people usually take translation for granted, as something that does not require any special effort, and at the same time, why translation is so challenging and full of possibilities.

There is nothing easy or simple about translation, even as there is nothing easy or simple about any human activity. It only looks easy because you are used to doing it. Anyone who is good at a certain activity can make it appear easy, even though, when we pause to think, we realize there is nothing easy about it.

Translation in the formal sense deals with human language, the most common yet the most complex and hallowed of human functions. Language is what makes us who we are. Language can work miracles. Language can kill, and language can heal. Transmitting meaning from one language to another brings people together, helps them share each other's culture and benefit from each other's experience, and makes them aware of how much they all have in common.

To pursue a translation career means to become a servant of language, a master well worth serving. But more importantly, it means serving your people and other people, bringing them closer together, working toward better understanding among people and nations everywhere. Linguistic isolation breeds xenophobia, prejudice, and fear. Translating means building bridges across all the chasms of ignorance and isolationism that surround us.

So if your work is not always appreciated, take heart. Notoriety is reserved for evil, while the recognition of good is almost always slow in coming. Over the ages, translators brought the world closer together, moved it from paganism to monotheism, from the Dark Ages to the Renaissance, from the rule of despots to the time of enlightenment and individual freedom, a process that is still going on and will continue for a long time to come. This handbook is an attempt to better define translation, and to help its practitioners improve and prosper. The author is offering this book to his colleagues as a token of appreciation for all the great work they have done and will continue to do in the service of their people and all people.

How to Get the Most Out of This Handbook

This handbook has many uses. Some parts of it can be read by both experienced and beginning translators to learn about certain aspects of translation, and other parts are informational in nature and will be of use when you look for a certain dictionary, a certain source of translation work, and the like. It is intended to serve as a sourcebook for all translators in all languages, both in the United States and abroad.

We urge all translators to read chapter 2, "Historical Overview of Translation." Little has been written about the history of translation, and for those of us who practice translation, it is important to have a historical perspective on our craft.

Beginners are encouraged to read chapters 3 and 4, "Requisites for Professional Translators" and "Translator's Self-Evaluation." These chapters should help the beginner get a better idea as to (1) whether or not to pursue translation in the first place, and (2) where one stands in one's development as a translator.

Having read those chapters, the beginner may want to continue with chapter 6, "Translation Techniques."

Chapter 7, "Translation, Computers, and the Internet," is must reading for the beginner and recommended for the advanced. Since it deals with digital technology, an area that is changing constantly, it is of equal importance to all of us, since we are all constant learners when it comes to this subject.

The rest of the chapters depend on individual needs. Certainly all of them are important for the beginner, as they deal with the key issues of translation work, and the advanced can use them selectively. It is our intention to keep them up to date, since things change so fast these days in all of these areas.

The second half of the book consists of appendices. These are meant to be used as a reference guide on resources for translators, such as dictionaries and dictionary sources, software in all languages and where to find it, publications for translators, and more.

Appendix 4 is of particular importance to freelance translators. Here we have provided information on hundreds of translation companies and other sources of translation work in the United States, with descriptions of the specific needs of many of them. They are arranged alphabetically, followed by a listing by state and city to help you find companies in your part of the country. This vital list has been completely updated since our previous edition.

Appendix 5 should be of interest to the beginner who is looking for translator training, and for the advanced who may wish to expand his or her horizons in a new area of translation.

The Uses of This Handbook

The world of translation is fast growing and fast changing. Since this handbook first appeared sixteen years ago, more has changed in the translation field than at any other time in the past. About every two years a new edition of this book has appeared, reflecting the many changes in the field.

Actually, this book has its origins in a smaller book that appeared almost eighteen years ago, titled *Guide for Translators*. For years I had felt the need for such a book, and since I couldn't find it anywhere, I decided to write it myself. I wrote it for my colleagues and for myself, and for all those who are interested in this fascinating field we call translation. The initial success of the *Guide* made it clear that a much expanded book was needed, and the idea of a handbook was born.

While the *Guide* remains largely valid and useful, and contains a great deal of material that will continue to be useful in the future, the *Handbook* attempts to cover as much of the field as possible, and it is the full intention of the publisher to continue to update it regularly, so that it can serve as an up-to-date sourcebook for translators, especially for freelancers, who depend on timely information to maximize their effectiveness in this fast-changing field.

The Nature of Translation

Many people assume that any literate person who knows more than one language can translate. Nothing is further from the truth. Translation is a talent few people possess, although many think they do. Without an innate aptitude for translation, one can go through the motions of replacing words with their equivalents in another language, but the results are likely to fall short of the intent and flavor of the original. Let me be quick to add that even the best translation is never a full and true reflection of its source, simply because no two languages in the world, not even the most closely related, are identical in their way of using words and nuances. The best one can hope for is a rendition close enough to the original not to alter any of its meaning; full enough not to omit any detail, no matter how seemingly insignificant; and elegant enough to provide at least some of the stylistic character of the original text.

Precisely because there is no such thing as a perfect translation of an original source, translation is always a challenge that requires skill, training, and experience. The purpose of this handbook is to help those who know at least two languages and have an aptitude for translating take the necessary steps to sharpen their skills through training and practice and, hopefully, go on to start acquiring the experience necessary to become truly productive and effective translators.

This handbook is the result of my fifty years of translation experience, as a biblical scholar and a literary translator with several book translations to my credit, later on as a technical translator for U.S. government agencies, and since 1983 as the founder and president of a translation service that engages hundreds of translators in over ninety different languages and dialects throughout the United States and abroad.

During the last thirty years, I have witnessed a dramatic change in the role of translators in this country and around the world. Opportunities for translators are growing as never before. This is due to the fact that the "global village" idea is becoming a fact of life with every passing day, thanks to the disappearance of the Iron Curtain, the advent of multinational alliances like the European Community, the growing global role of the United Nations, the globalization of business, and the miracle of modern communications. The Internet enables translators to receive text that was sent, say, from Washington to Athens by fax, translate it, and send it back to Washington over the Internet, all at an affordable cost and without wasting any valuable time in transit.

The constant improvements in the computer field have tripled and quadrupled the output of the professional translator, and have made the task of translating much easier. It is quite clear that computers will play an even greater role in the translation field in years to come, making translation more affordable and widely used. (A word of caution: those who maintain that computers will soon replace human translators altogether are not familiar with all the facts. The general consensus among the experts today is that computer technology will continue to enhance translation, but only as an aid to, rather than a replacement for, human translation.)

For Whom Is This Handbook Intended?

This handbook is designed to be used by anyone who has an interest in translation. This includes the professional as well as the occasional translator; the freelancer and the career translator; the oral interpreter engaged in escort, consecutive, simultaneous, or conference interpretation; and, last but not least, the translation student.

It is designed both as a learning and a reference tool. By reading its text thoroughly, you are certain to acquire a familiarity with the translation field, both theoretical and practical. By using the appendices, you will be able to find your way through the complex world of translation equipment, dictionaries, and sources of translation assignments. The material presented here is timely, and it is constantly under revision. It will be updated in each new edition of this book, which comes out every two years. Combined with the author's website (www .MordecaiSchreiber.com), it will enable you to be in constant touch with this fast-changing and dynamic field.

There are thousands of students in American colleges and universities who major in foreign languages. Many of them wonder what to do with their degree once they graduate. Many consider the possibilities of translation, only to find out there is little opportunity to break into this field, since there seems to be a gap between the formal education stage and the professional stage of working as a trained or accredited translator. They, too, can benefit from this handbook, which is designed to bridge this gap by offering information that, combined with a training program geared to help improve the aspiring translator's skills, will provide the necessary preparation for a professional translation career. This handbook will point anyone interested in translation in the right direction. The rest is up to you. Once you begin to pursue your own translation career, you will start formulating your own guidelines, develop your own techniques, and be ever on the lookout for new words, new knowledge, new linguistic sources, and a better understanding of how to communicate words and ideas, which, after all, is what translation is all about.

....

From ancient Egypt to the Renaissance to today's world, translators have played a key role in moving the world from one stage of civilization to the next.

....

2

Historical Overview of Translation

The purpose of this chapter is threefold: first, to give you a bird's-eye view of the history of translation since the beginning of time; second, to show you how universal translation is, encompassing every corner of the earth; and third, to make you realize how important translation is for human progress.

In the history of the Judeo-Christian-Islamic world, there are three key periods which have determined and defined those three civilizations, and all three periods are characterized by a high level of activity in the field of translation. The first is the beginning of the Christian era, at which time many languages, most important among them Hebrew, Aramaic, Greek, and Latin, interacted to create the new Christian civilization and the transformed Judaic civilization. The second begins with the birth of Islam in the seventh century and culminates in the twelfth and thirteenth centuries, notably in the city of Toledo, Spain, where Christian, Muslim, and Jewish scholars and translators from all parts of Europe and the Middle East undertook the enormous task of translating the Greek and Arabic classics into the new languages of Europe and in effect laid the foundation of those new languages and cultures, providing the bridge to the Renaissance and the Modern World. The third key period is today. All the major civilizations of the world are at present in a state of flux. The world as a whole is being transformed as never before in recorded history, and at the same time languages are being transformed, and translation has taken on a new significance unlike anything since the end of the Middle Ages.

Translation is one of the oldest occupations in the world. One of the earliest dictionaries known to us was discovered in 1974 by Italian archeologists in the ancient town of Ebla, in the Middle East. It dates back anywhere between 6,000 and 10,000 years, to the dawn of civilization. It is chiseled in clay tablets, using a writing method known as cuneiform. There, on the face of the tablet, are two parallel columns of words, in two different ancient tongues, related to taxation (tax collecting is also one of the oldest occupations).

Before there was writing, there was speaking. Neighboring tribes and nations have always spoken different dialects and even totally different languages. And yet they had to talk to each other in order to engage in trade, threaten each other, and after the folly of fighting was over, talk peace. To do this, they needed oral interpreters, those linguistically gifted individuals who had managed to master one or more tongues other than their own. From the beginning of time, those interpreters were considered an important asset for the community, or for the leader of the tribe or nation. They played a vital role in both trade and the affairs of state. Quite often, they became confidants of the ruler and enjoyed special privileges.

There was, however, a downside to the life of the interpreter. Since the interpreter was often at the center of important events, taking part in crucial negotiations and decisions, if things went wrong, if a deal failed, or worse yet, if a battle was lost, the interpreter was often used as a scapegoat. Examples of this unfortunate turn of events abound throughout the history of interpretation as well as translation. Writing, as mentioned before, has been around for at least 10,000 years, probably longer. In ancient Egypt, the court scribe was one of the most important officers of the Pharaoh's court. He was a highly cultivated person and most likely knew more than one language. In the Old Testament there is no clear distinction between the scribe and the interpreter or translator. When the Assyrians lay siege to Jerusalem, a Hebrew scribe served as an interpreter between the Hebrew-speaking Judeans and their Aramean-speaking enemies.

Human beings have long been fascinated, intrigued, and even intimidated by the great variety of languages and dialects in the world. This phenomenon is reflected in the legends and oral traditions of nearly every culture. The biblical story of the tower of Babel is a case in point. Originally, according to this story, everyone spoke the same language. Then people became so presumptuous that they began to build a tower reaching to heaven. Subsequently, the tower was destroyed and the mortals were punished by being made to speak many different languages. In the late nineteenth century, a new language called Esperanto was created by Ludwig Zamenhoff, intended to be the international language. It has enjoyed a certain measure of success, but only among small circles of scholars. In our time, however, the language that comes closest to being an international language is English. Be that as it may, the other languages of the world will not be disappearing any time soon. Clearly, in an ideal world there will be no need for translators, or, for that matter, for physicians, lawyers, as well as hundreds of other occupations. But in the real world, we need all of them.

Translating the Bible

The history of translation, not unlike the history of culture itself, begins with religion and eventually leads into secular culture. Language has always been a critical element of religion. To every culture, its language has always been sacred. It was the means of maintaining and transmitting traditions, and of communicating with the higher powers. Therefore, the issue of translating one's sacred writings and prayers into another language was always a very critical decision, which was never taken lightly. It took the Catholic Church centuries before it decided in the 1960s to allow celebrating Mass in the vernacular, rather than in Latin. Jews and Muslims, on the other hand, still consider praying in languages other than Hebrew and Arabic, respectively, questionable.

The Judeo-Christian-Muslim world derives its culture from a common source, namely, a set of books originally written in Hebrew, known to Christians as the Old Testament, to Muslims as the Holy Books, and to Jews as the Tanakh (acronym for Torah, Prophets, and Writings). The Hebrew Bible was created over a period of some one thousand years, roughly 1300 to 300 BC. By the time it was completed, its originators had begun to disperse around the Middle East and spoke several languages other than Hebrew, including Aramaic and Greek. The original Hebrew text became canonized, hence sacred, but for practical purposes it had to be recited and written in the Aramaic so that masses of believers in places like Babylonia, Syria, and even Palestine could understand it. Thus, several Aramaic translations of the Scriptures emerged, of which the most celebrated is the one attributed to Onkelos.

> Translators, humble servants of knowledge, often nameless, seldom acknowledged, more erred against than erring, forever looking for the right word.
>
> Where would we be without them? How would we in the West enjoy the Rubaiyat without Fitzgerald? How would Europe know the Bible without St. Jerome? How would nations interact, how would they enrich each other's culture and language without their translators and interpreters?
>
> —Anonymous

While Jewish life and learning flourished in and around Babylonia, with Aramaic as its main language, a major Jewish community prospered in Alexandria, Egypt. Here the dominant culture was Greek, and the main language spoken by the Jews was Greek. This gave rise to the first great translation of the Hebrew Bible, known as the Septuagint. While attributed to Ptolemy II, the Greek king of Egypt, it was most likely originally created to serve the needs of the Jewish community of Alexandria. The Septuagint was to play a crucial role in the development of Christianity. It was, in effect, the conduit through which Hebrew beliefs and civilization reached the pagan world about to become Christian, and, despite its imperfections, it continued to exert influence on the development of such diverse Christian cultural and linguistic groups as the Ethiopic and Coptic in Africa, the Slavonic in Eastern Europe, and the rest of Europe through the Latin versions of the Catholic Church.

No translator in history achieved greater honor and acclaim than St. Jerome (347–420), the patron saint of translators in the Catholic Church. Jerome translated both the Greek and Hebrew versions of the Bible into Latin, and produced the Vulgate, the standard Bible of the Church for the next thousand years. Throughout his life in Europe and in the Middle East, translation was his great passion, and despite adversity, he managed to leave the Church a vast corpus of translations and commentaries which were pivotal for the development of Christian civilization.

From a linguistic standpoint, an even more remarkable story related to the development of language and culture is the story of two brothers, St. Cyril and St. Methodius. The two are credited with introducing Christianity to the Slavic world in the ninth century. To do so, they actually had to devise a new alphabet, based on Greek characters, which eventually became the Cyrillic alphabet, used today in Russia and other Slavic countries. They translated the Holy Scriptures into the language later known as Old Church Slavonic, and in effect laid the foundation for the Slavic cultures.

The ninth century also saw the beginning of Bible translation into English under Alfred the Great; into French under Charlemagne, founder of the Holy Roman Empire; and into German through the efforts of von Weissenburg and others. Here again, biblical translation is closely linked to the development of national cultures during this pivotal period in European history.

However, the great impetus for Bible translation in Europe came immediately after the Reformation in the sixteenth century. The main force behind it was Martin Luther, who not only broke away from Rome and helped establish Protestantism, but also paid close attention to the principles of translation, and to the establishment of the German language as a functional language, ready to pick up where Latin had left off. Indeed, some of Luther's basic translation principles, such as paying close attention to the transmission of meaning to the target language, and the emphasis on clarity and simplicity of translation, have remained valid to this day.

The impact of Luther's translation of the Bible was soon felt in other parts of Europe. Translations of Scriptures were soon to follow in Danish, Norwegian, Swedish, and Icelandic, as well as in Slavic languages such as Slovene, Serbian (and Croatian, which is basically the same language), and Czech. The Kralice Bible in the Czech language (1579–1593) is considered the greatest example of classical Czech. All these translations made a seminal contribution to the development of the national cultures of these peoples.

The history of biblical translation in England is particularly fascinating. While it has its beginning with Alfred the Great in the ninth century (as was mentioned before)—the same Alfred who actually rescued the English language from foreign invaders such as the Danes and ensured its future—it is once again in the sixteenth century that biblical translation in England reached the level of high drama. In the spirit of the time, affected by both the Reformation and the invention of the printing press, the scholar William Tyndall, who was at home in both Greek and Hebrew (and a few other languages), translated both the Old and the New Testaments into English, with a view to replacing the Latin, which he considered less adequate for conveying the Bible to his people than their native tongue. Tyndall, who like Luther (whom he met in Germany) put an emphasis on clarity, also emphasized good functional English, which he helped fashion. Politically, however, he was out of favor with the "powers that be" (an expression coined by Tyndall) in England and had to flee to Belgium where Charles V's hit men reached him and managed to have him strangled *and* burned at the stake.

Human rulers can kill people, but they cannot destroy ideas. Despite the concerted effort in England to eliminate Tyndall's work, including the efforts of Henry VIII, who broke off with Rome and reintroduced the English Bible, which was largely Tyndall's work, without giving the martyred scholar any credit, it survived all the vicissitudes of the sixteenth century. In fact, when what became the Authorized Version of the Bible in England, namely, the King James Version, was published in 1611, the product of some fifty-four scholars, it was largely Tyndall's translation. This version marks a cultural as well as a religious turning point in English history. Together with the work of Shakespeare, it stands at the apex of English culture. Ironically, the authorship of both the Bard's plays and the King James Scriptures has been disputed, distorted, claimed, and reclaimed for the past four centuries.

The history of Bible translations is similarly intertwined with the development of national languages and cultures throughout the rest of Europe and many other parts of the world. The Bible is the most translated book in the world, having been translated into over 2,000 languages and dialects. Every year new translations of the Bible appear all over the world. The American writer Ernest Hemingway said that he learned to write by reading the Bible. My suggestion to aspiring translators—as well as to seasoned ones—is to keep reading the Bible, not only because of its timeless message, but because of its genius for clarity, brevity, and simplicity, the attributes of all superior translations.

Translation in the East—Islam, Hinduism, and Buddhism

In Islam, the Qur'an is considered untranslatable. This is why millions of Indonesian Muslims, for example, study it or use it for worship in the original Arabic, rather than in Indonesian. There are, in effect, hundreds of translations of the Qur'an, but officially they are considered "explanations" rather than "authorized versions," as would be the case with the Bible in a country like England. Arabic to the Muslim, like Hebrew to the Jew, is the language of revelation. Having said this, however, it is interesting to note that during the centuries of classical Islam, from roughly the seventh to the thirteenth century, translators played a critical role in making Islam the standard bearer of civilization as medieval Europe was sinking into ignorance and backwardness.

Soon after the spread of Islam throughout the Middle East, North Africa, and Spain, the new Muslim empire undertook ambitious programs of translating the classics, notably Greek philosophy, astronomy, and medicine, giving rise to such prominent translators as Hunayn ibn Ishaq (808–873), one of the early great translators of Baghdad, where translation flourished for the next four centuries (until the Mongolian conquest). In retrospect, by translating and preserving the works of Aristotle, Plato, and other Greek philosophers, poets, and scientists, Islamic scholars served as a bridge between antiquity and the modern world. Our scientific world has its roots in ancient Greece and Rome, but many of its branches have grown on the trunk of Islamic culture, which, in addition to transmitting the knowledge of the ancients through translation, added a great deal to it in areas such as mathematics and medicine.

Linguistically, the subcontinent of India is one of the most varied parts of the world, with more than 1,500 languages and dialects, including 16 official languages, the most prominent being Hindi and English. The leading religion is Hinduism, but there are also millions of Muslims, Christians, Buddhists, Sikhs, Jains, and Parsis. Needless to say, in such a linguistic kaleidoscope, translation is a thriving industry, moving in many different directions. The most translated work of Hinduism is arguably the Bhagavad Gita, originally written in Sanskrit. This religious work has been translated down to our time as a means of promoting the teachings of Hinduism. Some of the more recent notable translations are by Tilak (early twentieth century) into Marathi, and by Mahatma Gandhi (early mid-twentieth century) into Gujarati.

Unlike Hinduism, with Sanskrit as its sacred language, Buddhism is more universal and ecumenical, and has spread its teachings throughout Asia in several languages. The sacred scriptures of Buddhism were translated from Sanskrit into Chinese by the Buddhist monk and pilgrim to India Hsuan-tsang (602–664), one of the great enterprising translators of all time. Upon his return to China, he translated a large body of Buddhist sacred literature, which he had brought back with him after a long journey through mountains and deserts. One of his students in China was the Japanese monk Dosho. While Hsuan-tsang's version of Buddhism proved too esoteric for the Chinese, his disciple Dosho had more luck with it in Japan. After he returned to his native land, Dosho established the Hosso school, which became the most influential of all the Buddhist schools in Japan.

Translators Opening the Door to the Modern World

The most glorious period in the history of translation is represented by the so-called School of Translators of Toledo, which flourished in that beautiful Spanish city during the twelfth and thirteenth centuries. Toledo in those years was the crossroads of the cultures of the world, both spatially and temporally. On one side was the Islamic Empire, now nearing the end of its centuries of political and cultural preeminence. On the other side was Christian Europe, striving to emerge from the Middle Ages. And in the middle were the Jews of Spain, experiencing a golden age in their own Judaic and Hebraic culture, unlike anything anywhere since biblical and Talmudic times. Best of all, all three religions, usually at odds with one another, enjoyed a prolonged time of peaceful interaction which often accounts for great intellectual achievements.

In Toledo, the cultures of antiquity, preserved in the Arabic language in thousands of volumes, were translated first into Latin and later into the new languages of Europe. This undertaking has been compared to the discovery of the New World. In fact, the great discoveries of Columbus and others might never have occurred without the transmission of knowledge and science that took place in Toledo in those years. The modern world as we know it today might not exist. What is truly remarkable about the Toledo school is that it attracted translators from all parts of Europe, the most prominent being the Italian Gerard of Cremona, the Englishman Adelard of Bath, and Herman the German. But most critical of all was the part played by the Spanish Jewish translators of that time, who had the advantage of being equally at home in Muslim and Christian cultures, not to mention their own Judaic culture. The most prominent among them was the ibn Tibbon family, a dynasty of translators. The founder, Yehudah ibn Tibbon, has been called the "patriarch of translators." His monument stands to this day in Granada, Spain. His grandson, Moses, translated Arabic works, helping disseminate Greek and Arab culture throughout Europe. The ibn Tibbon dynasty remains to this day the exemplary translators of Judaism, not only because of their great cultural achievements, but because they formulated a theory of translation, based on the knowledge of the source and target languages as well as the knowledge of the subject matter, which has remained valid to this day.

Translation in the New World

The story of translation in the New World is, for the most part, not a happy one. During the age of the Great Discoveries, great explorers such as Columbus, Pizarro, Cortes, and others came into contact with new, hitherto unknown cultures and languages, those of the natives of the New World and other parts of the globe. Here again interpreters became the bridge between the white man and the other races. Cortes, the conqueror of Mexico, might have failed in his ruthless mission had it not been for a local native woman who served as his interpreter. The same was true of many other conquerors and discoverers. The great civilization of the ancient Maya of Central America was made known to us through the translation into Spanish of such Mayan classics as the *Popol Vu*.

The conquest of new worlds by the nations of Europe did not, however, result in an attitude of respect on the part of the conquerors toward the conquered, whereby the languages of the latter might have been studied by the former, and their oral or written traditions translated into such languages as Spanish, English, French, and so on. Instead, the colonizers looked upon their new subjects as heathens whose language and culture were worthless, and imposed their own language, culture, and religion on those who survived the many massacres inflicted upon them by their enlightened conquerors. It would not be until many years later that valuable cultural assets, such as Indian dialects of North America, African languages, and many other oral and written traditions, would be treated with respect, studied, and translated, as is finally beginning to happen in our time, in some cases after the originators of those cultures have all but disappeared.

Nor, for that matter, is the history of translation in the United States particularly uplifting. The European colonists who settled this continent had little need for translation and soon developed an insular attitude still reflected to this day in the political attitudes of American isolationists. No one has characterized this attitude better than Mark Twain in the celebrated exchange between Huck Finn and Jim, in which the runaway slave wonders why the French can't speak "like the rest of us." One of the great anomalies of American life to this day is the fact that while no other country in history has had a more culturally varied population coexisting as effectively as the population of the United States, translation has a long way to go to become as well established here as it is in other parts of the world.

The Twentieth Century

Translation in the present century has seen some good times and some bad times. Translation has fared the worst under totalitarian regimes such as Fascism, Communism, and Nazism. The history of Communist Russia, Fascist Italy, and Nazi Germany abounds with the suppression and persecution of translators. A more recent totalitarian regime, namely that of Iran, has engaged in active terrorism against translators, in this case against the translators of the Indian-born British author Salman Rushdie, one of whom was murdered by Iranian agents, and the other wounded.

When the Republic of Ireland was formed in 1922, a major translation program was launched which sought to revive the use and study of the Irish language, or Gaelic. Since the English language and culture had already been deeply entrenched in Ireland, to this day the dominant language remains English. But the example of Ireland is being emulated at present throughout the world.

Another national language that was reintroduced programmatically to both daily life and literature is Hebrew, the same biblical Hebrew we have encountered at the dawn of civilization, now transformed by many old and new cultural influences. Israeli Hebrew is one of the great linguistic success stories of all time. Not only has it become the spoken language of several million people who arrived in the new state from over one hundred different countries, but, using American English as its working model, it is constantly adding current expressions as well as technical and scientific terminology which has enabled the new society to use Hebrew in all fields of contemporary science and technology.

As the twentieth century came to a close, two linguistic phenomena became clearly dominant. The first is the growing incursion of American English into nearly all the languages of the world, mostly because of American pop culture and high tech. This is bound to have a lasting effect on languages in general in the twenty-first century. The second phenomenon is the reemergence of national languages throughout the world. Until a few years ago the Soviet Union, encompassing many nations and cultures, conducted all of its affairs in one language: Russian. With the breakup of the USSR, there are now dozens of official languages all the way from the Baltic Sea to the Far East. In Africa many languages are emerging as well, but there the trends are still hard to define. What is clear at this time is that linguistic diversity as well as a growing influence of one international language, namely English, stands to characterize the beginning of the next century.

What all of this means for translators is that we are standing on the threshold of a new golden age for translation, not unlike the one in Spain at the end of the Middle Ages. There is a new cultural openness in today's world, brought about by several factors, the most notable being the end of the Cold War between the West and the former Communist Bloc; the incredible progress in global communications, including such technologies as satellite communications, computers, modems, faxes, e-mail, and the Internet; and the fast-growing international trade throughout the entire world, as well as the new international awareness of many languages and cultures that for centuries were subjugated and suppressed. The world today, rather than being dominated by a few colonialist languages such as French, English, or Spanish, is finally reaching a stage of linguistic and cultural—albeit not quite yet social and economic—equality, whereby literally hundreds of languages and dialects are beginning to play a part in the global tapestry of human interaction. As a result, hundreds of new dictionaries are being published all over the world, language courses are being offered everywhere in an unprecedented number of languages, and the demand for competent translators is growing at a steady rate.

As the twenty-first century begins to unfold, the role of the translator will once again, as happened before during ancient and premodern history, become critical in shaping history and helping civilization make the transition into the next age.

How History Is "Translated" by the Young

From the neighborhoods of Chicago comes an unidentified document that purports to be a history of the world "pasted together . . . from genuine student bloopers collected by teachers throughout the U.S., from 8th grade through college level." Excerpts follow:

- Ancient Egypt was inhabited by mummies, and they all wrote in hydraulics. They lived in the Sarah Dessert and traveled by Camelot.
- David was a Hebrew king skilled in playing the liar. He fought with the Finkelsteins, a race of people who lived in biblical times. Solomon, one of his sons, had three hundred wives and seven hundred porcupines.
- The Greeks were a highly sculptured people, and without them we wouldn't have history. They invented three kinds of columns, corinthian, ironic, and dorc, and built the Apocalypse. They also had myths, which is a female moth.
- Queen Elizabeth was the Virgin Queen. When she exposed herself to her troops, they all yelled "hurrah." Then her navy went out and defeated the Spanish Armadillo.
- During the Renaissance, America began. Columbus was a great navigator who discovered America while cursing about the Atlantic. His ships were called the Nina, the Pinta, and the Santa Fe. . . . Sir Francis Drake circumcised the world with a one-hundred-foot clipper.
- Meanwhile in Europe, Voltaire invented electricity and also wrote a book called "Candy." Gravity was invented by Isaac Newton. It is chiefly noticeable in the fall, when apples are falling off the trees.
- Johann Bach wrote a great many musical compositions and had a large number of children. In between, he practiced on the old spinster, which he kept up in his attic.
- The sun never sets on the British Empire because the British Empire is in the east and the sun sets in the west.

3

Requisites for Professional Translators

Any person who knows more than one language has the ability to explain a word or a sentence in what translators call "the source language" (the language you translate from) by using an equivalent word or sentence in what they call "the target language" (the language you translate into). This, in effect, is the beginning of translation. But it is only the beginning. It does not automatically turn a person into an accomplished translator. Along with the knowledge of the source and the target language, a translator must have an aptitude for translation. Some people are endowed with a talent for translation. It is not an acquired skill, like riding a bicycle. It is rather a talent, like playing the violin. Some people have it, and some don't. It is not necessarily an indication of a lower or higher IQ. Nor is it an indication of how linguistically gifted one is. It is an inborn skill that enables a person to change a text from one language into another quickly and accurately, or, if you will, to think in more than one language at the same time. If you possess this skill, then it behooves you to develop it and make use of it, because there is never an overabundance of good translators, and it is almost axiomatic that the good ones can always find either full-time or part-time work.

The first requisite for the working translator is a thorough knowledge of both the source and the target languages. There is no point in billing oneself as a translator if one is not fully familiar with both languages, or does not possess a vocabulary in both equal to that of a speaker of those languages who has a university education or its equivalent.

The second requisite is thorough "at-homeness" in both cultures. A language is a living phenomenon. It does not exist apart from the culture where it is spoken and written. It communicates not only the names of objects and different kinds of action, but also feelings, attitudes, beliefs, and so on. To be fully familiar with a language, one must also be familiar with the culture in which the language is used, indeed, with the people who use it, their ways, manners, beliefs, and all that goes into making a culture.

Third, one must keep up with the growth and change of the language and be up to date on all of its nuances and neologisms. Languages are in a constant state of flux, and words change meaning from year to year. A pejorative term can become laudatory, and a neutral term can become loaded with meaning. Thirty years ago the English word "gay" simply meant "joyous." Now it is used to define an entire segment of society. We once spoke of the "almighty dollar." Now as we travel abroad we may find out the dollar is not necessarily everyone's preferred currency.

Fourth, a distinction must be made between the languages one translates from and into. Generally speaking, one translates from another language into one's own native language. This is because one is usually intimately familiar with one's own language, while even years of study and experience do not necessarily enable one to be completely at home with an acquired language. The exceptions to this rule are usually those people who have lived in more than one culture, and have spoken more than one language on a regular basis. Such people may be able to translate in both directions. There are also rare gifted individuals who have mastered another language to such a degree that they can go both ways. They are indeed extremely rare. Given all of this, one should allow for the fact that while the ability of the accomplished translator to write and speak in the target language (i.e., one's native tongue) may be flawless, that person may not necessarily be able to write excellent prose or give great speeches in the source language (i.e., the language from which one translates). Then again, it is not necessary to be able to write and speak well in the language one translates from, while it is to be expected that a good translator is also a good writer and speaker in his or her native language.

Fifth, a professional translator has to be able to translate in more than one area of knowledge. Most professional translators are called upon to translate in a variety of fields. It is not uncommon for a translator to cover as many as twenty or thirty fields of knowledge in one year, including such areas as political subjects, economics, law, medicine, communications, and so on. Obviously, it would be hard to find a translator who is an economist, a lawyer, a medical doctor, and an engineer all wrapped into one. In fact, such a person probably does not exist. One does not have to be a lawyer to translate legal documents. Many a professional translator has been able to gain enough knowledge and acquire sufficient vocabulary in a variety of technical fields to be able to produce perfectly accurate and well-written translations in those fields. This is not nearly as difficult as it may seem, since most technical fields utilize a well-defined number of terms that keep repeating themselves, and as one keeps translating the same subject, these terms become more and more familiar to the translator. One must, however, have a natural curiosity about many different areas of human knowledge and activity, and an interest in increasing one's vocabulary in a variety of related as well as unrelated fields.

Sixth, an effective translator must have a facility for writing or speaking (depending on whether the method used is writing, speaking, or dictation), and the ability to articulate quickly and accurately, either orally or in writing. Like a reporter, a translator must be able to transmit ideas in real time, and in good understandable language. Translation is a form of writing and speech making, and a translator is, in a sense, a writer and an orator.

Seventh, a professional translator must develop a good speed of translation. There are two reasons for this: First, most clients wait until the last minute to assign a translation job. As a result, they turn to a translator or a translation service with what is perhaps the most typical question in this business: "How soon can you have this job ready for me?" The professional translator has to be prepared to accept that long job with the short turnaround time, or there will be no repeat business from that particular client, or from most other clients, for that matter. Second, translation is generally paid by the word. The more words one can translate per hour, the more income one will generate. Translating 50 words per hour can land a translator in the poorhouse. Serious translation starts at 250 words per hour and can reach as high as 1,000 words per hour using word processing, and close to 3,000 words per hour using dictation (the author actually knows such a translator). High-volume translators are the ones who will be the most successful.

Eighth, a translator must develop research skills and be able to acquire reference sources that are essential for producing high-quality translation. Without such sources, even the best of translators cannot hope to be able to handle a large variety of subjects in many unrelated fields. Dedicated translators are the ones who are always on the lookout for new reference sources, and over time develop a data bank that can be used in their work.

Ninth, today's translator cannot be a stranger to hardware, software, fax, modem, the Internet, and the latest developments in all those media. Translation has become completely dependent on electronic tools. Gone are the days of handwriting, the typewriter, and all the other "prehistoric" means of communication. The more one becomes involved in translation, the more one finds oneself caught up in the latest high-tech developments.

Tenth, a translator who wishes to be busy on a fairly regular basis doing translation work must carefully consider the fact that certain languages are in high demand, say, in Washington or in Los Angeles, while others are not. Thus, for example, there is high demand for Japanese, German, Spanish, French, Chinese, Arabic, Russian, and Italian in both Washington and Los Angeles, but not nearly as much for Bulgarian, Farsi, Czech, or Afrikaans. If your language falls within the second group, it is extremely advisable to also have language expertise in one of the languages of the first group, or to seriously consider whether your particular language has enough of a demand to warrant a major investment of time and effort on your part. One should always check and see what kind of a potential one's language specialty has in a given geographic area.

The above ten points are the essential criteria for developing a translation career. There are many other considerations, but none as important as these. If you feel that you can meet all of the above criteria, then you should continue reading this handbook and put it to good use.

The Well-Rounded Translator

The main division in the translation field is between literary and technical translation. Literary translation, which covers such areas as fiction, poetry, drama, and the humanities in general, is often done by writers of the same genre who actually author works of the same kind in the target language, or at least by translators with the required literary aptitude. For practical reasons, this handbook will not cover literary translation but will instead focus on the other major area of translation, namely technical translation. High-quality literary translation has always been the domain of the few and is hardly lucrative (don't even think of doing literary translation if your motive is money), while technical translation is done by a much greater number of practitioners and is an ever-growing and expanding field, with excellent earning opportunities. This chapter discusses the characteristics of the well-rounded technical translator.

The term "technical" is extremely broad. In the translation business it covers much more than technical subjects in the narrow sense of the word. In fact, there is an overlap between literary and technical translation when it comes to such areas as the social sciences, political subjects, and many others.

One way of defining technical translation is by asking the question, does the subject being translated require a specialized vocabulary, or is the language non-specialized? If the text being translated includes specialized terms in a given field, then the translation is technical.

The more areas (and languages) a translator can cover, the greater the opportunity for developing a successful translation career. Furthermore, as one becomes proficient in several areas, it becomes easier to add more. Besides, many technical areas are interrelated, and proficiency in one increases proficiency in another. In addition, every area breaks down into many subareas, each with its own vocabulary and its own linguistic idiosyncrasies. Thus, for example, translating in Arabic does not make one an expert in all spoken Arabic dialects, yet a knowledge of several of those dialects is very beneficial for the professional Arabic translator.

How does one become a well-rounded translator? The answer can be summed up in one word—experience. The key to effective translation is practice. Since human knowledge grows day by day, and since language keeps growing and changing, the well-rounded translator must keep in touch with knowledge and language on a regular basis. The worst thing that can happen to a translator is to be out of touch with the source language for more than a couple of years. What the rusty translator may find out is that new words, new concepts, and new ways of using those words and applying those concepts have come into being during that period of "hibernation," and one's old expertise is no longer reliable.

Translation, therefore, is a commitment one makes not for a limited period of time, but rather long term. It is to be assumed that anyone who becomes a translator is the kind of person who loves words and loves the challenge of using words effectively and correctly. Such a person will not become an occasional translator, but will make translation a lifelong practice.

Stories Translators Tell

Two new immigrants from the Far East meet on the street in Miami.

"I heard your nephew, who moved to Miami last year, is becoming Americanized very quickly."

"How so?"

"He speaks fluent Spanish."

* * *

José goes back to South America after a short stay in the States.

"The gringos are very nice people," he tells his friends. "I went to Yankee Stadium. There were no seats left, so they told me to stand by the flagpole. Suddenly everyone got up, turned to me, and sang in chorus: "José, can you see?"

Good and Bad Translation Habits

The accomplished translator can develop good as well as bad habits. Starting with the bad, we have already pointed out one—losing touch with the source language for long periods of time. Another bad habit is taking illegitimate shortcuts while translating. There are several types of such shortcuts. The most typical is failing to look up a word one is really not sure how to translate. Being 90 percent sure of a word's meaning is not good enough in professional translation. If one is not sure of a word's meaning, even after all available means have been exhausted, then one must put in a translator's note to that effect, or make it known in some other way that there is a problem with translating that particular word. Anything less would be deceptive.

Another illegitimate shortcut is summarizing a paragraph instead of providing a *full* translation. There is such a thing as summary translation of a paragraph or a document. If a summary is called for, then this is precisely what the translator is expected to provide. But the most common form of translation is what's known in the business as a verbatim translation, which is a full and complete rendition of the source text. When verbatim translation is ordered, anything less than a full translation is an illegitimate shortcut. Unfortunately, some translators tend to overlook this from time to time, especially when they undertake more work than they can accomplish by a given deadline and decide to summarize rather than miss that deadline.

Perhaps the worst habit for a translator is to decide at a certain point in time that his or her knowledge of either the source or the target language is so good that it cannot possibly stand any improvement. The moment one stops growing linguistically, one is no longer on the cutting edge of one's profession. The good translator is a perennial language student, always eager and willing to learn more and to keep up with the latest.

As for good habits, the most important, perhaps, are the ones we obtain by reversing the above-mentioned bad habits. But there are many more. One excellent habit is to read professional literature in the field one will be called upon to translate in with reasonable frequency. One good example is *Scientific American*, which can help anyone who translates subjects of science and technology to learn the style or styles used in scientific writing. People who work in the field of translating business documents should definitely read business periodicals, not the least of which is the *Wall Street Journal*. One does not have to be a scientist to translate scientific articles, or have a business degree to translate business documents, but a general understanding of the subject goes a long way toward providing an accurate translation of the subject.

Another excellent habit is to translate not only for profit but also for enjoyment and experience. Most people, unfortunately, are not so taken with their daily work that they would want to continue doing it after hours for fun or practice. But an accomplished translator is someone who will on occasion translate simply for the sake of sharpening his or her skill, or accept a very small fee because of personal commitment to the subject matter, or because of a personal interest. This writer, for example, enjoys translating poetry because of the challenge of doing what is perhaps the most difficult type of translation, and, quite simply, because of the enjoyment of poetry.

Yet another good habit is always to be on the lookout for dictionaries. Many dictionaries are hard to find and are available in few places. This writer in all his travels across the United States and abroad always stops in bookstores to look for dictionaries. One can also order dictionaries from bookstores and from publishers, but then one has to know what to order and from whom (see appendix 2).

The last good habit I would like to mention is the practice of compiling word lists and building a reference library. Dictionaries do not have all the words and terms a translator needs, nor do they contain all the information that specialized references may have. There are aids for translators put out by certain organizations, and there is professional literature in every field. In recent years there has been a growing awareness of the need for terminology management (see chapter 8), and with the constant advances in computer technology, databases have been proliferating, making the work of the translator much easier than ever before.

Good references are worth their weight in gold when they are needed for a specific translation, and over time the experienced translator develops an extensive library of glossaries which become essential for any translation assignment.

....

Reading poetry in translation is like kissing a woman through a handkerchief.—Haim Nachman Bialik

Kissing a woman through a handkerchief is actually not so bad.
—Yehudah Amichai
....

4

Translator's Self-Evaluation

The following criteria were developed some years ago by a U.S. government agency for determining the skill level of a potential translator whom that agency might have liked to hire. You may want to read this chapter carefully to try to make an honest determination as to where on this scale you find yourself at this time. If you are below Level 2+, you need to keep practicing. If you are at Level 3 or higher, you can start doing some professional translating. After Level 4 you are ready for some serious translating, and at Level 5 you can start making a living as a translator.

Translator Skill Levels

Level 0
No functional ability to translate the language. Consistently misunderstanding or cannot comprehend at all.

Level 0+
Can translate all or some place names (i.e., street or city designations), corporate names, numbers, and isolated words and phrases, often translating these inaccurately.

In rendering translations, writes using only memorized material and set expressions. Spelling and representation of symbols (letters, syllables, characters) are frequently incorrect.

Level 1
Sufficient skill to translate the simplest connected written material in a form equivalent to usual printing or typescript. Can translate either representations of familiar formulaic verbal exchanges or simple language containing only the highest-frequency grammatical patterns and vocabulary items, including cognates when appropriate. Translated texts include simple narratives of routine behavior; concrete descriptions of persons, places, and things; and explanations of geography and government such as those simplified for tourists. Mistranslations are common.

In rendering translations, writes in simple sentences (or clauses), making continual errors in spelling, grammar, and punctuation, but translation can be read and understood by a native reader used to dealing with foreigners attempting to translate his/her language.

Level 1+
Sufficient skill to translate simple discourse for informative social purposes in printed form. Can translate material such as announcements or public events, popular advertising notes containing biographical information or narration of events, and straightforward newspaper headlines. Has some difficulty with the cohesive factors in discourse, such as matching pronouns with referents.

In rendering translations, writing shows good control of elementary vocabulary and some control of basic syntactic patterns, but major errors still occur when expressing more complex thoughts. Dictionary usage may still yield incorrect vocabulary of forms, although can use a dictionary to advantage to translate simple ideas. Translations, though faulty, are comprehensible to native readers used to dealing with foreigners.

Level 2
Sufficient skill to translate simple authentic written material in a form equivalent to usual printing. Can translate uncomplicated but authentic prose on familiar subjects that are normally present in a predictable sequence, which aids the translator in his/her work. Texts may include description and narration in context, such as news items describing frequently occurring events, simple biographical information, social notices, formatted business letters, and simple technical material written for the general reader. The prose is predominantly in familiar sentence patterns. Some mistranslations.

In rendering translations, has written vocabulary sufficient to perform simple translations with some circumlocutions. Still makes common errors in spelling and punctuation, but shows some control of the most common formats and punctuation conventions. Good control of morphology of language (in inflected languages) and of the most frequently used syntactic structures. Elementary constructions are usually handled quite accurately, and translations are understandable to a native reader *not* used to reading the translations of foreigners.

Level 2+
Sufficient skill to translate most factual material in nontechnical prose as well as some discussions on concrete topics related to special professional interests. Has begun to make sensible guesses about unfamiliar words by using linguistic context and prior knowledge. May react personally to material, but does not yet detect subjective attitudes, values, or judgments in the material to be translated.

In rendering translations, often shows surprising fluency and ease of expression, but under time constraints and pressure, language may be inaccurate or incomprehensible. Generally strong in either grammar or vocabulary, but not both. Weaknesses or unevenness in one of the foregoing or in spelling results in occasional mistranslations. Areas of weakness range from simple constructions, such as plurals, articles, prepositions, and negatives, to more complex structures, word order, and relative clauses. Normally controls general vocabulary, with some misuse of everyday vocabulary still evident. Shows a limited ability to use circumlocutions. Uses dictionary to advantage to supply unknown words. Translations are understandable to native readers not used to dealing with foreigner's attempts to translate the language, though style is obviously foreign.

Level 3

Able to translate authentic prose on unfamiliar subjects. Translating ability is not dependent on subject matter knowledge. Texts include news stories similar to wire service reports, routine correspondence, general reports, and technical material in his/her professional field, all of which include hypothesis, argumentation, and supported opinions. Such texts typically include grammatical patterns and vocabulary ordinarily encountered in professional reading. Mistranslations rare. Almost always able to correctly translate material, relate ideas, and make inferences. Rarely has to pause over or reread general vocabulary. However, may experience some difficulty with unusually complex structures and low-frequency idioms.

In preparing translations, control of structure, spelling, and general vocabulary is adequate to convey his/her message accurately, but style may be obviously foreign. Errors virtually never interfere with comprehension and rarely disturb the native reader. Punctuation is generally controlled. Employs a full range of structures. Control of grammar good, with only sporadic errors in basic structures, occasional errors in the most complex frequent structures, and somewhat more frequent errors in low-frequency complex structures. Consistent control of compound and complex sentences. Relationship of ideas presented in original material is consistently clear.

Level 3+

Increased ability to translate a variety of styles and forms of language pertinent to professional needs. Rarely mistranslates such texts or rarely experiences difficulty relating ideas or making inferences. Ability to comprehend many sociolinguistic and cultural references. However, may miss some nuances and subtleties. Increased ability to translate unusually complex structures and low-frequency idioms; however, accuracy is not complete.

In rendering translations, able to write the language in a few prose styles pertinent to professional/educational needs. Not always able to tailor language to suit original material. Weaknesses may lie in poor control of low-frequency, complex structures; vocabulary; or the ability to express subtleties and nuances.

Level 4

Able to translate fluently and accurately all styles and forms of the language pertinent to professional needs. Can translate more difficult prose and follow unpredictable turns of thought readily in any area directed to the general reader and all materials in his/her own special field, including official and professional documents and correspondence. Able to translate precise and extensive vocabulary, including nuances and subtleties, and recognize all professionally relevant vocabulary known to the educated nonprofessional native, although may have some difficulty with slang. Can translate reasonably legible handwriting without difficulty. Understands almost all sociolinguistic and cultural references.

In rendering translations, able to write the language precisely and accurately in a variety of prose styles pertinent to professional/educational needs. Errors of grammar are rare, including those in low-frequency complex structures. Consistently able to tailor language to suit material and able to express subtleties and nuances.

Level 4+

Increased ability to translate extremely difficult or abstract prose. Increased ability to translate a variety of vocabulary, idioms, colloquialisms, and slang. Strong sensitivity to sociolinguistic and cultural references. Increased ability to translate less than fully legible handwriting. Accuracy is close to that of an educated translator, but still not equivalent.

In rendering translations, able to write the language precisely and accurately, in a wide variety of prose styles pertinent to professional/educational needs.

Level 5

Can translate extremely difficult and abstract prose (i.e., legal, technical), as well as highly colloquial writings and the literary forms of the language. Translates a wide variety of vocabulary and idioms, colloquialisms, slang, and pertinent cultural references. With varying degrees of difficulty, can translate all kinds of handwritten documents. Able to understand how natives think as they produce a text. Accuracy is equivalent to that of a well-educated translator.

In rendering translations, has writing proficiency equal to that of a well-educated native. Without nonnative errors of structure, spelling, style, or vocabulary, can translate both formal and informal correspondence, official reports and documents, and professional/educational articles, including writing for special purposes, which might include legal, technical, educational, literary, and colloquial writing.

....

Some years ago, when President Carter went to Poland, he said to an audience, "I love you." His American-Polish interpreter translated it as "I lust after you," which elicited loud laughter from the audience. The reason for the mistranslation: the hapless linguist had been away from his native land for over twenty years, during which time some basic Polish expressions had changed.

....

5

Translation Problems

Generic Language Problems

Human language is an extremely complicated means of communication. This may well be the reason why misunderstandings among individuals and groups of people are so common, and why the human species continues to experience so much conflict with so many tragic consequences. We the members of this species tend to oversimplify the complex phenomena that surround us, and one of the things we greatly oversimplify is what human language is all about. First, we make the erroneous assumption that when we use a basic word like "water," it means exactly the same thing to anyone who speaks English. Nothing is farther from the truth. To a chemist, water is H_2O, or a chemical substance. To a city dweller, it is a substance usually mixed with chlorine, while to a seashore dweller, the word "water" always raises the question of freshwater or seawater. This is the first source of translation problems. Translation is more than the replacement of one word in the source language with another word in the target language. It is a decision-making process involving a judgment regarding every single word translated, and the best way to translate it.

Second, we tend to oversimplify the relationships among different languages. This is particularly true of Americans, who, unlike Europeans and others, live in a vast country that basically speaks one language. When an American travels around the world, he/she expects every word spoken in a foreign language to mean exactly what it means in American English. The word in Latin American Spanish for "now" is "ahora." When an American tourist in certain parts south of the border is told, "I'll bring it to you now," he/she takes it to mean "right away." "Ahora," however, does not mean "right away." In the local idiom, "now" is not measured in "seconds" or a few minutes, but rather anywhere from a few minutes to several hours. The word for "right away" is "ahorita," or, for more emphasis, "ahoritita." And even then there are no guarantees. Let us add in passing that even in the United States, "right away" is not what it used to be. Perhaps respect for words and keeping one's word is not what it used to be. But this is another matter.

As the twenty-first century begins to unfold, languages around the world are becoming more complicated by the day. Not because human beings wish them to be more complicated. Quite the contrary. As we mentioned before, the common human attitude is to simplify. But because the world is becoming more complicated, and because things are changing so fast these days, the need for new words and for new and different meanings for old ones is becoming overwhelming. Moreover, the unprecedented close interaction among different languages around the world, particularly between American English and all the other languages, is altering the character of languages everywhere, with literally thousands of American words being adopted by other languages, creating a whole new challenge for the contemporary translator not only of language pairs involving English, but also of other language pairs, such as, for example, German-French, trying to decide when and how to use those American words in the context of a language such as German or French.

Add to this the fact that the written word is, after all, a record of the spoken word. It is a set of combined symbols, namely letters and characters, or in some languages ideograms, put together to produce syllables and words and phrases, which invariably fail to convey most of the nuances of the spoken word. When you say a simple word like "really," you can inflect, modulate, and resonate in countless ways, which causes the word to convey almost any meaning you wish, from question to affirmation, from sorrow to derision. Writing is incapable of doing this. When an actor looks at a written script of a play, he/she must decide how to pronounce, or rather how to act out the words. When a translator looks at a text in a source language, he/she must decide whether the author is serious, or whether there is subtle or not-so-subtle humor or some other attitude in what the author says. A misjudgment can result in a bad translation.

Another generic problem with the written word is the fact that a writer always has a specific audience in mind when he/she writes a piece, be it general or technical. That audience, to begin with, speaks the same language as the author. Moreover, the audience consists of a specific segment or segments of the population that speaks that language. The author often assumes that his target audience shares a certain body of knowledge with him/her, and therefore does not always spell out everything, but rather alludes or refers to it by implication. Here the knowledge of the language alone will not stand the translator in good stead. He/she also must share the writer's cultural background and understand the subtleties of the source language text. When an American suspense novel writer has his/her character say, "Let's rock and roll," it does not necessarily refer to dancing, but rather to engaging in some aggressive action.

An even better example of this problem is the use of acronyms. Some acronyms, such as UN and USA, are universally known. But many acronyms are very subject specific and can easily throw off the best translator.

These, then, are some of the generic problems facing the translator. There are many more. My intention in bringing these problems to your attention is not to discourage you from pursuing this craft. Rather it is to help you understand what you are up against as a translator so that you can be better prepared to face these problems as they occur.

The following sections discuss specific languages and their translation problems vis-à-vis English.

....

Levels of Translation

Keep in mind that not all translation is done on the same level. Be sure to find out before you start a translation assignment whether it needs to be merely a rough draft, a fully correct translation for in-house use, or actually ready for publication.

....

Spanish
....

Arguably, Spanish is the most translated language in the United States today. In some parts of the country, such as South Florida, Southern California, and parts of New York City, Spanish is no less dominant a language than English. The Hispanic population in the United States has been growing steadily in recent years, and American business now has a major stake in reaching this important market segment, as well as its countries of origin, notably in Latin America.

While generically Spanish is one of the easiest languages to translate into English, in actual fact, Spanish-English technical translation is much more problematic than, say, German-English, or French-English, or even Japanese-English.

This may come as a great surprise to many. But as can be attested to by anyone who has been working with a large variety of technical materials in which Spanish is either the source or the target language, quite often there is hardly a safe way to translate a given text from or into Spanish in a way that would satisfy one's client or one's target audience.

The main reason for this is that there is really no single version of Spanish. There are major differences between the Spanish of Mexico, Central America, northern South America, and southern South America, not to mention such places as Puerto Rico, and, of course, the motherland, Spain. Since we have large populations in the United States today hailing from all these parts of the Hispanic world, there is no way of translating a given text in a way that would fully satisfy all of these people.

And this is only the beginning. There is also the problem of the new hybrids of Spanish spawned here in the United States. Thus, we have Chicano Spanish in places like Texas, New Mexico, and California. We have Cuban-American Spanish in Miami, and Puerto Rican–American Spanish in New York. We even have such "exotic" mutations as Salvadoran Spanish in Washington, a new dialect combining American English and Central American Spanish spoken by a community with a distinctive cultural character.

Let's consider a commonplace item such as eyeglasses. A New York manufacturer of eyeglasses wants to promote its product in the Hispanic communities in the United States. One community refers to eyeglasses as *anteojos*, a second community calls them *gafas*, a third, *espejuelos*, and a fourth, *lentes*. In the promotion mailing, which Spanish word should be used? No one word will fit all. Well, one answer is to customize the translation, namely, provide several versions, based on geography, and use each of the synonyms for its appropriate target audience. This will require market research at considerable expense. Moreover, many common everyday items are referred to by Hispanics living in the United States by the English, rather than Spanish, name. A can of spray, for instance, becomes "espray." An electric drill is, quite simply, a "drill." Any attempt to be a purist and provide the real Spanish word for spray or drill will result in a drop in sales.

An added problem is the fact that while English and Spanish are, in many respects, such similar languages, in many technical areas there is a wide gap between the two. Since the Hispanic world is not as industrialized as the English-speaking world, and since the high-tech/digital/information revolution of our time is being played out and defined mainly in American English, the problems of technical translation from and into Spanish, rather than diminishing, continue to grow.

There is no easy solution in sight. The worst one can do is to pretend these problems do not exist. Or, for that matter, make a case for some kind of a standard, universal Spanish that can satisfy everyone's needs, when, in effect, no such Spanish exists, certainly not when it comes to technical translation. One has to come to terms with these problems and do the best one can in any given situation.

Spanish translators constitute the largest of any group of translators in the United States. They range from very basic communicators of the written and spoken word to some highly trained and skillful technical and literary translators. As in any other language, it is important for the Spanish technical translator to specialize in a particular technical area or areas, such as law, medicine, communications, or what have you. In addition, it is very important to gain familiarity with the main varieties of Spanish alluded to in this chapter. In this day and age of global communications, almost anything we do transcends the boundaries of our immediate community, and so it is important to know how Spanish is used in other parts of the United States and the world. There are now specialized dictionaries for regional Spanish (and more keep coming out), which are a great help in this respect (see appendix 1).

In conclusion, Spanish translation is definitely a career worth pursuing in the United States, provided one approaches it cautiously and with a sense of realism and long-term commitment.

German

German is one of the world's leading languages in all technical subjects and in all areas of human knowledge. In addition, the German-speaking world generates an enormous amount of technical literature that is routinely translated into English. Conversely, a great deal of English-language literature in many fields is translated every year into German. All of which translates into one simple fact: if you can translate German, you are in the right profession.

While it is important in any language pair to have excellent familiarity with the subject matter one translates in, in German it is especially important. This is because German tends to say certain things—even those of a straightforward technical nature—in a less than straightforward way. Unless one is very familiar with the subject at hand, there is a clear and present danger of missing the point and making a fool of oneself. Therefore, it is not recommended for the beginner to plunge into complex subjects when translating German. A period of apprenticeship and some real hands-on experience are required to produce truly accurate German translations.

German lexicography is quite advanced, which means that good dictionaries are available to the German, particularly the German-English (either way) translator. One should have access to the major, latest-edition linguistic sources in one's area(s) of expertise, keeping in mind, of course, that some tend to be expensive.

There are usually good career opportunities for German translators in the United States, and plenty of freelancing opportunities. One has to be alert and make many contacts—with companies, law firms, government agencies, translation services, and so on. The more the better.

This writer feels quite confident that the opportunities for German translators in the United States will continue to grow at a good pace. This is due to the fact that those areas where there has been the greatest rate of growth—computers, telecommunications, international trade, life sciences, the automotive industry, scientific research, and so on—are areas in which Germany is either a producer or a major consumer, and the exchange of ideas and information between the two cultures is extremely vital. As all the aforementioned areas become more specialized and more advanced, the need for highly competent and accomplished translators in the two languages becomes more critical. As in any other language, there is never an overabundance of good German translators, and those who apply themselves and make a commitment to pursue a career of German translation seriously, with long-term objectives, stand to benefit from it.

French

French is a very popular language among language students in the United States, as it is around the world. For many years, French has been recognized as one of the world's leading languages, playing a dominant role in all fields of human endeavor, notably in the arts, sciences, and technology, and has dominated such major areas as diplomatic relations among nations. With the decline of France as a world power after the two world wars, however, French no longer enjoys the preeminence it once did, as American English has taken over many of its previous domains. Nonetheless, French continues to enjoy the status of being one of the languages most often translated, and both professional and freelance translators have been known to make a decent living practicing French translation.

There seem to be four primary geographical sources of French documents that require English translation. They are France, Francophone Canada, Haiti (where the line blurs between Creole and French), and the French-speaking parts of Africa.

France has made many gains in recent years in many areas, including high tech and international trade, in fact too many areas to be enumerated in this limited space. The upshot of all of this is that French documents in a great many subjects require translation, and it behooves the practitioners of French translation to remain *au courant* in all matters pertaining to French technical terminology, neologisms, and so on.

Unlike many other languages, including such major languages as German and Japanese, French has been resisting the incursion of American English in such areas as computers, telecommunications, and advertisement. It is very important, therefore, when translating from English into French, to keep this in mind.

Another area that requires special attention is the difference between European and Canadian French. The influence of the English language is much greater in the case of Canada than France. This is due to two reasons: The main language of Canada itself is English, and Canada's only land neighbor is the United States. As a result, the infamous English word "tax" can appear in Canada as either "impôt" or "tax," while in France it is more likely to be "impôt." The good news is that the Canadian government has developed many good French-English technical dictionaries and glossaries.

Matters become more complex when it comes to African or Haitian French, particularly the latter. It is highly recommended that one have personal experience in these varieties of the language, to make sure that local dialect, idioms, and special expressions are not missed.

Secondary sources of French would be such places as the French part of Switzerland, some Caribbean islands, and other places around the world where French is spoken. These, however, rarely come into play in the American translation marketplace.

There are excellent sources of French dictionaries and other technical references that make the job of French into/from English translation manageable. It is expected that more and more French language sources will be available on electronic media, and now is a good time to look into this kind of resource and consider adding them to your arsenal.

Russian

For some seventy years—from the end of World War I to the 1990s—the relationship between the Soviet Union and the West was basically adversarial. In addition, Soviet society was culturally repressed, and there was hardly any free cultural and scientific exchange of ideas and knowledge between the Communist Bloc and the West. As a result, the West concentrated more on monitoring the Soviet empire and arming itself against it than on any peaceful pursuits, all of which was closely reflected in the kind of Russian-English translation work that took place during those years.

All of this changed radically around 1992. As the Cold War ended, Russia divested itself of its empire and started a new era as a nascent democracy seeking to do the things all democracies do—focusing on economic, legal, and cultural issues rather than on the arms race. All of a sudden, those translators who had spent years translating from Russian into English found themselves tackling new fields—finance, insurance, and legal issues, to mention only a few. This radical change is the main source of the problems we encounter today in translating Russian into or from English. We translators are dealing with areas of human endeavor for which the Russian language did not develop sufficient terminology during the twentieth century, presenting a challenge for the Russians themselves and for anyone who translates from or into Russian.

The Russians, fortunately, have not been sitting on their hands for the past ten years. They are hard at work publishing new Russian-English and English-Russian dictionaries for business, law, computers, telecommunications, and many other long-neglected areas (see appendix 1). The Russian language, always resourceful and resilient, is adjusting itself to the new realities. While Russia as a society is undergoing political unrest and a prolonged economic crisis, a great deal of interaction between Russia and the West (one of the best examples is the Russian-American joint space program) is taking place, which forces the two sides to participate in the transformation of the Russian language from a tool of Communist propaganda to a free-market-economy language.

What persists through all these great changes are the inherent difficulties of the Russian language, by no means an easy language for English speakers to master. Unlike English, which has a rather uncomplicated and relaxed grammar, Russian has a very complex grammar, especially in regard to cases. Very often students of Russian in the West fail to master all the six cases of modern Russian, and as a result they are not able to produce a fully accurate translation. Conversely, Russian natives who translate English into Russian are not always thoroughly familiar with all the nuances of the vast vocabulary of American English, particularly with colloquial American expressions, and they too often fail to convey the exact meaning of American texts.

In today's Russian-English translation environment, my advice to translators in these languages is threefold: first, keep in close touch with both current Russian and current American English, through reading and verbal interaction with both languages; second, acquire as many of the new technical dictionaries as you can that are now being published in the areas you translate; and third, pay close attention to the case form in Russian, and to the complexities of both technical and colloquial American English.

Japanese

Japanese is one of the leading languages in today's world in science, technology, industry, and business. A great deal of technical, scientific, and business documentation is generated in Japanese and translated in the United States. At the same time, similar English-language documentation is regularly being translated into Japanese. There are no exact statistics on this subject, but it is safe to assume that along with Spanish, German, French, and Russian, Japanese is one of the top five most frequently translated languages in the United States.

A growing number of American college students choose Japanese for their foreign language requirement, or even major in this language. From all indications, given the popularity of the Japanese language and the continued economic importance of Japan, Japanese should continue to play a significant role on the international scene in the new century.

This means that developing one's skills as a Japanese translator is time well spent. The United States and Japan continue to interact in all areas of commerce, science, and technology. Documentation and literature flow between the two countries in a steady stream. As the global village becomes more of a reality with every passing day, the interaction between Japanese and English intensifies and requires an ever-growing volume of translation in real time.

Having said this, it comes as a surprise that Japanese-English lexicography is not well developed. There is a great shortage of subject-specific Japanese-English technical dictionaries, which makes it difficult to acquire working glossaries in certain areas. The few good Japanese-English dictionaries available are very expensive, beyond the reach of many freelancers. This is a problem that cries out for a solution.

Another important consideration is the cultural differences between Japan and the West. There are two basic styles of writing in Japanese—polite, personal writing, and a more formal, precise, informative writing. For scientific texts, the second style is always used. For general topics, one must choose between the two and then stick to it.

The Japanese lexicon is extremely rich. This wealth of vocabulary can be divided into three main categories: (1) words of Chinese origin, normally written in Kanji; (2) native Japanese words, written in Kanji or Kana; and (3) Western loan words, normally written in Katakana unless they have been in Japan so long that their foreign origin has been forgotten (e.g., "tobacco," often written as "*tabako*"). An understanding of these distinctions is helpful because it assists you in looking up new vocabulary.

Another aspect of Japanese text that requires special attention on the part of the translator is sentence and paragraph structure. The internal organization of a written text can be quite different in Japanese and English. One Asian writer has described English as "linear," with individual sentences moving a central idea forward one step at a time. Japanese writers who have not been influenced by Western notions of writing, however, sometimes adopt a "spiral" approach, repeating what has already been said as they gradually converge on their target. This can result in an extended paragraph with only one period and countless commas. The task of the translator is then to grasp what the target is, organize the paragraph into segments of suitable length, eliminate redundant portions, and render what is left into English.

Finally, Japanese and English do not operate in quite the same way. In Japanese, the verb comes at the end, while in English it is normally in the middle of the sentence. In fact, in translating Japanese into English, you have to jump back and forth to pick up the subject and the verb, and reorganize the whole thing. Most notorious is the disregard Japanese has for the plural form, for definite and indefinite articles, and for verb tenses, all of which are often ignored and have to be figured out from the context.

Despite these difficulties, more than a few Westerners have already succeeded in pursuing an effective career as translators of this particular language pair, and the study of Japanese in the West is increasing.

Chinese

More than 1.3 billion people speak various dialects of Chinese in the People's Republic of China. Another 7 million speak Cantonese in Hong Kong. An additional 23 million or so Chinese live in Taiwan. And there are countless Chinese communities spread throughout Southeast Asia and the rest of the world. Despite differences in accent and dialect, the written language has historically been the unifying element of the widely dispersed Chinese community.

The written language, however, has split into two. Prior to World War II, the Chinese characters in use throughout the Chinese-speaking world were essentially the same. In the 1950s, with the avowed goal of shortening the road to literacy, the Communist government began issuing simplified characters. Chinese communities outside mainland China, however, with the exception of Singapore, have for the most part continued to use traditional characters. For instance, in the United States, the vast majority of Chinese newspapers are still published in traditional characters—including the overseas edition of the 人民日报.

In addition, there are regional differences in terminology that go beyond the distinction between simplified and traditional characters. For instance, much of China refers to a bicycle as 自行车. A term often heard in Taiwan is 腳踏車, while people whose primary dialect is Taiwanese/Fukianese will be familiar with the terms 孔明車 and 鐵馬. Speakers of Cantonese often employ the term 單車. The fact that this list is by no means exhaustive provides some insight into the tremendous breadth of vocabulary in Chinese, even for simple, everyday objects.

This diversity is reflected in a generation of modern technological vocabulary as well. A computer, even in a scientific text, may be referred to as a 计算机 or a 電腦. A hard disk is sometimes referred to as an 硬盤 and sometimes as an 硬碟. Software is known as 軟件 and 軟體. The list goes on and on.

The bottom line is that, to be competitive, a Chinese-English translator needs to be able to read both simplified and traditional characters fluently, and to have a sensitivity for the rapid, sometimes overlapping coining of new words in the Chinese language.

In recent years a growing number of major American companies, as well as other companies from around the world, have been setting up operations in China. The need for technical translations from and into Chinese has been growing accordingly, and many experts maintain that China will play a major global role in the next century. All of this means that the need for Chinese-language translators and interpreters will continue to grow, and if anyone is looking for a language to pursue as a career, Chinese certainly is a good choice.

Italian

The volume of Italian translation in the English-speaking world is not nearly as great as, say, German or French. Nevertheless, Italian is one of the world's major languages, and there is hardly a field of human endeavor where Italian influence has not been felt. This is true of everything from fine arts to science and technology, from fashion to high tech, and other fields too numerous to mention. Whether or not one should pursue a full-time career as an Italian translator in the English-speaking world is hard to say. Certainly there is always a need for Italian freelancers, if only on a part-time basis, and there are indeed people who have successfully pursued full-time careers as Italian translators in countries like England and the United States. But clearly their numbers are not legion. As a general rule, if one happens to know Italian and has a flair for translation, it is certainly worthwhile to sharpen one's translation skills. If, on the other hand, one chooses to major in Italian in an American college or university with a view to making Italian translation a career, one should first examine the range of opportunities.

We would be remiss not to mention at this point that Italians have always excelled in the field of translation. Italian lexicography is excellent, and the practitioner of Italian-English translation has the advantage of outstanding general and technical dictionaries and references (see appendix 1). The kinship between the Italian language and the rest of Western culture, and the distinction of this language as arguably the most beautiful of European languages, makes the task of Italian translation a unique challenge and a delight.

Portuguese

Portuguese is a language spoken by over 200 million people around the world. The great majority of these people live in Brazil, while only some 10 million live in Portugal itself. Most of the documents translated from Portuguese into English or vice versa originate in Brazil. Brazilian Portuguese differs from European Portuguese in several respects, including several sound changes and some differences in verb conjugation and syntax. For example, object pronouns occur before the verb in Brazilian Portuguese, but after the verb in European Portuguese. Brazilian Portuguese seems to be developing at a faster rate than its progenitor, and the gap between the two continues to widen. This impacts on the work of the translator, who has to be aware of the differences between the two.

Portuguese-English lexicography is not nearly as advanced as that of other major Romance languages, which hampers the work of the translator in this language pair. Nor is Portuguese technical terminology as well developed in many areas as, say, French. This too makes it difficult at times to do technical translation into or from Portuguese. Nevertheless, Portuguese is a major language representing a major culture and a large segment of the world's population, and it is to be expected that its lexicography and technical vocabulary will continue to develop in the years ahead.

The volume of Portuguese translation in the English-speaking world is not nearly as great as, say, German or Spanish. Nevertheless, the need for Portuguese translation is by no means insignificant. Certainly there is a need for Portuguese freelancers, if only on a part-time basis, and there are indeed people who have successfully pursued full-time careers as Portuguese translators in places like England and the United States. But clearly their numbers are not legion. As a general rule, if one happens to know Portuguese and has a flair for translation, it is certainly worthwhile to sharpen one's translation skills in this language. If, on the other hand, one chooses to major in Portuguese in an American college or university with a view to making Portuguese translation a career, one should first examine the range of opportunities.

Arabic

Arabic is one of the world's major languages. It is the official language of eighteen countries in North Africa and the Middle East, and the mother tongue of at least 165 million people. It is also the language of the Qur'an, which makes it the second language for millions of Indians, Iranians, Indonesians, and other inhabitants of largely Muslim nations, and the holy tongue of all of the above. Historically, it has been one of the major repositories and catalysts of world culture.

The conscientious Arabic translator is aware of the generic difficulties in working with two languages as different from each other as English and Arabic. First, there are vast cultural differences between a Western language such as English and a Semitic language such as Arabic. One cannot translate these languages without paying attention to these cultural differences. In a way, translating between two disparate cultures like these often necessitates explication in

addition to direct rendition of words and phrases. Furthermore, Arabic characters create the problem of correct spelling of personal, place, and other proper
names, compounded by the absence of some basic consonants in Arabic, such as
p or v. This writer once came across the name "Davy Crockett" spelled in Arabic,
which sounded like "Daffy Crookit." It took several minutes to figure out who
this historical personality was.

In addition, Arabic is in the process of developing technical terminologies for
new areas such as computers and telecommunications, and the precise term is not
always readily available. Add to this the fact that there are several spoken Arabic
dialects that are not always mutually intelligible, such as Syrian and Egyptian, and
the fact that even the official written Arabic has different terms and usages in different Arab countries. What all this means is that very often the Arabic translator
needs to engage in some additional research to produce a truly accurate translation of Arabic into or from English. When all is said and done, however, meeting
the challenge of translating Arabic accurately and elegantly can be a source of
great satisfaction.

The volume of Arabic translation in the English-speaking world is not nearly
as great as, say, that of German or Spanish. Nevertheless, there is always a need
for accomplished Arabic translators. Whether or not one should pursue a full-
time career as an Arabic translator in the English-speaking world is hard to say.
Certainly there is always a need for Arabic freelancers, if only on a part-time basis,
and there are indeed people who have been successfully pursuing full-time careers
as Arabic translators in countries such as England and the United States. As a general rule, if one happens to know Arabic and has a flair for translation, it is certainly
worthwhile to sharpen one's translation skills. If, on the other hand, one chooses to
major in Arabic in an American college or university with a view to making Arabic
translation a career, one should first examine the range of opportunities.

Hebrew

Of all the languages discussed in this chapter, Hebrew is the only one that is not
spoken by a particularly large population. Roughly five million people in Israel
speak Hebrew, and less than a million in the rest of the world. But the importance
of Hebrew on the world scene should not be measured quantitatively, but rather
qualitatively. The Hebrew language represents one of the world's major cultures
and civilizations, at the center of which one finds the Hebrew Scriptures, and at
its most recent stages of development, a fast growing and developing contemporary language vigorously engaged in all facets of culture, science, and technology.

Some sixty years ago, when the new state of Israel was born and Hebrew was
still struggling to take its place among the languages of the world, the celebrated
writer Arthur Koestler compared the attempt to modernize Hebrew as "attach-
ing parts from a Cadillac to a Canaanite chariot." One thing Koestler advocated

at the time was to give up the Hebrew script and use Latin characters instead, as was done by Atatürk in Turkey earlier in the century. Much to many people's amazement, Hebrew did become a "full-service" modern language even though it did not give up its ancient Hebrew script. It is safe to say that it is easier today to translate Hebrew into and from English than it was sixty years ago, because literally thousands of basic words and technical terms which did not exist in Hebrew back then have now become part of the everyday language and the technical vocabulary.

This is not to say that translating Hebrew into or from English is easy. Hebrew is not a European, but rather a Semitic language. Its cousins are Arabic, Aramaic, and other languages of the Middle East. Like Arabic, it operates in a linguistic and cultural world different from the West, notwithstanding the great involvement of present-day Israel with Western civilization. One cannot translate a text directly from or into Hebrew without explicating certain words, terms, and phrases, or finding suitable equivalents. As happens today with other languages, very often in doing a technical translation from English into Hebrew, one is forced to keep a certain English term in the Hebrew so as not to lose the meaning. These are some of the challenges facing the practitioner in this particular language pair.

Most Israelis are quite at home with English, and much of Israeli business is conducted in English, which reduces the need for Hebrew-English translation, a phenomenon similar to what occurs in India, where English is the second official language after Hindi, or in Sweden, a nation well versed in English. Pursuing a full-time career as a Hebrew translator in the English-speaking world may not be the most sensible choice of career. But certainly if one is equally at home in Hebrew and English and has a flair for translation, it makes good sense to pursue translation in this language pair as a sideline.

Some final thoughts: This chapter has covered the most salient languages of "technically active" language groups, namely Germanic, Romance, Slavic, Sino-Japanese, and Semitic. There are additional translation problems specific to other languages within each of these groups, which hopefully will be treated in future editions. Some examples are North and South Korean, the languages of the Balkans, and Slavic languages in Central Europe. Also, there are other important languages in Europe, Asia, and Africa that were not discussed here: Turkish, Greek, Hindi, Indonesian, Swahili, and Amharic come to mind. It should come as no surprise to anyone if in the twenty-first century some of these will be herein discussed.

....

Today as always, if a talented translator does not get any assignments, the fault is the translator's.

....

6

Translation Techniques

The first five chapters of this book were devoted to the background, requisites, and problems of translation in general and with certain languages in particular—in other words, the more theoretical aspects of translation. The rest of this handbook is devoted to the "nuts and bolts" of the translation craft and business, the techniques, equipment, tools, and so on. The last part of the book consists of appendices which provide extensive information on dictionaries and where to find them, current sources of translation work, translation study programs, accreditation for translators, and publications of interest to translators. The present chapter discusses the best ways to handle translation assignments.

Preliminary Considerations

You are given a text to translate. Before you commit yourself to doing any work on it, you must ask yourself a few preliminary questions. They are:

1. Is the text legible?
2. Am I familiar enough with the subject to tackle it?
3. Do I have the linguistic resources (dictionaries, human contacts) to decipher unfamiliar words?
4. Is the text complete, or are there any missing parts?
5. Can I do it within the requested time frame?
6. Do I have a good reason for doing it (doing it as a learning experience, or because you enjoy it, or to help a friend, or because you are properly compensated for doing it)?

Once you have answered all the above questions to your own satisfaction, you are ready to proceed with the translation.

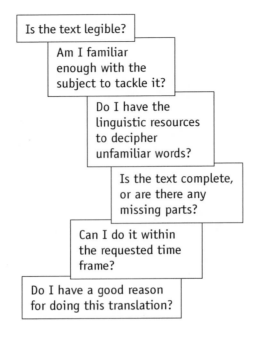

Is the text legible?

Am I familiar
enough with the
subject to tackle it?

Do I have the
linguistic resources
to decipher
unfamiliar words?

Is the text complete,
or are there any
missing parts?

Can I do it within
the requested time
frame?

Do I have a good reason
for doing this translation?

Effective Approaches

There is no single effective approach to translation, and over time translators develop personal techniques that enhance the quality and the speed of their translation. No one set of rules applies equally to everyone, but there are certain methods and means of translation that can help almost any translator achieve greater accuracy and output. The following is a review of some of the key techniques that are becoming almost universal among professional translators.

The first and foremost question a translator must deal with today is what kind of equipment to use in the process of translating. In the days of the pen and the typewriter, this question was much less crucial. Today, however, translation has become almost totally dependent on computers, for several good reasons: (1) word processing allows far greater flexibility in producing text than any other contemporary means; the output of most translators has been tripled and quadrupled through the use of computers; (2) computers allow text to be stored on a disk and reprinted or modified later on, a function that is invaluable in the translation field; (3) clients nowadays are getting used to asking for translation on electronic files, since it allows them to edit, reprint, modify, and enhance the physical appearance of a document; (4) if more than one translator is involved in a given translation project, the text from the various translators can be accessed by an editor and equalized or manipulated as necessary, without having to redo any particular portion thereof.

In addition, it is becoming more common every day to use electronic means such as e-mail or fax to transmit and receive text. These tools are no longer a luxury. Their cost has been coming down, and more and more translators are acquiring them. Many people today are saying they cannot imagine how translators were ever able to manage without them. The answer is very simple: manage we did, but it took us ten days to two weeks to do what we can now receive, translate, and deliver in two or three days.

The next question when approaching a translation assignment is, am I qualified to do this particular translation? Only an honest answer will do. If one is not sure, then chances are one should not tackle that particular task. One must feel confident about a particular assignment if the results are to be satisfactory. The exception to this rule is a case where a client cannot find anyone else to do that particular job, and for some good reason is either willing to take a chance or to receive less than a complete and fully accurate rendition. In such a case, it should be made clear between translator and client that the translation is not legally binding.

Once the commitment is made to proceed with the job, the translator will spend some time going over the entire document—even if it is book length—and do a realistic assessment of the following points:

1. How long will it take to translate the document?
2. What reference tools are needed to get it done?
3. What kind of preliminary steps are needed prior to the actual work of translating?
4. What special problems are related to the document, such as legibility of blurred or poorly copied text or difficult handwriting?
5. Does the document contain text in a language or languages other than the main source language, and if so, can the translator handle that language?

Regarding the question of time, one can do a quick estimate of the length of the document by averaging words per line, times lines per page, times number of pages. An experienced translator has a pretty good idea of the number of words per hour he or she can translate. This is an essential feature of undertaking a professional translation job, since most clients have tight deadlines and tend to give repeat business to those translators known for keeping to their deadlines.

As for reference tools, if, for example, one is given a document about telecommunications, one should make use of one's own resources in that field or borrow from other sources whatever one needs to accomplish the task.

Preliminary steps prior to actual translation can include a consultation with an expert in a specialized technical field regarding a difficult term, phrase, paragraph, or concept that the translator does not feel comfortable with. Having access to such experts is one of the translator's most cherished assets. It can make all the difference in the world between a correct and effective translation and one

How long will it take to translate the document?

What reference tools are needed to get it done?

What preliminary steps are needed prior to the actual work of translating?

What special problems are related to the document, such as legibility, blurred or poorly copied text, or difficult handwriting?

Does the document contain text in a language other than the main source language, and, if so, can the translator handle this language?

that misses the main point of the entire text. Another preliminary step is a trip to the local, regional, or even specialized library to do some research on the subject. Alternately, one can do preliminary research on the Internet (see chapter 7).

The problem of legibility should be identified *before* one begins the task, not after. Sometimes the problem may start in the middle of the document and be so severe as to render the translation of the first part useless. In that case, the translator may have wasted a great deal of time. Sometimes the problem is minor and does not affect the overall outcome of the translation. In other cases, the client may decide to proceed with the translation and simply put the designation "[illegible]" (between brackets rather than parentheses) wherever a word or part of the text cannot be deciphered.

Unbeknownst to client and translator, when a translation job is first assigned, there may be portions of text inside the source document in a language other than the main language of the document. This can happen in commercial, scientific, and scholarly documents. It even happens in Tolstoy's novel *War and Peace*, when the author starts using French instead of Russian. This too should be detected prior to commencing the translation work, and a decision has to be made regarding the following questions: (1) Does that text need to be translated? (2) Can the translator handle it? (3) Is it necessary to assign it to another translator?

Some Common Misconceptions about Translation and Translators

1. Anyone with two years of high school language (or anyone who lived in another country for three years during early childhood) can translate.
2. There's no difference between translation, transcription, and transliteration.
3. A good translator doesn't need any reference literature.
4. Translators will soon be replaced by computers.
5. Translators don't need to know how to spell, since they can use the spell-checker on their computer.
6. A good translator gets it right the first time, without any editing or proofreading.
7. Good translators are a dime a dozen.
8. If you can type in a foreign language, then you are an accomplished translator.
9. Translators can translate both ways just as easily.
10. A one-hundred-page technical manual that took four months and three people to write can be translated into another language by one translator in two days.

Once all this preliminary work has been done, one is ready to proceed with the actual translation work.

Depending on the particular text, one should either start translating at this point, or, in the case of a text containing highly specialized terminology which may send the translator on frequent trips to the dictionary, one should first go through the document and make a list of as many unknown or uncertain terms as possible, and then spend some time looking them up and making a word list. This technique saves a great deal of time, since once a list is completed, it is much easier to sail through the text, and the time spent initially on making the list is very short compared to the time wasted on repeated interruptions to look up words. Moreover, by first mastering the more difficult terminology of the text, one gains a much better understanding of the subject and is certain to produce a better translation. From the very start, make it a habit to compile word lists and glossaries of subject-specific terminologies, and keep them in a computer database program for future reference. In time, these lists will become your most valuable translation tool.

One should also follow good work habits. Some translators, particularly those engaged in freelance work, tend to overdo it, especially during their "busy season," when they can generate a large income during a relatively short period of time. They will go for twelve or more hours a day, and before they know it, they will start complaining of stiffness in the neck and shoulders, blurred vision, and ongoing fatigue. One should not translate more than eight hours a day. Six is ideal. Eight is tolerable, provided one takes a few short ten- to fifteen-minute breaks. Ten is pushing it. Over ten is definitely hazardous to your health.

Before you get ready to submit your translation, go over it again, using the following checklist:

Omissions—did you fail to translate any particular word or phrase, or even paragraph?

Format—does your format follow the original (breaking into paragraphs, for instance)?

Mistranslations—did you mistranslate any particular word?

Unknown words—were there words you were not able to translate which you would like to explore further?

Meaning—did you miss the meaning of any phrase or sentence?

Spelling—did you misspell any word which the spell-check function on your computer did not catch?

Grammar—did you make any grammatical mistakes?

Punctuation—did you mispunctuate or miss any punctuation marks?

Clarity—did you fail to clearly convey the meaning of any particular part of the text?

Consistency—did you call something by one name and then by another without any good reason?

"Sound-alike" words—did you mistranslate a word because it looks or sounds like a word in your target language but in reality has a different meaning?

Style—are you satisfied with the way your translation reflects the style of the original text (for example, the original is written in a clear, direct style, while the translation sounds more complex and indirect)?

This checklist is by no means exhaustive, but it does cover the main areas a translator must pay attention to.

As was already explained, your personal computer is your best friend when it comes to translating, editing, and producing a final copy. One can learn a few basic commands in Microsoft Word and start using the computer. But there is much more to software than entering, deleting, and inserting text. The better acquainted with software you become, the more it will help you with translation. Learn how to do columns and tables, how to use special technical and scientific symbols, do graphic functions, use the spell-check and the thesaurus, create databases for glossaries and for your own administrative records, and you will tackle a great variety of technical text in many fields at a speed that will amaze you. Remember: speed in translation is the most important thing next to language proficiency. Without it you will not be profitable, and you will be overrun by the competition. With an established record of fast, accurate translation, you can write your own ticket.

After a few years of using the computer, you may want to consider dictation. Personally, I prefer a mix of PC and dictation. When I have an unusually long job and not enough time to do it in, I may revert to dictation. Otherwise, I prefer word processing. One could argue that by dictating one gets more done and earns more, but there are other things to consider, such as the cost of transcription, the need to edit transcription, and the better control one has over writing than speaking. Some of us are natural speakers; others are writers.

One continues to develop translation techniques over time. One of the most wonderful things about translation, in my opinion, is the fact that your mind is never idle, never in a rut, but rather always being challenged by new tasks, new subjects, new knowledge, and the need to keep up with new developments in language, with different fields of human knowledge, and with the events of the world. As a translator in the Washington area since the late 1970s, I have found myself in the middle of world events, beginning with the peace treaty between Egypt and Israel in 1979, when I met Begin, Sadat, and Carter, and, more recently, in my daily dealings with events in post–Cold War Eastern Europe; the strife-torn Middle East; the famine in Somalia; the new North American Free Trade Agreement (NAFTA) between the United States, Canada, and Mexico; and the growing involvement of the U.S. space program with the space programs of other nations. Very few people cover as broad an area as a translator. Every day we in the translation business find new challenges and have to solve new problems. As a result, we are always developing new techniques and finding new answers.

7

Translation, Computers, and the Internet

Digital technology as it relates to translation and to almost anything else in today's world is in a constant state of change. In the nearly two years since this handbook was last revised, computers have become more dominant in the translation craft. More work is now being transmitted electronically by e-mail attachment rather than by fax. The Internet has become a routine tool for translators—from work search to word search. And a growing number of translators have become involved in the translation of such computer-based material as websites, a process now generally referred to as localization. All this has resulted in this newly revised and expanded chapter that looks at all of the above developments and how they benefit or fail to benefit translators.

Once you have read this chapter you will be glad to find out that one thing has not changed, which should come as no surprise: translation continues to be a human, rather than a machine function. Computers are no closer now to replacing human translation than they were three years ago, or at any other time in the past. Notwithstanding the great benefits translators are deriving from the digital revolution, computers continue to be the tools rather than the decision makers of the translation process.

Computers and Related Equipment

As was mentioned before, only a few years ago a translator would use a pen or a typewriter to translate. In 1980, for example, the ultimate text-producing tool in the world was the IBM Selectric electric typewriter, which we thought we would proudly bequeath to our children and grandchildren. All of this changed forever with the birth of the word processor, and more specifically, the PC, or personal computer, which is getting better every year, as if it were a magical tool with boundless possibilities. Certainly the PC has changed the lives of translators, increasing their productivity and profitability three- and fourfold, and enabling them to receive and transmit work, look for answers to linguistic questions, communicate around the world, and take advantage of computer-assisted tools (see below) that in certain cases can save a great deal of time and effort.

Bare Minimum Hardware and the Wish List

The electronic age offers a great deal more than the word processor. There is the fax, modem, optical scanner, e-mail, smart phones, iPad, various types of translation software such as translation memory, and last but not least, the Internet. No doubt, it all seems quite overwhelming. Which is the best tool? How much should I spend? How much do I need?

The first thing you are going to buy is a personal computer. Whether you are going to buy a desktop or a laptop is a matter of choice. The obvious difference is that one is portable and the other will have to sit on your desk. Laptops have now larger screens, full keyboards, DVD burners, good audio, and graphics cards just like their PC counterparts. A PC is just easier to troubleshoot and more scalable than a laptop. The best solution is to have both, just in case something goes wrong with the laptop.

One more thing: the standard computer for translators is the PC. The Mac, or Macintosh (also known as Apple), is extremely user friendly and very reliable, but because of its price, it is not nearly as often used in our field, so we will concentrate here on the former.

Whether you use a desktop or a laptop, be sure to have sufficient data storage space on your hard drive, as well as an external storage device (minimum 500 GB) that can be plugged into your computer and used to back up your files in real time (external HDDs are shipped with backup software).

If you use a laptop, be sure to also buy one or two LCD monitors (your eyes and back will thank you!). Your laptop should of course be wireless. This will enable you to use your computer in many more places than your desk, where your computer is stationary. As of this writing, the dominant PCs as well as laptops on the market are Hewlett Packard, Dell, Lenovo, Sony VAIO, and Toshiba. Be sure to read reviews before buying a PC or a laptop. You can visit websites like ZDNet, CNET, or user review sites. As translation software is memory hungry, you need as a minimum configuration for your PC or laptop the following: an Intel i3 (or more) processor, 4 GB of RAM, a 500 GB HDD, and a good 1 GB graphics card. You will of course have to add an LCD monitor or two to your PC or laptop. As the size matters, choose them large enough, like twenty-two to twenty-four inches. The best brands are Dell, LG, Samsung, and ViewSonic. My favorites are the Samsung, which are the most technologically advanced and have the best colors of all. There again, read reviews before buying anything. Also, to get the best deals on the Web, type the reference number of the item you favor in Google, or visit websites such as www.dealnews.com, www.amazon.com, www.newegg.com, www.tigerdirect.com, or www.frys.com.

As for printers, the choice is large, including Brother, HP (Hewlett Packard), Canon, Lexmark, Samsung, and Xerox. Choose any black-and-white laser printer, which are now very cheap and, best of all, the ink does not have to dry. Besides, laser printer toner does not need to be replaced very often. Choose a multifunction printer, which allows you to copy, print, scan, and fax at the same time.

Nowadays, you can find a Canon ImageClass (or equivalent) for $150. Check the brand websites to see which are the new models and learn their specifications. As the models change quickly, I am not going to recommend any one in particular. Do your homework, and check the above websites.

When purchasing a computer or peripherals, first decide exactly what configuration you are looking for. Then look around at retail outlets, mail-order catalogs, and Internet sources. Get the best deal you can get when you are ready to make a purchase.

As a translator, you will be making extensive use of your e-mail service. You will send and receive documents by e-mail attachment, and you will communicate with your clients and translation providers by e-mail.

What Kinds of Software?

The English-language word-processing software most commonly used in translation is Microsoft Word. Whatever language you are translating into, the U.S. version of Word can do it, as most languages use Unicode, a code that Word handles very well. Microsoft Excel is also very commonly used by translation companies and should be installed on your machine. You might also get requests for Microsoft Publisher files. As Microsoft Publisher is part of the MS Office suite, you are well advised to buy the whole package rather than separate versions of each component of the bundle. The Microsoft Office 2010 Home Edition is more than enough to accommodate your translation needs. The major weakness of Office is its spell-checker, a tool commonly used by all translators. For that reason, I would recommend the purchase of add-ons that independent software vendors have developed and that do work well with the Office suite.

A lot of translation companies and clients require the use of translation memory applications. The principle of these tools is pretty simple and can be summed up in one sentence: "Translate once, reuse many times." The most commonly used is SDL Trados 2007, and its newest version SDL Studio 2011, which is even more user friendly than its predecessors. When you buy the latest, you will also get SDL Trados 2007 in the bargain, which does make sense, as most companies have yet to make the move to Studio 2011. Trados is used by 90 percent of the translation community and should be preferred to other tools such as Wordfast, Atril Déjà Vu, or Kilgray MemoQ. They all have their pros and cons, but Trados is the oldest and best known (already twenty years old). Together with your translation tool, I would recommend using a terminology database application like SDL Multiterm, which allows you to build, update, and query your term lists. Besides, Multiterm works jointly with Trados, to which it can be seamlessly integrated.

If your translation work has graphic components, such as illustrations, photos, and the like, or includes book-sized projects, you may need graphics and desktop software such as PageMaker (the latest version is called InDesign), or Quark for desktop publishing, and Photoshop for graphics.

Machine Translation vs. Human Translation

Machine translation, or MT, is the term used to describe translation performed by a computer software program, as an alternative to human translation (HT), performed by a human translator. Machine translation belongs in the area of artificial intelligence. Artificial intelligence is the branch of computer science that deals with using computers to simulate human thinking. Its purpose is to create programs that can solve problems *creatively* rather than merely responding to commands—in other words, they operate just like the human brain.

In the late 1950s, programmers in organizations such as the U.S. Air Force believed that computers would soon be programmed to accept human language input and translate it into English or into any other language. During the ensuing fifty years, many millions of dollars were spent by the Air Force and by other entities in the hope of enabling computers to replace human translation. So far, the results have been quite limited, for two main reasons: (1) while computers have a seemingly unlimited capacity for processing data, they are far from being able to think creatively like human beings, and (2) human language is not merely a collection of signs and symbols that can be easily programmed, manipulated, and computerized. This is true of human language used not only in poetry and philosophy, but also in technical subjects, in which language expresses thought processes far more complicated than merely "one plus one equals two."

In recent years several companies in the United States and around the world have produced software designed to translate from one language into another. This software varies from a very basic word finder for the tourist to complex programs for translating technical and scientific data. Some of the latter range in price from as low as $250 to as high as $250,000 and have been sold to governments and international organizations. One important lesson, however, has been learned by both the makers of those programs and their consumers. Machine translation does not replace human translation. At best, the former can achieve around 60 percent accuracy, when the goal is as close to 100 percent as possible. Consequently, the expectations regarding MT have been modified, and it is now recognized that to achieve full accuracy, such translations must be postedited by a human translator.

All of the above notwithstanding, machine translation does have its uses. Certain limited language environments do allow for machine translation. One example is the Canadian weather bureau, which transmits weather reports in both English and French. The number of words involved in the daily weather report is very limited and can be easily programmed into a computer for translation from one language into another. Another example is official forms, which contain simple basic questions. An organization such as NATO can desire to have forms put out in ten different languages and set up a program to automatically translate each form into those languages. A third example is the Caterpillar corporation in Illinois that sells its agricultural machinery around the world and maintains operation manuals in various languages. This company has invested millions in its in-house translation software which allows it to update and modify its technical literature in a cost-effective way. In all of the above examples, the software was customized for one particular work environment where repetition is the common denominator.

Another use of machine translation is for processing a large body of a foreign-language text to find out what the gist of it is—rather than to achieve a fully accurate translation in order to decide whether or not to select parts of it for accurate (viz., human) translation. This process is only partially reliable.

Translators for the most part are not fond of postediting machine translation. Often the pay is not adequate, and the work can be harder and more time consuming than translating directly from the original. This certainly applies to freelancers, but also to in-house translators who are on a salary.

At the present time, the ones who benefit the most from machine translation are not those who buy such services, but rather the companies who develop and manufacture the software and the translators who work on those machine translation projects either as developers of the programs or editors of the machine-translated text. In other words, machine translation has not made translation cheaper for the average consumer of translation services and therefore does not pose a real threat to translators.

Machine translation is becoming more reliable than it used to be a few years ago. The only thing is, it needs to be properly trained. A machine translation engine, especially if it is a *rule-based engine*, needs to be "taught" by coding grammatical rules, do-not-translate expressions, terminology, and so forth into the engine. MT needs a lot of attention before it can give good results, but this can be achieved after patient work and with the help of computational linguists. Some popular rule-based engines are Systran, Promt, Lucy Software, IBM Websphere, Toshiba (Japanese), and CCIT (Chinese). On the other hand, MT *statistical engines* are trained on patterns found in texts, documents, or books existing in a pair of languages. A minimum of 50 million words are needed to train a statistical engine in order to get acceptable results. Language Weaver (SDL owned) has known a lot of success with the technology, especially in Arabic documents translated by the U.S. Department of Defense. The new trend is to combine both statistical and rule-based engines to create hybrid MT engines to improve the results. Asia Online is a good example, and despite its name, it has developed engines and can develop customized ones for all languages in the world.

Translation Memory

One computer tool commonly used today in the area of computer-assisted translation (CAT) is called translation memory. Here sentences and other parts of translated texts are stored and can be used again when the same or a similar translation is required. This tool can be applied to any kind of project, large or small, provided the text will be updated in the future. It makes even more sense for bigger projects, such as software manuals, heavy machinery guides, legal codes, and safety data sheets that are updated or modified on a regular basis, where most of the text remains the same while certain sentences or paragraphs are changed. It allows greater consistency, as one can search the TM with the help of the concordance feature while translating. If even part of a sentence has been translated in the past, you will be able to locate it and reuse it, thus saving time. A new feature called "advanced leveraging" automates the search and will try to find and replace phrases for you. These tools have been widely used in the localization industry for the past twenty years, and translators are well advised to invest in one, as not having it limits the number of prospective clients.

Translation memory provides great help for the translator, and it is not an obstacle to anyone's creativity. Its aim has never been to replace the human brain.

Localization

Localization is defined as the process of creating or adapting a product to a specific locale, that is, to the language, cultural context, conventions, and market requirements of a specific target market. With a properly localized product, a user can interact with the product using his or her own language and cultural conventions. It also means that all user-visible text strings and all user documentation (printed and electronic) use the language and cultural conventions of the user. Finally, the properly localized product meets all regulatory and other requirements of the user's country or region.

Clearly, this definition takes us out of the strict realm of translation into the domain of computer programming and international business. It alludes primarily to the localization of websites (as well as software) in other languages and cultures. Two other terms often used in conjunction with localization are "internationalization" and "globalization." The first refers to the preparation of computer text to be used in localization in such a way that it meets the requirements of the target language and culture. The second generally refers to both processes together, namely internationalization and localization.

With the fast proliferation of websites and the rapid growth of many kinds of computer software, a growing number of translation companies have ventured into the field of localization, and more than a few computer hardware- and software-producing companies (including giants like IBM and Microsoft) have turned to the field of translation as a function of localization.

Thus, localization has been presenting translators with new opportunities and some difficult questions. On the one hand, there is a huge volume of text these days in website and software development that necessitates multilingual translation. On the other hand, for a translator to become involved in localization, a specialized knowledge of computers is usually required, since website and software localization requires not only language translation but also adaptation of computer commands to the requirements of the target language. Hence, a translator may want to carefully consider how far he or she wishes to become involved in technical computer work that requires skills and training beyond the scope of actual translation work.

It should be mentioned that localization in the sense of translating a text and adapting it to another culture existed long before the computer age. Thus, for example, an American advertisement company in the precomputer era that planned an international ad campaign for a company such as Coca-Cola had to study the cultures of other countries and customize the ads not only in terms of the target language, but also the cultural conventions, preferences, and taboos of the target country. Furthermore, the act of translating itself is in a sense a form of localization, since language does not exist separately from its culture.

Website and software localization has been around now for several years. It relies heavily not only on human translation but also on machine and machine-assisted translation tools, such as translation software and translation memory. Given the limitations of these tools, the often unrealistic expectations of the marketplace, and the eagerness to process a large volume of material in record time, localization has been experiencing many problems, and the goals its pursuers have set for themselves are yet to be realized. One should keep all of this in mind before getting involved in this area of translation.

The Internet has opened up opportunities for translators unlike anything before in human history.

The Uses of the Internet for Translators

The translation field has become increasingly "wired," witnessing a proliferation of sites relating to professional activities, job hunting, commercial products, and online reference materials for translators. It is not an exaggeration to say that translators do themselves (and potentially their clients) quite a disservice by ignoring the virtual translation community.

This section will introduce you to a selection of highly regarded and well-maintained sites of use to translators. It assumes basic web literacy. Of course, the Internet's ever-changing nature guarantees that certain websites will decline or disappear, while new ones will emerge by the time this book becomes available.

So please be aware that you will probably have to do some updating of the following information on your own.

The Almighty Google

One of the latest verbs in English is "to Google." The incredible reach of www.google.com is such that we can no longer live without it. To Google somebody means to type the person's name into the Google website and find out instantly everything (well, almost) there is to know about that person, which applies not only to people but to everything else under the sun. On Google's home page, you will find a function called "Language Tools." It allows you to find words and translate text in several major languages from and into English. As in all machine translation, the rate of accuracy here is much less than 100 percent, but at least it helps you orient yourself through text and terminology.

Professional Activities

Translators wishing to learn about the state of their profession will benefit from a visit to the American Translators Association's site, www.atanet.org. I discuss the ATA in greater detail in chapter 15. Its website includes information on the association's formal activities such as conferences, publications, and certification procedures. Even if you are not an ATA member, the site is useful because it can guide you to other translation-related sites.

Another major website of interest to translators is the site of the international umbrella organization of the world's translator associations, the International Federation of Translators, found at www.fit-ift.org.

Aquarius, at www.aquarius.net, claims to be "the world's language network." This commercial website lists translation agencies seeking translators and interpreters, who in turn can post resumes to make their services known. It also links to other translation sites.

More recent websites of this kind are www.proz.com, which bills itself as "the world's leading enabling and sourcing platform for language professionals"; www.planettranslation.com, which is useful for both translators and translation service buyers and also provides tips and terminology; and www.translatorscafe.com, which provides useful functions for translators looking for work and resources.

Networking with Other Translators

Translators these days often communicate with one another on the Internet, sharing knowledge, passing on information, checking terminology, or just griping about not being paid on time. It all started with what used to be called "chat rooms," which morphed into various kinds of translation forums located in the United States and around the world.

One kind of forum for translators is the newsgroup: subscribers post messages and receive answers (say, to a specialized translation query). One newsgroup for translators is http://www.faqs.org/faqs/language/translation-faq.

Also, you will find it useful to join social networking like www.linkedin.com, where you can post your profile and enroll in numerous newsgroups related to translation in general, machine translation, LISA, Trados, job offers, and the like.

Reference Materials

The Translator's Home Companion at www.lai.com/companion.html provides a great deal of useful information for translators. The Human Languages Page at www.june29.com/IDP provides links to other translation-related sites, including some listed here, and to dictionaries.

Online Dictionary Services

Inter Active Terminology for Europe (IATE) at http://iate.europa.eu is a very useful service. It handles the twenty-seven official languages of the European Union, including Spanish, Portuguese, French, German, Italian, English, Danish, and Dutch. It features many specialized dictionaries in nontechnical, legal, and technical areas.

Termium Plus at www.termiumplus.gc.ca is an extremely good terminology database. It has been developed by the government of Canada and contains millions of terms related to a wide range of fields. You can use it mostly for French and English. Spanish has been recently added and contains a good number of entries.

The Grand Dictionnaire Terminologique de l'Office Québécois de la langue française at www.oqlf.gouv.qc.ca/ressources/gdt.html is a very useful terminology database for all the French-to-English and English-to-French translators. It covers a wide variety of subjects and is fairly comprehensive.

Linguee at www.linguee.com "is a unique translation tool combining an editorial dictionary and a search engine with which you can search through hundreds of millions of bilingual texts for words and expressions." This is a very useful tool if you use the following languages: French, English, German, Spanish, and Portuguese.

Online Dictionaries at www.yourdictionary.com covers a far greater range of languages than the above site. It provides links to dictionaries and translations in many specializations.

Glossaries

There are many mediocre glossaries out there in cyberspace, so use caution with this type of online resource. Here is one of the better ones: http://www.termisti .refer.org/termisti.htm. U.S. government agencies provide some very useful glossaries; for example, www.epa.gov/glossary (for environmental terminology).

Finding Cultural Information

A quick way to access cultural and historical information on other countries is via the Electronic Embassy at www.embassy.org. This service provides links to embassy and/or United Nations home pages for many nations. Most countries' pages include links to cultural resources such as online newspapers, libraries, and so on. You may have to do some digging to find the information you're after, but if it exists online, you will probably find it by starting here. Also the foreign ministries of various countries are a good source for all sorts of information related to a particular country.

Shopping for Dictionaries

A prime source for dictionaries is www.schoenhofs.com. Major virtual bookstores also have good selections of dictionaries. Examples: www.barnesandnoble.com and www.amazon.com. You may also wish to consult these websites of major dictionary publishers: Elsevier at www.elsevier.com, Routledge at www.routledge.com, and McGraw-Hill at www.mcgraw-hill.com.

Freelancers can find out about the payment practices of translation agencies. For the most part they are free, but you have to join to be able to use them. See www.paymentpractices.net and www.tcrlist.com.

The Power of Language

Once, in the "good old days," the Russian Czar decided to grant clemency to one of his unfortunate subjects who had been sentenced to death. He ordered his communications expert to send a telegram to the prison in Siberia, stating: "Clemency, period, no execution."

The careless clerk at the telegraph office did not proofread the telegram. It came out as: "Clemency no, period, execution."

8

Dictionaries, Reference Literature, and Terminology Management

Dictionaries

No translator, no matter how accomplished or well versed in both the source and the target languages, can do without dictionaries and reference literature. If either language or knowledge were static, remaining the same over a long period of time, then one could conceivably reach a level of expertise where references become marginal. The fact remains that this is not the case, certainly not in our day and age, when both language and knowledge are changing almost daily. If, for instance, you specialize in translating medical subjects, and you stop doing it for a few months, you may find out that there are new names of drugs, medical concepts, and procedures which did not exist at the time you stopped translating. Therefore, you need current reference sources that will enable you to handle current medical subjects.

By the same token, the best of dictionaries and reference sources become dated the day they are published, and will never answer all your questions. This handbook—for that matter—will have to be revised almost every year if it is to keep up with all the information it seeks to provide.

What all this means to you as a translator is that even if you possess the best of linguistic and technical references, as indeed you should, you may want to get in the habit of compiling your own glossaries and databases in subjects you frequently translate, to keep yourself up to date, and always be on the lookout for new reference sources.

When you start out in this business, you soon discover that the acquisition of good dictionaries and reference literature is quite an expensive proposition. The best general and technical dictionaries in such major languages as Spanish, German, French, and Japanese range in price from $100 to over $300 each. Good technical reference books in specialized subjects are not much cheaper. As a beginner, you may not be independently wealthy, and you may get an assignment which would require a couple of expensive dictionaries, but the money you earn from the assignment will not cover the cost. What are you to do?

What I did when I started out some years ago as a freelance translator of Spanish and Hebrew was to go to my regional public library, where they had some of the reference sources I needed. It was not as convenient as having my own, but it worked. Then, as I started earning more money from translation, I gradually acquired the dictionaries I needed. I must confess, sometimes I over-indulged myself and bought dictionaries which weren't so good, and which I should have checked out more carefully. But my general policy has been to stay within my budget, and the times when I was able to acquire some of my best and most expensive reference sources were when I got an assignment in one of my languages of expertise big enough to justify the expense.

In this work, when it shall be found that much is omitted, let it not be forgotten that much likewise is performed. —Samuel Johnson's comment upon completion of his dictionary in 1755

As of this writing, there is a growing trend in the publishing world to produce dictionaries and references as electronic media, best known as e-books. Does this mean we should stop buying dictionaries? This is hard to predict. Books are not going to disappear in the next few years, if ever, but e-books in general are becoming more and more popular and user friendly on handheld electronic devices. Typically, a professional translator engaged in a highly technical translation job will be surrounded by dictionaries and reference sources and will be looking up things in as many as ten or twelve different books at the same time. To do all of this on computer would necessitate a ten- or twelve-part split screen, with a great deal of keypunching or mouse-clicking, which may be more time consuming than simply having the good old books spread around you. On the other hand, e-books are virtually weightless and do not occupy any space, making them great tools for the translator on the go. How all of this will play out in the immediate future is a little hard to predict.

For recommendations of good dictionaries and reference sources, see appendix 1. For major dictionary outlets, see appendix 2.

Reference Literature

Besides dictionaries, a working translator needs reference books for the subjects being translated. First, there are general references covering general knowledge, data, and language. Then there are specific reference works geared toward a given field, such as medicine. This includes medical dictionaries, encyclopedias, handbooks, journals, and various compilations of medical data, in both the source and the target language. The third major source of information today is the Internet. Use it extensively.

Terminology Management

Dictionaries and electronic equipment are not sufficient to produce high-quality translations. With language changing almost daily, you have no choice but to compile your own glossaries in specific subject areas. Indeed, every new job will add words to your lists. This has always been the case, and today it is more so than ever before. The more extensive a glossary you develop as you go along, and the more accessible you make it, the better your translations will be, and the easier your life will become as a translator.

In the "old days" we simply jotted words on pieces of paper and kept them inside the dictionary, either in the front or in the back. When we translated a specialized item, such as farming equipment or coal mining, we would write down the difficult and unknown terms, do some research, and write down the English equivalents of the foreign terms (or vice versa). Each time we did another piece of translation on the same subject, we would refer to that list and get good use out of it.

Now, however, we have become much more sophisticated. We do what is known in professional linguistic circles as "terminology management." To manage all of our glossaries and specialized terminology we rely on two key elements—smart terminology organization, and smart use of the computer.

Types of Terminology

Terminology falls into different categories. The most obvious category is the *main subject area*. Each field of human knowledge and activity has its own terminology. This is particularly true of such areas as law, medicine, computers, engineering, and so on. Very often, the same word used in each of those fields takes on a different meaning (a "host" used in a medical sense is different from any other sense). In organizing your glossaries, it is best to start out by putting them into clearly defined categories. You need to identify the categories you will be working in, and put them in alphabetical order, starting with an area such as agriculture, and ending with zoology. There are many ways of organizing information on computer, and you can choose one depending on the extent of your terminology management needs. The simplest way is to use your word-processing program, which can automatically alphabetize your entries. At the other end of the scale are programs especially designed for translation management, which tend to be quite costly. They are mostly used in very large translation projects involving teams of translators. Whichever program you use, the idea is to have the information organized in such a way that it is very accessible and easy to use. You should store it on your working drive, create a backup, and also keep a hard copy.

Within each subject there are *subject subspecialties*. Thus, for example, there is real estate law, criminal law, computer law, and so on. If you do a great deal of legal translation, you need to segregate your glossaries and keep them according to these subspecialties. The same holds true in chemistry, medicine, and a great many other areas.

Another major area of terminology is *organizational language*. This refers to major corporations, not-for-profit organizations, and government agencies, all of whom develop their own terminology, which becomes extremely critical in doing translation work. Here you need to organize your glossaries according to clients, with the above categories organized within these client categories. If, for instance, you do a great deal of work for IBM, you need to follow their usage very closely, and be consistent each time you do a translation job for them. What has become very common for large organizations is to produce their own glossaries, word lists, lists of acronyms, and so on. More often than not they will give you those valuable tools at the beginning of their relationship with you. But sometimes they forget, and an experienced translator will always ask for them up front. Very often they only have them in hard copy, and you can either urge them to convert those items into electronic files, so that you can use them on your computer, or else do it yourself (here an optical scanner comes in very handy). Quite naturally, you will be able to keep expanding those official lists.

The other aspect of organizational language is *preferential usage* and *corporate style*. This is not a matter of right or wrong terminology, but of the choice of words and the style of writing of a particular organization. The U.S. government, for instance, publishes a style manual which reflects the standard usage of the federal government, from punctuation to the use of ambiguous words. The best way to master a specific corporate style is to read a few documents generated by that organization prior to embarking on a translation assignment.

Another major area of terminology management, which every translator is familiar with, is *acronyms* and *initialisms*. More than ever before, documents today are saturated with acronyms and abbreviations. Some are universally known and are used daily in the media, since any educated person knows them (UN, NATO, UNESCO, etc.). Some are known to any translator working in a specific area (a translator of computer literature is bound to know the meaning of CD-ROM, RAM, etc.). A great many, however, are either too esoteric, are only used by one particular organization, or are too recent to be widely known. Compiling lists of acronyms and abbreviations and organizing them in a systematic and accessible manner is one of the most important functions of technical translation in today's world. One important aspect of your list of acronyms is the indication whether it is to be left untranslated (for an objective reason or because of an organizational preference), or whether it is to be translated or transliterated.

Creating New Terminology

It is not common for translators to create new terminology. This work is done by specialists in either academia, private industry, or government, and by the language academies of various countries. But there are occasions when a translator finds him/herself breaking new ground, and there is no choice but to create new terms. This writer was once involved in one such case, when his translation agency was given an assignment by the U.S. government to translate a book from Japanese about protecting highways against snowstorms. The Japanese government had embarked a few years ago on a major study that combined civil engineering and meteorology, studying the properties of snow in relation to the condition of highways, bridges, and tunnels under severe snow conditions. As a result, the Japanese broke new ground in the study of snow, which required new Japanese terminology describing the nature and behavior of snow under certain conditions. In translating this five-hundred-page study into English, it became clear that there were no equivalent words in English for all the newly coined Japanese words. As a result, the translators, one of whom had a degree in civil engineering, and the other a background in meteorology, had to coin new words. This was explained to the contact person at the U.S. government agency which had requested the translation, who instructed the translators to go ahead with the work. Usually one of two things happens in a case like this. Either the new terms are effective, and will become official, or else someone may improve upon them and provide better terms.

To sum up, terminology management is probably the most critical aspect of technical translation. It often makes the difference between a good translator and an excellent one. The better you manage terminology, and the more extensive your up-to-date terminology sources are, the higher your chance is to be looked upon as a truly reliable translator in a given field.

Some Uncomplimentary Statements about Translators

It is difficult in following lines laid down by others not sometimes to diverge from them, and it is hard to preserve in a translation the charm of expressions.—St. Jerome

Traduttori, traditori [Translators are traitors].—A traditional Italian adage

Some hold translations not unlike to be The wrong side of a Turkey tapestry.—James Howell

Les traductions augmentent les fautes d'un ouvrage et en gâtent les beautés [Translations increase the faults of a work and spoil its beauties]. —Voltaire

Nor ought a genius less than his that writ attempt translation.
—Sir John Denham

9

Key Translation Areas

Some translators spend a lifetime translating basically only one subject. This is true of a translator with a major corporation like Ford, who only translates automotive subjects, or with a government agency like the National Institutes of Health (NIH), who only translates medical subjects. I say "basically," because in reality there is no such thing as a purely automotive or medical translation. Every technical subject is "tainted" by other subjects, notably legal, financial, and so on. But still, the translators in the aforementioned examples do concentrate on one major area.

But as was mentioned before, the typical freelancer has to know a variety of subjects if he or she wishes to make a living translating. The question to ask oneself is, which subjects? Not all subjects were created equal when it comes to translation. Some are translated constantly, and others infrequently. The practical thing to do is ask yourself, which are the most commonly translated subjects? And do I have enough expertise in at least two or three of those subjects so that I can give myself a good start in this business?

There are no absolute answers to these questions, since subjects vary from place to place. In a place like the area between San Jose, California, and Seattle, Washington, computer-related subjects are very prominent, while in Detroit automotive subjects are prevalent, and so on. But there is a fairly general consensus on certain areas that are more common than others. Here is a working list which is by no means exhaustive, but certainly representative:

Advertising
Aerospace
Automotive
Business/Finance
Chemistry
Civil engineering
Computers
Electrical/Electronic engineering
Environment
Law

Medicine
Military Subjects/Martial Arts
Nautical Subjects
Patents
Social Sciences
Telecommunications

The above are very inclusive areas. They break into many subareas, and often are mixed together. But let's take a quick look at each one of them, and try to gain a general idea as to what is required to work in those areas.

Advertising

This is a very specialized field. To borrow a term from software translation, to translate advertising copy really means to "localize." One has to go beyond a straight translation of text. Advertisement is in effect an effort to impress people with a few words, and get them to buy something which they may or may not buy otherwise. The key to advertising is the "target audience." The moment one translates any advertising text, it is clearly targeting a different audience, which speaks a different language. Most likely, it will differ from the original audience in more aspects than just speaking another language. There will be cultural, political, and even religious or economic differences. All of this has to be factored in when doing this type of translation. By the same token that it takes a special type of creativity to write advertising copy in the first place, it takes a similar creativity to render that copy in another language. Clearly, translating advertising text requires experience, and it is not something a beginner should jump into.

Aerospace

Here a distinction should be made between aeronautics and space subjects, which are often thrown together these days under the heading of aerospace. Aeronautics is an older subject than space sciences. Both are highly technical, with the difference being that space subjects are in the process of developing, and therefore present a higher degree of linguistic difficulty than aeronautics. As space exploration continues to develop, entirely new sciences are being created, such as space medicine, space engineering, and so on. One cannot enter this field of translation cold, but rather must go through a process of apprenticeship, unless one already has a background in either aeronautics or space studies or both. On the other hand, the terminologies and nomenclature in these areas are accessible, and with good terminology management, one can learn how to operate in these areas fairly quickly.

Automotive

This is a relatively easy technical field for a translator to work in, provided one has good sources of terminology and contact with the technical people involved in the subject. In all major languages, there are very good dictionaries for automotive subjects, mechanical and electric engineering, and all other subjects related to cars. The important thing here is to pay close attention to the actual usage of car-related terminology in the geographical area where the translation is to be used, so that the end-users of your product can use it safely and efficiently in their work.

Automotive Terminology in Spanish; or, How a Car's Trunk Changes Names throughout the Hispanic World

Spain—maletero
Chile—maleta
Argentina—baúl
Paraguay—valijera

Bolivia—maletera
Costa Rica—joroba
Mexico—cajuela

Business/Finance

This is a highly specialized area of translation. It is not recommended to get involved in translation of financial subjects, such as banking, insurance, the stock market, or real estate, without a background in those subjects. Here the question is not only knowing the terminology, as in the case of automotive subjects, but also understanding the subject one is translating. It is common in financial subjects to have a great deal implied in the text, rather than spelled out. People who write on these subjects generally assume that their readers have a good understanding of the topic, and so they allude to a great many things without bothering to explain them. You will hardly ever see the term "gross national product" spelled out in a financial text. It is known as GNP, and the average reader of this kind of material is expected to know what it means. In American English in particular, there is a very rich jargon of financial terms, which must be closely adhered to if one is to provide a translation that makes sense to, say, a stockbroker or a financial planner. For that matter, all major languages have their own specific terms, phrases, and concepts that flow out of the economic and financial reality of their societies or regions that are not easy to master. Here good dictionaries are only useful up to a point, but they are certainly not sufficient for coming up with all the answers. In sum, this is an area one should not walk into too hastily but should be prepared to approach carefully and selectively. (See appendix 1 for business dictionaries by Morry Sofer in Arabic, Chinese, French, German, Italian, Japanese, Korean, Portuguese, Russian, and Spanish.)

Chemistry

Many of us had chemistry in high school and/or college. But if you talk to a chemist these days, you'll find out that there is no longer one subject known as chemistry, or one kind of chemist. More perhaps than any other science, chemistry has become a multitude of sciences, each with its own specialized nomenclature, terminology, units, abbreviations, jargon, typographical organization, and databases. To cite a few examples: polymers and copolymers, space-related chemistry, geochemistry, petrochemistry, and stereochemistry, not to mention such areas as pharmacology, where chemistry reaches into the field of medicine.

Unlike financial subjects, however, things here are laid out quite explicitly, and with good terminology management, one can become an effective translator of chemical subjects in a relatively short time. Since chemical subjects are one of the largest sources of translation in the world, those who are interested in this field are well advised to invest in the resources necessary for doing this kind of work, which consist of electronic databases available from government, academic, and private organizations; good specialized dictionaries in specific areas of chemistry; and publications that help translators keep in touch with the field. For translators of Arabic, for instance, it certainly pays to specialize in petrochemistry; for translators of German, in nearly any area of chemistry; and so on. Once you have identified the possibilities available to you in this field, you can begin to work on improving your capabilities in it, and you should be getting steady work.

Civil Engineering

This field can be approached in one of two ways. If you already have a background in civil engineering, you are ahead of the game. If you don't, you can ally yourself with a civil engineer who would go over your translation and make technical corrections. The field of civil engineering offers some large translation projects, which can be quite lucrative, and since few translators in any given language happen to be civil engineers themselves, it is quite common for a technical translator to ally him- or herself with a civil engineer to ensure the quality of the final product. As in all branches of engineering, here too, terminology can be easily managed once you have the right resources and know how to organize them.

Computers

Computers are arguably the fastest-growing field in the translation profession. For a translator, familiarity with computers does not only mean having the right tools to maximize productivity, but also having access to subject matter which provides a large volume of translation work. Computer literature during the past ten years has grown phenomenally. It includes how-to books; manuals for computers, printers, and software; articles about computers; and books and articles about the Internet, to mention only the most commonly known items. Translating computer subjects presents both an opportunity and a challenge. The opportunity is working in a fast-growing field. The challenge is the fact that computer subjects are changing and growing daily, and last year's computer dictionary is near obsolete this year. Thus, to be a truly specialized computer translator, one needs to be in ongoing touch with computer publications and computer columns in the general press, and try out new equipment and programs. Like chemistry, computers represent one of the most active fields of translation and cannot be ignored by anyone who wishes to develop a successful freelance business.

Electrical/Electronic Engineering

American companies play a dominant role in the global market of electrical and electronic products. As a result, there is a great need for translation of these subjects around the world. The translation of these documents requires a good understanding of the basic principles of electronics and the correct use of terminology. These documents follow well-established rules which must be adhered to very closely, and are typically full of acronyms and abbreviations, measurement units, scientific symbols, and descriptions of pieces of equipment, their components, and all their pieces down to the smallest subcomponents. Fortunately, there are excellent dictionaries for these subjects both in English and in most major language pairs from/into English. Translators who work regularly with these subjects tend to develop extensive glossaries and are often known for their good terminology management, which is the key in this field. As a major technical area of translation, this area is definitely worth pursuing.

Environment

Environmental studies is a relatively new field, yet its importance around the world is quite evident. Unlike some of the other technical fields mentioned here, this subject is not well defined and in effect encompasses several disciplines, such as biology, chemistry, forestry, hydrology, and civil engineering, to mention only a few. It is not quite clear how one goes about specializing in translation of environmental subjects. My suggestion is you shouldn't waste too much time trying to figure it out. You should only be aware of the fact that this is an important field, and if you should have the opportunity to work on translations related to environmental subjects, you will have to judge for yourself whether the particular document is within your area or areas of expertise.

Law

Translation of legal subjects is practically an inescapable feature of technical translation, just as all aspects of your daily life, from driving to getting married to buying a piece of property, have legal implications. Nearly all the subjects discussed in this chapter get mixed with legal text (a chemical patent, a business contract, medical insurance, etc.). The law is one thing none of us can drop from our personal agenda, so we have to learn how to deal with it as best we can.

For translators, that means paying special attention to legal documents, and developing good legal reference resources. In addition, we have to be aware of the following aspects of legal translation: (1) the legal system of each country is different, and therefore you cannot translate every legal term directly from one language to the next; (2) there are different specialties within the legal field, such as business law, patent law, criminal law, constitutional law, and even computer law, and each has its own specialized terminology; (3) translations of legal documents can be used in court and are often used outside the court system (for naturalization, marriage, etc.), and thus become legal documents in their own right, and therefore must be handled with extreme attention to accuracy and completeness.

Legal translation is by far one of the most if not *the* most common type of translation, not only in the United States but around the world. Most legal documents are not too difficult to translate, although some do tend to be turgid, or purposely ambiguous. Once you become regularly involved in a specific type of legal translation, such as contracts, depositions, or divorce decrees, you find out that they invariably follow the same formula, and your work becomes much easier than when you first started out. In addition, legal translation requires good writing skills, and your command of your target language is being tested when you do this type of translation. Finally, while some types of legal translation may be tedious, many are quite interesting.

Medicine

Much of what was said before about chemical subjects also applies to medicine. Here, too, we have a large number of subjects all grouped under the general heading of "medicine," which includes life sciences, pharmacology, and even space medicine. Another major area related to medicine is health care, which has become a huge source of translations in the United States, especially in Spanish.

This field has its own jargon, with terms such as "copayment," "health care provider," "delivery," and so on. Mastering this jargon in both the source and target languages is time well spent.

One does not have to have a medical degree to translate in this field, but clearly terminology management is a key to effective translation in all biomedical subjects. The trend today in this field is TDB, or terminology database, which allows storing a vast body of information and manipulating it in a variety of ways. While physicians are notorious for their poor handwriting and hard-to-decipher transmission of medical information, the task of the translator is to render medically related data in a clear and concise fashion, with the highest degree of accuracy.

The good news about medical translation is that the reference literature and the computerized TDBs are getting better every year, and there is nothing to prevent a translator in the world's major languages from developing good skills as a medical translator.

How English Is (Mis)Used around the World

In an Acapulco hotel: "The manager has personally passed all the water used here."

In a Japanese hotel: "You are invited to take advantage of the chambermaid."

In a Vienna hotel: "In a case of fire, do your utmost to alarm the hotel porter."

In a Bangkok drycleaner's: "Drop your trousers here for best results."

In a Hong Kong dress shop: "Ladies have fits upstairs."

Military Subjects

Translation of military subjects has always been a huge industry. The trend in the world today is to move away from armed conflicts toward peaceful pursuits, but the world unfortunately is still far from being free from conflict, and the need for expert translators of military subjects is still very real. This field covers an enormous array of subjects, ranging from military history to military technology, the art of war, human issues involving the military, and much more. Most military materials are written in a concise and factual style which does not require special literary skills. The underlying theme of military subjects is getting the job done quickly and efficiently. This is why much of military translation is done by people with a military background.

Over the years, The U.S. Department of Defense has been a major source of military-related translation in all languages. Many people have made a career of such translation work, and some still do. There is no one piece of advice for people who look to enter this field, since it is so broad and diffuse. But a general acquaintance with and understanding of military theory and operations is necessary to work in this field effectively. Thus, for example, a soldier does not "shoot" but "fires," and his or her personal weapon is not a "gun" but a "rifle." The military does have its own way of saying things, and like all professionals, they too insist on respect for their language.

Nautical Subjects

This field covers naval subjects, which are part of the military field, and civilian navigation, which includes anything from a small sailboat to huge oil tankers. Seafaring has one of the richest vocabularies in the English language, and people who are not directly involved in sailing and nautical activities can easily get lost in this linguistic environment. Some areas of nautical translation, however, such as cartography, are not all that vocabulary intensive and can be mastered by "landlocked" translators. In approaching nautical subjects, one must first see how technical the particular document is, and whether one has sufficient background to handle it.

Patents

Patent translation is one of the main growth areas of translation around the world. This is particularly true if you are a Japanese-into-English translator, since the bulk of patent registration in the United States consists of Japanese patents. German and French come a distant second and third, with the rest of the major languages of the world trailing behind. Most patents relate to either medical, chemical, or mechanical subjects. The legal part of the patent translation is fairly well defined and straightforward and does not require a great deal of training. The text itself can be difficult at times and requires a certain degree of subject understanding. Most patents are only a few pages long and make for a comfortable assignment—not too short to be unprofitable, and not too long to monopolize all your time. Many translators have developed a good system of doing patent translation, and the field is open to new players.

Social Sciences

This term is used here in the broadest sense, to include such areas as politics, international relations, and basically all social subjects which may be considered general rather than technical. For the most part, this type of translation, which includes books, newspaper and periodical articles, essays, speeches, and so on, does not require specialized technical knowledge, but rather a broad education and a familiarity with the contemporary world. If you routinely translate, for example, articles concerning social and political events in Germany, you may want to subscribe to some German newspapers and magazines to keep up with the latest trends in the German language. You should also read books about your subject and take a personal interest in it beyond your translation assignments.

It should be pointed out that translations of this kind are not as prevalent as truly technical translations, and therefore a freelance translator who seeks to build his or her practice purely on this type of translation may find it difficult to secure a steady flow of assignments. Most technical translators look upon social-sciences-related translation as a bonus, an occasional opportunity to do something most of them enjoy doing but do not expect to do on a regular basis.

Telecommunications

This subject is closely related to electronics, computers, and at times marketing and advertising. The activity in this field around the world today is enormous, as giant telecommunications companies from the United States, England, Germany, France, and other countries compete for their share of the pie in the world markets. Here in the United States, the competition among telecommunications companies is rather severe, as the laws regulating telecommunications services have been changing dramatically, and as the advent of the Internet has forced the traditional telephone companies to invest in looking for a share in this new world of communications. It is by no means an easy field to work in as a linguist, since there are new linguistic developments almost every week, and one needs to keep constantly abreast of all the new concepts and new terminology which this field keeps generating, not only in English but in other languages as well. But it is worth getting involved in and gaining expertise in, since its volume of translation is growing at a very rapid rate. A word of advice to those who get into this field: stay in close touch with your client, and make sure the two of you have a good understanding as to the terminology you are expected to use, the degree of localization (adjusting the text to the particular country where it will be used), how much is to be left in the original language to avoid confusion, the use of acronyms, and the corporate style of the client, which needs to be reflected in the translation. If you'll excuse the pun, in this type of work you certainly don't want to have any breakdown in communication.

For a successful translation career, the knowledge of two or more languages is not enough. One should also pursue a major technical area, such as law, medicine, or business.

10

How to Operate Successfully as a Freelance Translator

So you've decided to try your hand at freelance translation. Congratulations! If this is indeed your calling, or your karma, or your destiny, or whatever you choose to call it (as a translator, you will always be compelled to choose the right word), stick to it, and your reward will be more than tangible. While not everyone may appreciate your work, since translation is—and has always been—one of the most misunderstood (sometimes even maligned) professions, if you maintain your professional integrity, you will always know your own self-worth, and your reputation will grow.

But getting down to reality, there are many mundane technical details one must master if one is to operate successfully as a freelance translator. Here are some of the most important ones.

Financial Issues

Self-Employment. As a freelancer, you are self-employed and have to pay your own taxes. Many freelancers tend to ignore this fact until they get their 1099 forms at the beginning of the new year and realize they have to pay taxes like everyone else. It is very important to set aside a portion of your income during the year and be ready for that infamous April 15. Otherwise, you may find yourself paying interest to pay taxes, which is not the best way to manage your finances.

Financial Records. You may want to consult your accountant on what kind of expenses you can deduct from taxes and keep records and receipts of those expenses. You will be able to deduct part of your house as an office, and all your phone, fax, office supplies, and work-related room and board. The laws have been changing in recent years, and a good accountant is essential to maximizing your deductions.

Pricing Yourself. One of the first lessons a freelance translator learns is that not all translation jobs are created equal. By that I mean, like a good businessperson, you learn how to price each job, and either accept it or reject it. I have dealt with many freelance translators in many different languages who decide beforehand that—like a lawyer at a high-powered law firm—they will not offer their services for less than, say, a hundred dollars an hour or twenty cents per word. Now, granted, there are a few translation and interpretation jobs around that will pay these high rates. But they are few and far between. I may be moving in the wrong circles, but quite frankly, while I have seen such rates being paid, they were quite exceptional, and I personally don't know any freelance translator who gets them on a regular basis.

The name of the game is earning money on a steady basis, not once in a blue moon. And to do so, one has to be flexible. Many a time I agreed to do a translation job for a client for less than it was worth, but my payoff often came when, soon thereafter, the same client, valuing the quality of my work and my near-fanatic adherence to deadlines, came back to me with another, often urgent job, and this time I charged a higher rate, which made up for the shortfall the first time around. In short, you quickly learn in this business that your potential clients—be they small or large companies, government agencies, or academic institutions, it makes no difference who—are almost always looking for a bargain. While they may not argue with their doctor or lawyer or even plumber about their rates, you can rest assured they will argue with you, and will always try at least one or two of your competitors, hoping to get a better rate. You have to be prepared to do "creative rate structuring" if you are to get that coveted job.

How do you know how much to charge for your services? There is no easy answer to this question, as any professional translator knows. A lot depends on who your clients are. As a general rule, for-profit organizations will pay more than not-for-profit, or public and government agencies. The rule of thumb is supply and demand. If the client can get it cheaper, you may not get that job. You have to establish for yourself what one may call a realistic rate.

To begin with, written translation work is normally charged by the word. I have known good, fast translators who made a good living getting as little as three or four cents per word. (Time is the real measure of your translation earning. The more words per hour you can translate accurately, the more you will earn.) Many translators will be shocked to hear this. They will call these rates "slave wages" and refuse to talk to me again. These days the range of seven to ten cents per word for translation from a foreign language into English, and eight to twelve cents per word for translation from English into a foreign language is considered normal. In California the rates are usually somewhat higher than on the East Coast, but then again, they pay higher taxes there. Rates have been changing in recent years, and will continue to change. Translation organizations in the United States are not allowed to set rates, or even suggest rates. To find out about going rates, you may want to talk to local colleagues.

To reiterate: try to charge your better-paying clients more, and those less capable of paying, less. Always look at the greater picture of your total yearly earnings, rather than getting yourself hung up on each case, giving the client and yourself a hard time. Flexibility is the secret weapon of the freelancer.

Getting Paid. Since most people do not have a good understanding of what translation is all about, and that includes some of the largest corporations and law firms in the country, they may decide after you perform your translation that your work is not up to snuff, and they will either withhold payment or try to reduce it. If indeed you did a less than acceptable job, well then, you have to bite the bullet and take a reduction in pay. But that often is not the case, and you can find yourself in the lurch. If you know and trust your client (you have worked with them before, or they are a very reputable entity in your community, etc.), then you just go ahead and do the work. But if you have the slightest doubt about getting paid, get something in writing from your client, such as a purchase order, or have the client sign a statement issued by you, stating your own terms, or even try to get some money down. Remember, you are now in business, not in a social or academic situation, and the business world is tough.

Equally important is keeping good records of your clients, and keeping notes on them, for two main reasons: first, you want to know a year or two from now if you had a problem with a client, so that you can act accordingly and not make the same mistake twice. Second, you want to keep in touch with your clients, letting them know you moved, or your phone number changed, or even drop them a card for the holiday season. Your goal is repeat business, which means steady income, and also validates your worth as a good translator.

Delinquent Accounts. Hopefully you won't take on too many bad clients. But having some bad clients is a fact of life and cannot be avoided. The question is what to do with those who, for no good reason, refuse to pay.

In the case of government agencies, the bad news is that they often take longer than they should to pay. But the good news is that eventually they do pay, unlike the private sector, where your client may go out of business. Since they make the laws, or are in charge of enforcing them, they cannot ignore them, and they pay. There are extreme cases—more than a few—when a payment drags on for months. My suggestion is that for the first three months you send friendly reminders and/ or make friendly phone calls. After that, you have the recourse of contacting the office of your congressperson, who is usually very responsive in contacting the delinquent person or office, and invariably you will get your money within thirty

---

English Goes Abroad

Outside of a Paris dress shop: "Dresses for streetwalking."

Hong Kong dentist advertisement: "Teeth extracted by the latest methodists."

In a Tokyo bar: "Special cocktails for the ladies with nuts."

days. You should only use this as a last resort, although, in some instances, you may be surprised to find out that a government employee would say to you, "My hands are tied, please feel free to contact your congressperson to make sure you get paid." Government never ceases to amaze those contractors who work with it.

In the case of private clients, you have the recourse of taking them to small claims court. While the judge cannot force the defendant to pay, the process usually does work well, since most people don't want to ruin their credit record or their business reputation. Then again, you may be dealing with a client who just went belly-up or skipped town. In this case you have a business loss and a tax write-off.

Since a great deal of freelance translation is done for law firms, let me state that the great majority of law firms and lawyers do appreciate translation work and pay on time, although some prefer to pay in sixty rather than thirty days. But then there are those exceptions, usually the smaller operators, who either experience chronic cash-flow problems or live high on the hog and are always short on cash. Some of those members of the bar either wait until their client pays them before they pay you, or make up an excuse to get out of paying altogether. You almost get the feeling they have learned a trick or two from their own clients. Now, as a freelancer, or as an independent contractor, you should never accept the argument "I'll pay you when my client pays me." You have absolutely no responsibility for someone else's clients, especially when it comes to a lawyer, many of whose clients are less than upright citizens. You are entitled to your money, and a lawyer of all people should know this. You give the attorney sixty days, and then you pull out your final weapon. You let your client know that if you don't get paid within three working days you will contact the ethics committee of the bar association he or she happens to belong to. In most cases, you will get your money very quickly. If you still don't get your money, you call the bar, and rest assured they will take some action.

Incidentally, what often happens in this type of delinquent account is that the lawyer may send you part of the payment with a note that this is "payment in full." Do not deposit or cash this check, since such action means that you agree with the letter and waive your right to the rest of the money. Finally, if it is clear to you that the lawyer in question has financial or cash-flow difficulties, you may want to suggest getting your money in the form of a few monthly payments.

Record Keeping. Many freelance translators are far from being well-organized individuals. I ought to know, since being disorganized was my problem for many years. Typically, you happen to wander into this type of work. You do an assignment, you find out you are good at it, and so you do another one. The next thing you know it is next year, you have done a fair number of assignments, and now you need to refer back to some of them, find out how you translated a certain phrase, or check some administrative detail, but you either can't find it or you didn't keep any records.

By now you get the picture. No one taught us in school how to keep records as freelancers, and so we have to learn from our mistakes. But rather than learn from your own mistakes, you will save a great deal of time and trouble if you learn from mine. In short, as soon as it becomes clear to you that you have started doing translation assignments regularly, start keeping records. On the next page we have included a sample translation log you can keep, preferably online with hard copies in an alphabetic file. Along with this form you should keep a hard copy of your original text and your translation, if at all feasible (some clients won't allow you to keep copies because of confidentiality, and some jobs may be too large and complex for you to be able to keep copies).

Good record keeping will yield countless benefits. Those benefits will fall into two categories: First, you will be building a library of your completed assignments, which will greatly facilitate your work in the future. Second, you will be able to measure your progress, plan ahead, keep track of clients, be aware of your strong points and your weaknesses and plan accordingly, and see the trends and have a better idea what to go after. Do not be afraid to develop a whole system of records, even if some duplicate each other to some extent. There is no such thing as being overorganized, certainly not in this field. Given the fact that ours is not a highly standardized profession, and that we all have different ways of doing our work, it is equally important that each one of us has his or her way of organizing oneself to do the best job possible.

Budgeting Yourself. Bear in mind that a freelancer has no job security, no steady biweekly or monthly paycheck, no tenure. You are in business for yourself, as a consultant, or a contractor, or a subcontractor. As such, you will experience periods of either feast or famine, and you will have to learn how to handle both.

I once knew a translator who did a large job, earned a few thousand dollars in less than two months, and spent the entire sum on an expensive notebook computer with a high-resolution color monitor, built-in fax, modem, and extra memory chips. Soon he ran into a long dry spell, and he needed the money to pay his bills. He had to sell his super-duper gadget at a considerable loss. He learned his lesson the hard way. He could have made do with a notebook half as expensive and kept at least two thousand dollars in the bank. This would have carried him through the dry spell until things started to pick up again (which they did). I believe he is now operating more prudently and doing quite well.

It seems all freelancers learn this lesson at some point. Like a squirrel, we stash away some of our acorns for a rainy day. We learn how to look farther down our professional road, and by the time we have to sit down and do our tax return, we feel a sense of satisfaction knowing we have provided well for ourselves and have put aside enough to pay Uncle Sam.

Translator/Client Relations

Cultivating and keeping clients is the key to freelance success. A freelance translator generally works with individual clients, companies, organizations, government agencies, and last but not least, translation agencies. Understanding your clients and their needs, and being able to give them what they need and having good communication with them, is the basis on which you should build your free-lance practice. This is not to say that you must please your clients no matter how unreasonable or unfair they happen to be, and never be willing to give up a client, but at the same time it is very important in doing translation work not only to do the best job possible but also to educate your clients and win them over.

Translation is one of the least understood professions around. Some people do not even refer to the process of transferring a text from one language to another as translation, but rather call it by all sorts of names, such as "transcription," "conversion," or simply "changing." Even well-educated people do not always make the distinction between "translating" and "interpreting." And certainly few people have a true appreciation of what a translator has to go through each time he or she confronts a translation assignment. Certainly the advent of the com-puter has not helped matters. In the popular mind, computers will soon replace human translators altogether, and this profession will disappear just like the old-time secretary, phone operator, and so forth. Given this state of affairs, it is quite obvious why translators, unlike lawyers or physicians, have a unique task of explaining themselves and paying special attention to client relations.

Unrealistic Promises. Some freelancers, especially when they start out, tend to promise more than they can deliver. You are offered a lucrative assignment and you hate to give it up. So you commit yourself to a timetable that is unrealistic, hoping that you may get an extension or make up an excuse at the other end of your timetable and get away with it. An experienced translator knows this is a sure prescription for losing a client and tarnishing one's reputation. Most transla-tions in the business world are needed on time, and quite often even sooner. In extreme cases, you may be asking for legal trouble, since you may cause loss of business or customers for your client. The first cardinal rule in translator-client relations is never to promise what you can't deliver. The right thing to do is explain to your client that the timetable is not realistic, and try to negotiate for more time. If this is not possible, suggest splitting the job among two or more translators. If there is no way you can find an accommodation with your client, then you have no choice but to turn down the job.

Establishing Credibility. With a new client, you have to establish credibility and gain the client's confidence in your work. If you have a potential major cli-ent, one who can give you steady work, you have to make every effort on that first assignment to do the best job possible, no matter how long it takes. If you have a problem with a term or a phrase, let the client know. Honesty is usually more appreciated than pretentiousness. If the term is indeed a problem which nearly any other translator will have trouble with, then your case is sound. You don't gain any points by sweeping the problem under the carpet.

Once you have established credibility, you have to keep up your quality assur-ance program. The client expects the best from you, not only the first time, but every time.

Keeping Up with Clients. Around the holidays it is always thoughtful to send your clients holiday greetings, to let them know you think of them. You want your clients to think of you as their source of translation services, who is always there when they need you. When you move, let them know. When you don't hear from them for an extended period of time, drop them a note, letting them know you have been doing some interesting work in their language or field, so as to show them you are still there for them. Establishing a personal relationship with your clients is the key to repeat business. Moreover, you will often work with companies and organizations where there is a turnover of personnel, and the person you worked with last time won't be there next time. You need to find out who your new contact person or potential contact person is, and either drop in on them to introduce yourself or say hello over the phone. A new person on the job usually appreciates that sort of attention, which makes her/his work easier and shows them that you are interested in working with them.

Legal Issues

There are several legal issues that affect translators, the two most prominent ones being the employment status of the translator in the fifty states and translator liability. Here is a brief review of both issues.

Independent Contractor. The status of the freelance translator in the United States has never been clearly defined. Since employment and unemployment issues are handled at the state level, there have been several court cases in recent years in states such as California, Colorado, New York, and New Jersey which involved the question of whether a freelance translator who provides translation services to a translation agency is an employee of that agency or an independent contractor. While a freelancer is in effect an independent contractor and prefers to operate as a self-employed individual or entity, there have been instances where a freelancer was not able to generate new assignments from an agency and chose to apply for unemployment insurance on the pretext of having been "laid off" by that agency. This would give rise to an audit of the agency by the state's unemployment office, resulting, in some cases, in that claimant being defined by the state as an employee of the agency, entitled to unemployment payments. Some agencies have taken this matter to court and won. Others have preferred to pay the unemployment tax and leave it at that. But in the final analysis, the interests of the freelancer are hurt, because no translation agency can survive by carrying a large number of freelancers on its books when, in effect, it is a small business engaged in a large variety of languages and subjects which require the services of many different individuals. This issue is far from resolved, and the best way to confront it is by maintaining professional integrity and not making false employment claims.

Liability Insurance. An even more worrisome issue for freelancers is that of liability. A medical interpreter, for instance, can find him or herself in the midst of a medical malpractice suit, in which an immigrant who does not speak English was given the wrong medicine because of poor translation, and now this person sues the doctor and the interpreter on the advice of his or her lawyer, figuring that they can win the case by proving one or the other to be at fault. The American Translators Association now offers liability insurance to its members. While translators have been clamoring for this type of insurance for a long time, so far there have been few takers. It is your call whether or not you feel the need for this kind of insurance.

In short, when it comes to legal issues, freelance translators are basically on their own. While the legal issues are very real and potentially dangerous, the answers are not quite there yet, and may be a long time in coming.

English Goes Abroad

In a Bucharest hotel lobby: "The lift is being fixed for the next day. During that time we regret that you will be unbearable."

In a Leipzig elevator: "Do not enter the lift backwards, and only when lit up."

In a Belgrade elevator: "To move the cabin, push button for wishing floor. If the cabin enter more persons, each one should press a number of wishing floor. Driving is then going alphabetically by national order."

11

Sources of Translation Work

If you choose freelance translation, you should consider yourself a one-person translation company. Your main concern will be where to find work. The need for freelance translation is greater than anyone can estimate and is clearly growing at a rapid rate. Worldwide, translation is a multibillion-dollar industry. But finding translation work on your own is easier said than done. The main problem is that translation is hardly ever a steady, ongoing function of any particular work source, such as an embassy, a company, a government agency, or even a publisher. None of those needs translation every day of the year. Each of them may need a great deal of translation all at once (more than any one person can handle within the given time frame), and then none for a long time. And if any one of them needs translation on an ongoing basis, chances are a decision will be made to hire an in-house translator rather than farm out the work.

The fact remains, however, that a well-rounded freelancer can earn well over $50,000 a year, and in the case of highly specialized technical translators in major languages like Spanish, German, Japanese, or Russian, even $100,000 or more. The secret to all of this is establishing for yourself a good clientele. There are two ways of doing this. The first, and by far the hardest, is finding your own clients and working with them directly. You may want to contact embassies, law firms, publishers, government agencies, and so on and solicit work directly from them. If you are fortunate enough to find some good, steady clients on your own, you will be doing quite well. But the problem often lies in the word "steady." What seems to be a steady client today may not be so steady tomorrow.

This brings us to the second, and by far the safer option, which is translation agencies. There are hundreds of them in the United States, and they handle huge amounts of translation business every year. In this chapter we will discuss translation agencies, as well as direct sources of translation available to the freelancer.

Translation Companies

Translation companies, also known as translation agencies, or translation bureaus, are for the most part privately owned commercial establishments ranging in size from one or two employees to ten or more, but hardly ever more than ten. Some are divisions of larger companies, offering translation as a secondary function. Some specialize in one language only, such as Spanish, German, or Japanese. Most offer several languages, and quite a few bill themselves as offering "all languages." This last type is somewhat pretentious, since there are more languages in the world than any one person can identify. But what they really mean is that they will make the effort to find a translator in almost any language they may be called upon to translate.

As a general rule, translation agencies employ relatively few in-house translators, since the flow of work in any given language is usually uneven. Instead, they rely on the services of a network of hundreds of freelancers who can handle a great variety of subjects. Those freelancers are located all over the United States and even abroad. The ones who are most reliable and professional get the major share of the work, and some of them earn the above-quoted figures.

As a freelancer, you need to cultivate at least one such agency, preferably two or three. The problem in working with only one is that, with few exceptions, there may not be a steady flow of work coming out of any given agency in any given language, in subjects you are equipped to handle. Two or three will give you better coverage and assure a better flow. On the other hand, you may find yourself in a situation where all three ask you to do something at the same time, and you may not be able to do it. You need to establish an understanding with your agencies that would make an allowance for such a scenario, so that you don't spoil your relationship with any one of them.

The worst thing you can do as a freelancer working with translation agencies is to overcommit yourself. Your most important personal asset is your reliability. Once you fail to meet deadlines (keep in mind, the agency stands to lose a client if deadlines are not met), your reliability becomes questionable, and if you do it once too often, you may soon find out that those phone calls from the agency offering you work assignments stop coming.

Where do you look for translation agencies? Appendix 4 offers a listing of hundreds of such agencies. You can find more on the Internet, or through the ATA (American Translators Association), which has local chapters around the country. My suggestion is to start with those close to home. In this day and age of international electronic communications, geographic distance is not a problem. But then again, working close to home has its advantages, because you can meet the people face to face, befriend them, and in some instances even avail yourself of their dictionaries and other resources.

Keep in mind that a translation company has overhead and also needs to make some profit to stay in business. They do the hard work of finding translation assignments and therefore share with you the profit from the job. You can usually make more money by going directly to the client, and if you have enough of your own clients, you don't need a translation company to send work your way. But most freelance translators do need those companies, which invariably provide a more steady flow of work than what a freelancer can get on his or her own.

The two things all translation companies appreciate and reward in a freelancer are honesty and loyalty. If you agree to a deadline, stick to it. Don't renege on it at the last minute. That's a sure prescription to spoil your association with your company. Equally important is not to go behind the company's back and try to solicit its own clients directly. Some companies will make you sign an agreement to this effect. Others will rely on the honor system. Don't abuse their trust. It usually doesn't pay off.

Direct Sources of Work

Working with translation agencies usually does not stop you from finding your own clients, as long as there is no conflict of interest with the agency's clients. It would be impossible to list here all the potential sources of direct translation work, since they include practically the entire human race (everyone needs a document translated at some point). But there are some major sources which ought to be mentioned, and here are some of the more important ones.

Law Firms

Law firms are a major source of translation work. Some of the larger firms hire full-time translators or staff members who are bilingual, especially if they do business on a regular basis with a foreign entity. Most firms use translators on an as-needed basis. Legal translation is a specialized field in which you need to acquire experience working with legal documents. There are several legal specialties, such as patent law, international law, immigration, and so on. Each specialty has its own style and terminology, which a translator needs to become acquainted with. As a freelancer, adding legal translation to your list of specialties is an excellent idea. You will find out that your volume of translation will increase considerably by doing so.

Quite often, a law firm needs both document translation and interpretation. Keep in mind that interpretation is a discipline separate from translation, and that there is a big difference between one-on-one consecutive interpreting and simultaneous conference interpreting (see chapter 14). If asked by a law firm to do both text translation and interpreting, be sure to find out first exactly what the assignments consist of.

Industry

Corporations doing business in other countries have to deal with documents originated in the languages of those countries or English documents that need to be translated into those languages. Here again we find the two approaches of either hiring translators or farming out work to freelancers and to translation services (or a combination of both). This field is perhaps the fastest growing source of translation in the new century. More and more major American companies are turning to international business as a way to offset the decline of business at home and to gain a share of the world market. Their need for translation is growing every day, and even those who have in-house translators are finding themselves using freelancers because of their volume of translation work. (See the list of major companies in appendix 4.)

If you are fortunate enough to form a relationship with a major company doing business overseas, you may find yourself in the enviable position of dealing with a major, steady source of translation.

How does one get work with major corporations? If you have a special expertise in their field of work, find out who handles outside vendors or services, and give them a call or drop them a note. It also helps to know someone in the company who can do some of the legwork for you and put you in touch with the right people. As a general rule, this is not easy to do. But persistence does pay off some of the time, and even if only a few respond, it is worth the effort.

The U.S. Government

For several decades following World War II, translation in the federal government enjoyed a boom. The onset of the Cold War resulted in large-scale translation activities on the part of the U.S. Department of Defense (DoD), all the branches of the service (particularly the Army, Navy, and Air Force), and the Central Intelligence Agency (CIA). In addition, such multilingual organizations as the Voice of America (which started broadcasting in 1942 in forty languages) sprang into being. These and other organizations employed a host of translators and farmed out millions of words every year to be translated. Looking back, those were the feast years of government translation. During the 1990s, however, a major shift has been taking place. Since 1992, there has been a sharp decline in government translations, and those translation agencies and freelancers who were dependent on government work for their bread and butter were hurting. This is not to say that the U.S. government is no longer a source of employment for translators. There are still many opportunities for translation in the government, offered by such bodies as the Language Services division of the U.S. Department of State (for in-house as well as freelance translators and interpreters), the Library of Congress, the U.S. Patent and Trademark Office, and so on. (See the list of U.S. government agencies in appendix 4.)

My translation company, Schreiber Translations Inc. (STI), started out in life as a full-service translation company for the federal government. This was in the early 1980s, when the boom was still on. We provided translation from and into over fifty languages and dialects, as well as interpreting, transcription, voice-over, graphics, and editing. Luckily for us, we realized early on that, as the world was changing, we were better off not being locked into government work, and we were able to develop a lucrative practice in nongovernmental sectors. At the same time, because we are located in the Washington, DC, area, and because we have gained the trust of government agencies, we continue to get a great deal of government work.

What are the pros and cons of translating for the government? For many linguists over the years, the government has offered job security. I know some fine translators who have worked for the government for many years and had interesting and fulfilling careers. On the other hand, career translators in the government are not paid exceptionally high salaries. Quite a few freelance on the side in an effort to supplement their income. As for freelancers who contract with the government, here we have mixed results. Some have found themselves a cozy niche and are kept busy on a fairly regular basis. Others go through the "feast and famine" syndrome. Some have been frustrated by spending a long time hunting for government assignments, with small results. To freelance effectively for the government, one should, in most instances, work in one of the top languages the U.S. government is interested in (Spanish, Russian, German, French, and Japanese, and currently also Chinese and Arabic).

State and Local Government

Government at all levels, from the municipal to the federal, needs translation. At the local level we find more and more city and county government translating their pamphlets, brochures, and other documents into the languages of their immigrant populations, notably Asian languages and Spanish. In addition, local government has an ongoing need for interpreters, mostly for the court system, but also for social services, hospitals, and other local institutions. At this time of tight budgets, this may not be the most lucrative field, but it is definitely worth exploring, since it is local and mostly uses local linguists.

Major Organizations

Among the largest organizations that use a great deal of translation one should mention the United Nations, the World Bank, the World Health Organization, and the Organization of American States, to cite only some of the better-known ones here in the United States. Surely there are more in Europe, such as the World Court, the European Community, NATO, and many more. Most of these organizations use in-house linguists and do not farm out translation work if they can help it. But quite often they have more documents to translate than they can handle in house, and they look for outside help.

For a list of such organizations and how to contact them, see the list of major organizations in appendix 4.

Publishers

Book publishers use freelance translators in many different ways. This is not an easy field to break into, particularly for the beginner. Many publishers turn to academia for translators, and if you are in academia and can translate from or into another language in your field of expertise, there is a chance you can get the work. Others turn to established translators with name recognition. But it is certainly worth trying to query publishers and find out if they need your services.

Software Localization Companies

A fast-growing area of translation is software localization, or translation of software-related text into other languages and adapting the text to the target culture. Software localization companies specialize in computer subjects and in English-into-foreign-language translation. They employ in-house translators, but they also use freelancers from time to time. Their work encompasses everything from computer manuals to localization of websites.

Networking

An excellent source of work for freelance translators is personal contacts with other translators. The ATA's local chapters are one place where translators meet and get to know each other. The annual conference of the ATA holds a networking session, which is very valuable. One also meets translators through personal contacts in the translation field.

The new way to meet translators is on the Internet. Language forums bring together translators from all over the world. All you need to do is post a message on one of those programs, and before you know it you get a response from someone in your own town or halfway around the world.

Keeping in touch with other translators is a prime means of finding out about work sources and assignments. There are clearly many advantages to networking in the translation field, and the more contacts one has the better.

Professional translators need to know more than a source and a target language. They also have to develop expertise in the subject areas they translate.

12

A Career as an In-House Translator

Translators are not as visible to the general public as dentists or police officers and therefore seem to be a rare breed. The fact is, thousands of translators work full time in international corporations and organizations, the U.S. Armed Forces, U.S. government agencies, law firms, medical organizations, and many other entities. I happen to know a large number of those translation professionals. Many of them seem to be quite happy and fulfilled in their career, and are paid respectable though not outrageous salaries.

If you would like to pursue a full-time translation career, there are several things to consider. Here are some of the most essential.

Level of Expertise

Besides being very proficient in both your source and target language, and having a good writing ability, you have to have expertise in the field you will be working in on a full-time basis. If, for instance, you become a full-time translator for the National Geographic Society, you will need a good background in geography, preferably a graduate degree in that field. Keep this in mind when you apply for an opening for a translator position in any given organization. Chances are they are looking for someone with a strong background in their field.

Translation Training

Potential employers will also be interested in your credentials as a professional translator. They may look for either a translation degree from an accredited institution, accreditation from an organization such as the ATA, or, in the case of U.S. government employment, for both training and experience. For courses and programs for translators in colleges and universities, and for ATA accreditation, see appendices 5 and 7.

I am not trying to imply that you cannot find full-time employment as a translator without the above training or accreditation. Unlike medicine or law, translation is not a fully regulated profession by any means. While the above are very helpful, they are not a must. You can find employment as a translator on your own personal merit, provided you can prove that you have an exceptional ability to translate and a thorough familiarity with your subject. The FBI, for instance, will test you to determine your exact level of expertise. Many a career translator started out in a totally different field, and somehow by virtue of his or her special skills in this field became recognized as a reliable and much-needed translator. This, of course, is up to you to discover about yourself.

The Right Language

If your language of expertise is Maltese (the language of the Island of Malta), your chances of finding full-time employment as a translator in the United States are slim to none. In all my years as a translation agency manager, I only had one request for Maltese (it came from the FBI, and they later changed their mind about doing it). I did find one person in the United States who could translate Maltese, but as I expected, it was not her full-time occupation.

Invariably, a full-time translation career is possible if you work in one of the major languages of the world, such as Russian, Spanish, German, French, Italian, Portuguese, Japanese, Chinese, or Arabic.

Multiple Languages

If you are fortunate enough to be fluent in several languages, particularly major ones, you may want to consider a full-time translation career. Many organizations look for individuals like yourself, not the least of which are international companies, law firms, government agencies, and the United Nations.

Pros and Cons

A full-time translation job means steady income, benefits, and everything else that goes with steady employment. But like all other jobs, it also has its drawbacks. Unlike the freelancer, you don't enjoy the same sense of freedom and flexibility. You become locked into one area and one subject, and at times you may find it quite repetitive and unchallenging. You are also part of an organization that, like all organizations, has its own politics which you may not always find to be to your liking. If you are fortunate enough to work for a congenial organization, you are lucky. But this is not always the case. Ultimately, the decision of which way to go is up to you.

Some Tips on Sending out Resumes for Translation Jobs

1. Proofread your resume ten times. In this business you cannot afford any typos, mistakes, or poor language in your introductory written effort.
2. Put your language and area of expertise in the first paragraph of your resume. This is the first thing the reader wants to know, and there is no sense burying it somewhere on the bottom.
3. Know your potential employers. Be sure you have the right qualifications for what they are looking for.
4. Stick to the point. Don't tell them you like to play tennis or hockey. They are too busy to be bothered with your personal life.
5. Capitalize on your experience, especially if it is relevant to what they are looking for.
6. Don't write a "threadbare" resume. Make it substantial, but only put in pertinent information.
7. Use good-quality laser printing paper, preferably the usual twenty-pound stock, and if possible a pleasing color such as light tan or beige.
8. Don't make it too fancy, just dignified and businesslike.
9. If you add a sample translation, make it short (one or two paragraphs) and effective.
10. Make it easy to read, crisply printed, with bold key words, such as your subject areas.

13

Training Programs

Several institutions, including universities, U.S. government agencies, and world bodies like the United Nations, provide translation education and training. Yet translator education in the United States is not nearly as advanced as it is in some other parts of the world. In fact, most working translators in America today were trained, so to speak, on the job. I happen to be one of them. My background includes five years of graduate school, but it was not in the field of translation (although in some ways related to it). I picked up translation on my own as a young teenager, as part of my lifelong flirtation with writing. During the past thirty years I have worked with literally hundreds of translators, and I have watched many of them grow and develop on the job, as I took part in providing them with professional tips and practical advice. This handbook is part of my own effort to put all that experience into a book for the benefit of present and future translators and students of translation. So if you wonder whether you have to take a course or pursue a study program in order to become a translator, the answer is not necessarily. There are, however, advantages to such programs, and if you have the opportunity to pursue them, you certainly should.

One very effective approach to translator education is to choose a practical field of knowledge where there is a growing need for translation, such as telecommunications, and get a degree in that field, while working on either a translation degree or improving your language and writing skills. There is always a need for a highly specialized technical translator in such a field, and if you establish a reputation for yourself as an authority in that area, you may find yourself very much in demand.

Appendix 5 provides a list of translator education programs around the country. The list is far from exhaustive, and you should consult your local college or university on this matter, since this type of program has been proliferating in recent years. You may also suggest to your local county or other type of government to invite a local senior translator to give an adult education class in translation, which can certainly benefit the community.

Proverbs from around the World

A proverb is a short sentence based on long experience.—Cervantes

The man who is surrounded by dwarves looks like a giant.—Jewish

Trust in Allah, but tie your camel.—Arabic

If you scatter thorns, don't go barefoot.—Italian

Even the lion has to defend himself against flies.—German

Good luck beats early rising.—Irish

Visits always give pleasure—if not the arrival, the departure.—Portuguese

14

Oral Interpretation

A field closely related to translation is oral interpretation. Many translators also work as interpreters, and many professional interpreters are known to do text translation as well. The two terms—translation and interpretation—are often confused, despite the fact that they represent two distinct ways of working with language. This handbook is primarily concerned with text translation, but a few words about oral interpretation are in order.

Oral interpretation is best suited for those who possess the following skills:

- exceptional articulation
- a high comfort level speaking in front of an audience
- public speaking experience
- complete ease in both languages
- the ability to retain one or more points while listening to new information, and then reproduce the entire message accurately in the second language
- the ability to summarize the main points of something that's being said
- experience in one or more technical areas (not always necessary, but helpful)

Interpreting requirements—depending on the type of interpreting one is engaged in—can range from simple, general conversation, to highly technical exposés and discussions. Most interpreting falls into the general categories of:

Consecutive interpreting
Simultaneous interpreting
Sight translation
Signing (sign language)

Interpreting can take place in the following environments:

Escort
Meeting
Phone
Courtroom
Conference

Consecutive Interpreting. This may be the most common form of interpreting, since it covers a wide variety of situations where the interpreter waits for the speaker to finish a sentence and then renders it orally in the target language. Some of the most common types of consecutive interpreting are court interpreting, where the interpreter waits for the witness, or any other foreign speaker, to finish each sentence or segment of presentation, and then repeats it in the language of the court; medical interpreting, in which the patient does not speak the target language and needs someone to mediate linguistically between patient and doctor or nurse; business negotiations interpreting, where the two sides sit around the table with an interpreter who helps them communicate by listening to each side and interpreting for the other side.

Other scenarios requiring consecutive interpreting include telecon interpretation, factory/construction site tours, and foreign visitor escort services. Consecutive interpreting requires formal training, and in such instances as court interpreting, certification as well. Court interpreting is a career that is growing in prominence in parts of the country that have large populations of nonspeakers or minimal speakers of English, such as Miami, Los Angeles, Chicago, and New York. It should be mentioned that federal and state exams for court interpreter certification require proficiency in simultaneous and sight modes of interpretation, in addition to the consecutive mode. If you find this type of work challenging and suitable to your temperament, you may want to look into training for it by either contacting the local court system or checking the various teaching programs (see appendix 5).

Escort Interpreting. This is usually the easiest form of consecutive interpreting, as it seldom involves very technical language. For the beginner, escort interpreting is a good place to start. A useful resource for learning more about government-related escort interpreting is the U.S. Department of State's Office of Language Services, which produces an escort interpreter manual. The manual deals with the basic functions and responsibilities of escorts assigned to the U.S. Information Agency's cultural exchange program. To request a copy of the manual, call the OLS's administrative office at (202) 647-4000.

Over-the-Phone Interpreting (OPI). Interpreting over the phone is probably as old as the phone itself, but it has been brought into prominence in recent years by the Language Line service (www.languageline.com). This is a seven-day-a-week, twenty-four-hour-a-day interpreting service, purportedly in 140 languages. The service enables speakers of different languages to communicate by telephone via a three-way conference call including an interpreter. Several translation companies around the country have now entered this field. They hire freelance interpreters who are on call to perform this service, which is used mainly for businesses (such as customer service centers), for 911 calls for the local police, and for public institutions such as school systems. These companies claim to be able to provide an interpreter over the phone within forty-five seconds and that nearly all requests for interpreters are filled.

Simultaneous Interpreting. This is a highly specialized form of interpreting, which requires a special aptitude. True simultaneous interpreting can only be done with the appropriate equipment. There are a few different types currently used, all of which are based on the premise that what the speaker says is transmitted into the interpreter's ear, while the interpreter repeats it into a microphone in the second language. One has to be able to listen to the speaker and repeat the same words in a different language almost at the same time. This takes a great deal of training and experience and is paid at a higher rate than consecutive interpretation. Everyone has seen heads of state on the news with an interpreter standing by, echoing every word uttered by the speaker in another language. No doubt this is a very challenging activity, and those who practice it deserve our admiration. It would not be advisable to undertake this type of interpreting without the proper training and experience. Examples of organizations that employ simultaneous interpreters are the United Nations and the U.S. Department of State.

Simultaneous interpretation may be required for such things as business or professional conferences, training seminars, or presentations. A simultaneous interpretation longer than two hours requires at least two interpreters to allow for rest periods.

Sight Translation/Document Comparison. During conferences and negotiations, there are often written documents that have to be explained, interpreted, and/or translated on the spot for immediate use. While it is understood that one cannot produce perfect translations under such conditions, nevertheless the interpreter on duty has to be able to provide a good working version of the text in question. This means that the interpreter in this particular situation has to be familiar with the subject matter of the documents and not have to look up every other word in the dictionary. Sight translation can be very taxing at times, but there is little one can do about it. It comes, as they say, with the territory of the interpreting craft.

An interpreter or a translator may occasionally be called upon to compare documents in the source and target languages in order to verify that the two versions are fully identical. This happens most often in the case of legal documents, such as contracts involving private parties, corporations, or international agreements, treaties, and the like, at various governmental levels. Discussion may take place in both languages, involving the interpreter, who now acts as a linguistic consultant. This is a highly responsible task which requires sensitivity and familiarity with both cultures and languages, and skills both as a translator and interpreter.

Another example of sight translation occurs when a client is faced with an overwhelming amount of material in a foreign language and needs someone to review the material and determine which documents or parts of documents are useful and require translation.

Sign Language. This discipline has grown in importance in recent years, as American society has become more sensitive to the needs of the disabled. It is common today to see sign interpreters for the deaf in lectures, conferences, and on television. Signing, at the same time, is an activity that has grown in popularity among American interpreters, and more are training for it now than ever before. As evidence of the field's growing pains, recent literature points to insufficient instructional materials and training programs for prospective sign interpreters.

Since it calls for working in the simultaneous mode, signing is a demanding form of interpretation. Nevertheless, this is undoubtedly one of the most rewarding forms of interpretation, as it helps an entire segment of the population participate in the normal activities the rest of us are engaged in. It speaks well for our society that sign language, which was first brought to this country in the last century by the Frenchman Thomas Hopkins Gallaudet, has become a familiar sight to all of us through the mass media, and that there is a regular demand for it in the courts, hospitals, and nearly any other area of human activity.

Bear in mind that people often confuse oral interpretation with written translation. Be sure when requested to do interpreting that they are not actually asking for translating.

The Pros and Cons of Interpretation

The field of interpreting can offer many challenges and rewards. It almost always puts the interpreter in an extremely high-pressure situation, both from the standpoint of having to come up with the correct way of saying something on a moment's notice, and because of the consequences of an error made on the part of the interpreter, which can be very serious.

A true commitment to an interpreting career, especially one in simultaneous interpreting, requires flexibility. One must be willing to do a lot of traveling, for example. Also, interpreting assignments are often required in the evenings, during dinners or functions, or on weekends, to meet or see off foreign visitors. A serious consideration with interpreting is the role that personality plays. Unfortunately, there are many instances where an interpreter is dismissed in the middle of an assignment, not because of any lack of skill, but simply because his or her personality rubs the client the wrong way. And yet, interpreting can present many exciting opportunities, including participation in world events, such as the Olympic Games, the launch of a spacecraft, the signing of a peace treaty, or meetings between world leaders.

When considering an interpreting assignment, keep several important factors in mind:

- Insist, and this cannot be emphasized enough, that you be given preparation materials. Whether the assignment is a business meeting or a technical presentation, the only way for you to familiarize yourself with the corporate- or industry-specific terminology in question is to review related materials beforehand. If the client absolutely cannot provide such materials, make sure to inform them that you will be operating at a disadvantage.

- Be sure to discuss fees ahead of time and to obtain some sort of contract from your client outlining these fees. If there is travel involved, there should be some sort of compensation for the travel time. If the preparation requires an unusual amount of time, there should be some sort of compensation for this as well. There should ideally be some prearranged fee for a last-minute cancellation, although if the work stems from the government this may not be possible.

- Confirm that your client is aware of the difference between simultaneous and consecutive interpreting, and if what they really need is simultaneous, that they will be providing the appropriate equipment and also the appropriate backup.

- Make sure you are given a single contact to report to. Often there is confusion when there are several people involved in a meeting or conference, and it is not always clear who has the authority to dismiss you.

- Make sure you are aware of any possible boundaries of your assignment. For example, if a foreign delegation member requests your help on a shopping trip after business hours, should you accompany this person? Will you be paid for your time?

Closing Remarks

Interpreting requires training different from written translation. I would encourage those who are interested in translation yet are more at ease speaking than writing to look into pursuing an interpreting career. To my knowledge, the professional field of interpreting is not nearly as vast as that of translation. But there are thousands of full- and part-time interpreters employed in the United States, mostly by the court system and by international bodies such as the United Nations, the World Bank, the International Monetary Fund, and various U.S.

government agencies, notably the U.S. Department of State. Since interpreters, unlike translators, regularly interact with people under less than easy conditions, it is important for interpreters to have a gregarious and pleasing personality, a good appearance, good manners, patience, social savvy, and a good sense of humor.

Bad Translation

Some years ago the Cincinnati Reds got to the World Series. The next day the following sign appeared all over town:

Darn tootin' we rootin'!

A newspaper reporter from a foreign country was in town that day. He didn't quite know what to make of this sign, and since he was too proud of his English expertise, rather than ask one of the locals to interpret, he came up with his own interpretation. He reported the event to his newspaper in these words:

Signs appeared yesterday all over Cincinnati, Ohio, saying: "Damn all those car horns! We are going back to our roots, namely, to the horse and buggy!"

15

Translators' Organizations

The American Translators Association (ATA)

The ATA is to the freelance translator in the United States what the AMA is to physicians, or the bar associations to lawyers. While the ATA does not have the status and prestige enjoyed by the AMA or the bar, it is a friendly, vigorous, and effective organization, where individual translators have a say and are able to grow together with their association as they work together on a better future for translators and for the translation profession. One may think I have a vested interest in the ATA, or that they paid me to say these things. Wrong on both counts. I am saying these things as someone who has never been active in ATA politics, and who by nature shies away from organizations. I am saying these things because during the past thirty years I have watched the ATA grow from 2,000 to some 10,000 members, with scant means, with little or no outside help, and I have watched its members work hard with a limited budget, producing, among other things, a great monthly professional periodical, the *ATA Chronicle* (which alone is worth the annual dues). Its working committees pursue issues of interest to translators, and its annual conference, which I have enjoyed for many years, is arguably the single best opportunity during the year for translators to expand their horizons.

The ATA was established in 1959 by two hardy and idealistic translators in New York. When I joined in 1979 it was headquartered in a town on the Hudson River in New York, but later on it moved to my "neighborhood," namely, the Greater Washington area (Alexandria, Virginia, to be precise). It has quite active regional chapters in North and South Carolina (Carolina Association: CATI), Atlanta (Atlanta Association: WAIT), Missouri (Mid-America: MICATA), Washington, DC (National Capital Area: NCATA), New York City (New York Circle of Translators: NYCT), Cleveland (Northern Ohio: NOTA), San Francisco (Northern California: NCTA), Los Angeles (Southern California: SCATIA), and Florida (Florida Chapter ATA: FLATA); cooperating groups in Colorado (Colorado Translators Association: CTA), Delaware (Delaware Valley Translators Association: DVTA), New Mexico (New Mexico Translators and Interpreters Association: NMTIA), and Seattle (Northwest Translators and Interpreters: NOTIS); and affiliated groups in Michigan (Michigan Association:

Matin) and Utah (Utah Association: URIA). Every ATA officer, director, division administrator, chapter officer, and committee member is an unpaid volunteer. For addresses and additional information on ATA chapters, see appendix 6. The ATA's website (see address below) also lists unaffiliated regional translation and interpretation organizations.

The ATA accepts all translators as members, as well as translation agencies and organizations involved in translation, such as academic institutions and corporations, but it encourages its individual members to become ATA-accredited. Currently certification is available into English from Arabic, Croatian, Danish, Dutch, French, German, Japanese, Portuguese, Russian, and Spanish, and from English into Chinese, Croatian, Dutch, Finnish, French, German, Hungarian, Italian, Japanese, Polish, Russian, Spanish, Swedish, and Ukrainian.

Membership is open to U.S. and foreign translators and translation students, as well as companies and institutions.

Address:
American Translators Association
225 Reinekers Lane, Suite 590
Alexandria, VA 22314
Phone: (703) 683-6100
Fax: (703) 683-6122
Website: www.atanet.org
E-mail: ata@atanet.org

FIT (Fédération internationale des traducteurs/International Federation of Translators)

This international organization does not accept individual membership, but rather organizational. Its members include the ATA and similar translator organizations worldwide. See appendix 6 for a list of addresses of FIT chapters and members.

Website: www.fit-ift.org

ALC (Association of Language Companies)

This is a U.S.-based association of translation companies which the individual translator ought to be familiar with. If you are a freelancer, chances are you are or will be doing work for one or more of its members.

Website: www.alcus.org

GALA (Global and Localization Association)

This is the worldwide localization organization. Their mission is to raise the profile of the language industry as a whole and to promote the interests of owners of language companies. Their members are Language Service Providers (LSPs), and it is fair to say that, generally speaking, companies who spend the time and money to belong to them are upstanding companies who promote best practices, including with regard to how they treat the freelancers with whom they work.

Website: www.gala-global.org

Translators without Borders

On a different note, Translators without Borders is also an organization freelancers should be aware of. Translators without Borders' mission is to support humanitarian work around the world by providing free translations. The organization works with professional volunteer translators around the world to provide free translations to support humanitarian NGOs by translating essential information into the languages of the people who need it most. Since 1993, Translators without Borders has provided over $2 million worth of humanitarian translations at no charge, and currently they provide about a million free words per year.

Translators without Borders has an ongoing need for translators, reviewers, web masters, computer experts, graphic designers, marketing experts, and fundraisers, and the organization accepts monetary donations as well.

Website: www.translatorswithoutborders.org

Other Organizations

There are several additional national, regional, and local organizations of translators and interpreters or both in the United States, and several foreign and international ones that have ties with U.S. translators. During my thirty years of intense involvement in translator affairs in the United States, I have seen very little evidence of their impact on the affairs or welfare of translators in this country, but since this handbook is committed to giving translators as full a picture as possible of the translation scene in the United States, I'll try to cover some of this ground.

National Association of Judiciary Interpreters and Translators (NAJIT)

Founded in 1978, NAJIT represents court interpreters throughout the United States who work in the federal and state court systems in both foreign and sign languages. It holds annual conferences and local workshops, and publishes a quarterly newsletter (*Proteus*) and other materials for interpreters. It helped design the federal certification exam mandated by the Court Interpreters Act of 1978.

Address:
NAJIT
1707 L Street NW
Washington, DC 20036
Tel: 202-293-0342
Website: www.najit.org

ALTA (American Literary Translators Association)
Operates out of the University of Texas at Dallas. It publishes the biannual *Translation Review*.

Address:
The University of Texas at Dallas
800 W. Campbell Road, Mail Station JO51
Richardson, TX 75083-3021
Phone: (972) 883-2093
Fax: (972) 883-6303
Website: www.utdallas.edu/alta

PEN American Center
This is the world organization of poets, playwrights, editors, and novelists, with an interest in literary translators.

Address:
PEN
588 Broadway, Suite 303
New York, NY 10012
Phone: (212) 334-1660
Fax: (212) 334-2181
Website: www.pen.org
E-mail: pen@pen.org

AMTA (Association for Machine Translation in the Americas)
Publishes *MT News International*.

Address:
AMTA
209 North Eighth Street
Stroudsburg, PA 18360
Phone: (570) 476-8006
Fax: (570) 476-0860
Website: www.amtaweb.org
E-mail: business@amtaweb.org

16

Translation: A Lifelong Career

The best thing about translation is that it is an activity you can pursue at different times of your life, and you can continue doing it or pick it up again even after you retire from your regular job. This has never been more true than today, in the age of digital communications. I wrote several parts of this handbook on the plane from Washington to San Diego, on the beach in Puerto Rico, and in other places I have lost track of, thanks to my three-pound notebook computer and my two-pound LaserJet printer, two small items that travel with me almost everywhere.

When I get up too early to go to the office, I do some translating. When I have some time to kill between engagements, I do some more.

Translation has put me in touch with more areas of human knowledge and endeavor than almost any other career is capable of doing. At one time or another, a translator becomes part of almost anything. During thirty years of providing translation for U.S. government agencies, I started with the State Department and the FBI, moved on to the Defense Department, and at one time or another interacted with almost every federal department and agency. I can think of few other careers more challenging and fascinating.

But best of all, a translator never stops learning. Language keeps changing, knowledge keeps increasing, and the professional translator stays on top of it all. Once you have developed good translation habits, you will enjoy the continuous activity of learning new words and terms, and being part of the latest advances in many areas of human knowledge. It is, indeed, a privileged position.

I hope you have enjoyed reading this handbook as much as I have enjoyed writing it, and that you will benefit from translation as much as I have. If that is the case, then my reward will be great indeed. I have felt for many years that translators deserve a better break than they have been getting in our largely insular, monolingual society. Most translators I have known were and are hardworking folk, decent and dedicated people, friendly and generous, and it has been a special privilege for me to be their colleague and friend, as well as teacher and provider of translation work. There is no doubt in my mind that ours is a profession that will become more and more prominent as the twenty-first century continues to unfold, and for several years now I have felt a sense of exhilaration knowing that I am part of one of the great adventures of our time.

Dictionaries and Reference Literature

The languages listed are:

Afrikaans	French	Pilipino/Tagalog
Albanian	Georgian	Polish
Amharic	German	Portuguese
Arabic	Greek	Romanian
Azerbaijani	Hebrew	Russian
Basque	Hindi	Serbian
Bengali	Hungarian	Serbo-Croatian
Bosnian	Icelandic	Slovak
Bulgarian	Indonesian	Slovene
Byelorussian	Italian	Somali
Cambodian	Japanese	Spanish
Catalan	Kazakh	Swahili
Chinese	Korean	Swedish
Creole	Kurdish	Tatar
Croatian	Lao	Thai
Czech	Latin	Turkish
Danish	Latvian	Ukrainian
Dutch	Lithuanian	Uzbek
Esperanto	Macedonian	Vietnamese
Estonian	Malay	Yiddish
Farsi (Persian)	Nepali	Yoruba
Finnish	Norwegian	

For a general discussion of dictionaries and reference literature, see chapter 8.

Translators use hundreds, perhaps thousands, of different dictionaries and reference books. The prices on these can vary significantly. It is not possible to list all of them, or to provide their current cost, but there are dictionaries and reference books that stand out, and a good number of those are listed here. Full reference information is provided wherever possible, and especially useful works are followed by comments.

GENERAL ENGLISH LANGUAGE REFERENCES
American English Dictionaries
Which is the best dictionary for American English? The answer, quite simply, is none. American English is long overdue for some truly comprehensive dictionary, not unlike the complete Oxford Dictionary of British English. In its absence, the following general American English dictionaries are recommended in order of preference:

Webster's Third New International Dictionary, Springfield, MA: Merriam-Webster 2003. This is the traditional "major" American-English dictionary. Though dated, it is still good to have around.
    American Heritage Dictionary, 4th ed., Boston: Houghton Mifflin 2000. An excellent one-volume all-around dictionary, beautifully illustrated.

Other large dictionaries of this kind are offered by Random House, Oxford University Press, and others, but they do not improve on the above two.
    For a smaller, very useful dictionary (of which there are many), we recommend *Webster's New World Dictionary*, Guralnik, D., New York: Simon & Schuster, many editions.
    A book which complements the standard dictionaries is the *American English Compendium*, 3rd ed., Rubinstein, M., Lanham, MD: Taylor Trade Publishing 2012. It covers proverbs, expressions, U.S. slang, U.S. vs. British English, foreign words in American English, acronyms and abbreviations, and other "odds and ends."

American English Reference Books
Most translations into English, particularly technical ones, require what is known as "good idiomatic English." There are general rules for what is considered good writing style and good usage. Here are some of the key books in this field:
ACS Style Guide: A Manual for Authors and Editors, American Chemical Society 2006.
The Chicago Manual of Style, 16th ed., Chicago: University of Chicago Press 2010. More popular with editors than translators.
Technical Editing: A Practical Guide for Editors and Writers, J. Tarutz, Reading, MA: Addison Wesley Longman 1992.
The Elements of Style, Strunk, W., and White, E.B., New York: Longman 2008. A classic and a must.
Modern American Usage, Follett, W., New York: Hill & Wang 1998. Old but useful. Many good tips on those English words, phrases, and terms that are often misused.
Roget's Thesaurus, Boston: Houghton Mifflin, many editions. Beware of the thesaurus! It may be useful as an intermediate step in your search for the right word, but not as the final authority.

Style Manual, U.S. Government Printing Office, Washington, DC 2010. A must for translators involved in U.S. Government translations. The government has its own rules of American English usage, which should be adhered to in this type of work.

Additional References

Random House Historical Dictionary of American Slang, Lightner, J.E., New York: Random House 1997. Only vols. 1 and 2 (A–O) are out.

Acronyms, Initialisms, & Abbreviations Dictionary, Mossman, J., Washington, DC: Gale Research 2002.

American Idioms, Makkai, A., New York: Barron's 2004.

The Handbook of Good English, Johnson, E.D., New York: Pocket Books 1991.

The Elements of Grammar, Shertzer, M.D., New York: Barnes & Noble 2001.

The Elements of Editing, Plotnik, A., New York: Macmillan 1982.

Handbook of American Idioms & Idiomatic Usage, Whitford, H.C., Prentice Hall 1987.

Colloquial English, Collis, H., New York: Regents 1981.

General Reference

This type of book is hard to recommend. The field is so vast it would fill a separate volume. Here are some handy ones:

Encyclopedia Britannica, the flagship of all English-language encyclopedias, is now available on such electronic devices as the iPad. Priced far below the hardcover set, it is a major, though not exhaustive, source of information.

Columbia Desk Encyclopedia, comes in different sizes and can help you (not always) with names, dates, and other bits of information.

Almanacs, many different kinds. Of limited use to translators.

Atlases, too many to enumerate. One of the best new ones is the *Times Atlas of the World*.

Business and Related Fields

Dictionary of Real Estate Terms, Friedman, J., New York: Barron's 2008.

Dictionary of Insurance Terms, Rubin, H., New York: Barron's 2008.

Dictionary of Business Terms, Friedman, J., New York: Barron's 2007.

Dictionary of Finance and Investment Terms, Downes, J., New York: Barron's 2010.

Dictionary of Banking Terms, Fitch, T., New York: Barron's 2006.

Chemistry/Life Sciences

Hawley's Condensed Chemical Dictionary, 15th ed., Hoboken, NJ: Wiley-Interscience 2007.

In addition to the above reference, you can find multivolume encyclopedias of chemistry in the public libraries that will answer many of your questions. But as your questions become more and more specific, you will need very specialized reference material in the many specialized areas of chemistry and life sciences, which are often published by government and by public and private organizations, such as the World Health Organization (www.who.int), pharmaceutical companies, and many more.

Computers and the Internet
Here the field changes almost daily. For some quick, handy sources of basic computer terminology, you might try the following:

Webster's New World Computer Dictionary, 10th ed., Pfaffenberger, B., New York: Macmillan 2003.

Newton's Telecom Dictionary, 25th ed., Newton, H., New York: Miller Freeman Books 2009.

Dictionary of Computer and Internet Terms, Downing, D., and Covington, M., New York: Barron's 2009.

Computer Desktop Encyclopedia, Freedman, A., New York: McGraw-Hill 2001.

Electric/Electronics
McGraw-Hill Electronics Dictionary, Sclater, N., New York: McGraw-Hill 1997.

Standard Dictionary of Electrical and Electronic Terms, Jay, F., New York: Institute of Electric and Electronic Engineers 1997.

Engineering
McGraw-Hill Concise Encyclopedia of Engineering, Parker, S., New York: McGraw-Hill 2005.

Law
Black's Law Dictionary, Black, H.C., St. Paul, MN: West Publishing 2006. The standard book in its field.

Merriam-Webster Dictionary of Law, 1996. A comprehensive guide to American law, including new terms, usage examples, and an appendix with an explanation of the American court system. Inexpensive.

Dictionary of Legal Terms: A Simplified Guide to the Language of Law, Gifis, S., New York: Barron's 2011.

Medicine
Stedman's Medical Dictionary, 28th ed., Baltimore, MD: Lippincott, Williams & Wilkins 2006. Highly recommended.

Stedman's Medical Dictionary for the Health Professions and Nursing, Philadelphia: Lippincott 2011.

Dorland's Illustrated Medical Dictionary, 32nd ed., Philadelphia: W.B. Saunders Co. 2011. Also an excellent reference.

Dictionary of Medical Terms, Rothenberg, M., New York: Barron's 2006.

Merck Manual, 18th ed., Merck & Co. 2006 (see also *The Merck Index*).
The Bantam Medical Dictionary, 6th ed., New York: Bantam 2009.
Blakiston's Gould Medical Dictionary, McGraw-Hill 1979. Highly regarded.

Military

For all military materiel, the Jane series (annual, London: Jane's Information Group) is the key source:
Jane's All the World's Aircraft.
Jane's Fighting Ships.
Jane's Weapon Systems.

Also recommended:
Encyclopedia of Modern U.S. Military Weapons, Laur, T., New York: Berkley Publishing Group 1998.
The Dictionary of Modern War, Luttwak, E., New York: HarperCollins 1998.
Encyclopedia of the U.S. Military, Arkin, W., New York: Harper & Row 1990.
The Harper Encyclopedia of Military History: From 3500 B.C. to the Present, Dupuy, R.E., New York: HarperCollins 1993.

Science and Technology

Dictionary of Science & Technology on CD-ROM, Academic Press 1996.
Van Nostrand Scientific Encyclopedia, 10th ed., Considine, D., New York: Van Nostrand Reinhold 2008.
McGraw-Hill Dictionary of Scientific & Technical Terms, 5th ed., Parker, S., New York: McGraw-Hill 2002. One of the finest one-volume references covering all science and technology. A must for any technical writer or translator.

Telecommunications

McGraw-Hill Illustrated Telecom Dictionary, Clayton, J., New York: McGraw-Hill 2002.
Data & Telecommunications Dictionary, Petersen, J., Boca Raton, FL: CRC Press 1999.

GENERAL AND SPECIALIZED DICTIONARIES IN LANGUAGES OTHER THAN ENGLISH

The following list is by no means exhaustive. Wherever I was able to examine a dictionary closely, we inserted a short comment. Otherwise, you should get additional information before purchasing a dictionary, to make sure it fulfills your needs.

AFRIKAANS

Afrikaans-English/English-Afrikaans Dictionary, rev. ed., Kromhout, J., Hippocrene Books 2001.

Afrikaans: Legal
English-Afrikaans Legal Dictionary, Hiemstra, V.G., Gaunt Inc. 1984.

ALBANIAN
Albanian-English Dictionary, Newmark, L., Oxford University Press 2000.
Albanian-English/English-Albanian Standard Dictionary, Hysa, R., Hippocrene 2004.

AMHARIC
Advanced Amharic Lexicon: A Supplement to Concise Amharic-English Dictionaries, Getahun, G., Lit Verlag 2004.
Concise Amharic Dictionary, Leslan, W., University of California Press 1996.
Phrase Book: English, Amharic, Tigrina & Arabic, Giorgis, A.G., 1998.

ARABIC
General Dictionaries
A Dictionary of Modern Written Arabic, Wehr, H., Ithaca, NY: Spoken Language Services 1993. This is one of the best general Arabic-English dictionaries around. Available in hardcover and paperback.
Al-Mawrid, Baalbaki, M., Kazi Publications Inc. 2007. Contains many modern words and idioms.
Arabic-English Lexicon, 8 vols., Lane, E.W., French and European Publications Inc. 2003.
The Oxford English-Arabic Dictionary of Current Usage, Doniach, N.S., Oxford: Oxford University Press 1992.
Al-Fara'id al-Durriyah, Hava, G., Beirut: Dar al-Mashriq 1982.
An Arabic-English Lexicon, 8 vols., Lane, E.W., Beirut: Librairie du Liban 1980.
Al-Qamus al-'Asri, Elias A., Cairo: Modern Press 1960.

Arabic: Dialects
NTC's Gulf Arabic-English Dictionary, Hamdi, A., Lincolnwood, IL: NTC Publishing Group 1999.
A Dictionary of Post-Classical Yemeni Arabic, Piamenta, M., New York: E.J. Brill 1997.
al-Qamus al-Arabi al-Shabi al-Filastini, Barghuthi, A., al-Lahjah.
al-Filastiniyah al-Darijah, Birah: Jamiyat Inash al-Usrah, Lajnat al-Abhath al-Ijitimaiyah.
A Dictionary of Iraqi Arabic: English-Arabic/Arabic-English (Georgetown Classics in Arabic Language and Linguistics), ed. by Clarity, B., Stowasser, K., Wolfe, R.G., Woodhead, D.R., and Beene, W., Washington, DC: Georgetown University Press 2003.
Dictionary of Egyptian Arabic, Hinds, M., Beirut: Librairie du Liban 1987. Egyptian terms.

An Arabic-English Dictionary of the Colloquial Arabic of Egypt, Spiro, S., Beirut: Librairie du Liban 1980.

A Dictionary of Moroccan Arabic: Moroccan-English & English-Moroccan (Georgetown Classics in Arabic Language and Linguistics), ed. by Harrell, R., Sobelman, H., and Fox, T., Washington, DC: Georgetown University Press 2004.

A Dictionary of Syrian Arabic: English-Arabic (Georgetown Classics in Arabic Language and Linguistics), ed. by Stowasser, K., and Ani, M., Washington, DC: Georgetown University Press 2004.

Arabic: Agriculture

Chihabi's Dictionary of Agriculture and Allied Terminology, Al-Khatib, A., 2000. English-Arabic.

Arabic: Botany

Botany and Microbiology Dictionary: English-Arabic, Safat, Kuwait: Kuwait Foundation for the Advancement of Sciences 1985.

Illustrated Polyglotic Dictionary of Plant Names, Bedevian, A., Cairo: Argus and Papazian Presses 1936.

Arabic: Business and Related Fields

Arabic Business Dictionary, Sofer, M., and Ettayebi, A., Lanham, MD: Taylor Trade Publishing 2012.

Islamic Economics and Finance: A Glossary, Khan, M.A., Routledge 2007. Arabic-English.

The Office Dictionary in English and Arabic, compiled by Multi-Lingual International Publishers Ltd., London: Oxford University Press 1987.

Management Dictionary (Arabic-Arabic-English), Ghattas, N., Brech, E., et al., Beirut: Librairie du Liban 1983.

English-Arabic Dictionary of Accounting and Finance, Abdeen, A., Beirut: Librairie du Liban, John Wiley & Sons 1982.

A Dictionary of Economics, Business & Finance (English-Arabic), Ghattas, N., Librairie du Liban Publishers; New Impression edition 2000.

Banking and Financial Dictionary: English, French, Arabic, El Assiouty, M.N., Cairo: Distributor, Investment Trustee Department, National Bank of Egypt 1980.

Dictionnaire des Termes Economiques et Commerciaux, Henni, M., Beirut: Librairie du Liban 1982. English-French-Arabic.

Arabic: Chemistry

Unified Dictionary of Chemistry Terms: English, French, Arabic, Tunis: Arab League Educational, Cultural and Scientific Organization 1992.

Kuwait Science Encyclopedia, Chemistry Dictionary, Kuwait: Book & Author Programme 1984.

Illustrated Dictionary of Chemistry in English with English-Arabic & Arabic-English Glossaries, Godman, A., Beirut: Librairie du Liban 1984.

Arabic: Civil Engineering
Arabic Dictionary of Civil Engineering, Kay, E., London: Routledge & Kegan Paul 1986.

Arabic: Communications
A Dictionary of Audio-visual Technology: English-Arabic, Sieny, M.E., Beirut: Librairie du Liban 1987.
Dictionary of Mass Communications: English-French-Arabic, Badawi, A.Z., Cairo: Dar al-Kitab al-Masri 1985.

Arabic: Computers
Encyclopedia of Computer and Internet Terms, English-Arabic, Hammad, A.E., 2008.
Arabic Encyclopedia of Library, Information, and Computer Terms: English-Arabic, Elshami, A.M., Academic Bookshop; al-Tab'ah 2001.
Computer Dictionary with CD-ROM (English-Arabic), Arab Scientific Publishers 2001. A computer dictionary of computer and software terms with CD-ROM which includes dictionary and Microsoft manual style for technical publications.
Encyclopedic Dictionary of Computer Terms, El-Zohairy, N., International Book Center 1996.
Encyclopedia of Computer Terms, Hammad, A.E., American Global Publishing 1994. English-Arabic.
English Arabic Computer Dictionary, Kashou, R., Reading, Berkshire, UK: University of Reading & Sagar Computers Ltd. 1992.
An Illustrated Dictionary of Data Processing, Computing, and Office Automation: English-Arabic with English Index, Cusic, D., Beirut: Librairie du Liban 1988.
Al-Kilani Dictionary of Computer & Internet Terminology, English-English-Arabic, Kilani, T., and Kilani, M., Beirut: Librairie du Liban 2003.
A Dictionary of Data Processing and Computer Terms: English-French-Arabic, Haddad, E.W., Beirut: Librairie du Liban 1987.
Illustrated Dictionary of Computing Science, Quentin, R.D., Beirut: Librairie du Liban 1996.
Arabic Computer Dictionary, Ghanayem, M.F., Texas: International House Publications 1986. Arabic-English.

Arabic: Diplomacy
A Dictionary of Diplomacy and International Affairs, el 'Adah, Samouhi Fawq, Librairie du Liban 1996. English-French-Arabic.

Arabic: Geography
Dictionary of Arabic Topography and Place Names, Groom, N., London: Librairie du Liban 1983.

Glossary of Arabic Place Names, Arabian American Oil Company, s.l.: ARAMCO 1978.

Arabic: Journalism
al-Qamus al-Ilami: Arabi-Inkilizi, Najm, A., Baghdad: Wizarat al-Thaqafah wa-a;-Ilam 1982.

Arabic: Law
Arabic-English Law Dictionary, Amin, S.H., Glasgow: Royston 1992.
Faruqi's Law Dictionary, 5th rev. ed., Faruqi, H., Beirut: Librairie du Liban 2005. English-Arabic.
Customs Dictionary: English-Arabic, Mahmoud, R., Cairo: published by author 1984.
Faruqi's Law Dictionary, Faruqi, H., Beirut: Librairie du Liban 2003. Arabic-English.
Law Dictionary: English-Arabic, al-Wahab, D.I.I., Beirut: Librairie du Liban 1988.

Arabic: Medicine
Marashi's Grand Medical Dictionary: English-Arabic. Marashi, M.O., Librairie du Liban Publishers 2003.
Hitti's Pocket Medical Dictionary: English-Arabic, Hitti, Y.K., Beirut: Librairie du Liban 2006.
A Modern Arabic Dictionary of Dental Terms: English-Arabic, Duyat, M., Amman: Dar al-Ibdaa 1990.
Concise Medical Dictionary, Allah, J., and Fawzi, M., Cairo: University Book Centre 1986.
Qamus Mustalahat Tibb al-Asnan, Mutayyam, K., s.n.: Matbaat al-Taqddum 1984.
The New Medical-Pharmaceutical Dictionary, Oweida, A.M., Cairo: Dar al-Fikr al-Arabi 1970.
Dictionary of Anatomy, Abadir, F.M., Princeton University Arabic Collection, Alexandria: Al Maaref Establishment 1968.
The Unified Dictionary of Anatomy English-Arabic, World Health Organization 2005.

Arabic: Military
Illustrated Military Dictionary (English-Arabic), Hadary, S. A., Madbouli 2004.
Modern Military Dictionary, Kayyali, M.S., Arab Institute for Research and Publishing, Beirut, London: Third World Center for Research and Publishing 1994. Arabic-English-Arabic.
Arabic Military Dictionary, Kay, E., London: Routledge & Kegan Paul 1986. English-Arabic-English.
Pocket Book of Military Terms, 6th ed., Badran, C., Cairo: Greater Egypt Publishers 1982. English-Arabic.

Al-Mu'jam al-'Askari al-Muwahhad, Committee for Standardizing Military Terminology for Arab Armies 1971. Arabic-English.

Al-Mu'jam al-'Askari al-Muwahhad, Committee for Standardizing Military Terminology for Arab Armies, Cairo: Dar al-Ma'arif 1970. English-Arabic.

Arabic: Nautical
Elsevier's Maritime Dictionary, Bakr, M., Elsevier Science 1987. English-French-Arabic.

Arabic: Oil
A New Dictionary of Petroleum and the Oil Industry, Al-Khatib, A., Beirut: Librairie du Liban 1990. English-Arabic.

Arabic: Psychology and Psychiatry
Mujam Ilm al-Nafs wa-al Tibb al-Nafsi: Injilizi-Arabi, Jabir, J., Cairo: Dar al-Nahdah al-Arabiyah 1988.
Mujam Ilm al-Nafs, Inkilizi-Faransi-Arabi, Aqil, F., Beirut: Dar al-Ilm lil-Malayin 1977.
Dictionary of Psychology: English-Arabic, Illustrated, Zahran, H., Cairo: Al Shaab Print House 1972.

Arabic: Science and Technology
Mustalahat al-Duru, Amman: al-Majma al-Lughah al-Arabiyah al-Urduni 1994. Dictionary of explosives.
al-Mujam al-Muwahhad Li-Mustalahat al-Riyadiyat wa-al-Falak: Injilizi, Faransi, Arabi, Tunis: al-Munazzamah 1990.
Unified Dictionary for Terminologies of General and Nuclear Physics: English, French, Arabic, Tunis: Arab League Educational, Cultural and Scientific Organization 1989.
A New English to Arabic Dictionary of Scientific and Technical Terms, Al-Khatib, A., Beirut: Librairie du Liban 2005.
Mujam al-Hayawan, Maluf, A., Beirut: Dar al-Raid al-Arabi 1980.
Dictionary of Zoological Terms, Unified Dictionary of Scientific Terms for General Education Levels, No.4, s.l.: Iraqi Academy Press 1976.
Dictionnaire des sciences de la nature, Ghaleb, E., Beirut: Imprimerie Catholique 1965. Arabic-English-French.
Space Dictionary, al-Laqqani, M., Cairo: Dar El-Hana Press 1962.

AZERBAIJANI
Azerbaijani-English English-Azerbaijani Dictionary and Phrasebook, ed. by Awde, N., Ande, N., and Ismailov, F., New York: Hippocrene 1999.
Azerbaijani-English Dictionary, O'Sullivan, P., Kensington, MD: Dunwoody Press 1995.

Azerbaijani-English, English-Azerbaijani Dictionary, Mamedov, S., New York: Hippocrene 1994.

BASQUE

Basque-English/English-Basque Dictionary & Phrasebook, Conroy, J., New York: Hippocrene 1998.

Basque-English/English-Basque Dictionary, Aulestia, G., and White, L., Reno: University of Nevada Press 1992.

BENGALI

Samsad Bengali-English Dictionary, Biswas, S., Calcutta: Sahitya Samsad 2006.

Dictionary of English, Bengali & Manipuri, French and European Publications 1992.

BOSNIAN

Bosnian-English/English-Bosnian Compact Dictionary, Nikolina Uzacanin, N., New York: Hippocrene 1996.

BULGARIAN

Complete Bulgarian-English Dictionary, Constantine Stephanove, Nabu Press 2010.

Bulgarian-English/English-Bulgarian Dictionary, Tchomakov, I., New York: Hippocrene 1997.

Bulgarian-English Dictionary, 2 vols., Atanassova, T., et al., Sofia: 1990.

Bulgarian: Medical

Medical Dictionary (English-Bulgarian), Assen, G., 1998.

Bulgarian: Technical

Technical Dictionary (English-Bulgarian), Sofia: Technika EOOD 1992.

English-Bulgarian Polytechnical Dictionary, French and European Publications 1993.

BYELORUSSIAN

Hippocrene Concise Byelorussian-English/English-Byelorussian Dictionary, Ushkevich, A., and Zezulin, A., New York: Hippocrene 1994.

CAMBODIAN

The New Oxford Picture Dictionary, English-Cambodian, Oxford: Oxford University Press 1999.

Cambodian-English/English-Cambodian Dictionary, New York: Hippocrene 1990.

Modern Cambodian Dictionary, Headley, R., Kensington, MD: Dunwoody Press 1997.

CATALAN

Catalan-English/English-Catalan Dictionary & Phrasebook, Britton, A.S., New York: Hippocrene 2011.

Catalan-English/English-Catalan Dictionary, Sabater, M.S., and Freixenet, J.A., New York: Hippocrene 2001.

Catalan Dictionary, London: Routledge 1994. English-Catalan/Catalan-English.

Diccionari anglés-català, Oliva: Encyclopedia Catalana 1983.

CHINESE

General Dictionaries

Oxford Chinese Dictionary, New York: Oxford University Press 2010.

Far East Medium Chinese-English Dictionary, Shih-chiu, L., Taipei: Far East Book Company (Cheng & Tsui Co.) 1999.

Handbook of Chinese Synonyms with Bilingual Explanations, Beijing: China Today Press 1992. Simplified characters.

Visual Dictionary, Corbeil, J.C., Hong Kong: Readers' Digest Association Far East Ltd. 1988.

English-Chinese Word-Ocean Dictionary, 2 vols., Wang Tungyi, Beijing Defense Industry Press 1987.

Reverse Chinese-English Dictionary, Beijing: Commercial Press 1999.

The Shogakukan Dictionary of New Chinese Words, Tokyo: Shogakukan 1985.

Chinese Idioms and Their English Equivalents, Chen Yongzhen and Spring Chen, Hong Kong: Commercial Press 2002. A must for anyone translating general Chinese text.

A Chinese-English Dictionary, Beijing Foreign Languages Institute, Chinese-English Dictionary Editorial Committee, Hong Kong: Commercial Press 1981. A very good midsized dictionary. Entries are arranged alphabetically, but there is also a character index.

A Dictionary of World Place Names, Shanghai: Shanghai Cishu Chubanshe 1981.

A Classified and Illustrated Chinese-English Dictionary, Hong Kong: Joint Publishing Company 1989.

Xinhua Cidian, Beijing: Commercial Press 1980. The most basic reference. Indispensable.

Chinese Cihai, Shanghai: Shanghai Cishu Chubanshe 1979. The staple reference of Chinese translators for years.

Xinhua Hanyu Cidian, Dictionary Editorial Department of the Chinese Academy of Sciences' Language Research Institute, Hong Kong: Commercial Press 1977.

Chinese-English Dictionary of Contemporary Usage, Wen-shun Chi, Berkeley: University of California Press 1977.

Handbook of Chinese-English Phrases, Beijing: Waiwen Chubanshe 1970.

Tung-Fang Kuo-Yu Tz'u-Tien, Taipei: Far East Book Company 1970.

Chinese: Aerospace/Aviation
English-Chinese Aviation Dictionary, Hua Renjie, Beijing: Shangwu Yinshuguan 1982.
Chinese-English Rocketry Dictionary, 7602nd Air Intelligence Group 1979.

Chinese: Agriculture
A Chinese-English Dictionary of China's Rural Economy, Broadbent, K., Farnham Royal, Bucks, England: Commonwealth Agricultural Bureau 1978.

Chinese: Biology/Life Sciences
English-Chinese Dictionary of the Life Sciences, Beijing: Zhongguo Kexuejishu Chubanshe 1992.

Chinese: Business and Related Fields
Chinese Business Dictionary, ed. by Sofer, M., and Guo, R., Lanham, MD: Taylor Trade Publishing 2012.
Global Business Dictionary: English-Chinese-French-German-Japanese-Russian, ed. by Sofer, M., Lanham, MD: Taylor Trade Publishing 2012.
Midland Group English-Chinese Dictionary of Finance, Adams, S.J., and Mathieson, T.I., AMCD (Publishers) Ltd., Hong Kong University Press 1991.
Dictionary of International Trade and Finance, Taipei, Taiwan: Chung-hwa Cheng-hsin-swo Inc. Publishing Department 1989.
New Chinese Dictionary of Economics and Trade, Harbin Press 1989.
Chinese-English Dictionary of Economic Terms, China Commercial Press 1988.
An English-Chinese Dictionary of Finance, Economics and Accounting, Chen Jinchi, Beijing Economics Institute, Beijing: Zhong-guo Caizheng Jingji Chubanshe 1987.
An English-Chinese Dictionary of Economics and Finance, Hu Xisen, Yu Jialai, and Qu Wanfang, Beijing: Shiyou Gongye Chubanshe 1986.
A Glossary of Economic and Commercial Terms (Chinese-English), Xie Zhenqing, Beijing: Zhongguo Duiwai Jingji Maoyi Chubanshe 1997.
Nichi-Ei-Chu Boeki Yogo Jiten, Shangwu Yinshuguan, Toho Shoten, Tokyo: Toho Shoten 1986. Japanese-English-Chinese.
Accounting Terminology in Use in the PRC & the USA, Lou Er-Ying and Farrell, J.B., Hong Kong: Joint Publishing Co., and Shanghai: Shanghai Renmin Chubanshe 1985.
A Chinese-English Textile Dictionary, Zhu Zhengdu, Lou Erduan, et al., Beijing: Fangzhi Gongye Chubanshe 1985.
An English-Chinese Glossary of International Finance and Trade, Beijing: Zhongguo Zhanwang Chubanshe 1996.
An English-Chinese Lexicon of International Economy, Beijing: Zhongguo Shehui Kexue Chubanshe 1984.
English-Chinese Economics Glossary, Chongqing: Zhongguo Shehui Kexue Chubanshe 1983.

English-Chinese Accounting Dictionary, Beijing: Shiyou Gongye Chubanshe 1982. Good, reputable reference.

A Dictionary of Economic Management Terms, Changchun: Jilin Renmin Chubanshe 1982.

Glossary of Foreign Exchange Terms, Caizheng Jingji Chubanshe 1980. Chinese-English-French-Russian-German.

English-Chinese, Chinese-English Dictionary of Business Terms, Chu Hsiu-feng, Hong Kong: Chi Wen Publishing Co. 1973.

English-Chinese & Chinese-English Accounting Dictionary, Ji Zehua, Hong Kong: Wan Li Book Co. 1964.

Chinese: Chemistry

English-Chinese Dictionary of Chemistry and Chemical Engineering, 4th ed., Beijing: Kexue Chubanshe 2000.

Chinese-English/English-Chinese Chemistry Dictionary on CD-ROM, Beijing: Chemical Industry Press.

Chinese-English-Japanese Glossary of Chemical Terms, Tokyo: Toho Shoten Ltd. 1980. Far from complete, but there are very few other such sources available in this field. Entries are arranged by number of strokes in a character.

Chinese: Civil Engineering

English-Chinese Dictionary of Civil and Architectural Engineering Terms, Hong Kong: Commercial Press 1989.

Chinese: Computers

English-Chinese Computer Software Dictionary, Zhou Hanzong, Changsha: Hunan Kexue Jishu Chubanshe 1986.

A Comprehensive IBM Computer Dictionary, Science Popularization Press 1985.

English-Chinese Computer Dictionary, Beijing: Renmin Youdian Chubanshe 1984.

Chinese: Electrical Engineering/Electronics

English-Chinese Dictionary of Data Communications Technology, Electrical Engineering Press 1990.

Chinese-English Dictionary of Electronics Technology, Gan Dayon, Beijing: Dianzi Gongye Chubanshe 1987. A valuable reference.

English-Chinese Dictionary of Electrical Engineering, Beijing: Kexue Chubanshe 1987.

English-Chinese Dictionary of Television and Electronics, Beijing: Kexue Chubanshe 1987.

English-Chinese Dictionary of Remote Sensing, Li Wenlan, Beijing: Kexue Puju Chubanshe 1986.

English-Chinese Dictionary of Television and Video Recording, Beijing: Renmin Youdian Chubanshe 1983.

DICTIONARIES AND REFERENCE LITERATURE

Chinese: Environmental Sciences
Chinese-English Dictionary of Environmental Sciences, Beijing: Zhongguo Huanjing Chubanshe 1993.

Chinese: Fiber Optics
English-Chinese Lightwave Communications and Optical Fiber Technical Dictionary, Li Guangqian, Beijing: Renmin Youdian Chubanshe 1985.

Chinese: Geology
Geology Dictionary, Ministry of Geology and Mineral Resources, Beijing: Dizhi Chubanshe 1983.
English-Chinese Comprehensive Geology Dictionary, Beijing: Kexue Chubanshe 1980.

Chinese: Highway Engineering
English-Chinese Dictionary of Highway Engineering, Beijing: Renmin Jiaotong Chubanshe 1978.

Chinese: Journalism
English-Chinese Glossary of Newspaper Terms, Hong Kong: Commercial Press 1986.

Chinese: Laser/Infrared Technology
English-Chinese Dictionary of Lasers and Infrared Technique, Zhou Rongsheng, Beijing: Kexue Chubanshe 1987.

Chinese: Medical
English-Chinese Medical Dictionary, Commercial Press 1988.
An English-Chinese Medical Dictionary, Lu Zai-ying, People's Medical 2006.

Chinese: Military
English-Chinese Military and Technical Dictionary, Jiang Kang and Lu Zuokang, Luoyang: Yuhang Chubanshe 1985.
Cihai, Military Supplement, Shanghai: Shanghai Cishu Chubanshe 1980. A must, as is the "Cihai" itself.

Chinese: Science and Technology
The Chinese-English Dictionary of Scientific and Technical Glossaries (Hanying keji dacidian), 2 vols., Beijing: Kexue Jishu Wenxian Chubanshe 1998. A good comprehensive general technical dictionary.
A Comprehensive Chinese-English Dictionary of Science and Technology, Beijing: Commercial Press 2003.
Chinese-English Dictionary of Scientific and Technical Terms, Harbin: Heilongjiang Renmin Chubanshe 1985. One of the best, but unfortunately not available from the publisher.

Comprehensive Chinese-English Dictionary of Science and Technology, Beijing: Kexue Chubanshe 1983.

A Modern Scientific and Technical Dictionary, Shanghai: Shanghai Scientific and Technical Publishing House 1980. Highly recommended.

An English-Chinese Dictionary of Technology, Qinghua University Specialist Group, Beijing: Guofang Gongye Chubanshe 2002. Recommended.

A Modern Science and Technology Dictionary, Shanghai: Shanghai Kexue Jishu Chubanshe 1980.

Chinese: Transportation
English-Chinese Dictionary of Railway Terms, Beijing: Renmin Tiedao Chubanshe 1977.

CREOLE
Haitian Creole Dictionary and Phrasebook: Haitian Creole-English, English-Haitian Creole, New York: Hippocrene 2008.

Haitian Creole-English Dictionary, Targete, V., Kensington, MD: Dunwoody Press 1998.

Creole-English/English-Creole Concise Dictionary, Ovide, S., New York: Hippocrene 1996.

Haitian Creole-English-French Dictionary, 2 vols., Valdman, A., Bloomington: Creole Institute, Indiana University 1981.

English Haitian Creole Word to Word (Bilingual Dictionaries), Vilsaint, F., Coconut Creek, Florida: Educa Vision Inc. 2006.

Creole: Medicine
Haitian Creole-English Pocket Medical Translator, International Medical Volunteers Association 1996.

CROATIAN, See Serbo-Croatian.

CZECH
General Dictionaries
Czech English Dictionary, 10th ed., Poldauf, I., French and European Publications 2001.

Czech-English Comprehensive Dictionary, Poldauf, I., New York: Hippocrene 1998.

Concise Czech-English/English-Czech Dictionary, Trnka, N., New York: Hippocrene 1991.

English-Czech Dictionary, 4 vols., Hais, K., et al., Prague Academia 1991.

Slovník spisovného jazyka českého, 4 vols., Hais, K., et al., Prague: Academia 1971.

Czech-English/English-Czech Dictionary, Chermak, A., Saphrograp.

DICTIONARIES AND REFERENCE LITERATURE

Czech: Chemistry
Anglicko-český a česko-anglický chemickotechnologický slovník, Jouklova, Z., Prague: SNTL 1967.

Czech: Computers
English-Czech Dictionary of Data Processing, Telecommunications & Office Systems, New York: i.b.d. Ltd. 1994.
Anglicko-český a česko-anglický slovník výpo cetní techniky, 2 vols., Minihofer, O., New York: i.b.d. 1994.

Czech: Economics
Česko-anglický obchodní slovník, Zavada, D., Prague: Orbis 1958.

Czech: Electronics
Dictionary of Electrical Engineering & Electronics (English-Czech/ Czech-English), Malinova, L., Prague: SNTL 1992.

Czech: Nuclear Physics
Czech-English/English-Czech Dictionary of Nuclear Physics, New York: i.b.d. Ltd. 1985.

Czech: Technical
Česko-anglický technický slovník, 3rd ed., Kluvdova, B., and Stackova, V., Prague: SNTL-Nakladatelství technick literatury 1983.
English-Czech Technical Dictionary, Bazant, Z.P., French and European Publications 1985.

DANISH
General Dictionaries
A Danish-English Dictionary, Ferrall, J.S., and Repp, T.G., Nabu Press 2010.
Danish-English Comprehensive Dictionary, Kjaerulft-Nielsen, B., New York: i.b.d. Ltd. 1994.
Danish Dictionary, Jones, W.G., London: Routledge 1995.
Nye ord i dansk, Petersen, P., Copenhagen: Gyldendal 1984. Danish-Danish.
Nudansk ordbog, 2 vols., Jacobsen, L., Copenhagen: Politikens forlag 1979.

Danish: Business and Related Fields
English-Danish Commercial Dictionary, Svenson, A.L., New York: i.b.d. Ltd. 1991.
Miniordbog i fanansietingsenggelsk: engelsk-dansk, dansk-engelsk, Norager, P., Copenhagen: Samfundslitteratur 1987.
Dansk-engelsk handels-og fagordbog for erhvervslivet, administrationen og forvaltningen, Bailey, I.E., Copenhagen: Det Schonbergske Forlag 1982.

Danish: Law
Retsplejeordbog (Legal Dictionary), Hjelmblink, S., Copenhagen: Munksgaard 1991 (Munksgaards ordboger).

Danish: Medicine
Danish-English/English-Danish Medical Dictionary, Pilegaard, M., and Baden, M., New York: i.b.d. Ltd. 1994.

Danish: Technical
English/Danish Technical Dictionary, Clausens, New York: i.b.d. Ltd. 1995.
Danish/English Technical Dictionary, Christensen, A.O., New York: i.b.d. Ltd. 1995.
Teknisk ordbog: dansk-engelsk, udarbejdet i samarbejde med Fonden for Fagsproglig Liksikografi, Copenhagen: Fonden for Fagsproglig Leksikografi og Grafisk Forlag 1990.

Dansk-engelsk teknisk ordbog, Warrern, A., Copenhagen: Clausen Boger 1988.

DUTCH
General Dictionaries
Langescheidt Universal Dictionary Dutch, Langenscheidy 2008.
Compact Dutch & English Dictionary, New York: McGraw-Hill 1999.
Wolters Handwoordenboek Nederlands-Engels, 20th ed., ten Bruggencate, K., Utrecht: van Dale Lexicografie 1997. English-Dutch volume also published 1997.
Wolters' Engels Woordenboek, 20th ed., 2 vols., Gerritsen, J., et al., Wolters-Noordhoff 1997.
Van Dale Dutch-English/English-Dutch Dictionary, Martin, W., and Tops, G.A.J., Utrecht, Van Dale Lexicografie 1999.
Dutch-English/English-Dutch Dictionary, Renier, G.G., and Renier, F.G., London: Routledge 2003.
Van Dale, Groot Woordenboek der Nederlandse Taal, 11th ed., 3 vols., Geerts, G., and Heestermans, H., Van Dale Lexicografie 1986.
Nijhoffs Zuid Nederlands Woordenboek, de Clerck, W., Antwerp: Martinus Nijhoff 1981.
Nederlands-Engels Woordenboek, 3 vols., Jansonius, H., Leiden: Nederlandsche Uitgeversmaatschappij 1972.

Dutch: Business and Related Fields
The Banking and Insurance Lexicon (Dutch-English), Voeten, M.E.C.M., and van den End, A., Gateway 1996. Excellent.
English-Dutch Dictionary of Financial Management, 5th ed., Van Amerongen, F., Samson 1994.

Dutch-English Reference Book on Business Terminology, 9th ed., Huitinga, T., 1993.

Dutch: Computers
Woordenboek Informatica, van Steenis, H., Sybex uitgeverij 2001.
Dutch-English Verklarend Informatica Woordenboek, van Uitert, C., and Kaspers A.M., 1989.

Dutch: Law
The Legal Lexicon (Dutch-English), van den End, A., Gateway, 1995. Excellent resource.

Dutch: Medicine
Medical Dictionary (Dutch-English/English-Dutch), Kerkhof, P.L.M., 2006.

Dutch: Military
Dutch-English Dictionary of Military and Associated Terms, Brokling, L.G., Menlo Park, CA: published by the author 1983.

Dutch: Technical
Dutch-English Great Polytechnic Dictionary, Schuurmans Stekhoven, G., New York: i.b.d. Ltd. 1997. Recommended.

ESPERANTO

Comprehensive English-Esperanto Dictionary, Benson, P.: Esperanto League for North America 1995.
Concise Esperanto and English Dictionary, Wells, J.C., Lincolnwood, IL: NTC Publishing Group 1992.

ESTONIAN
General Dictionaries
Langenscheidt Picture Dictionary (Estonian/English), Langenscheidt 1994.
Hippocrene Concise Estonian-English/English-Estonian Dictionary, Kyiw, K., New York: Hippocrene 2002.
Estonian-English Dictionary, Saagpakk, P.F., New Haven, CT: Yale University Press 1982.
Estonian-English Dictionary, Silvet, J., New Jersey: French and European Publications 1993.

Estonian: Business and Related Fields
English-Estonian/Estonian-English Business Dictionary, Aule, A., et al., Tallinn: TEA 1993.

FARSI (PERSIAN)

Farsi-English/English-Farsi Concise Dictionary, Miandji, A., New York: Hippocrene 2003.

The Larger English-Persian Dictionary, Haim, S., Tehran: Farhang Moaser 2004. English-Persian/Persian-English.

A Dictionary of Common Persian and English Verbs: With Synonyms & Examples, Amuzgar, H., Ibex Publishers 2005.

Combined New Persian-English and English-Persian Dictionary, Aryanpurkashani, A., Costa Mesa, CA: Mazda Publishers 1986.

Comprehensive Persian-English Dictionary, Steingass, F., London: Routledge 2005.

FINNISH

General Dictionaries

Langescheidt Universal Finnish Dictionary, Langenscheidt 2008.

NTC's Compact Finnish and English Dictionary, Sovijarvi, S., NTC Publishing Group 1999.

Suomi-Englanti-Suomi Sanakirj, Reikiaro, I., and Robinson, D., Jyväskylä: Gummerus 1992.

Lyhennesanakirja, Helsinki: Otava 1985.

Finnish-English General Dictionary, Hurme, R., et al., Helsinki: Werner Söderström 1996.

Nykyslangin sanakirja, Karttunen, K., Osakeyhtiö: Werner Söderström 1979.

Suomalais-englantilainen suursanakirja, Alanne, V.S., Helsinki: Werner Söderström 1974.

30,000 Lyhennettä, Helsinki: Otava 1970.

Finnish: Business and Related Fields

Stock Exchange Dictionary (Estonian-English-Finnish-German-Russian), Liivaku, U., New York: i.b.d. Ltd. 1994.

Finnish-English Technical and Commercial Dictionary, Talvitie, J.K., New York: i.b.d. Ltd. 2000.

Ajankohtainen sihteerin perussanasto, Porko, L., Helsinki: Gaude-amus 1988.

Finnish: Electronics

Finnish-English Dictionary of Electronics, Hukki, P., New York: i.b.d. Ltd. 1995.

Finnish: Medicine

Medical & Scientific Terms Dictionary, Pesonar, N., New York: i.b.d. Ltd. 1987. English-Finnish.

Finnish: Military

Sotilaslyhennesanasto, Poroila, E., Kirjapaino: Mikkeli 1960. Finnish-English/English-Finnish.

Finnish: Technical
Englanti-suomi suuri kuvasanakirja: A visual glossary, Helsinki: Söderström 1981.

FRENCH
General Dictionaries
Dictionnaire electronique du français, French ed., Nicolato, L., Kindle edition 2011.

Harrap's New Standard French & English Dictionary, 4 vols., London: George G. Harrap & Co. Ltd. 1989. This is the best French-English/English-French dictionary for all-around translation use, and perhaps one of the finest examples of lexicography in any language. One can only wish this kind of a dictionary existed in every language.

HarperCollins Robert French Unabridged Dictionary, 8th ed., New York: HarperCollins 2007. Arguably the best one-volume French-English/English-French all-around dictionary for translators.

Le Petit Larousse illustré, Larousse 2008.

Le Petit Robert, Paris: Robert 2000. French-French. Also available on CD-ROM.

Nouveau dictionnaire étymologique, 1st ed., Jacquenod, R., 1996.

Dictionnaire des faux amis, Van Roey, J., et al., Louvain-la-Neuve: Duculot 2004. French-English/English-French.

Dictionnaire encyclopédique, 2 vols., Maubourguet, P., et al., 1994. Includes illustrations and atlas.

Oxford Hachette French-English/English-French Dictionary, Correard, M.H., 2010. Also available on CD-ROM. Highly recommended.

Larousse grand dictionnaire anglais-français/français-anglais, Garney, F., 2000.

Dictionnaire de l'argot, Colin, J.P., Paris: Larousse 2001.

Dictionnaire des mots contemporains, Gilbert, P., Paris: Robert 1989.

Dictionnaire des néologismes officiels, Fantapie, A., Franterm 1984. French-English/English-French.

Dictionary of Modern Colloquial French, Hérail, R.J., and Lovatt, E.A., London: Routledge 1990.

The Oxford-Duden Pictorial French-English Dictionary, Oxford: Clarendon Press 1983.

Dictionnaire usuel illustré, Flammarion 1983.

Lexique général, New York: United Nations Publications. English-French. Used by all United Nations translators.

Dictionnaire des expressions et locutions figurées, Rey, A., and Chantreau, S., Paris: Robert 1979. French-French.

Lexis, Dictionnaire de la langue française, Larousse 2003.

Dictionnaire français-anglais de locutions et expressions verbales, Dubois, M., Larousse.

A Dictionary of Colorful French Slang and Colloquialisms, Deak, E., and Deak, S., New York: Dutton 1961.

French: Aerospace/Aviation
Aeronautics Abbreviations Glossary (French-English), Delol, J., 1997.
Aeronautic Dictionary (English-French/French-English), 3rd ed., Lambert R., 2001.
Dictionnaire de l'aéronautique et de l'espace/Dictionary of Aeronautics & Space Technology, Goursau, H., St. Orens-de-Gameville: published by author; French-English volume 1990; English-French 1992.
Dictionnaire de télédétection aérospatiale, Paul, S., Paris: Masson 1982. French-English.

French: Architecture
Dictionary of Architecture & Construction (French-English/English-French), 3rd ed., Forbes, J., 2003.

French: Automotive
Glossary of Automotive Terminology, Chrysler Corporation, Warrendale, PA: SAE Publications French-English/English-French.

French: Business and Related Fields
French Business Dictionary: The Business Terms of France and Canada, ed. by Sofer, M., Lanham, MD: Taylor Trade Publishing 2012.
Global Business Dictionary: English-Chinese-French-German-Japanese-Russian, ed. by Sofer, M., Lanham, MD: Taylor Trade Publishing 2012.
Economic, Finance & Accounting Dictionary, Esposito, M., 2005. French-English/English-French.
French Dictionary of Business, Commerce and Finance, London/New York: Routledge 1996. French-English/English-French. CD-ROM 1999.
Dictionary of Financial and Stock Market Terminology (English-French/French-English), Freeland, C., published by author 2006. Highly recommended.
Dictionnaire financier anglais-français, Whettem-Leysen, V., and Adams, S., Cheshire, England: AMCD (Publishers) Ltd. 1995.
Economic, Business & Finance Dictionary (French-English/English-French), Marcheteau, M., 1995. Small paperback, but still a good reference.
Dictionary of Accounting (English-French), Ménard, L. 1994. Excellent.
Dictionnaire de banque et bourse, Crozet, Y., Paris: Armand Colin 1993.
Dictionnaire économique et juridique anglais-français, 3rd ed., Baleyte et al., Navarre 1992.
Le Robert & Collins du management (commercial, financier, economique, juridique), Péron, M., and Shenton, G., Paris: Dictionnaires Le Robert 1999. French-English/English-French. Very fine reference.
Dictionary of Business: English-French, French-English, Collin, P.H., Teddington, Middlesex: Peter Collin Publishing Ltd. 2002.
Economics Dictionary (French-English/English-French), Greenwald, D., 1987.

French-English/English-French Accounting, Fiscal and Finance Dictionary, De Saxcé, F., 2007.

Glossaire des communauts européennes, Conseil des communautés européennes 1987.

Delmas/Harrap Business Dictionary, Delmas/Harrap, London: Harrap 1979.

Dictionnaire des affaires, Peron, M., Paris: Librairie Larousse 1968.

Dictionnaire de la comptabilité, Sylvain, F., Toronto: Institut Canadien des Comptables Agréés 2004.

French: Chemistry

Chemical French, Dolt, M.L., Nabu Press 2010.

A French-English Dictionary for Chemists, Google ebook, New Jersey: John Wiley & Sons 2007.

French-English Dictionary for Chemists, Patterson, A.M., New York: John Wiley & Sons 1921.

French: Communications

English to French Dictionary of Telecommunications and the Internet (Dictionnaire anglais et français des telecommunications et de l'internet), de Luca, J., French and European Publications 2004.

French Dictionary of Telecommunications, New York: Routledge 1997. Available on CD-ROM, summer 1998. French-English/English-French.

Dictionnaire de multimédia/Multimedia Dictionary, 2nd ed., Notaise, J., 1996.

Dictionary of Media & Multimedia (French-English/English-French), Chevassu, F., Presse Pocket 1995.

English-French Dictionary of Telecommunications and the Internet, de Luca, J., 2004.

French: Computers

English to French Dictionary of Telecommunications and the Internet (Dictionnaire anglais et français des telecommunications et de l'internet), de Luca, J., French and European Publications 2004.

Dictionary of Computing and Information Technology, 2nd ed., 1996.

Dictionnaire d'informatique français-anglais, 6th ed., Ginguay, M., Paris: Masson 2001.

Dictionnaire de la microinformatique, Fantapie, A., Paris: Franterm 1984. French-English.

Dictionnaire de l'informatique, Morvan, P., Paris: Librairie Larousse 1981.

Harrap's French and English Dictionary of Data Processing, Camille, C., London: Harrap 1985.

French: Electronics

Encyclopedic Dictionary of Electronics (English-French), Fleutry, L., 1991.

International Electrotechnical Vocabulary, General Index, Geneva: International Electrotechnical Commission 1979. English-French/French-English.

French: Environment
French Dictionary of Environmental Technology, New York: Routledge 1997. French-English/English-French.

French: Journalism
Newspaper French: A Vocabulary of Administrative and Commercial Idiom, Ritchie, A., University of Wales Press 1991.

French: Law
Dahl's Law Dictionary French-English/English-French, St. Dahl, H., William S. Hein Co. 2008.
Vocabulaire juridique, 6th ed., Cornu, G., Presse universitaire de France 2003. Excellent; covers civil and private law.
L'Anglais juridique/Legal English, Dhuicq, B., Presse Pocket 2001.
The Council of Europe Legal Dictionary (French-English), Bridge, F.H.S., Council of Europe Publications 1994. Highly regarded.
Economic & Legal Dictionary (French-English/English-French), Baleyte, J., et al., 2000.
Dictionnaire juridique français-anglais, Quemner, Th. A., Paris: Editions de Navarre 1977.
Dictionnaire juridique et économique, Doucet, M., Paris: La Maison du Dictionnaire 1980.

French: Medicine
Dictionary of Medicine, French-English with English-French Glossary, 2nd ed., Djordjevic, S.P., Rockville, MD: Schreiber Publishing 2004. The most complete and updated French-into-English medical dictionary available.
English and English to French Dictionary of Medical and Biological Terms and Medications, Hill, G.S., French and European Publications 2005.
Dictionnaire anglais-français des sciences medicales et paramedicales, Gladstone, W.J., 2002.
Dictionnaire médical du chirurgien dentiste, 1st ed., Girard, P., et al., Masson 1997.
Medical Dictionary (French-English), Garnier, M., 1995. Excellent.
Medical Dictionary (French-English), Hamburger, J., Flammarion 1994. Also very useful.
Dictionnaire français-anglais/anglais-français des termes médicaux et biologiques, Lepine, P., Paris: Flammarion Médecine-Sciences 1992.
Medical Dictionary (French-English/English-French), Delamare, J., Maloine: 1992.
Dictionnaire de médecine, Hamburger, J., Flammarion 1982.

French: Military

A French-English Military Technical Dictionary, Willcox, C., Ross & Perry 2001.

Lexique militaire, Ottawa, Canadian Forces Headquarters 1982. English-French/French-English.

Glossaire militaire, Imprimerie Nationale 1982. English-French/French-English.

French: Mining

The Oxford-Duden Pictorial French-English Dictionary, Oxford: Clarendon Press 1983.

French: Oil

Dictionary of Petroleum Technology (French-English/English-French), Moureau, M., and Brace, G., Editions Technip 2008. Recommended.

French: Political

Dictionnaire français-anglais/anglais-français (Collection Saturne), Dubois, M.-M., Paris: Larousse.

French: Technical

French Technical Dictionary, 2 vols., London: Routledge 1997. French-English/English-French. Very comprehensive. Also available on CD-ROM and diskette.

Words Techniques: Dictionnaire thématique anglais: industrie, technologies, ingénierie, Gusdorf, F., Ellipses 1998.

Dictionnaire général de la technique industrielle, Tome IX: French-English, Ernst, R., Wiesbaden: Brandstetter 1982.

Dictionnaire international d'abbréviations scientifiques et techniques, Azzaretti, M., La Maison du Dictionnaire 1978.

Dictionnaire technique anglais-français, Malgorn, G., Dunod 1976.

Dictionnaire technique français-anglais, Malgorn, G., Dunod 2003.

GEORGIAN

General Dictionaries

Georgian-English/English-Georgian Dictionary & Phrasebook, New York: Hippocrene 2010.

Kartuli enis ganmartebiti leksikoni, Chikobava, A.S., Tbilisi: Georgian Academy of Sciences Linguistics Institute 1986.

Inglisur-kartuli leksikoni, Gvarjaladze, T., and Gvarjaladze, I., Tbilisi: Izd. Sabchota sakartvelo 1975.

GERMAN

General Dictionaries

Dictionary German-English, German ed., Eichhorn, D., Kindle eBook 2011.

Langenscheidts Enzyklopädisches Wörterbuch (Der Große Muret-Sanders), 4 vols., Berlin: Langenscheidt 2000. The best all-around German-English, English-German dictionary. Quite expensive, but definitely a good investment for the German-English translator.

Duden Deutsches Universal Wörterbuch, Mannheim: Dudenverlag 2003. German-German.

Deutsches Wörterbuch, Wahrig, G., Gütersloh: Bertelsmann Lexikon-Verlag 1999. German-German. Excellent reference.

Brockhaus-Wahrig-Deutsches Wörterbuch, Brockhaus, F.A.,Wiesbaden: 1994.

Grosses Abkürzungsbuch, Koblischke, H., Leipzig: VEB Bibliographisches Institut Leipzig 1994.

Collins German-English/English-German Dictionary, Terrell, P., New York: HarperCollins 2004.

HarperCollins Unabridged Dictionary (German-English/English-German), New York: HarperCollins 1991.

Duden Wörterbuch der Abkürzungen, 2nd rev. ed., von Werlin, J., Mannheim: Dudenverlag 2006. Recommended.

Langenscheidts Grosswörterbuch, Messinger H., Berlin: Langenscheidt 1982.

The Oxford-Harrap Standard German-English Dictionary, Jones, T., Oxford: Clarendon Press 1977.

English-German/German-English Dictionary, 2 vols., Wildhagen H., Wiesbaden: Brandstetter Verlag 1972. Though dated, it is still outstanding.

German: Acoustics
Dictionary of Acoustics, Langenscheidt 1998. English-German/German-English.

German: Advertising/Marketing
Concise Dictionary of Advertising (German-French-English), Koschnick, W.J., 1994.
Dictionary of Advertising and Marketing, Gruber, C.M., 1977.

German: Aerospace/Aviation
Luftfahrt-Definitionen Englisch-Deutsch/Deutsch-Englisch/Glossary of Aeronautical Terms English-German/German-English, 2nd ed., Cescotti, R., Stuttgart: Motorbuch Verlag 1993.
Aeronautic & Space Technology Dictionary (Russian-German-English), Kotik, M., 1986.

German: Agriculture
Dictionary of Agriculture/Forestry/Horticulture, 2 vols., Langenscheidt. Vol. 1 (English-German) 1990; vol. 2 (German-English) 1998.

German: Automotive
Pons Fachwörterbuch der Kfz-Technik, 2 vols., Schmitt, P., Stuttgart/Dresden: Ernst Klett 1992. German-English/English-German. Highly recommended.

German: Biology

German Dictionary of Biology, 2 vols., Eichhorn, Routledge/Langenscheidt 1998. Vol. 1 (German-English, 1st ed.); vol. 2 (English-German, 2nd ed.) on CD-ROM 2005.

Dictionary of Human Biology: English/German, German/English, Reuter, P., Birkhauser 2001.

German: Business and Related Fields

German Business Dictionary, ed. by Sofer, M., Lanham, MD: Taylor Trade Publishing 2012.

Global Business Dictionary: English-Chinese-French-German-Japanese-Russian, ed. by Sofer, M., Lanham, MD: Taylor Trade Publishing 2012.

German Dictionary of Business, Commerce and Finance, London: Routledge 2002. Also on CD-ROM. German-English/English-German.

Dictionary of Business & Economics (German-English/English-German), 5th ed., 2 vols., Schäfer, W., Vahlen F. Verlag 1997 (German-English), 1996 (English-German). Highly recommended; a condensed version is available on CD-ROM.

Management & Marketing Dictionary (English-German/German-English), 2 vols., Schäfer, W., 1995. Also available on CD-ROM.

English-German Dictionary of Banking and Stock Trading, Zahn, H.E., 2007.

Financial Dictionary (German-English/English-German), Schäfer, W., DTV Verlag 1992.

Dictionary of Banking & Finance: English-German (Bilingual Specialist Dictionaries), Collin, P.H., Torkar, E., and Livesey, R. Peter Collin Publishing Ltd. 2005.

Dictionary of Legal, Commercial and Political Terms, Dietl, C.-E., Moss, A. A., and Lorenz, E., Verlag C.H. Beck 2005. German-English/English-German. Highly recommended.

Business German, Clarke, S., New York: HarperCollins 1992.

Financial & Economic Glossary (English-German), Zahn, H. 1989.

Wörterbuch Wirtschaftsenglisch, Hamblock, D., and Wessels, D., German-English 1989; English-German 2002.

Cambridge-Eichborn German Dictionary, Cambridge: Eichborn/Cambridge University Press 1983. German-English/English-German.

Wörterbuch der Rechts-und Wirtschaftssprache, Romain, A., München: Verlag C.H. Beck 2002. German-English/English-German.

German: Chemistry

English to German Dictionary of Chemistry and Chemical Technology, Technical University of Dresden Staff 2003.

German Dictionary of Chemistry & Chemical Technology, 2 vols., Gross, H., Routledge/Langenscheidt. Vol. 1 (German-English) 6th ed., 1997; vol. 2 (English-German) 5th ed., 1997. Also on CD-ROM 1998.

German Dictionary of Analytical Chemistry, Knepper et al., Routledge/ Langenscheidt 1997; CD-ROM 1998.
Dictionary of Chemistry (German-English/English-German), 2 vols., Wenske, G. German-English 1993; English-German 1992. The best.
Chemie und chemische Technik, Technische Universität, Dresden: VEB Verlag Technik 1992. German-English. Recommended.
Dictionary of Chemical Engineering, Lydersen, A.L., and Dahl, I. New York: John Wiley and Sons 1992. English-German-Spanish-French.

German: Civil Engineering
English to German Dictionary of Building and Civil Engineering, Gelbrich, U., French and European Publications 2004.
Dictionary of Building and Civil Engineering, 2 vols., Langenscheidt. Vol. 1 (English-German, 2nd ed.), 1995; vol. 2 (German-English, 1st ed.).

German: Computers
Dictionary of Computing (German-English/English-German), Ferretti, V., 2004. Highly recommended.
Computer Dictionary German-English/English-German, Microsoft Pr Deutschland; book and CD-ROM edition 2000.
German Dictionary of Information Technology, London/New York: Routledge 1996; CD-ROM 1997.
Computer Englisch Schulze, Herbert, H., Hamburg: Zohwohlt Taschenbuch Verlag 1997. German-English/English-German.
Computer Englisch (German-English/English-German), Schulze, H., 1997.
Lexikon Informatik und Datenverabeitung/Informatics and Data-Processing Lexicon, 4th ed., Schneider, H.J., 1997. German-English with English-German index.
Dictionary of Artificial Intelligence, Langenscheidt 1998. English-German/ German-English.
Technische Kybernetik, Junge, Berlin: VEB Verlag Technik 1982. English-German/ German-English.
Fachausdrücke der Text-und Datenverarbeitung, IBM Deutschland 1978. English-German.
Fachwörterbuch Energie-und Automatisierungs-Technik, 2 vols., Siemens. German-English.
Routledge German Dictionary of Information Technology (CD-ROM), Seeburger, U., London: Routledge 1998.

German: Construction
German Dictionary of Construction, London/New York: Routledge 1998.

German: Electronics

English to German Dictionary of Electrical Engineering and Automation, Bezner, H., French and European Publications 2003.

German Dictionary of Electrical Engineering and Electronics, 2 vols., Budig, P.-K., Langenscheidt/Routledge 1998. Vol. 1 German-English (6th ed.); vol. 2 (5th ed.); also on CD-ROM.

German Dictionary of Microelectronics, Bindmann, W., Routledge/Langenscheidt 1998. German-English/English-German.

Dictionary of Electronics, Computers & Telecommunications (German-English/English-German), 2 vols., Ferretti, V., 1992.

Dictionary of Microelectronics & Microcomputer Technology, Attiyate, Y. H., and Shah, R., VDI Verlag 1984.

Lexikon der Elektronik, Nachrichten und Elektrotechnik, Wernicke, H., Deisenhofen: Verlag H. Wernicke 1979. German-English-German.

German: Environment

German Dictionary Environmental Technology, Newland, A., Routledge, 1st ed. 2001.

German Dictionary of Environmental Technology, London/New York: Routledge 1997; also on CD-ROM.

Dictionary of Applied Ecology, Langenscheidt 1998. English-German/German-English.

German: Food Technology

Dictionary of Food Technology (English-German), Bratfisch, R., Berlin/Paris: Verlag Alexandre Hatier 1994.

German: Law

Rechtswörterbuch. Buch und CD-ROM, 19th ed., Creifelds 2007.

Legal Terminology Handbook (Anglo-American-German), Heidinger, F., 1996. Recommended.

Dictionary of Legal & Commercial Terms, Romain, A., German-English 2004; English-German 1989.

Dictionary of Legal, Commercial and Political Terms, 2 vols., Dietl, C.-E., Moss, A. A., and Lorenz, E., Verlag C.H. Beck 2005. German-English/English-German. Recommended.

Der Grosse Eichborn Legal and Economic Dictionary, Eichborn, R., German-English 1986; English-German 1981.

German: Medicine

German Dictionary of Medicine, London: Peter Collin 2002.

German Dictionary of Medicine, 2 vols., Nöhring, F.-J., Routledge/Langenscheidt 1997. Vol. 1 (German-English); vol. 2 (English-German). Also on CD-ROM.

Dictionary of Medicine, Schick, E., New York: i.b.d. Ltd. 1998.
Compact Dictionary of Clinical Medicine (English-German), Reuter, P., and Reuter, C. 1997.
Dictionary of Veterinary Medicine (German-English/English-German), 2nd ed., Mack, R., 2002.
Hexal Wörterbuch Medizin German-English/English-German, Walburga, R.B., 1995.
English-German Medical Dictionary, Reuter, P., and Reuter, C., Stuttgart/New York: Georg Thieme Verlag 1995.
Roche Lexikon Medizin, Urban & Schwarzenzberg 2003.
Medizinisches Wörterbuch, Unseld, D., German-English/English-German 1978.
Wörterbuch für Ärzte (Dictionary for Physicians), Stuttgart: Georg Thieme Verlag German-English.

German: Nautical
Schiffstechnisches Wörterbuch, Dluhy, R., Vincentz Verlag 1999. English-German/German-English.
Schiffahrts Wörterbuch, Hamburg: Horst Kammer 1987. German-English-French-Spanish-Italian.

German: Nuclear Energy
Engineering, Freyberger, G.H., Stuttgart/New York; Georg Thiemig Verlag 1979. English-German/German-English.
Wörterbuch der Kraftwerkstechnik, Konventionelle Dampfkraft-werke, Kernkraftwerke, Stattmann, F., Stuttgart/New York: Georg Thiemig Verlag 1971.

German: Optics
Dictionary of Optics and Optical Engineering, 2nd ed., Langenscheidt 1998. English-German/German-English.

German: Patents
Dictionary of Patent Practice, Üxeküll, J.-D., 1977. German-English/English-German.

German: Physics
German Dictionary of Physics, 2 vols., Sube, R., Routledge/Langenscheidt. Vol. 1 (German-English) 1999; vol. 2 (English-German) 1999. CD-ROM 1999.

German: Technical
German Technical Dictionary/Universal-Wörterbuch der Technik Englisch, 2 vols., London/New York: Routledge 2004. German-English/English-German. Also available on CD-ROM and diskette.

Fachwörterbuch/Technik und angewandte Wissenschaften German/English, 5th ed., Walther, R., Berlin/Paris: Verlag Alexandre Hatier 1993.

Last Resort Dictionary of Technical Translations (German-English/English-German), Walker, B., 1992.

Dictionary of Engineering and Technology, Ernst, R., Oxford University Press 1990. Recommended.

Fachwörterbuch Energie und Automatisierungstechnik, Bezner, H., Siemens Aktiengesellschaft 1999. German-English.

The Oxford-Duden Pictorial German-English Dictionary, New York: Oxford University Press 1995.

The Compact Dictionary of Exact Science and Technology, Kucera, A., Wiesbaden: Brandstetter Verlag 1982. English-German.

Anglo-American and German Abbreviations in Science and Technology, Wennrich, P., New York: Bowker 1976–1978.

Solid-State Physics and Electronic Engineering, Bindman, W., 1972. German-English/English-German.

German-English Technical & Engineering Dictionary, 2nd ed., De Vries, L. and Herrmann, T., New York: McGraw-Hill 1994. A must for every serious student and translator.

GREEK
General Dictionaries

Langenscheidt Greek (Modern) Standard Dictionary, Berlin: Langenscheidt 2005.

Neo Lexiko tis Elliniki, Stafylidis 1995. Greek-Greek.

Hyper Lexicon, Stafylidis 2005. Greek-English/English-Greek. Contains examples of use and information on the changes of meaning according to the field of use. Very accurate.

Ellinoanglikon Evrilexikon, Tsambounara, P., Athens 1987.

NTC's New College Greek & English Dictionary, Nathanail, P., NTC Publishing Group 1996.

The Pocket Oxford Greek Dictionary, Pring, J., Oxford 2002. Greek-English, English-Greek

Hyper lexiko tis Ellinikis Glossas, 5 vols., Pagoulatos 1985. Greek-Greek.

Mega Sigkhronon Ellino-Anglikon Lixikon, Genikon kai Emborikon-Oikonomikon-Tekhnikon-Allilografias, Elevtherios Arkhondakis 1974.

Mega Ellino-Anglikon Lexikon, Crighton, W., Athens: G. K. Elevtheroudakis A.E. Supplement to the above, more up to date, but still not quite caught up with current coinage.

Greek: Biology/Medicine

Mesh-HELLAS Vioiatriki orologia, Vita Iatrikes Ekdosis, Medical Studies Association 1995. The latest in biomedical terminology. Award winner.

Lexiko tis Viologias, Malliaris Pedia, HarperCollins 1994. Contains explanations of terms and illustrations.

Greek: Economics
Lexiko tis Iconomias, Malliaris Pedia, HarperCollins 1994. With explanations of terms and an introduction to economics.

Greek: Law
Introduction to Greek Law, Kerameas et al., Sakoulas Publications 2008. From the top publisher of legal literature in several languages. Great source of documentation in law, economics, and commerce.

Greek: Physics
Lexiko tis Fysikis, Malliaris Pedia, HarperCollins 1994. Contains explanations of terms and explanatory diagrams.

Greek: Technical
Michigan Press Ellino-Anglikon (Lexikon) Epistimonikon Kai Tekhnikon Oron, Giannakopoulou, E.S., Athens: Monotoniko, Ekdotikai Viomikhanikai Epikhirisis P. Koutsoumbos A.E. 1984.

HEBREW
General Dictionaries
The Oxford English-Hebrew Dictionary of Current Usage, Kahane, A., and Doniach, N., Oxford University Press 1998.
Milon Hazuti/Visual Dictionary, Hebrew-English, Hebrew ed., Sar'el, B., Jerusalem: Carta Publishing 1992.
TEXTON Electronic Dictionary (English-Hebrew-English), Tel Aviv: Kravitz Technology Ltd. 1991. A handheld electronic dictionary.
Oxford Student's Dictionary for Hebrew Speakers (English-English-Hebrew), Hornby, A.S., and Reif, J., Tel Aviv: Kernerman Publishing Ltd. 1985. Intended for Hebrew speakers. Entries in English give English definitions and Hebrew equivalents.
Dictionary of Israeli Slang—Milon ha-slang ha-makif, Rosenthal, R., Jerusalem: Keter 2005.
The Megiddo Modern Dictionary, Sivan, R., Tel Aviv: Megiddo 1982. English-Hebrew/Hebrew-English. Newer than the Alkalai, but not as good.
The Complete English-Hebrew/Hebrew-English Dictionary, Alcalay, R., Tel Aviv: Masada 2000. Hebrew-English/English-Hebrew. Good general source, somewhat dated.
Milon Olami L'ivrit meduberet, Ben-Amotz, D., Jerusalem: Levin-Epstein 1972. An excellent source of Israeli slang.
Milon Ivri Shalem, 3 vols., Alkalai, R., Ramat Gan: Masada 1969. Hebrew-Hebrew. A good authority on contemporary Hebrew.

DICTIONARIES AND REFERENCE LITERATURE

Otzar Hasafa Haivrit, Stuchkov, N., New York: Schulsinger 1968. A major Hebrew thesaurus.

Yad Halashon, Avineri, Y., Tel Aviv: Izraeel 1964. A treasury of Hebrew elucidations.

Konkordantzya LaTanakh, Mandelkern, S., Tel Aviv: Schocken 1969. The guide to finding every word and phrase in the Bible.

The Comprehensive Hebrew Calendar, Spier, A., New York: Feldheim 1996. The Hebrew and general calendars, 1900–2100.

A Dictionary of the Targumim, the Talmud Babli and Yerushalmi, and the Midrashic Literature, Jastrow, M., New York: Pardes 2007. Hebrew-English. The guide to classical Hebrew and Aramaic.

Hebrew: Computers
Online computer glossary: http://zionism.bravehost.com/Hi-Tech-Glossary.htm.
English-Hebrew Hebrew-English Dictionary, New York: i.b.d. Ltd. 1992.
Dictionary of Electronic and Computer Terms, Bick, J., Bnei Brak: Steimatzky 1991. Hebrew-English/English-Hebrew.
The Up-to-Date Technical Dictionary, Bick, J., Tel Aviv: Sifri 1998.

Hebrew: Economics
Milon Munakhim, Yakir, A., Tel Aviv: Heshev 1989. Hebrew-English.

Hebrew: Law
Legal Dictionary, Shaked, E., Bnei Brak: Steimatzky 1992.
Legal Dictionary, Moses, E., Tel Aviv, 17 Shprintzak St. 64738.

Hebrew: Medicine
Dictionary of Medical & Health Terminology, New York: Simon & Schuster 1991.

Hebrew: Military
Lexicon Dvir, Munakhim Tzvaiim, Burla, Y., Tel Aviv: Dvir 1988.
Dictionary of Military Terms, Akaviya, A., Haifa: Magen 1951.

Hebrew: Political
Diplomatic Hebrew: A Glossary of Current Terminology, Marwick, L., Washington, DC: Library of Congress 1980.

Hebrew: Technical
Milon Lemunahim Tekhniyim, Be'er, H., Hata'asiya Hatzva'it 1984.
The Technical Dictionary, 2 vols., Gafni, H., Jerusalem: Keter Publishing House 1978. Hebrew-English/English-Hebrew.
Technical Dictionary, Ettingen, S.G., Tel Aviv: Yavneh 1972. Hebrew-English-French-German-Russian.

HINDI
General Dictionaries
The Oxford Hindi-English Dictionary, McGregor, R.S., Oxford University Press 2010.
Hindi-English English-Hindi Standard Dictionary, Mladen, D., New York: Hippocrene 1996.
Hippocrene Practical Hindi-English/English-Hindi Dictionary, Tiwari, U., New York: Hippocrene 1991.
A Practical Hindi-English Dictionary, Chaturvedi, M., and Tiwari, B.N., New Delhi: National Publishing House 1992.
Angrezi-Hindi Kosh (English-Hindi), Bulcke, C., New Delhi: Chandra & Co. Ltd. Publishers 1987.

Hindi: Business and Related Fields
Glossary of Audit & Account Terms (English-Hindi), Office of the Comptroller & Auditor General of India, New Delhi 1985.

Hindi: Political
Rajniti Vigyan Kosh, Om Prakash Gaba, Delhi: B.R. Publishing Corporation 1982. English-Hindi.

HUNGARIAN
General Dictionaries
Hungarian-English Dictionary, Akademiai Kiado. Book and CD-ROM edition 2006.
Hungarian Practical Dictionary: Hungarian-English English-Hungarian, Szabo, E., Hippocrene 2005.
NTC's Hungarian-English Dictionary, Magay, T., and Kiss, L., Lincolnwood, IL: NTC 1998.
English-Hungarian Deluxe Dictionary, Orszagh, L., Arthur Vanus Co. 1992.
Magyar-Angol Szotar, 2 vols., Orszagh, L., Budapest: Akademiai Kiado 1982.
Idegen szavak & Kifejezesek szotara, Bakos, F., Budapest: Akademiai Kiado 1973.

Hungarian: Business and Related Fields
Angol-Magyar Bank es Tozsdeszotar, Peter, N., Budapest: Akademiai Kiado 1993.
Longman Dictionary of Business English, Longman Angol-Magyar Business Szotar, Adam, J., Czobor Zsuzsa, Budapest: Akademiai Kiado 1993.
Angol-Amerikai Kozgazdasagi Kifejezesek Ertelmezo Szotara, Budapest: Muszaki Fordito Vallalat 1992.
Magyar-Angol Kereskedelmi, Penzugyi es Bankszotar, Budapest: Muszaki Fordito Vallalat 1991.
Negynyelvu kozgazdasagi szotar, Kelen, B., Budapest: Kozgazdasagi & Jogi Kiado 1974.

Hungarian: Computers
Hungarian-English Dictionary of Computer Technology, Kovacs, M., New York: i.b.d. Ltd. 1991.
Az adatfeldolgozas Fogalommeghatarozasai es Tobbnyelvu Szotar, Budapest: Magyar Szabvanyugyi Hivatal 1982.
Adatfeldogozas, computerek, irodagepek, Verlag Technik, Berlin: Verlag der Ungarischen Akademie.

Hungarian: Geography
Magyar Helysegnev-Azonosito Szotar, Lelkes, G., Budapest: Balassi Kiado 1998.
Magyar Neve Hatarokon tuli helysegnev-szotar, Sebok, L., Budapest: Arany Lapok 1990.

Hungarian: Law
Magyar-Angol Jogi Szotar, Mora, I., Budapest: Muszaki Fordito, Vallalat 1992.

Hungarian: Medical
English-Hungarian Medical Dictionary, Veghelyi, P., New York: i.b.d. Ltd. 1991.

Hungarian: Technical
Angol-Magyar Muszaki es Tudomanyos Szotar I–II, Magay, T., and Kiss, L., Budapest: Akademiai Kiado 1993.
English-Hungarian Technical Dictionary, Nagy, E., New York: i.b.d. Ltd. 1997.
Muszaki Ertelmezo Szotar: Elektronika, Hiradastechnika, Vacuum-technika, 2 vols., Oldal, R., Budapest: Akademiai Kiado 1983.
Magyar-Angol Muszaki Szotar, 4th ed., Budapest: Akademiai Kiado 1980.
Angol-Magyar Muszaki Szotar, 5th ed., Budapest: Akademiai Kiado 1980.
English-Hungarian Dictionary of Science and Technology on CD-ROM, Magay, T.

ICELANDIC
English-Icelandic online glossary: http://www.dicts.info/2/english-icelandic.php.
English-Icelandic Dictionary, Mladen, D., New York: Hippocrene 1996.
Icelandic-English English-Icelandic Dictionary, Sigurdsson, A., New York: i.b.d. Ltd. 1976.

Icelandic: Mathematics
English-Icelandic Mathematical Dictionary. Axelsson, R., University of Iceland Press 1997.

INDONESIAN
Tuttle's Concise Indonesian Dictionary, Kramer, A.L.N., Rutland, VT: Charles S. Tuttle Co. 2007.

An Indonesian-English Dictionary, Echols, J.M., New York: Cornell University Press 1995.

ITALIAN
General Dictionaries
Collins Italian Concise Dictionary 5th Edition Text Only, HarperCollins Publishers 2010.
Cassell's Italian Dictionary: Italian-English English-Italian, Rebora, P., New York: Macmillan 1994.
Italian Encyclopedic Universal Dictionary, 1994.
Il Nuovo manuale de stile, Lesina, R., 1994.
Visual Dictionary (Italian-English/English-Italian), Corbeil, J.C., 1992.
Sansoni-Harrap Italian-English/English-Italian Dictionary, 4 vols., Macchi, V., London 1991. Extensive, expensive.
HarperCollins Sansoni Italian Unabridged Dictionary, Kramer, A.L.N., Rutland, VT: Charles Tuttle 2005.
Dizionario Italiano Ragionato, D'Anna, G., Florence: Sintesi 1988.
Grande Dizionario Hazon Garzanti, Garzanti Editore S.p.A. 2001. English-Italian/ Italian-English.
Il nuovo Zingarelli vocabolario della lingua italiana, Zingarelli, N., Bologna: Nicola Zanichelli 1983. Italian-Italian.
La nuova enciclopedia universale, Garzanti 1982. Italian-Italian.
Collins/Sansoni Italian Dictionary, Macchi, V., Glasgow/Firenze: Collins 1981. Italian-English/English-Italian.
Dizionario della lingua italiana, Devoto, G., Firenze: Le Monnier 1980. Italian-Italian. Excellent reference.
Prontuario dei termini politici, economici, sociali in uso in Italia, Ferrau, A., Roma: Zingarelli Editore S.p.A. 1974.
Il Ragazzini (Biagi Concise Dizionario), Zanichelli, N., Bologna: Nicola Zanichelli 2007. English-Italian/ Italian-English.
Streetwise Italian Dictionary/Thesaurus, McGraw-Hill 2005.

Italian: Business and Related Fields
Italian Business Dictionary, ed. by Sofer, M., Lanham, MD: Taylor Trade Publishing 2012.
Nuovissimo dizionario commerciale, Ragazzini, G., and Gagliardelli, G., Milan: Mursia 1992. English-Italian/Italian-English.
Italian-English/English-Italian Finance & Commercial Dictionary, Picchi, F., Zanichelli 1990.
Dictionary of Commerce (Italian-English/English-Italian), Motta, G., Milan: Carlo Signorelli Editore 1978.
Italian-English English-Italian Dictionary of Economics and Banking, Codeluppi, L., New York: i.b.d. Ltd. 2001.

Italian: Law

Dizionario Giuridico, de Francis, F., English-Italian (based on British Law), Italian-English (based on American Law) 1996. Very fine reference.

Italian: Medicine

New English and Italian Dictionary of the Medical Sciences, Biology and Biotechnology, Italian-English and English-Italian/Nuovo Dizionario Enciclopedico di Scienze Mediche e Biologiche e di Biotecnologie Inglese-Italiano e Italiano-Inglese, French and European Publications 2003.

Medical & Biological Dictionary (Italian-English/English-Italian), Delfino, G., Zanichelli 1996.

Italian-English/English-Italian Medical Dictionary, Petrelle, M., Le lettere 2007.

Italian-English/English-Italian Medical Dictionary, Lucchesi, M., Cortina Rafaello 1987.

English-Italian Dictionary of Medical Phraseology, Marino, V., New York: i.b.d. Ltd. 1985.

Dizionario medico, Lauricella, E., Firenze: Sadea 1961. Italian-Italian.

Italian: Military

Military Dictionary: English-Italian, U.S. Government Staff, Ross & Perry 2002.

Italian: Nautical

Grande dizionario di Marina, Silorata, M.B., Cava dei Tirreni: Di Mauro 1970. English-Italian/Italian-English.

Italian: Technical

Technical Dictionary, Marolli, G., New York: i.b.d. Ltd. 2001. English-Italian/Italian-English. Excellent reference, now on CD-ROM.

English-Italian/Italian-English Technical Dictionary, Ragazzini, G., et al., Milano: Mursia 1983.

Dizionario tecnico, Denti, R., Milano: Ulrico Hoepli Editore 1991. Italian-English/English-Italian.

McGraw-Hill Zanichelli Dizionario enciclopedico scientifico e tecnico, Bologna: Nicola Zanichelli 1998. English-Italian/Italian-English.

JAPANESE

General Dictionaries

Tuttle Pocket Japanese Dictionary: Japanese-English English-Japanese, Tuttle Publishing 2008.

Kodansha's Furigana English-Japanese Dictionary, Yoshida, M., and Nakamura, Y., New York: Kodansha America Inc. 1999.

Kojien Shinmaru, Izuru, Tokyo: Iwanami Shoten 1991.

Waei Honyaku Handbook, Murata, S., Tokyo: Japan Times Ltd. 1991.

Japanese Family Names in Chinese Characters: A Guide to Their Readings, Nihon Seimei, Yomifuri Jiten Sei no Bu, Tokyo: Nichigai Associates 1990. This or a similar name dictionary is a must.

Japanese Given Names in Chinese Characters: A Guide to Their Readings, Nihon Seimei, Yomifuri Jiten Mei no Bu, Tokyo: Nichigai Associates 1990. See note above.

Shin Gijutsu Ryakugo Jiten, Aoyama, K., Tokyo: Kogyo Chosakai Publishing Co. 1985.

Nichibei Hyogen Jiten, Iwazu, K., Tokyo: Shogakkan 1984.

Shin Eiwa Daijiten, Koine, Y., Tokyo: Kenkyusha 1983.

Shin Waei Daijiten, Masuda, Ko, Tokyo: Kenkyusha 1981. Highly recommended. Includes many examples of usage.

Nichibei Kogo Jiten, Seidensticker, E., Tokyo: Asahi Shuppansha 1978.

Nandoku Seishi Jiten, Ono, S., and Fujita, Y., Tokyo: Tokyodo 1977.

Iwanami Kokugo Jiten, Nishio, M., Tokyo: Iwanami Shoten 1971.

Nihon Chimei Hatsuon Jiten, Nihon Hoso Kyokari, Tokyo: Nihon Hoso Shuppan Kyokai 1959.

Japanese: Business and Related Fields

Japanese Business Dictionary, ed. by Sofer, M., Lanham, MD: Taylor Trade Publishing 2012.

Global Business Dictionary: English-Chinese-French-German-Japanese-Russian, ed. by Sofer, M., Lanham, MD: Taylor Trade Publishing 2012.

Japanese Business Language, Mitsubishi: Staff, London: Routledge 1994.

A Dictionary of Japanese Financial Terms, Williams, D., University of Hawaii Press 1995.

Advanced Business English Dictionary, rev. ed., Kobayashi, H., Tokyo: Pacific Management Consultants, Global Management Group 1987.

New Japanese-English Dictionary of Economic Terms, Tokyo: Oriental Economist 2000.

Keizai Yogo Jiten, Hasegawa, H., Tokyo: Fujishobo 1985.

Japanese Directory of Professional Associations, Tokyo: Intercontinental Marketing KK 1984.

Nihon Shoko Keizai Dantai Meibo, Tokyo Chamber of Commerce and Industry 1982.

Waei Keizai Eigo Jiten, Hanada, M., Tokyo: Japan Times Ltd. 1976.

Seikai Kancho Jinjiroku, Tokyo: Toyo Keizai Shinposha.

Japanese: Computers

Illustrated Computer Dictionary Super, Express Media 2005.

English-Japanese Japanese-English Dictionary of Computers and Data-Processing Terms, Ferber, G., Mitsubishi Press 1989.

Japanese-English Computer Dictionary, New York: i.b.d. Ltd. 1989.

Japanese: Medicine
Suteddoman Igaku Jiten, Medical View 2002. Translation of *Stedman's Medical Dictionary*.

Japanese: Technical
Kagaku Gijutsu 35-Mango Daijiten, 2 vols., 3rd ed., Tokyo: Interpress 1990. A most comprehensive general-purpose Japanese technical dictionary. A reliable source of scientific terms.
Kagaku Daijiten, Tokyo: Maruzen 1989.
Nikkei High-Tech Dictionary, Tokyo: Nihon Keizai Shimbunsha 1983.
Magurokiru Kagaku Gijutsu Yogo Daqiten: McGraw-Hill Science and Technology Dictionary, Tokyo: Nikkan Kogyo Shimbunsha 1982.

KAZAKH

A Learner's Dictionary of Kazakh Idioms, Washington: Georgetown University Press 2012.
Kazakh (Qazaq)-English Dictionary, Krippes, K.A., Kensington, MD: Dunwoody Press 1995.

KOREAN
General Dictionaries
Korean Standard Dictionary, New York: Hippocrene 2009.
NTC's Compact Korean Dictionary, Rhie, G., and Jones, B.J., Lincolnwood, Illinois: NTC 1996.
Essence Hanyong Sajon, Korean-English Dictionary, Kim Chol-hwan, Seoul: Minjung Sorim 1996.
Hyondai Hwaryong Okp'yon-Ch'osinp'an, Seoul: Tong-A Chulpansa 1985.
The New World Comprehensive Korean-English Dictionary, Seoul: Sisa Yong-osa 1985.
Essence Yonghan Sajon, Kim Myong-hwan and Kim Chol-hwan, Seoul: Minjung Sorim 1984.
Hyondai Choson-mal Sajon, Pyongyang: Kwahak, Paekkwa Sajon Chulpansa 1981. Korean-Korean.
Kugo Taesajon, Yi Hui-sung, Seoul: Minjung Sorim 1981. Korean-Korean.
Yongcho Sajon, English-Korean, Kim il-Song University, chollima Yong-o Kwangjwa Oegukmun Toso Chulpansa 1976.
Choson Munhwa-o Sajon, Pyongyang: Linguistics Research Institute, Academy of Social Sciences 1973.

Korean: Business and Related Fields
Korean Business Dictionary, Sofer, M., Lanham, MD: Taylor Trade Publishing 2012.
Kyongje Sino Sajon, Chang Tae-hwan, Seoul: Daily Economic Press 1989.

Korean: Nuclear Energy
Wonjaryok Yongo Sajon, Seoul: Hanguk Wonjaryok Sanop Hoeui Chulpansa
1983. English-Korean/Korean-English.

Korean: Technical
Kigye Yongojip, Seoul: Tongmyongsa 1976. Korean-Chinese-English/English-
Korean-Japanese.
Kigye Yongo Sajon, Seoul: Songan-dang 1985. English-Korean/Japanese-Korean/
Korean-Japanese-English.

KURDISH
Kurdish-English/English-Kurdish Dictionary, Amindarov, A., New York:
Hippocrene 2006.

LAO
Historical Dictionary of Laos, Stuart-Fox, M., Lanham, MD: Scarecrow Press 2008.
Lao-English Dictionary, Kerr: White Lotus 1992.
English-Lao/Lao-English Dictionary, Marcus, R., Rutland, VT: Charles E. Tuttle 2001.

LATIN
Cassell's Latin Dictionary, Simpson, D.P., New York: Macmillan 1987.
Langenscheidt Pocket Dictionary (Latin-English/English-Latin), Berlin:
Langenscheidt 1978.
Latin Dictionary, Lewis, C.T., and Short, C., Oxford University Press.

LATVIAN
General Dictionaries
Practical Latvian-English/English-Latvian Dictionary, Sosare, M., New York:
Hippocrene 1998.
Latvian-English Dictionary, Turkina, P.E., Riga: Avots 1991.
Renyi Bilingual Picture Dictionary Latvian, Forest Publishing House 1994.

LITHUANIAN
General Dictionaries
Lithuanian/English-English/Lithuanian Concise Dictionary, New York:
Hippocrene 2004.
English-Lithuanian Dictionary, Piesarkas, B., and Baravykas, V., New York:
Routledge 1995. Lithuanian-English, English-Lithuanian.
Lithuanian-English Dictionary, Vilnius: Mokslas 1979.

MACEDONIAN
General Dictionaries
Macedonian Dictionary, Mircevska, S., New York: Routledge 1998.

Anglisko-makedonski recnik, Crvenkovski, D., and Grujić, B., Skopje: Nasa Kniga 1993.

Makedonsko-angliski recnik na idiomi, Murgoski, Z., Skopje: Tabernauka 1993.

Macedonian-English/English-Macedonian Concise Dictionary, Mladen, D., New York: Hippocrene 1997.

MALAY

Comprehensive Malay Dictionary, Weatherhill Inc. 2004.

English-Malay Malay-English Dictionary, French and European Publications 1992.

Standard Malay-English/English-Malay Dictionary, rev. ed., Coope, A.E., New York: Hippocrene 1993.

NEPALI

A Practical Dictionary of Modern Nepali, Boston: Schoenhofs 1999.

Nepali-English/English-Nepali Dictionary, Prakash, A.R., New York: Hippocrene 2003.

Concise Nepali-English/English-Nepali Dictionary, Raj, P.A., New York: Hippocrene 1992.

NORWEGIAN

General Dictionaries

Norwegian Practical Dictionary: Norwegian-English/English-Norwegian, New York: Hippocrene 2011.

Norwegian Dictionary (Norwegian-English/English-Norwegian), London: Routledge 1994.

Aschehoug og Gyldendals store norske ordbok, Guttu, T., Oslo: Kunnskapsforlaget 1991.

Engelsk-norsk ordbok, 2nd ed., Svenkerud, H., Cappelen 1988.

Norsk-engelsk administrativ ordbok: Navn og termer fra offentlig virksomhet, Chaffey, P., Oslo: Universitetsforlaget 1999.

Norsk-engelsk ordbok, stor utgave, Kirkeby, W.A., Oslo: Aschehoug-Gyldendal 1986.

Bokmålsordboka: Definisjons-og rettskrivningsordbok, Landrφ, M.I., and Wangensteen, B., Oslo: Universitetsforlaget 2001. Norwegian-Norwegian.

Definisjons- og rettskrivingsordbok, Hφvdenak, M., et al., Oslo: Det Norske Samlaget 1986. Norwegian-Norwegian. This book and the above are the most comprehensive, single-volume N-N dictionaries.

ADNOM: norsk-engelsk glossar, Oslo: Universitetsforlaget 1984.

Norwegian-English Dictionary, Haugen, E., Madison: University of Wisconsin Press 1984.

Norsk slang, Tryti, T., Oslo: Universitetforlaget 1984. Norwegian-Norwegian. Government administration and private association names and terms.

Nyord i norsk, 1945–1975, Nor.-Nor., Norsk Språkråd, Oslo: Universitetsforlaget 1982. Contains cross-references among Danish, Norwegian, and Swedish.
Norsk-engelsk handelsordbok, Gabrielsen, E.D., Oslo: Kunnskapsforlaget 1978.

Norwegian: Agriculture
Norsk landbruksordbok utgitt av Nemnda for Norsk land-bruksordbok, Rφmmetveit, M., Oslo 1979.

Norwegian: Automotive
Norwegian-English/English-Norwegian Dictionary of Motor Vechicle and Traffic Terminology, Kirkeby, W.A., New York: i.b.d. Ltd. 1978.

Norwegian: Business and Related Fields
English-Norwegian Dictionary in Social Economics, Hansen, E., Scandinavian Press 1992.
Norwegian English Commercial Dictionary, Gabrielsen, E.D., New York: i.b.d. Ltd. 1987.

Norwegian: Law
Norsk-engelsk juridisk ordbok: strafferett, straffeprosess og andre termer; med engelsknorsk register, Chaffey, P., and Walford, R., Oslo: Universitetsforlaget 1999.
Norsk-engelsk juridisk ordbok, Craig, R.L., Oslo: Universitetsforlaget 1999. Contract law.
Norsk-engelsk juridisk ordbok: sivilrett og strafferett, Lind, A., Oslo: Bedriftsφknomens Forlag 1992.

Norwegian: Medical
Norwegian-English/English-Norwegian Medical Dictionary, Kåss, E., New York: i.b.d. Ltd. 1993.

Norwegian: Military
English-Norwegian Military Dictionary, Ark, O.J., Oslo: Grφndahy & Son Forlag A.S. 1985.
Engelsk-amerikansk-norsk militær ordbok, Marm, I., Oslo: Fabritius 1977.

Norwegian: Oil
Petroleums-ordliste: engelsk-norsk, norsk-engelsk, utarbeidet ved Norsk termbank, Universitetet i Bergen, Oslo 1988.
Olje Ordliste, Rådet for Teknisk Terminologi Norsk Språkåd, Universitesforlaget 1982.

Norwegian: Technical
Engelsk-Norsk teknisk ordbok, 6th rev. ed., Ansteinsson & Reiersen, F. Bruns bokhandels forlag 1994.

DICTIONARIES AND REFERENCE LITERATURE

Miljøleksikon: energi, helse, natur, økologi, Pleym, H., Bekkestua: NKI 1991.
Norsk teknisk fagordbok, Hjulstad, H., and Norevik, B., Bergen: Universitetsforlaget 1984.
Norsk dataordbok, 3rd ed., Norsk språkråds komite for dataterminologi, Bergen: Universitetsforlaget 1984. Norwegian-English.
Teknisk, illustrert ordbok, Arleij, R., oversatt av Hacheim, O., and Eidnes, T., Oslo: Yrkesopplæring 1983. Contains English, French, Spanish, Finnish, Polish, Serbo-Croatian, Turkish, Vietnamese, and Urdu equivalents.
Ordbok for automatiseringsteknikk, Rådet for teknisk terminologi, Oslo 1978.

PILIPINO/TAGALOG
Pilipino: General Dictionaries
Tagalog-English/English-Tagalog (Filipino) Standard Dictionary, Gavez Rubino, C., New York: Hippocrene 2002.
Pilipino-English/English-Pilipino Phrase Book and Dictionary, New York: Hippocrene 1996.
Vicassan's Pilipino-English, Santos, V.C., Manila: National Book Store 1995.
Hippocrene Concise Pilipino-English/English-Pilipino Dictionary, Bickform, S., New York: Hippocrene 2005.

Tagalog: General Dictionaries
English-Tagalog/Tagalog-English Pocket Dictionary, Enriques, L., Colton Book Imports 2005.
Tagalog Dictionary, Ramos, T.V., Honolulu: University of Hawaii Press 1990.
English-Tagalog Dictionary, English, L.J., Manila: Congregation of the Holy Redeemer 1997.

POLISH
General Dictionaries
Larousse Pocket Polish-English/English-Polish Dictionary, 2007.
Polish-English Dictionary, vols. 1–3, Pogonowski, I., New York: Hippocrene 1996.
Collins Polish-English/English-Polish Dictionary, 2 vols., Fisiak, J., Warsaw: Polska Oficyna Wydawnicza BGW 1996.
Mały słownik subkultur młodzieżowych, Peczak, M., Warsaw: Semper 1992. Youth, subculture, and slang idioms.
Słownik języka polskiego, 3 vols., Warsaw: Państwowe Wyd. Naukowe 1992. Polish-Polish.
Wielki słownik pol.-ang./ang.-pol., 2 vols. each, Stanislawski, J., Warsaw: Wiedza Powszechna 1993.
Encyklopedia popularna PWN, Warsaw: Państwowe Wyd. Naukowe 1980. Polish-Polish.
Słownik poprawnej polszczyzny, Doroszewski, W., Warsaw: Państwowe Wyd. Naukowe.

Słownik wyrazow obcych, Tokarski, J., Warsaw: Państwowe Wyd. Naukowe.
Mały słownik języka polskiego, Skorupka, S., Warsaw: Państwowe Wyd. Naukowe 1968.
The Kosciuszko Foundation Dictionary, 2 vols., Bulas & Whitfield, New York: Kosciuszko Foundation 2005. Polish-English/English-Polish.

Polish: Aerospace
Słownik lotniczo-kosmonautyczny (pol.-ang.-ros.), Czerni, S., Warsaw: Wyd. Komunikacji i Łączności 1984.

Polish: Agriculture
Mała encyklopedia rolnicza, Warsaw: Wyd. Rolnicze i Lesne 1964.

Polish: Business and Related Fields
Słownik handlu zagranicznego, Bialecki, Klemens, et al., Warsaw: Państwowe Wydawnictwo Ekonomiczne 1993.
Słownik pięciojęzyczny ekonomiczno-handlowy, Ratajczak, P., Zielona Góra: Kanion 1993. Multilingual. Has English, French, German, and Russian for Polish terms.
Podręczny słownik menedżera, Woytowicz-Neyman, M., and Pulawski, M., Warsaw: Państwowe Wydawnictwo Ekonomiczne 1992. English-Polish/Polish-English.
Podręczny słownik polsko-niemiecko-angielski rachunkowości i bankowości, Jaruga, A., et al., Lodz: Towarzystwo Gospodarcze RAFIB 1992.
Międzynarodowy słownik finansow, Bannock, G., and Manser, W., Warsaw: Wydawnictwo Andrzej Bonarski 1992.
Leksykon finansowo-bankowy, Jaworski, W., et al., Warsaw: Państwowe Wydawnictwo Ekonomiczne 1991.
Słownik terminologii prawniczej i ekonomicznej angielsko-polski, Jaslan, J., and Jaslan, H., Warsaw: Wiedza Powszechna 1991. Designed for lawyers and economists.
Mały słownik biznesmena, Rumowska, E., and Czerniawski, R., Warsaw: Poltext 1991.
Słownik skrotow, Paruch, J., Warsaw: Wiedza Poszechna 1990. A listing of acronyms and abbreviations.
Leksykon rachunkowości, Niewiadoma, M., Skierniewice: Centrum Kreowania Liderów, Boguslaw J. Feder. English-Polish.
Pocket Business Dictionary, Polish-English/English-Polish, 2 vols., Woytowicz-Neyman, M., and Malec, J.
Słownik handlowo-ekonomiczny polsko-angielski, Świeżewska, W., Warsaw: Państwowe Wyd. Ekonomiczne 1970.
Mały słownik ekonomiczny, Drewanowski et al., Warsaw: Polskie Wyd. Gospodarcze 1958.

DICTIONARIES AND REFERENCE LITERATURE

Polish: Computers
Terminoow I Komunikatoow Komputerowych, Sikorski, W., Warsaw: Mikom 1995.
Dictionary of Computer Science (English-Polish), Marciniak, A., et al., Warsaw: Wydawnictwo Naukowe PWN 1993.

Polish: Environment
Dictionary of Environmental Protection (Polish-English), Czekierda, K., 1996.

Polish: Law
Police and Legal Dictionary (Polish-English-French-German-Russian), Sostek, G., 1996.
Słownik prawniczy polsko-angielski, Cracow: Wyd. Polskiej Akademii Nauk 1986.

Polish: Medicine
Polish-English/English-Polish Medical Dictionary, Słomski, P., New York: i.b.d. 2003.
Lexicon Medicum (English-Russian-French-German-Latin-Polish), Złotnicki, Warsaw: 1971.

Polish: Military
Leksykon wiedzy wojskowej, Warsaw: Wyd. Ministerstwa Obrony Narodowej 1979.
Mała encyklopedia wojskowa, 3 vols., Wyd. Ministerstwa Obrony Narodowej 1970.
Ilustrowany wojskowy słownik techniczny (Polish-Russian-English-French), Zlomanov, A.A., Wyd. Ministerstwa Obrony Narodowej 1968.
Angielsko-polski słownik wojskowy, Wyd. Ministerstwa Obrony Narodowej 1960.

Polish: Nautical
Maritime Dictionary (English-Polish/Polish-English), Milewski, S., Warsaw: Wyd. Naukowo-Techniczne 1969.

Polish: Technical
Technical Dictionary (Polish-English/English-Polish), reprint, Skrzynska, M., et al. 1997.
Angielsko-polski słownik skrótów-elektronika, informatyka, teleinformatyka, Bosakirski, B., Warsaw: Wydawnictwo Naukowo-Techniczne 1992.
Słownik naukowo-techniczny polsko-angielski/angielsko-polski, 2 vols., Czerni, S., and Skrzynska, M., Warsaw: Wyd. Naukowo-Techniczne 1992.
Leksykon naukowo-techniczny, Warsaw: Wyd. Naukowo-Techniczne 1983.

PORTUGUESE
General Dictionaries
Brazilian Portuguese-English Dictionary, Kindle ed., Saase, V., 2011.

The Oxford-Duden Picture Dictionary: English-Brazilian Portuguese, Oxford University Press 2000.

Dicionário de Expressões Populares Portugueses, Simões, G.A., Lisbon: Dom Quixote 1993. Portuguese-Portuguese.

The New Michaelis Dictionaries, São Paulo: Edições Melhoramentos 2000. A series of dictionaries. The *Novo Michaelis* Portuguese-English, English-Portuguese is a good comprehensive dictionary.

Dicionário Escolar de Português-Inglês/Dicionário Escolar de Inglês-Português, 2 vols., sold separately, Lisbon: Porto Editora 2001.

Novo Dicionário Aurélio da Língua Portuguesa, 2nd ed., Buarque de Holanda, A., Ferreira: J.E.M.M. Editores, Ltda. 2001. Portuguese-Portuguese. Essential.

A Portuguese-English Dictionary, Taylor, J., Stanford University Press 1970.

A Dictionary of Informal Brazilian Portuguese, Chamberlain, B., Washington, DC: Georgetown University Press 2003.

Webster Dicionário Inglês-Português, Houaiss, A., and Cardim, I., Record 2005.

Dicionário de Expressões Idiomáticas, Pugliesi, M., Editora Parma Ltda. 1981. Portuguese-Portuguese.

The New Appleton Dictionary of the English and Portuguese Languages, Houaiss, A., New York: Appleton-Century-Crofts 1967.

HarperCollins Portuguese Concise Dictionary, 2nd ed., HarperCollins 2002.

Dicionário Estrutural, Estilístico e Sintático da Língua Portuguesa, Ramalho, E., Porto: Lello & Irmão. Though published in Portugal, it is still useful for Brazilian texts.

Portuguese: Business and Economics

Portuguese Business Dictionary, ed. by Sofer, M., Rockville, MD: Schreiber Publishing 2006.

Dicionário de Termos de Negócios Inglês-Português/Português-Inglês, Pinho, M.O.M., Editora Atlas 2005.

Michaelis Dicionário Executivo Inglês-Português, Melhoramentos 1999.

Dicionário Bancário Português-Inglês, Correia da Cunha, A., Portugal: Publicações Europa-América 1988. Excellent but small.

Dicionário de Economia e Gestão, Lima, G., et al., Porto: Lello & Irmão, Editores 1984.

Dictionary of Economic and Commercial Terms, Cavalcante, J.C., Marques 1982. English-Portuguese.

Dicionário Técnico Contábil, Altmann, M.R., 1990. English-Portuguese/Portuguese-English.

Portuguese: Computers

Computer Dictionary: English-Portuguese/Portuguese-English, French and European Publications 1998.

DICTIONARIES AND REFERENCE LITERATURE

Dicionário de Informática, Inglês-Português, Português-Inglês, Microsoft Press, Editora Campus 1993.

Dicionário Enciclopédico de Informática, Fragomeni, A.H., 1986. English-Portuguese/Portuguese-English.

Dicionário de Informática, Society of Computer and Peripheral Equipment Users, Rio de Janeiro 1985.

Dicionário de Informática, Lisbon: Publicações Dom Quixote 1984.

Portuguese: Law

Enciclopédia do Advogado, 5th ed., Soibelman, L., Rio de Janeiro: Luso-Brazilian Books 1995. Portuguese-Portuguese. Essential for legal translation.

Noronha Legal Dictionary/Dicionário Jurídico, de Noronha Goyos, D., Editora Observador Legal 2006. Portuguese-English/English-Portuguese. An absolute necessity.

Dicionário Jurídico Português-Inglês/Inglês-Português, Chavez, M., Rio de Janeiro: Barrister's Editora 1989.

Vocabulário Jurídico, 2 vols., DePlacido e Silva, Rio de Janeiro 2002. Portuguese-Portuguese.

Portuguese: Medicine

Medical Dictionary: English, Spanish, Portuguese, Notte-Schlegel, I., New York: Springer-Verlag 2008.

Dicionário Médico, Rio de Janeiro: Editora Guanabara-Koogan 1979.

Dorland (Pocket) Dicionário Médico, New York: i.b.d. Ltd. 2004.

Portuguese: Metallurgy

Dicionário Metalúrgico, Inglês-Português, Português-Inglês, Taylor, J.L., São Paulo: Assoc. Brasileira de Matais 2004.

Portuguese: Technical

Dicionário Verbo de Inglês Técnicos e Científico, Farinha dos Santos Tavares, J., Lisbon: Editorial Verbo 1994. English-Portuguese/Portuguese-English.

Dicionário de Termos Técnicos, Mendes Antas, L., São Paulo: Traco Editora 1980.

DePina Dicionário Técnicos (Inglês-Português/Português-Inglês), Araujo, A.D.P., Makron Books, Editora McGraw-Hill 1978.

ROMANIAN

General Dictionaries

Romanian-English/English-Romanian Practical Dictionary, Miroiu, M., New York: Hippocrene 2010.

Romanian-English/English-Romanian Dictionary, New York: Hippocrene 2002.

NTC's Romanian and English Dictionary, Bantas, A., Lincolnwood, IL: NTC 1995.

Dictionar de neologisme, Marcu, F., and Manca, C., Bucharest: Editura Academici 1978.

Dictionarul explicativ al límbii române, Coteanu, I., Seche, L., and Seche, M., Bucharest: Academy of the Republic of Romania 1975.

Dictionar engléz-român, Levitchi, L., Bucharest: Academy of the Republic of Romania 1974.

Dictionar român-engléz, 3rd ed., Levitchi, L., Bucharest: Editura Stiintifica 1973.

Dictionarul límbii române modérne, Macrea, D., Bucharest: Academy of the Romanian Republic 1958. Romanian-Romanian. Later editions may be available.

Romanian: Business
Business Dictionary, London: Peter Collin 1999.

Romanian: Technical
Dictionar tehnic român-engléz, Bucharest: Editura tehnică 1970.

RUSSIAN
General Dictionaries
English-Russian Dictionary with Transcriptions, Kindle ed., Pushkin, A., Relintech 2010.

The Oxford Russian Dictionary, Unbegaun, B., Oxford: Oxford University Press 2007.

English-Russian/Russian-English Dictionary, 2nd ed., Katzner, K., New York: John Wiley & Sons 1999. Also available on CD-ROM. Good for American English.

Russian-English Dictionary of Verbal Collocations and Translation, Benson, M., and Benson, E., Amsterdam/Philadelphia: John Benjamins 1993.

Russian-English Translator's Dictionary, Vedeneeva, C., and Zimmerman, M., 1991.

Elsevier's Russian-English Dictionary, 4 vols., Macura, P., Amsterdam: Elsevier 1999. One of the major all-around Russian-English dictionaries. Expensive.

Slovar russkogo yazyka, Ozhegov, S.I., Moscow: Russkiy yazyk 2000. Russian-Russian. A good one-volume general dictionary.

Russian-English Dictionary of Interjections and Response Phrases, Kveselevich, D.I., and Sasina, V.P., Moscow: Russkiy yazyk 1990.

New English-Russian Dictionary, Galperin, I.R., Moscow: Russkiy yazyk 1988. Reliable, one of the best in the field.

Russko-angliyskiy slovar, Smirnitskiy, Moscow: Russkiy yazyk 1987.

Krylatyye slova: Literaturnyye tsitaty: Obraznyye vyrazheniya, Ashukin, N.S., Moscow: Khudozhestvennaya Literature 1986.

Dictionary of Russian Abbreviations, Scheitz, E., New York: Elsevier 1985. A must. Abbreviations and acronyms are a plague of the Russian language, and a translator's nightmare.

Russian-English Dictionary, Taube, A.M., Moscow: Russkiy yazyk 1975, 1982, 1985.

The Oxford Russian-English Dictionary, Wheeler, M., Oxford: Clarendon Press 1992. Excellent, but not as extensive as the Elsevier.

Slovar russkogo yazyka, Rus-Rus., 4 vols., Yevgenyeva, W.P., Moscow: Russkiy yazyk 1981, 1983, 1984. A first choice for many translators.

Slovar russkikh lichnykh imyen, Petrovskiy, N.A., Moscow: Russkiy yazyk 1984.

Sovetskiy entsiklopedicheskiy slovar, Prokhorov, A.M., Moscow: Sovetskaya entsiklopediya 1984.

Russian-English Dictionary of Abbreviations and Initialisms, Shipp, J.F., Philadelphia: Translation Research Institute 1982. Out of print.

Slovar trudnostey russkogo yazyka, Rozental, D.E., Moscow: Russkiy yazyk 1976. Very helpful for translation into Russian.

Solzhenitsyn's Peculiar Vocabulary: Russian-English Glossary, Carpovich, V. V., New York: Technical Dictionaries Co. 1976.

Frazeologicheskiy slovar russkogo yazyka, Molotov, A.I., Moscow: Sovetskaya entsiklopediya 1967.

Russian: Agriculture

Elsevier's Dictionary of Agriculture and Food Production, Rakipov, N., and Geyer, B., Elsevier Science B.V. Russian-English 1994.

English-Russian Dictionary of Agriculture, Kozlovsky, V.G., and Rakipov, N.G., Moscow: Russkiy yazyk 1997.

Russko-angliyskiy selskokhozyaystvenniy slovar, Ussovskiy 1977.

Russian: Aviation/Aerospace

Elsevier's Dictionary of Civil Aviation, Beck, S., and Aslezova, S., Elsevier 2002.

Dictionary of Aeronautics and Space Technology, Goursau, H., and Novitchkov, N., Saint-Orens-de-Gameville, France: Goursau 1994. English-Russian.

English-Russian Dictionary of Civil Aviation, Marassanov, V.P., Moscow: Russky Yazyk Publishers 1989.

Aeronautics & Space Technology Dictionary (Russian-German-English), Kotik, M., 1986.

English-Russian Aviation & Space Dictionary, Murashkevich, A.M., Moscow: Voyenizdat 1974.

Russian: Botany

Russian-English Botanical Dictionary, Macura, P., Columbus: Slavica 1979.

Russian: Business and Related Fields

Russian Business Dictionary, ed. by Sofer, M., Rockville, MD: Schreiber Publishing 2005.

Global Business Dictionary: English-Chinese-French-German-Japanese-Russian, ed. by Sofer, M., Rockville, MD: Schreiber Publishing 2005.

Elsevier's Dictionary of Economics, Business, Finance and Law: Russian-English, Elsevier 2007.

Russian-English, English-Russian Business Dictionary, Zagorskaya, A., and Petrochenko, N.P., New York: John Wiley 1996.

Dictionary of Economics and Finance (English-Russian), Anikin, A., 2004.

Russian-English Foreign Trade and Foreign Economic Dictionary, Zhdanova, I.F., Moscow: Russkiy yazyk 1991.

A Russian-English Social Science Dictionary, Smith, R.E.F., Birmingham: Institute for Advanced Research in the Humanities 1990.

Ekonomiko-matematicheskiy slovar, Fedorenko, N.P., Moscow: Nauka 1987.

Kratkiy ekonomicheskiy slovar, Belik, Yu. A., Moscow: Politizdat 1987.

Ekonomicheskiy morskoy slovar-spravochnik, Kotlubay, M., Odessa: Izd. Mayak 1976.

Russian: Chemistry
Dictionary of Chemistry (Russian-English), Macura, P., 1993. Recommended.

Russian: Civil Engineering
Elsevier's Dictionary of Civil Engineering, Bhatnager, K.P., Amsterdam: Elsevier 1988.

Russian: Computers
The Comprehensive Russian-English Dictionary of Computer Terms, Druker, P., IEEE Computer Society Press 1999.

English-Russian Explanatory Dictionary of Abbreviations in the Field of Computer Terms, Sevastyanov 1995.

Russian: Education
Lingvo-stranovedcheskiy slovar: narodnoye obrazovaniye v SSSR, Denisova, M.A., Moscow: Russkiy yazyk 1978.

Russian: Electronics
Anglo-russkiy slovar po radioelektronike, Lisovskiy, F.V., Moscow: Russkiy yazyk 1987. A valuable and comprehensive reference in the field. Contains a Russian index.

Russian-English Dictionary of Electrotechnology and Allied Sciences, Macura, P., Melbourne, FL: Robert E. Krieger Publishing Company 1986.

Anglo-russkiy slovar po mikroelektronike, Prokhorov, K., Moscow: Russkiy yazyk 1985.

Russian: Geography
English-Russian, Russian-English Geographical Dictionary, Gorskaya, M., Rockville, MD: Kamkin 1994.

Russian: Geology
Russko-angliyskiy geologicheskiy slovar, Sofiano, T.A. 1984.
Geologicheskiy slovar, 2 vols., Moscow 1978. Russian-Russian.

Russian: Law
English-Russian Dictionary of American Criminal Law, Braun, M., and Clothier, G., Greenwood Press 1998.
Legal Dictionary (Russian-English), Butler, W.E., 2001.
Legal Dictionary (English-Russian), Mamulyan, A.S., and Kashkin, S., 2005.
English-Russian Law Dictionary, Rockville, MD: Kamkin 1993.
Encyclopedia of Soviet Law, Amsterdam: Martinus-Jijhoff Publishing Co. 1985.

Russian: Maritime
English-Russian Dictionary of Navigation, Hydrography and Oceanography, Sorokin, A.L., Rockville, MD: Kamkin 1984.

Russian: Mathematics
Russian-English Dictionary of Mathematics, Efimov, O., Boca Raton, FL: CRC Press 1993.
Russian-English Mathematical Dictionary, Milne, L.M., Madison, WI: University of Wisconsin Press 1962.
Russian-English Dictionary of the Mathematical Sciences, Lohwater, A.J., Providence, RI: American Mathematical Society 1990.

Russian: Medicine
Comprehensive Russian-English Medical Dictionary, 3rd ed., Russo 2005.
Stedman's English-Russian Medical Dictionary, Moscow: Géotar 1995. Recommended.
Russian-English Medical Dictionary & Phrase Book, Petrov, V., et al. 1993.
English-Russian Dictionary of Medical and Biological Abbreviations, Akzhigitov, G.N., Rockville, MD: Kamkin 2001.
Anglo-russkiy slovar po immunologii i immunogenetike, Petrov, Moscow: Russkiy yazyk 1990.
Anglo-russkiy slovar po biotekhnologii, Drygin, Moscow: Russkiy yazyk 1990.
Anglo-russkiy meditsinskiy slovar, Akzhigitov, G.N., Moscow: Russkiy yazyk 1988. The above four dictionaries are an absolute must for translating medical texts.
Entsiklopedicheskiy slovar meditsinskikh terminov, Petrovskiy, Moscow: Sovetskaya entsiklopediya 1983. Russian-Russian.
Russian-English Medical Dictionary, Yeliseyenkov, Yu. B., Moscow: Russkiy yazyk 1975.
Russian-English Biological-Medical Dictionary, Carpovich, New York: Technical Dictionaries 1960.

Russian: Metallurgy
English-Russian Metallurgical Dictionary, Lerlov, N.I., Isteyev, A.I., Tyurkin, V.A., et al., Moscow: Russkiy yazyk 1985.

Russian: Military
Russian-English Glossary of Military Terms and Abbreviations, 2nd ed., Office of Naval Intelligence, June 1993.
English-Russian Dictionary of Antimissile & Antisatellite Defense, Novichkov, N.N., Moscow: Voyenizdat 1989.
English-Russian Military Dictionary, 3rd ed., Shevchuk, V.N., and Polyukhin, V.M., Moscow: Voyenizdat 1987. Classic. Contains media jargon on military themes.
Voyennyy Entsiklopedicheskiy slovar, 2nd ed., Akhromeyev, S.F., Moscow: Voyenizdat 1986.
Spravochnik ofitsera nazemnoy artillerii, 2nd ed., Lebedeb, V. Ya., Moscow: Voyenizdat 1984.
Russian-English/English-Russian Military Dictionary, London: Her Majesty's Stationery Office 1983. British usages.
Anglo-russkiy voyenno-morskoy slovar, Moscow: Voyenizdaat 1962.

Russian: Mining
Gornoye delo: terminologicheskiy slovar, 4th ed., Lidin, G.D., et al., Moscow: Nedra 1990.
English-Russian-English Dictionary on Mining Polyglossum 3.52 (On CD), Manyshev, V.P., ETS Publishing House 2005.

Russian: Oil
Wavetech Russian/English Oil & Gas Translator: Abbreviations, Parameters, and Units, Pennwell 1996.
Woods' Illustrated English-Russian Petroleum Technology Dictionary, Serednytsky, L., et al., Dallas/Kiev: Albion Woods Publishers 1997.
Petrologicheskiy anglo-russkiy tolkovyy slovar, Marakushev, A.A., Moscow: Mir 1986.
Russko-angliyskiy razgovornik dlya neftekhimikov i khimikov-neorganikov, Kuznetzov, Yu. I., and Sloushcher, V.M., Moscow: Russkiy yazyk 1985.
Russko-angliyskiy neftepromyslovyy slovar, Stoliarov, D.E., Moscow: Russkiy yazyk 1982.
Anglo-russkiy slovar po khimii i pererabotke nefti, Kedrinskiy, V.V., Moscow: Russkiy yazyk 1979.

Russian: Physics
Russian-English Physics Dictionary, Emin, I., New York: Wiley & Sons 1963.

Russian: Technical

Dictionary of Science & Technology (Russian-English), Callaham, L.I., 1996.

Elsevier Dictionary of Science and Technology, Chakalov, G.G., Amsterdam: Elsevier 1993.

The Comprehensive English-Russian Scientific and Technical Dictionary, 2 vols., Barinov, S.M., et al., Moscow: Russkiy yazyk 2007.

Science and Engineering Dictionary, Carpovich, E.A., and Carpovich, V.V., Technical Dictionaries Co. 1988. Excellent, even indispensable.

Russko-angliyskiy politekhnicheskiy slovar, Kuznetsov, B.V., Moscow: Russkiy yazyk 1986.

Kratkiy illyustrirovannyy russko-angliyskiy slovar po mashinostroyeniyu, Shvarts, V.V., Moscow: Russkiy yazyk 1983.

Anglo-russkiy slovar po sistemnomu analizu, Vyshinskaya, Ye. V., 1982.

Politekhnicheskiy slovar, Ishlinskiy, Moscow: Sovetskaya entsik-lopediya 1980.

Anglo-russkiy slovar po nadezhnosti i kontrolyu kachestva, Kovalenko, E.G., Moscow: Russkiy yazyk 1975. A comprehensive work for anyone engaged in this field.

Russko-angliyskiy tekhnicheskiy slovar, Chemukhin, Moscow: Voyenizdat 1971.

Russian-English Scientific and Technical Dictionary, 1st ed., Alford, M.H.T., and Alford, V.L., Oxford: Pergamon 1970.

SERBIAN, See Serbo-Croatian.

SERBO-CROATIAN

Note: While Serbian and Croatian are now being treated as two separate languages, most dictionaries for those languages are still known as Serbo-Croatian dictionaries. Serbian and Croatian dictionaries are included in this category.

General Dictionaries

Standard English-SerboCroatian, SerboCroatian-English Dictionary, Benson, M., Cambridge University Press 2008.

Srpskohrvatsko-engleski recnik, 3rd ed., Benson, M., Belgrade: Prosveta 1991.

English-SerboCroatian and SerboCroatian-English Dictionary, Benson, M., Cambridge, UK: Cambridge University Press 1990.

The New Standard Dictionary (English-Serbo-Croatian/Serbo-Croatian-English), Grujic, B., and Srdevic, I. 1990.

Serbo-Croatian-English/English-Serbo-Croatian Dictionary of Synonyms & Antonyms, 3rd ed., Dajkovic, J., 1989.

The Oxford-Duden Pictorial Serbo-Croat & English Dictionary, Oxford: Clarendon Press 1988.

Hrvatsko ili srpsko engleski rjecnik, Drvodelic, M., Zagreb: Skolska Knjiga 1982.

Veliki rjecnik stranih rijeci, Klaic, B., Zagreb: Zora 1972.

Recnik u slikama: Engleski i srpskohrvatski, Beograd, G., Zagreb: Naprijed 2002.

Serbo-Croatian: Business and Related Fields
Croatian Dictionary of Business and Government, Ivir, V., New York: i.b.d. Ltd. 1993.
English-Serbo-Croatian and Serbo-Croatian-English Economic Dictionary, Gligorijevic, V., Belgrade 1986.

Serbo-Croatian: Law
English-Croatian Criminal Justice Grammar and Dictionary, Gacic, M., New York: i.b.d. Ltd. 1992.

Serbo-Croatian: Maritime
Serbo-Croatian-English Maritime Dictionary, Pricard, B., New York: i.b.d. Ltd. 1991.

Serbo-Croatian: Technical
Serbo-Croatian-English/English-Serbo-Croatian Dictionary of Naval Architecture, Mechanical Engineering and Nuclear Energy, Bartolic, L., New York: i.b.d. Ltd.
Rečnik tehničkih izraza, Belgrade: Tehnička knjiga 1961.

SLOVAK
General Dictionaries
English-Slovak and Slovak-English, Andricik, M., Pezolt 2005.
English-Slovak Dictionary, Haraksimova, E., Bolchazy-Carducci Publishers 2001.
Slovak-English/English-Slovak Pocket Dictionary, New York: i.b.d. Ltd. 1995.
Krátky slovník slovenského jazyka, Kacala, J., et al., Bratislava: Vgda 1997.
Hippocrene Concise Slovak-English/English-Slovak Dictionary, New York: Hippocrene 1998.
Česko-slovensk slovník, Horak, G., Bratislava: Vgda 1979.
Slovak-English Dictionary, Konus, J.J., Passaic, NJ: Slovak Catholic Sokol 1969.
Slovensko-anglick slovník, Vilikovska, et al., Bratislava: SPN 1964.
Anglicko-slovensk a slovensko-anglick vreckov slovník, Bratislava: Slovenske padagogicke nakladatel'stvo 1963.

Slovak: Technical
Vreckov anglicko-slovensk a slovensko-anglick technick slovník, Novak & Binder, Slovenské vydavatel'stvo technickej literatury 1961.

SLOVENE
English-Slovene/Slovene-English Modern Dictionary, Komac, D., New York: Hippocrene 2005.
Veliki Slovensko-Angleski Slovar, Grad, A., Ljubljana: Drzavna Zolozba Slovenije 1982.

Slovene: Business
Slovene Business Dictionary, London: Peter Collin 1999.

SOMALI
Somali: Somali-English, English-Somali Dictionary & Phrasebook, Ande, N., New York: Hippocrene 1998.
English-Somali/Somali-English Dictionary, Korshel, M., New Delhi: Star Publications 2002.

SPANISH
General Dictionaries
Diccionario de la lengua española, 22nd ed., Madrid: Real Academia de la Lengua Española 2010. Spanish-Spanish. Available in one-volume hardcover deluxe edition, also two-volume economic hardcover; CD-ROM edition forthcoming. This is the official dictionary of the Spanish language. The new twenty-second edition incorporates for the first time foreignisms (mainly English) as well as many Latin American colloquialisms, making this dictionary a must for Spanish translators.
Collins Spanish Concise Dictionary, 6th ed., Collins Reference 2010.
HarperCollins Spanish-English/English-Spanish Dictionary, Bradley, D., New York: HarperCollins 2005. Contains 230,000 references and 444,000 translations.
The Oxford Spanish Dictionary, Jaman, B.G., and Russell, R., Oxford: Oxford University Press 2008. Thumb indexed. Spanish-English/English-Spanish (also on CD-ROM). Very good.
Diccionario internacional Simon and Schuster, de Gamez, T., New York: Simon & Schuster 1997. English-Spanish/Spanish-English. Contains many Latin Americanisms.
Multicultural Spanish Dictionary, 2nd ed., ed. by Sofer, M., Lanham, MD: Taylor Trade Publishing 2012. Everyday Spanish words as they differ from country to country.
Libro de Estilo "El País," 14th ed., 1998.
The Interpreter's Companion (Spanish-English/English-Spanish), Mikkelson, H., Acebo: 2000. Compilation of terms not found in other dictionaries, covering legal, medical, drugs, weapons, profanity, and slang terms.
Diccionario Ideas Afines, Corripio, F., 1994. Recommended.
Collins Spanish-English/English-Spanish Dictionary, Unabridged, 3rd ed., Smith, C., New York: Harper-Collins 2006. Widely considered one of the best of its kind.
Visual Dictionary, Corbeil, J.C., New York: Facts on File 2006.
Qué es qué (What's What), Enciclopedia visual bilingüe, Maplewood, NJ: Hammond 1988. A pictorial dictionary.
The Collins Spanish Dictionary, Barcelona: Ediciones Grijalbo 1988. Good for Spanish for Spain.

Diccionario de dudas y dificultades de la lengua española, Seco, M., Madrid: Espasa-Calpe 2004.

Diccionario de uso del español, 2 vols., Moliner, M., Madrid: Editorial Gredos 2004. Spanish-Spanish. Excellent; also available on CD-ROM.

Gran diccionario español-inglés, Garcia Pelayo y Gross, R., Ediciones Larousse 2004. Very comprehensive. European oriented.

2001 Spanish and English Idioms, Savaiano, E., and Winget, L., Woodbury, NY: Barron 2008. Not exhaustive, but quite useful.

Diccionario de los idiomas inglés y español, Velázquez, M., Englewood Cliffs, NJ: Prentice Hall 1972. Spanish-English/English-Spanish. Old, but still useful.

Sinónimos castellanos, Garcia, R., and Sopena, R., Buenos Aires 1967. Spanish-Spanish.

Diccionario español de sinónimos y antónimos, Sainz de Robles, F.C., Spanish-Spanish 2006.

Buenas y malas palabras, Orellana, M., Chile: Editorial Universitaria 1998.

General Regional Spanish Dictionaries
Mexican Spanish, London: Lexus 1996.

In progress: Cuban and Peruvian Spanish dictionaries by Anthony T. Rivas (Ref. ATA).

The Dictionary of Chicano Spanish, Galvan, R.A., Lincolnwood, IL: NTC 1995.

La traducción del inglés al castellano, Orellana, M., 1994.

Nuevo diccionario lunfardo, Gobello, J., 2005. Colloquial language of Buenos Aires by a noted author on the subject.

Lexicón de colombianismos, 2 vols., Banco de la Republica, Bogota: Biblioteca Luis-Angel Arango 1983.

Diccionario de venezolanismos, vol. 1, A–I, Academia Venezolana de la Lengua, Universidad Central de Venezuela, Facultad de Humanidades y Educasión, Caracas: Instituto de Filología Andrés Bello 1983.

Bilingual Dictionary of Mexican Spanish, 3rd ed., Hamel, B.H., Los Angeles: Bilingual Book Press 2002.

Diccionario de americanismos, Steel, B.

Diccionario de mejicanismos, Santamaria, F., Mexico City: Editorial Porrua 1993. Very useful for any Mexico-related translation.

Spanish: Aviation/Aeronautics
Diccionario aeronáutico civil y militar inglés-español, Velasco, Madrid: Paraninfo 1995.

Spanish: Business and Related Fields
Spanish Business Dictionary, ed. by Sofer, M., Rockville, MD: Schreiber Publishing 2005. Multicultural business Spanish with varying terms from major Spanish-speaking countries such as Spain, Mexico, Venezuela, Chile, and Argentina.

Spanish Dictionary of Business, Commerce and Finance, London, New York: Routledge 1997; CD-ROM 1998.

Nuevo diccionario bilingüe de economía y empresa, Lozano, J.M., Madrid: Ediciones Piramide 2005. English-Spanish/Spanish-English.

Dictionary of Business, Collin, P.H., Middlesex, UK 1993. English-Spanish/ Spanish-English.

English-Spanish Banking Dictionary, Esteban, R.G., Madrid: Editorial Paraninfo 1993.

Diccionario Enciclopédico Profesional de Finanzas y Banca, 3 vols., 1992.

World Bank Glossary (Spanish-English/English-Spanish), 1996.

Dictionary of Accounting (Spanish-English with S-E/E-S vocabulary), Kohler, E., 2005.

Harrap's Glossary of Spanish Commercial and Industrial Terms, Rodrigues, L., London: Harrap 1990. English-Spanish/Spanish-English.

Diccionario comercial inglés-español/español-inglés, Giraud, A., Barcelona: Editorial Juventud 1990.

Dictionary of Modern Business, Robb, L., Washington, DC: Anderson Kramer Associates 1960. English-Spanish/Spanish-English.

Spanish: Chemistry
Hawley—Diccionario de química y de productos químicos, Sax, I., Barcelona: Ediciones Omega 1993. Best of its kind.

Spanish: Communications
Spanish Dictionary of Telecommunications, London/New York: Routledge 1998. Spanish-English/English-Spanish.

Diccionario del video inglés-español, Perales, Madrid: Paraninfo.

Diccionario para Electrónica, Telecomunicaciones e Informática, Buenos Aires: EMEDE, S.A. 1986.

Diccionario terminológico de los medios de comunicación, Prieto, F., Marid: Ediciones Piramide English-Spanish.

Spanish: Computers
Online: http://www.wordreference.com/es/translation.asp?tranword=information %20technology, 2011.

Dictionary of Information Technology (Spanish-English/English-Spanish), Vollnhals, O., 1997. Very good.

English-Spanish, Spanish-English Dictionary of Electrical and Computer Engineering, Kaplan, S., New York: John Wiley 2001.

Computer Dictionary (English-Spanish), Freedman, C., 1994.

Diccionario comentado de terminología informática, Aguado, G., Madrid: Editorial Paraninfo 1994.

Diccionario de informática inglés-español/español-inglés, Madrid: Ediciones Diaz de Santos 1993.
Diccionario de informática inglés-español, Olivetti, Barcelona: Editorial Paraninfo 1993. Rather small and limited.
Dictionary of Computer Terms, Chiri, A., New York: Hippocrene 1993.
Diccionario de micro informática inglés-español, Tapias, R., Barcelona: Editorial Noray 1985. Old but useful.

Spanish: Electronics
Diccionario de electrónica español-inglés, Amós, Madrid: Paraninfo 1988.
Diccionario de electrónica y técnica nuclear, Markus, J. Spanish-English 1993.

Spanish: Engineering
Electrical and Computer Engineering Dictionary, Kaplan, S., New York: John Wiley & Sons 2001. English-Spanish/Spanish-English.
Diccionario técnico inglés-español, Malgorn, G., Madrid: Paraninfo 2006.
Dictionary of Environmental Engineering, J. Villate, Miami: Ediciones Universal 1979.
Engineers' Dictionary, Robb, L., New York: 2004. English-Spanish/Spanish-English. Still considered one of the best.

Spanish: Environment
Spanish Dictionary of Environmental Technology, London/New York: Routledge 1998. Spanish-English/English-Spanish.
Spanish-English Dictionary of Environmental Science and Engineering, Headworth, H., New York: John Wiley 1997.

Spanish: Law
English-Spanish, Spanish-English Legal Dictionary, Kaplan, S., New York: John Wiley 2008.
Legal Dictionary (Spanish-English/English-Spanish), Alcarez Varo, E., 2007. Highly recommended.
Diccionario jurídico inglés-español, Saint Dahl, H., McGraw-Hill 2003.
Bilingual Dictionary of Criminal Justice Terms, Benmaman, V., Connolly, N., and Loos, S., Longwood, FL: Gould Publications Inc. 1996. English-Spanish. Small but good.
Diccionario de Derecho, Duran, R., 2005.
El inglés jurídico, Alcarez Varo, E., 2004.
Diccionario jurídico, Moro, T., 2003.
Diccionario jurídico español-inglés, Cabanellas de las Cuevas, G., and Hoague, E.C., Austin, TX: Butterworth Legal Publishers 1991. Spanish-English/English-Spanish. Highly recommended; complements the Alcarez Varo (see above).

Dictionary of Law, Economics and Politics, Navarro, R.L., Madrid: Editoriales de Derecho Reunidas 1989.

Diccionario de Derecho, de Pina, R., and de Pina Vara, R., Mexico City: Editorial Porrua 1985.

Diccionario de términos legales, Robb, L., Mexico: Editorial Limusa 1980.

Diccionario de ciencias jurídicas, políticas y sociales, Ossorio, M., Heliasta S.R.L 2005.

Spanish: Maritime

Nautical Dictionary (Spanish-English/English-Spanish), Malagón Ortuondo, J.M., 2007.

Diccionario marítimo y de construcción naval, Perez, J.A., Barcelona: Ediciones Garriga 1976.

Spanish: Medicine

Medical Dictionary: English, Spanish, Portuguese, Nolte-Schlegel, New York: Springer-Verlag 2008.

English-Spanish/Spanish-English Medical Dictionary, Rogers, G., New York: McGraw-Hill 2006.

The Delmar English-Spanish Dictionary for Health Professionals, Kelz, R.K., Delmar Publishers 1996.

Medical Dictionary (Spanish-English/English-Spanish), McElroy, O.H., et al., 2005. Good, small paperback.

Mosby's Medical Dictionary (Spanish-English with E-S/S-E Vocabulary), De Teran Bleiberg, E., 2003. Extensive explanations and illustrations.

Bilingual Glossary for Medical and Healthcare Translators: Oncology, Hematology, and Radiotherapy: English-Spanish-English, Albin, V., and Coggins, M., Houston: PCM Translation Resources 1994.

Medical Encyclopedic Dictionary (Spanish-English), 2 vols., Dorland 1992. Excellent.

Diccionario de términos médicos, Torres, R., Madrid: Alhambra 2002. Spanish-English/English-Spanish.

Diccionario de los Términos Técnicos de Medicina, Garnier, M., and Delamare, V., 1981.

Spanish: Military

Diccionario técnico militar, Gomez, A., Madrid: Ediciones Agullo 1980.

Diccionario moderno de tecnología militar, Wells, R., Fairfax, VA: Lexicon Press 1977.

Spanish: Mining

Glossary of Mining Terms (Spanish-English/English-Spanish), Diaz Preto, P., 1995.

Spanish: Psychiatry
Glossary of Psychiatric Terms (Spanish-English/English-Spanish), Nemiah, J.C, 1996.
Dictionary of Psychology and Psychiatry (Spanish-English/English-Spanish), Kaplan, S., 1997.

Spanish: Real Estate
Dictionary of Real Estate Business, Salles, M., Dearborn: 1997.

Spanish: Technical
Polytechnic Dictionary of Spanish and English Languages, rev. ed., Beigbeder Atienza, F., 2003. Highly recommended.
Routledge Spanish Technical Dictionary, 2 vols., London/New York: Routledge 1996. Vol. 1 (Spanish-English); vol. 2 (English-Spanish). CD-ROM 1998.
The Contractors Dictionary of Equipment, Tools and Techniques, Kennedy, F., New York: John Wiley 1996.
Technical Glossary for Bilingual Technical Writers and Translators: English-Spanish/Spanish-English, Rodríguez, H., published by author, 1996.
Diccionario técnico, Rafael Garcia Diaz, Mexico: LIMUSA, S.A. 1996.
Glosario Internacional para el Traductor (Spanish-English/English-Spanish), reprint, Orellana, M., 1998. Very useful for translators.
Diccionario de términos científicos y técnicos, 5 vols., Barcelona: McGraw-Hill Boixarev 1981. A translation of the excellent McGraw-Hill *Dictionary of Science and Technology* (see General References).
Spanish-English/English-Spanish Encyclopedic Dictionary of Technical Terms, 3 vols., Collazo, J.L., McGraw-Hill 1980.
Glosario español-inglés de términos técnicos, 5 vols., Thomann, A.E., Armco Steel Corporation 1975. Spanish-English/English-Spanish.

SWAHILI
Swahili-English, English-Swahili Practical Dictionary, Awde, N., Hippocrene 2000.
Concise Swahili and English Dictionary, Perrot, D.V., Kent, UK: Hodder and Stoughton Ltd. 1965.

SWEDISH
General Dictionaries
Swedish-English English-Swedish Practical Dictionary, Hille, H., New York: Hippocrene 2011.
English-Swedish Comprehensive Dictionary, New York: Hippocrene 1997.
Norstedts stora englesk-svensk/svensk-englesk ordbok, Andra uppla-gan, Petti, V., Rider, I.H., Berglund, B.M., Martinsson-Visser, Y., Swedenborg, L., and Wiman, M., Stockholm: Norstedts Förlag 1993. Recommended.

Svengelsk ordbok (Acta Wexionensia. Ser. 3, Language & Literature; 1), Selten, B., Stockholm: Almquist & Wiksell International 1987. English loanwords and words with English elements with correct Swedish spellings and definitions in Swedish.

Fökortningsordbok: åtta tusen svenska och internationella förkortningar med förklaringar, Collinder, B., and Svenblad, R., Andra utökade upplagan, Malmo: Liber 1987. Acronyms and abbreviations.

Nyord i svenskan fran 40-tal till 80-tal; Svenska spraknamnden; textredigering, Swedenborg, L., Stockholm: Esselte Studium 1986. Swedish-Swedish.

Svensk ordbok/utarbetad vid språkdata, Göteborgs universitet, Sture, A., vetenskaplig ledare, Solna: Esselte Studium 1986. Swedish-Swedish.

A Modern Swedish-English Dictionary (Swedish-English/English-Swedish), 2 vols., 4th rev. ed., Stockholm: Prisma 1984.

Stora engelsk-svenska ordboken, Santesson, R., Stockholm: Esselte Studium 1984. Comprehensive.

Svensk-engelsk ordbok, Santesson, R., Stockholm: Esselte Studium.

Bonniers svenska ordbok, Swedish-Swedish, Malmström, S., Györki, I., and Sjögren, P., Stockholm: Albert Bonniers Förlog 1990.

Svensk slangordbok, Andra Upplagan, Gibson, H., Stockholm: Esselte Studium 1983.

Nysvensk ordbok, 5 vols., Ostergren, O., Stockholm: Wahlström & Widstrand 1981. Swedish-Swedish.

Nya förkortningordboken, Larsson, W., Halmstad: Bokförlaget Spektra AB 1975.

Illustrerad svensk ordbok, Molde, et al., Natur och Kultur 1970. Swedish-Swedish.

Swedish: Business and Related Fields

Dictionary of Business: English-Swedish, Collin, P.H., Malmström, L., and Fox, R., Teddington, Middlesex: Peter Collin Publishing Ltd. 1998.

755 Svenska organisationer pa fyra språk: Engelska, franska, tyska, finska, Heyum, J., Stockholm: Addax Språkförlag 1987.

Ekonomi ordbok: svensk-engelsk fackordbok for ekonomifunktionen med begreppsförklaringar, Edström, N.F., and Samuelson, L.A., Stockholm: P.A. Norstedt & Söners Forlag 1987.

Svensk-engelsk affärslexikon, Stockholm: J. Sanders och Affärsförlaget 1980.

Svensk-engelsk fackordbok, 2nd rev. ed., Gullberg, P.A., Norstedts & Söner Förlag 1977.

Swedish: Law

Juridisk ordbok: Svensk-engelsk fackordbok, Martinger, S., Stockholm: Norstedts Förlag 1987.

Swedish: Nuclear Energy

Karnergiordlista, Stockholm: Tekniska nomenklaturcentralen och Sveriges Mekanstandardisering 1990. Nuclear energy terms—Swedish, English, French, and German equivalents.

Swedish: Technical
Norstedts dataordbok, Darcy, L., and Boston, L., compilers, Schroder, J., translator, Stockholm: P.A. Norstedt & Söners Förlag 1987.
Svensk-engelsk teknisk ordbok (Swedish-English/English-Swedish), 2 vols., 10th ed., Engström, E., AB Svensk Trävarutidning Förlaget 1983. English-Swedish volume newly revised 1997.

TATAR
Concise Tatar-English/English-Tatar Dictionary, Shahmayer, S., New York: Hippocrene 1994.

THAI
Thai-English/English-Thai Dictionary & Phrasebook, Higbie, J., New York: Hippocrene 1999.
The Oxford-Duden Pictorial Thai and English Dictionary, Oumah, C., New York: Oxford University Press 1998.

TURKISH
General Dictionaries
Langenscheidt New Standard Dictionary: Turkish-English/English-Turkish, Akdikmen, R., Langenscheidt 2006.
Turkish-English/English-Turkish Dictionary, New York: Hippocrene 2002.
The Oxford Turkish Dictionary, Fahir, I., et al., Oxford: Oxford University Press 1992.
Turkish Grammar, Lewis, G., Oxford University Press 2001.
Redhouse Yeni Turkce-Ingilizce Sozluk, Istanbul: Redhouse Press.
Buyuk Turkce-Ingilizce Sozluk, Tuglaci, P., Istanbul: Inkilap ve Akar Publishing House.

Turkish: Computers
Dictionary of Information Technology, Turkish-English/English-Turkish, French and European Publications 1999.

Turkish: Technical
Dictionary of Technical Terms, Turkish-English, French and European Publications 1999.

UKRAINIAN
New English-Ukrainian and Ukrainian-English Dictionary, Zhluktenko, J., A.S.K. 2005.
English-Ukrainian/Ukrainian-English Dictionary, Bikhovets, N., et al., Rockville, MD: Kamkin 1995.

Hippocrene Practical Ukrainian-English/English-Ukrainian (with Menu Terms), Hrabovsky, L., New York: Hippocrene 1991.

English-Ukrainian Dictionary, Toronto: University of Toronto Press 1990.

Hippocrene Standard Ukrainian-English/English-Ukrainian Dictionary, New York: Hippocrene.

Ukrayinsko-anhliyskyy slovnyk, Zhluktenko, Yu. O., et al., Kiev: Radyanska Shkola 1987.

Ukrayinsko-anhliyskyy slovnyk, Andrusyshen, C.H., Toronto: University of Toronto Press 1981.

Slovnyk ukrayinskoyi movy, 11 vols., Academiya nauk, Keva: Naukova dumka 2001.

Slovnyk inshomovnykh Sliv, Melnychuk, O.S., Kiev: URE 2000.

Slovnyk Ukrayinskykh idiom, Udovychenko, G.M., Kiev: Radyanskyy pysmennyk 1968.

Ukrainian: Business

Ukrainian-English Dictionary of Business, Kronglov, A., McFarland 1997.

UZBEK

Uzbek-English/English-Uzbek Dictionary, Khakimov, K., New York: Hippocrene 1993.

Uzbek-English Dictionary, Waterson, N., Oxford: Oxford University Press 1980.

VIETNAMESE

Tuttle Concise Vietnamese Dictionary: Vietnamese-English English-Vietnamese, Giuong, P.V., Tuttle 2008.

NTC's Vietnamese-English Dictionary, Nguyen, D., Lincolnwood, IL: NTC 1995.

Vietnamese-English/English-Vietnamese Dictionary, Le-Ba-Khanh, New York: Hippocrene 1991.

Tu Dien Tieng Viet, Hanoi: Vien Khoa Hoc Xa Hoi Viet Nam, Vien Ngon Ngu Hoc, Trung Tam Tu Dien Ngon Ngu 1992. Vietnamese-Vietnamese.

Tu Dien Viet-Ahn, Bui Phung, Hanoi: Hanoi University 1986.

Tu Dien Tieng Viet, Van Tan, Hanoi: Nha Xuat Ban Khoa Hoc Xa Hoi 1986.

Thanh Ngu Tieng Viet, Nguyen Luc, Hanoi: Nha Xuat Ban Khoa Hoc Xa Hoi 1978. Contains correct rendition of proverbs.

Tu Dien Anh Viet, Huu Chi et al., Hanoi: Nha Xuat Ban Khoa Hoc Xa Hoi 1975. English-Vietnamese.

Tu Dien Hoc Sinh [Cap II], Nguyen Luong Ngoc, Hanoi: Giao Duc 1971.

Vietnamese-English Student Dictionary, Nguyen Dinh Hoa, Carbondale: Southern Illinois University 1971.

Vietnam Tu Dien, 2 vols., Le Van Duc, Saigon: Khai tri 1970. Available in United States.

Tu Dien Thanh Ngu Dien Tich, Dien Huong, Saigon: Khai Tri 1981.

YIDDISH

Yiddish-English-Hebrew Dictionary, Harhavy, A., New York: Schocken Books, YIVO Institute for Jewish Research 2005. (Reprint of 1928 expanded 2nd ed.)

English-Yiddish/Yiddish-English Dictionary, Harduf, D.M., Ontario, Canada: published by author 1985.

Modern English-Yiddish/Yiddish-English Dictionary, Weinrich, U., New York: Schocken Books 1990.

YORUBA

Yoruba-English/English-Yoruba Concise Dictionary, Yai, O.B., New York: Hippocrene 1996.

Where to Find Dictionaries

Dictionaries are becoming ever more available in general bookstores and in bookstore chains such as Barnes & Noble, and on the Internet via amazon.com, barnesandnoble.com, and more. The following is a partial list of book sources that specialize in dictionaries, particularly hard-to-find technical ones. Some will order a great many technical dictionaries for you from sources in both the United States and abroad. Some of the British, European, and other overseas bookstores listed here are excellent and well worth contacting.

The best way these days to shop for dictionaries is on the Internet.

U.S. Sources of Dictionaries

Blackwell Book Services, Blackwood, NJ	www.blackwell.com
Cheng & Tsui Co., Boston, MA	www.cheng-tsui.com
China Books & Periodicals Inc., San Francisco, CA	www.chinabooks.com
French & European Publications Inc., New York, NY	www. frencheuropean.com
Hippocrene Books, New York, NY	www.hippocrenebooks.com
John Wiley & Sons, New York, NY	www.wiley.com
Kinokuniya Bookstores, San Francisco, CA	www.kinokuniya.com
Kinokuniya Bookstores, New York	www.kinokuniya.com
McGraw-Hill, New York, NY	www.mcgraw-hill.com
Polish Bookstore and Publishing, Brooklyn, NY	www.polbook.com
Rizzoli International Book Store, New York, NY	www.rizzoliusa.com
Routledge, New York, NY	www.routledge.com
Rowman & Littlefield, Lanham, MD	www.rowman.com
Schoenhofs Foreign Books, Cambridge, MA	www.schoenhofs.com
Szwede Slavic Books, Redwood City, CA	www.szwedeslavicbooks.com
Western Continental Book Inc., Denver, CO	www.continentalbook.com

Foreign Dictionary Sources

Argentina
Editorial Planeta, www.editorialplaneta.com.ar

Australia
Kinokuniya Bookstores, www.kinokuniya.com

Chile
Editorial Universitaria, Santiago, Chile. www.universitaria.cl

France
La Maison du dictionnaire, Paris, France. www.dicoland.com
Editions du CNRS, Paris, France. www.cnrseditions.fr
Editions Klincksieck, Paris, France. www.klincksieck.fr

Germany
Kubon & Sagner, Munich, Germany. www.kubon-sagner.de
Langenscheidt, www.langenscheidt.com

Hong Kong
Joint Publishing Company, Central District, Hong Kong. www.jointpublishing.com

Mexico
Editorial Planeta, www.editorialplaneta.com.mx

Malaysia
Kinokuniya Bookstores, www.kinokuniya.com

Singapore
Kinokuniya Bookstores, www.kinokuniya.com

Spain
Editorial Planeta, www.editorial.planeta.es

Sweden
Tekniska Litteratursallskapet, Stockholm, Sweden. www.tls.se

Thailand
Kinokuniya Bookstores, www.kinokuniya.com

United Kingdom
B. H. Blackwell Ltd., Oxford, UK. www.blackwell.co.uk
Multilingual Matters, www.multilingual-matters.com
Oxford University Press, Oxford, UK. www.oup.co.uk

Foreign-Language Software Sources

This appendix is designed for translators who translate documents *from* English *into* another language. Word-processing software in languages other than English is produced both in the United States and in the country of the target language. Translators in the United States, however, have to be aware of the compatibility of the software with U.S. word-processing software. Microsoft's dominance in English-language word processing extends to its localized products, which have the obvious advantage of being compatible with their English versions and with one another, in addition to the considerable number of languages they cover. We start, therefore, with a listing of Microsoft foreign-language products, followed by other sources. This is by no means an exhaustive listing, but rather a sampling of sources to help translators who have a need for software in a given language start the process of looking for the product that best meets their needs.

Microsoft Foreign-Language Software and Product Support

(Website: microsoft.com/worldwide)

Arabic
Microsoft Egypt, Smart Village, Kilo 28, Cairo/Alex Desert Road
Abou Rawash, Cairo, Egypt
Phone: +202 35393333 Fax: +202 35390303

Chinese
Microsoft (China) Co., Ltd., 19/F, Millennium Tower, 38 Xiaoyun Road,
    Chaoyang, Beijing 100027, P.R. China
Phone: 011-86-10-8453-8989 Fax: 011-86-10-8453-8509

Croatian
Microsoft Hrvatska d.o.o., Turinina 3/IV, HR—10010 Zagreb, Croatia
Phone: 385 1 4802 500 Fax: 385 1 4802 525

Czech
Microsoft s.r.o., BB Centrum, budova Alpha, Vyskocilova 1461/2a, 140 00 Praha
  4, Czech Republic
Phone: +420 2611 97 111 Fax: +420 2611 97 100

Danish
Microsoft Danmark ApS, Tuborg Boulevard 12, 2900 Hellerup, Denmark
Phone: (45) 44 89 0100 Fax: (45) 44 68 5510

Dutch
Microsoft B.V., Evert van de Beekstraat 354, 1118 CZ Schiphol, Netherlands
Phone: +31 (0)20-5001500 Fax: +31 (0)20-5001999

French (Canadian)
Microsoft Canada Co., 1950 Meadowvale Blvd., Mississauga, Ontario L5N 8L9
Phone: (877) 568-2495 Fax: (800) 933-4750

French
Microsoft France, 18 Avenue du Québec, Zone de Courtaboeuf 1, 91957 Courta-
  boeuf Cedex, France
Phone: (33) 825 827 829 Fax: (33) 1 64 46 06 60

Finnish
Microsoft OY (Suomi), Keilaranta 7, 02150 Espoo, Suomi
Phone: 358 (0) 9 525 501 Fax: 358 (0) 9 878 8778

German
Microsoft Deutschland GmbH, Konrad-Zuse-Str. 1, D-85716 Unterschleissheim
  (Munich), Germany
Phone: +49/(0)89/3176-0 Fax: +49/(0)89/3176-1000

Greek
Microsoft Hellas S.A., 221 Kifisias Ave., 151 24, Athens, Greece
Phone: +30 211 1206 000 Fax: +30 211 1206 003

Hebrew
Microsoft Israel Ltd., Ha'Pnina st. 2, Ranana 43107, Israel
Phone: 972-9-7625400 Fax: 972-9-7625200

Hungarian
Microsoft Magyarorszag Kft., Graphisoft Park 3 (Zahony u.), 1031 Budapest,
  Hungary
Phone: +36 1 437 2800 Fax: +36 1 437 2899

Italian
Microsoft, Centro Direzionale San Felice, Palazzo A, Via Rivoltana 13, 20090—
Segrate (MI), Italy
Phone: 39 02 70 398 398 Fax: 39 02 70 392 020

Japanese
Microsoft Company Ltd., Odakyu Southern Tower 2-1, Yoyogi 2-Chome
Shibuya-ku, Tokyo 151-8583, Japan
Phone: 81-3-4332-5300

Korean
Microsoft Korea, 6th Floor, POSCO Center, 892 Daechi-Dong, Kangnam-Gu,
Seoul, 135-777, South Korea
Phone: 82-2-531-4500 Fax: 82-2-555-1724

Norwegian
Microsoft Norge AS, Postboks 43, Lilleaker, 0216 Oslo, Norway
Phone: (47) 22 02 25 00 Fax: (47) 22 95 06 64

Polish
Microsoft Sp. z o.o., Al. Jerozolimskie 195a, 02-222 Warszawa, Poland
Phone: (+48) 22-594-1000 Fax: (+48) 22-594-1002

Portuguese
MS Portugal, Edifício Qualidade C1–C2, Av. Prof. Doutor, Aníbal Cavaco Silva,
Tagus Park, 2744-010 Porto Salvo, Portugal
Phone: (351) 21 440-92-00 Fax: (351) 21 441-21-01

Russian
Microsoft Russia, 17 Ul. Krylatskaya, 121614, Moscow, Russia
Phone: +7 (495) 9678585 Fax: +7 (495) 9678500

Serbian and Montenegrin
Microsoft Software d.o.o., Makedonska 30/VI, 11000 Belgrade, Serbia
Phone: +381 11 330 66 00 Fax: +381 11 330 66 01

Slovene
Microsoft d.o.o., Ljubljana, Smartinska c. 140, SI—1000 Ljubljana, Slovenia
Phone: +386 (0)1 5 846 100 Fax: +386 (0)1 5 846 122

Spanish (Mexican)
Microsoft Mexico, S.A. de C.V., Paseo de Tamarindos 400 A Piso 29, Col.
Bosques de las Lomas, Mexico D.F. C.P. 05120, Mexico
Phone: +52 (55) 5267-2000 Atencion a clientes: 01800 5272000
Fax: +52 (55) 5258-0225

Swedish
Microsoft AB, Box 27, S-164 93 Kista, Sweden
Phone: +46 8 7525600 Fax: +46 8 7505158

Tagalog
Microsoft Philippines Inc., 16th Floor, 6750 Ayala Office Tower, 6750 Ayala
    Avenue, Makati City 1200, Philippines
Phone: (63 2) 860 8989 Fax: (63 2) 860 8920

Thai
Microsoft (Thailand) Limited, 37th Floor, Unit No. 1–7, CRC Tower, All Seasons
    Place, 87/2 Wireless Road, Lumpini, Pathumwan, Bangkok 10330, Thailand
Phone: 66-2257-4999 Fax: 66-2257-0099

Turkish
Microsoft Bilgisayar Yazilim, Hizmetleri Limited Sirketi, Barbaros Plaza Is
    Merkezi, 145-C, Kat 21, Emirhan Caddesi, Dikilitas, Besiktas 80700, Istanbul,
    Turkey
Phone: 90-212-326-5000 Fax: 90-212-258-5954

Vietnamese
Microsoft Vietnam, 9th Floor, Hanoi Tung Shing Square, 2 Ngo Quyen, Hanoi,
    Vietnam
Phone: +844-825-1955 Fax: +844-826-1222

Sources of Translation Work

There are three major sources of translation work in the United States: the government sector, the public sector, and the private sector.

The government sector includes the city, county, and state governments in addition to the federal government. All of them need translation work on a fairly regular basis, and all of them are worth contacting. It is not always easy to find the right person or office to contact, but perseverance does pay off. One good place to start your search is the procurement or contracting office of any given government entity. They usually know who in the system needs what, and they can often tell you whether they've heard lately of someone in the system needing translation. Again, you need to have a great deal of patience with these folks, who are not known for their alacrity.

The U.S. government, or the "Government" with a capital G, is a huge source of translation. It is hard to put a dollar figure on it, but it certainly goes into the many millions of dollars per year. Government translation requests come in three main forms:

1. *Translation contracts.* Various government agencies issue a request for a bid on a one- to five-year translation contract. Those usually require several languages, and most freelancers cannot handle them on their own. To find out about those contracts, read the government publication *Commerce Business Daily* (found online at http://cbdnet.gpo.gov). You may want to monitor the contract office handling the particular contract and have them tell you (under the Freedom of Information Act) which company is awarded the contract. You can then contact that company and offer your services in your particular areas of expertise.

2. *Translation requirements in a nontranslation contract.* The government may need a company to monitor drug dealers who speak Spanish. It contracts with a company specialized in electronic monitoring. That company will then subcontract the translation portion of its prime contract to a translation company. Here again you can follow this process and offer your services.

3. *One-time translation order.* The Department of Energy may need to translate a Russian book on power plants. They will look for someone who has a good

knowledge of Russian and English, and experience in this kind of technical translation. They usually turn to a translation company, but they may also contract with an individual. This type of assignment is very hard to find, since the agency will rarely advertise what they call a "small purchase" (which to a freelancer can be quite big), and will instead contact an established translation company.

The *public sector* includes many organizations, academic institutions, foundations, and so on. All of them, at one time or another, need translation work. The question is how to find out who needs what and when. I wish I had the answer, but I don't. The same holds true for the *private sector*, which consists of commercial and industrial entities, law firms, and individuals.

All of which leaves you with the *translation companies*, who in effect act as a broker between you and the work sources. They develop many contacts, they bid on contracts, they advertise in the media and in the Yellow Pages, and they provide millions of dollars worth of translation work for freelancers every year.

The following is a list, arranged alphabetically, of translation companies. It is followed by a state-by-state regional index. A word of caution: not all of them are financially sound, and they do not always pay on time or treat freelancers with the professional respect they usually deserve. *Inclusion in the ensuing list does not mean in any way that we endorse any of the companies listed.* We leave it to you to check out any company you may be interested in, draw your own conclusions, and establish your own relationship with them.

The information contained in the following list is based on survey questionnaires sent to translation agencies. The amount of detail corresponds to the amount of information given us by those agencies that responded and does not reflect any judgment on the editors' part as to the quality of those agencies. We have attempted to fill in as much information as we could for those agencies that did not respond to our survey.

U.S. TRANSLATION COMPANIES

-A-

A Foreign Language Service, 40 West Baseline, #202, Mesa, AZ 85210
Phone: (480) 813-4242 Fax: (480) 323-2324
E-mail: bill@aflscorp.com Website: www.aflscorp.com
Contact: Bill Peters / Member: ATA

A-Z Friendly Languages Inc., 3818 Brookdale Circle, Brooklyn Park, MN 55443
Phone: (763) 566-4312 Fax: (763) 503-3977
E-mail: azfl@friendlylanguages.net
Contact: Natasha Geilman, President / Member: ATA

A2Z Global Language Solutions, 230 East Cuthbert Boulevard, Haddon Township, NJ 08108
Phone: (856) 833-0220 Fax: (856) 854-0491 Mobile: (609) 968-6699
E-mail: tlandgren@a2zglobal.com Website: www.a2zglobal.com
/ Member: ATA
Contact: Theodora Landgren (only for executive issues or sales) / Member: ATA
   Full service LSP offering worldwide services for translation, editing, publishing, proofreading, narration, and interpreting in most languages. Strengths especially in all aspects of engineering for Asian languages, audio files, high quality only. Languages often needed: Scandinavian, European, Japanese, Korean, simplified and traditional Chinese. Subject matter mostly: medical devices, all aspects of defense contracts, IT. Types of material: marketing, technical, software, and legal materials to support the product.

ABC Worldwide Translations & Interpretations, 8306 Wilshire Boulevard, Suite 200, Beverly Hills, CA 90211
Phone: (310) 260-7700 Fax: (310) 260-7705
E-mail: info@wordexpress.net Website: www.wordexpress.net
Contact: Muriel Redoute / Member: ATA

ABS Translation & Interpreting Service, 1685 Hampton Road, Abington, PA 19001
Phone: (215) 886-2219 Fax: (215) 886-7671
E-mail: ABStrans@aol.com
Contact: Aram Sarkisian / Member: ATA

Academy of Languages Translation & Interpretation Services, 216 1st Avenue South, Suite 330, Seattle, WA 98104
Phone: (206) 521-8601 Fax: (206) 521-8605
E-mail: translate@aolti.com Website: www.aolti.com
Contact: Olivier Fabris / Member: ATA

Accent on Languages, 2418 5th Street, Suite B, Berkeley, CA 94710
Phone: (510) 644-9470 Fax: (510) 644-9590
E-mail: services@accentonlanguages.com Website: www.accentonlanguages.com
Contact: Francine Kuipers, Treasurer / Member: ATA

Access Interpreters LLC, 4094 Pathfield Drive, Columbus, OH 43230
Phone: (614) 402-0258 Fax: (609) 939-1187
E-mail: accessint05@yahoo.com
Contact: Yana Schottenstein, General Manager / Member: ATA

AccessOnTime, 3210 Lake Emma Road, Suite 3090, Lake Mary, FL 32746
Phone: (888) 748-7575 Fax: (407) 330-7959

E-mail: blima@accessontime.com Website: www.accessontime.com
Contact: Anabela Lima, Human Resources Director

Accu Trans Inc., 4517 Minnetonka Boulevard, Suite 200, Minneapolis, MN 55416
Phone: (952) 927-7277 Fax (952) 925-4772
E-mail: nadia@accutransinc.biz Website: www.proz.com/pro/51070
Contact: Nadia Oparista / Member: ATA

Accurapid Translation Services Inc., 806 Main Street, Poughkeepsie, NY 12603
Phone: (845) 473-4550 Fax: (845) 473-4554
E-mail: mail@accurapid.com Website: www.accurapid.com
Contact: Gabe Bokor, President
   Founded 1978. Member: ATA. Translates German, Spanish, French, Hungarian, Portuguese, Russian, Chinese, and Japanese both from and into English. Emphasis on engineering, patents, law, business, and finance translation. Prospective translators should demonstrate competence and a professional attitude. Resumes are filed for future reference. The company pioneered the use of technological tools in the industry. The company maintains a pool of over six hundred professional freelance translators from Europe, Asia, and the Americas.

Accuworld LLC, 200 West Madison Street, Suite 930, Chicago, IL 60606
Phone: (312) 641-0441 Fax: (312) 641-7370
E-mail: accuworld@accuworld.com
Contact: Human Resources Department
   Founded 1968. Member: ATA. Translates all languages, both from and into English. Covers all areas, with specialties in foreign-language voice-overs, health care, pharmaceuticals, insurance, and technical manual translation. Resumes are compiled in a database according to area of expertise. The company, headquartered in Hartford, Connecticut, has over three hundred worldwide locations. It provides language training, cultural training, translation/interpretation services, and foreign-language typesetting and voice-overs. Maintains a pool of 800+ translators.

ADA Inc., 2401 Shannon Place SE, Washington, DC 20020
Phone: (202) 889-0123 Fax: (202) 678-2770
E-mail: lguzman@adainc.net Website: www.adainc.net
Contact: Leonid Guzman, Project Director / Member: ATA

Adams Globalization, 10435 Burnet Road, Suite 125, Austin, TX 78758
Phone: (512) 821-1818 Fax: (512) 821-1888
E-mail: HR@adamsglobalization.com Website: www.adamsglobalization.com
Contact: Allan W. Adams, President; Mark Brown, Sales / Member: ATA

Advanced Communication and Translation Inc. (ACT), 4332 Montgomery
Avenue, Suite A, Bethesda, MD 20814
Tel: (301) 654-2890 Fax: (301) 654-2891
E-mail: act@act-translate.com Website: www.act-translate.com
Contact: Monique-Paule Tubb / Member: ATA

Advanced Language Translation Inc., 25 North Washington Street, Rochester,
NY 14614
Toll Free: (800) 218-9024 Phone: (585) 697-0462 ext. 18 Fax: (585) 697-0467
E-mail: info@advancedlanguage.com Website: www.advancedlanguage.com
Contact: Scott Bass, President / Member: ATA

AE Inc.—Translations, 15995 North Barkers Landing, Suite 111, Houston, TX
77079
Phone: (281) 870-0677 Fax: (281) 556-9737
E-mail: translations@aetrans.com Website: www.aetrans.com
Contact: Stephen D. Ross / Member: ATA

Affinity Language Services, 101 South Fairview Avenue, Wind Gap, PA 18091
Phone: (610) 863-3955
E-mail: info@affinitylanguages.com Website: www.affinitylanguages.com
Contact: Michelle Zuccarini
  Founded 1998. Member: ATA. Works in Spanish, German, French, Italian,
and Dutch. Also in Japanese. Main areas: technical, sci-tech, legal, medical, and
business. Also provides interpretation, editing, proofreading, transcription, and
copywriting. Uses translators worldwide.

Affordable Business Services Inc., 490 Broadway, Suite 5, Somerville, MA 02145
Phone: (617) 776-7353 Fax: (617) 628-5267
Contact: Pierre P. Joas, Assistant Vice President / Member: ATA

Agencia Internacional, 599 Central Street, Lowell, MA 01852
Phone: (978) 452-2934 Fax: (978) 441-0346
Contact: Manuel Melo, Owner / Member: ATA

Agnew Tech-II, 741 Lakefield Road, Suite C, Westlake Village, CA 91361
Phone: (805) 494-3999 Fax: (805) 494-1749
Contact: Irene Agnew
  Founded 1986. Member: ATA, NAWBO, WBENC, WITI. Translates Spanish,
Chinese, French, German, Japanese, Russian, Vietnamese, and more from
English. Also does scripts and voice-overs. Covers all technical areas. Prospective
translators should have a B.A. degree or higher and two to three years experience.
Resumes received via e-mail are reviewed, graded, and scheduled for a translation

test. The company is a full-service translation bureau, as well as providing desktop publishing, web page design, multimedia, and audiovisual services. Maintains a pool of three hundred to four hundred translators.

aiaTranslations—a division of Atkins International Associates Inc., 54 Old Highway 22, Suite 302, Clinton, NJ 08809
Phone: (908) 735-8577 Fax: (908) 735-2277
Toll Free: 1-888-ATKINS-1
Websites: www.aiaTranslations.com or www.atkinsinternational.com
E-mail: molly.naughton@atkinsinternational.com
Contact: Molly Naughton, MBA, Vice President, Translations
Founded 1995. Member ATA. Agency focuses on health care and pharmaceutical-related translations in all languages. Requires translators with medical and marketing expertise. Freelancers are asked to complete online form at www.atkins international.com/workwithus.asp in lieu of sending resume.

Alamex Translation Services LLC, 301 Randolph Avenue, Suite 200, Huntsville, AL 35801
Phone: (256) 532-4050 Fax: (256) 536-1834
E-mail: alamex@alamexllc.com Website: www.alamexllc.com
Contact: Patrick Castle / Member: ATA

Alanguage Bank Inc., 159 West 25th Street, 6th Floor, New York, NY 10001
Phone: (212) 213-3336 Fax: (212) 343-2940
E-mail: info@alanguagebank.com Website: www.alanguagebank.com
Contact: Pei Wen Shih / Member: ATA

Albors and Associates Inc., PO Box 5516 Winter Park, FL 32793
Phone: (800) 785-8634 Fax: (407) 657-7004
E-mail: rene@albors.com Website: www.albors.com
Contact: René A. Albors, President
Founded 1996. Member: ATA, NAJIT, Hispanic Chamber of Commerce, Orlando Chamber of Commerce. Translates Spanish, French, Portuguese, Japanese, German, Chinese, Russian, Polish, Arabic, and Italian, both from and into English. Emphasis on legal, medical, and business translations. Prospective translators should be experienced, expert with terminology, and prompt in their delivery of finished work. Accepts unsolicited resumes for translation and interpretation. Resumes are computer filed, and a letter of thanks is sent to acknowledge receipt. Maintains a pool of 5,300 translators.

ALC Inc./AllWorld Language Consultants Inc., 172 Rollins Avenue, Rockville, MD 20852
Phone: (301) 881-8884 Fax: (301) 881-6877

Website: www.ALCINC.com
Contact: Carlos A. Scandiffio / Member: ATA

Alexandria Translations, 8827 Fort Hunt Road, Alexandria, VA 22308
Phone: (703) 799-7606 Fax: (703) 799-7607
E-mail: info@alexandriatranslations.com Website: www.alexandriatranslations
.com
Contact: Lidia Terziotti / Member: ATA
Translates and edits documents in a variety of languages.

All Global Solutions International, PO Box 3634, Lantana, FL 33465
Phone: (561) 889-6488 Fax: (530) 658-4882
E-mail: alexm@allgsi.com Website: www.allgsi.com
Contact: Alexandre Monot, Founder and President / Member: ATA

All Language Translations, 2214 Garden Drive, Niskayuna, NY 12309
Phone: (518) 857-2848 Fax: (518) 372-6804
E-mail: cezary@ix.netcom.com
Contact: Cezary Drzymalski / Member: ATA

Allen Translation Service, PO Box 1529, Morristown, NJ 07962
Phone: (973) 292-2737 Fax: (973) 292-3954
Contact: Kevin Hudson / Member: ATA

Allslavic Translation Services, 4930 NW 84th Avenue, Fort Lauderdale, FL 33351
Phone: (800) 775-5504 Fax: (954) 741-3898
E-mail: info@slavprom.com Website: www.allslavictranslations.com
Contact: Stanka Moskov / Member: ATA

Alpha Tech Communications, 4440 Chastant Street, Suite E, Metairie, LA 70002
Phone: (504) 454-6554 Fax: (504) 454-6717
E-mail: alphaTC@aol.com
Website: www.alphatechtranslations.com or www.ustranslations.com
Contact: Claudia Adamcewicz, Director of Sales and International Language Services
    Founded 1998. Member: ATA. Alpha Tech Communications translates
many languages including English into Spanish, French, German, Portuguese,
Chinese, and Arabic. Along with translating English into these languages, they
translate them back into their respective language. They also translate Italian-
English, Japanese-English, Greek-English, Russian-English, and so forth. Their
main subjects of translation are medical handbooks and legal documents.
They deal with a wide variety of documents, from journal articles to technical
documents. They do accept resumes and they do use freelance. The resumes are
reviewed, evaluated, classified, and kept in their data files to contact freelancers

when necessary. They require you to have a good command of the language pair(s) you work with. Experience, commitment, and responsibility are requirements. Computer programs and Internet tool skills are a plus. They have one in-house translator and about twenty freelancers. They also offer interpreting equipment rental/sales, video narration, transcription, proofreading/editing, and ESL training.

ALTA Language Services, 3355 Lennox Road NE, Suite 510, Atlanta, GA 30326
Phone: (404) 920-3838 Fax: (404) 920-3839
E-mail: translations@altalang.com
Contact: Robert Jones
   Founded 1982. Member: ATA, AAIT. Uses freelance translators and interpreters. Accepts unsolicited resumes. Resumes are filed by language. Requires outstanding translation skills. Main languages (both ways) are Spanish, German, French, Japanese, Portuguese, Dutch, Italian, Chinese, Korean, and Russian. Main subjects are legal, medical, and general. Does multilingual typesetting in addition to translation and interpretation. Engages around three hundred translators.

ALTCO Translations, 1426 Ridgeview Road, Columbus, OH 43221
Phone: (614) 486-2014 Fax: (614) 559-6682
E-mail: trudypeters@sbcglobal.net
Contact: Trudy E. Peters, Owner
   Founded 1982. Member: ATA. Uses freelancers for translation and interpretation. Only experienced translators' applications accepted. Main languages: all European languages. Main subjects are patents, business, IT, manuals, brochures, advertising, and medical/pharmaceutical.

Alticor Inc., Corporate Communication, 77-2X, 7575 East Fulton Road SE, Ada, MI 49355
Phone: (616) 787-7372 Fax: (616) 787-7956
Contact: Tieu O'Brien / Member: ATA

Always Ready Translation Services, 11026 Ventura Boulevard, Room 10, Studio City, CA 91604
Phone: (800) 240-6601 Fax: (818) 755-8959
E-mail: language@worldnet.att.net
Contact: Dan Prescott, President
   Founded 1985. Accepts resumes. Translates Spanish, Asian languages, Russian, Armenian, and other European languages.

American Bureau of Professional Translators (ABPT), 8989 Westheimer Road, Suite 116, Houston, TX 77063

Phone: (713) 789-2500 Fax: (713) 789-8920
E-mail: chetna@abpt.com or abpt@abpt.com Website: www.abpt.com
Contact: Ms. Chetna Patel, General Manager / Member: AATIA, ALC, ATA, BBB, HITA, NCTA

American Education Research Corporation, PO Box 996, West Covina, CA 91793
Phone: (626) 339-4404 Fax: (626) 339-9081
E-mail: aerc@verizon.net Website: www.aerc-eval.com
Contact: Martha Alvarez / Member: ATA

American ESL Inc., 89 North Main Street, Randolph, MA 02368
Phone: (781) 963-1114 Fax: (781) 963-1171
E-mail: w.wisetrans@verizon.net Website: www.a-esl.com
Contact: Kenneth Paquette, President / Member: ATA

American Evaluation and Translation Service Inc., 407 Lincoln Road, Suite 11–J, Miami Beach, FL 33139
Phone: (786) 276-8190 Fax: (786) 524-0448
E-mail: info@aetsinternational.com Website: www.aetsinternational.com
Member: ATA

American International Business and Associates Inc., 4693 West Flager Street, Miami, FL 33134
E-mail: abc1021@aol.com
Contact: Rita Benet, Vice President / Member: ATA

American Language Technologies Inc., 3941 Legacy Drive, #204, PMB 199A, Plano, TX 75023
Phone: (972) 517-2700 Fax: (469) 429-0020
E-mail: jay@americanLT.com Website: www.americanLT.com
Contact: Jay Forte, CEO / Member: ATA
Based out of Dallas, Texas, but servicing nationally, American Language Technologies Inc. is a full service translation and interpreting company providing translations, interpreting, and voice talent in ninety-five different languages. Work focuses on but is not limited to the human resources departments (especially operations, ethics, and HR manuals), marketing, and legal departments. They also provide transcription services. Their main client is the U.S. federal government, and they continually search for DEA and DHS cleared monitors for T3 lines.

American Translation Partners Inc., 175 Paramount Drive, Raynham, MA 02767
Phone: (617) 350-9988 Fax: (508) 823-8854
E-mail: info@americantranslationpartners.com

Website: www.americantranslationpartners.com
Contact: Scott Crystal
Founded 1998. Member: ATA, NAJIT, NETA, MMIA, LPDAM, FIT, TTI, LISA, AIIC. Accepts resumes. Requires language proficiency and experience as well as computer proficiency. Translates Spanish, Portuguese, French, German, Italian, Japanese, Chinese, Korean, Vietnamese, Haitian Creole, Afrikaans, and all Indian dialects. Works in government, legal, medical, insurance, technical, financial, and software subjects in more than two hundred language pairs. Has 1,500 translators in New England and 3,500 worldwide.

Americlic LLC, 200 Eagle Road, Suite 106, Wayne, PA 19087
Phone: (877) 254-2587 Fax: (484) 654-1041
E-mail: kmaynard@americlic.com
Contact: Karin Maynard, VP Operations / Member: ATA

APS International Ltd., 7800 Glenroy Road, Minneapolis, MN 55439
Phone: (952) 831-7776 Fax: (952) 831-8150
E-mail: trans@civilactiongroup.com
Contact: Ann Mickow / Member: ATA

Arabic Dialects, 8117 South Lemont Road, #1, Darien, IL 60561
Phone: (773) 406-1234 Fax: (630) 427-1224
E-mail: ashraf@egypttours.com Website: www.arabic-interpreter.com
Contact: Ashraf Michael, President / Member: ATA

ArchiText, a division of Translations.com, 23 Main Street, 3rd Floor, Andover, MA 01810
Phone: (978) 409-6112 ext. 116 Fax: (978) 409-6096
E-mail: jdoyle@architext-usa.com Website: www.architext-usa.com
Contact: John J. Doyle

Argo Translation Inc., 2420 Ravine Way, Suite 200, Glenview, IL 60025
Phone: (847) 901-4070 Fax: (847) 901-4075
E-mail: sales@argotrans.com Website: www.argotrans.com
Contact: Jacqueline LaCarelli
Founded 1995. Member: ATA. Uses freelance translators and interpreters. Accepts unsolicited resumes. Works in all languages and subjects, viz., medical, technical, legal, commercial. Always on the lookout for professional translators. Has 575 translators.

Around the World Inc., 23612 West 52nd Street, Shawnee, KS 66226
Phone: (913) 422-1030 Fax: (913) 422-1032
E-mail: atwtranslation@sbcglobal.net Website: www.atwtranslation.com
Contact: Gary West

Founded 1998. Member: ATA, BBB. Translates all languages, mainly technical, advertising, business, and legal. Translates and typesets for private and business sectors. Utilizes over 5,000 translators.

Arthur International Inc., 900 IDS Center, 80 South 8th Street, Minneapolis, MN 55402
Phone: (952) 474-3300
E-mail: sales.usa@arthurint.com Website: www.arthurint.com
Contact: Pierre deShasta / Member: ATA

Artra International Corporation, 1 East Broward Boulevard, Suite 700, Fort Lauderdale, FL 33301
Phone: (877) 517-7727 Fax: (877) 517-8568
E-mail: mail@ARTRAinternational.com Website: www.artrainternational.com
Contact: Natalie Zlochevsky / Member: ATA

ASET International Services Corporation, 2009 North 14th Street, Suite 214, Arlington, VA 22201
Phone: (703) 516-9266 Fax: (703) 516-9269
E-mail: khendzel@asetquality.com Website: www.asetquality.com
Contact: Kevin S. Hendzel, Director of Language Services
Founded 1987. Member: ATA. Translates in over one hundred languages, both from and into English. Emphasis on equipment manuals, pharmaceuticals and medical equipment, software localization, nuclear, chemical, industrial and structural engineering, law and legislation, regulations and codes, education, and consumer goods translation. Prospective translators are required to have ten years professional translating experience and formal technical training in a specialty area. Resumes are archived in a database and assignments given when an appropriate match arises. Resumes must be faxed or submitted by e-mail. The company also works with engineering drawings and specifications and possesses full AutoCad and full-color printing capabilities. They provide interpreting services and are an authorized master distributor for the Bosche interpreting equipment series. The company also handles rentals, sales, and repair of Bosche interpreting equipment as well as customized installations of interpreting equipment. ASET also has a full-scale in-house audio/video production studio and extensive expertise in complete localization of software, courseware, and web materials, including computer-based training. In-house staff of 83. Welcomes voice-over talent. Maintains a pool of 2,000+ translators, interpreters, testers, and voice talent.

Asian Link Corporation, 1108 West Valley Boulevard, Suite 4, Alhambra, CA 91803
Phone: (626) 300-9191 Fax: (626) 300-8955
E-mail: sophia@asialink.com
Contact: Sophia N. Yang / Member: ATA

Asian Pacific Development Center-Interpreters Bank, 1544 Elmira Street,
Aurora, CO 80010
Phone: (303) 365-2959 Fax: (303) 344-4599
E-mail: interpretersbank@apdc.org Website: www.apdc.org
Contact: Eed Cefkin / Member: ATA

Asian Translation Service, 392 North 1410 East, Lehi, Utah 84043
Phone: (801) 565-8281 Fax: (801) 365-6560
E-mail: ats@asiantranslation.com Website: www.asiantranslation.com
Contact: Steve Stevens
　　Founded 1992. Member: ATA. Translates English into Hmong, Vietnamese,
Cambodian, Thai, Korean, Japanese, Chinese, Tagalog, Malay, and Indonesian,
mainly health related, business, personal documents, and product catalogs.
Provides full range of translation and interpretation. Uses about thirty translators.

ASIST Translation Services, 4663 Executive Drive, Suite 11, Columbus, OH 43220
Phone: (614) 451-6744 Fax: (614) 451-1349
E-mail: asist@asisttranslations.com
Contact: Elena Tsinman, President
　　Founded 1983. Member: ATA. Uses freelance translators and interpreters.
Accepts unsolicited resumes. All resumes are entered in a database. If quali-
fied, translator is contacted immediately. Applicant must be experienced, native
speaker, and have a university degree. Main languages are English into French,
Spanish, Chinese, Japanese, Russian, Arabic, German, Somali, Portuguese, and
Italian. Additional languages are Dutch, Swedish, and Danish. Does two to three
million words a year. Also does typesetting, website translation, software translation, localization, audio-visual productions, and desktop publishing. Maintains
pool of 2,000 translators.

Atlantic International Translators Inc., 4956 Vermack Road, Atlanta, GA 30338
Phone: (770) 350-9050 Fax: (770) 350-9051
E-mail: atlanticit@aol.com Website: www.atlanticitinc.com
Contact: Rogelio Cipriano / Member: ATA

Atlas Language Services Inc., 8700 West Bryn Mawr Avenue, Suite 800-South,
Chicago, IL 60631
Phone: (888) 816-0577 Fax: (866) 816-0578
E-mail: kevin@atlasls.com Website: www.atlasls.com
Contact: Kevin J. McQuire / Member: ATA

Atlas Translation Services, 805 North Central Avenue, Suite 200, Glendale, CA
91203
Phone: (818) 242-2400 Fax: (818) 242-2475

E-mail: translations@atlaspvs.com
Contact: Sorina Kalili
Founded 1993. Uses freelancers for translation. Accepts unsolicited resumes. Main languages (both ways) are Farsi, German, Spanish, French, Arabic, Chinese, and Japanese. Main subjects are legal, business, and scripts. Also does legal interpretation.

ATS—Acclaim Technical Services, 101 Main Street, Suite 400, Huntington Beach, CA 92648
Phone: (714) 596-8704 Fax: (714) 596-8734
E-mail: info@acclaimtechnical.com Website: www.acclaimtechnical.com

Audio to Go Inc., 42 West 89th Street, Apt. E, New York, NY 10024
Phone: (212) 721-1183 Fax: (212) 721-1273
E-mail: info@a2g.com Website: www.a2g.com
Contact: Gayle Goldfarb
Founded 1991. Member: NYCT. Accepts resumes. Requires certification, experience, native speakers in target language. Translates all languages. Translates audio and video programs with narrators in their native language.

Auerbach International Inc./dba Translations Express, 64 Mercedes Way, San Francisco, CA 94127
Phone: (415) 592-0042 Fax: (415) 592-0043
E-mail: translations@auerbach-intl.com Website: www.auerbach-intl.com
Contact: Philip Auerbach / Member: ATA

Auracom International Inc., 996 South Main Street, Suite 2A, Main Floor, Stowe, VT 05672
Phone: (802) 253-8911 Fax: (802) 253-7322
E-mail: info@auratrans.com Website: www.auratrans.com
Contact: Matt Lulofs / Member: ATA

Avantext, 2991 Shattuck Avenue, Suite 200, Berkeley, CA 94705
Phone: (510) 644-3490 Fax: (510) 644-3492
E-mail: info@avantext-usa.com Website: www.avantext-usa.com

Avantgarde Translations, 525 Sedgewood Lake Drive, Charlotte, NC 28211
Phone: (704) 362-3757 Fax: (704) 362-3937
Website: www.avantgardetranslations.com
Contact: Memuna Williams / Member: ATA

Avantpage, 1138 Villaverde Lane, Davis, CA 95618
Phone: (530) 750-2040 Fax: (530) 750-2024

E-mail: luis@avantpage.com Website: www.avantpage.com
Contact: Luis Miguel, CEO
    Founded 1996. Member: ATA, ALC. Accepts resumes. Requires three years experience, certification/accreditation where available. Translates English into Spanish, Japanese, Chinese (simplified and traditional), Korean, French, German, Vietnamese, Arabic, Hebrew, Italian, and Portuguese. Also Farsi, Thai, Tagalog, and more. Main areas are health care, education, government, and marketing.

Avid Translation, 235 East 3rd Avenue, Suite 202 San Mateo, CA 94401
Business line: (650) 525-9896 Fax: (650) 525-9822 Client line: (800) 858-1146
Website: www.avidtrans.net

-B-

Babel Trans-Media Center, 1720 Ala Moana Boulevard, Tradewinds, Suite A5
    Honolulu, HI 96815
Phone: (808) 946-3773 Fax: (808) 946-3993
E-mail: tmc@babeltmc.com Website: www.babeltmc.com
Contact: Tomoki Hotta / Member: ATA

Babel Tower Inc., PO Box 491023, Fort Lauderdale, FL 33349
Phone: (954) 731-9180 Fax: (954) 731-1366
E-mail: babeltower@bellsouth.net Website: www.babeltowerinc.com
Contact: Sandra Fernandez
Founded 1996. Member: ATA. Translates all languages.

Back to Basics Learning Dynamics Inc., 6 Stone Hill Road, Wilmington, DE
    19803
Phone: (302) 594-0754 Fax: (302) 239-9589
E-mail: beverly@backtobasicslearning.com
Website: www.beverlystewart.com
Contact: Beverly Stewart, M.Ed., President/Director
    Founded 1985. Member: ATA. Winner of many local, regional, and national awards and recognition. Education and business consultant.

Barinas Translation Consultants Inc., 800 Hop Tree, San Antonio, TX 78260
Phone: (210) 545-0019 Fax: (210) 545-3735
E-mail: info@barinas.com Website: www.barinas.com
Contact: Sonia Barinas, President
    Founded 1980. Member: MPI, AAHA, TSHE, SATC, San Antonio Chamber of Commerce, GSHMA, ISMP, THMA. Uses freelance translators and interpreters. Accepts unsolicited resumes. Resumes are checked for quality and experience,

then filed by language and areas of expertise. Please submit sample with resume and indicate degree in translation and/or interpretation. Degree in law, medicine, or the like is a plus. Main language pairs are Spanish-English, French-English, French-Spanish, Portuguese-English, German-English, Chinese-English, Japanese-English. Main subjects are legal, medical, technical, and telecom. Specializes in simultaneous interpretation for meetings and conventions. Does about 350 projects a year. Uses hundreds of freelancers.

Baystate Interpreters Inc., 32 Pleasant Street, Gardner, MA 01440
Phone: (978) 632-1662 Fax: (978) 632-1772
E-mail: service@baystateinterpreters.com Website: www.baystateinterpreters.com
Contact: Darrin Brooks / Member: ATA

Beacon Worldwide, 30 South Wacker Drive, 22nd Floor, Chicago, IL 60606
Phone: (312) 466-5671 Fax: (312) 466-5601
E-mail: info@beacon-ww.com Website: www.beacon-ww.com

Berkeley Scientific Translation Service Inc., PO Box 150, Berkeley, CA 94701
Phone: (510) 548-4665 Fax: (510) 548-4666
E-mail: marlo@berksci.com Website: www.berksci.com
Contact: Dr. Marlo R. Martin
Founded 1974. Member: ATA. Translates Japanese, Korean, Chinese, and other major European and Asian languages, both from and into English. Emphasis on mechanical, automotive, chemical and chemical engineering, computers and software, electronics, biotechnology, pharmaceuticals, physics, and patent translations. Prospective translators should be able to produce authoritative translations into their native language within a specialized area. Resumes are screened for educational background and subject expertise as related to translation experience. The company was founded by a physicist and engineer and seeks translators with similar qualifications. Maintains a pool of seventy to one hundred translators.

Betmar Languages Inc., 6260 Highway 65 NE, Suite 308, Minneapolis, MN 55432
Phone: (763) 572-9711 Fax: (763) 571-3467
E-mail: best@betmar.com
Contact: Elizabeth A. Loo / Member: ATA

Better Communications, 3700 Wilshire Boulevard, #695, Los Angeles, CA 90010
Phone: (213) 387-1166 Fax: (213) 387-1163
E-mail: jean@bettercomm.com
Contact: Jinah Song, Office Manager / Member: ATA

Bilingual Professional Agency Inc., 1663 East 17th Street, Brooklyn, NY 11229
Phone: (718) 339-5800 Fax: (718) 339-8433
E-mail: translations@comprehensivenet.com Website: www.comprehensivenet.com
Contact: Leah Schlager / Member: ATA

BioMedical Translators, 3477 Kenneth Drive, Palo Alto, CA 94303
Phone: (650) 494-1317 Fax: (650) 494-1394
E-mail: biomed@biomedical.com
Contact: Monique Vazire
Founded 1992. Member: ATA, NCTA. Main languages translated are French, German, Italian, Spanish, Dutch, Swedish, Portuguese, Danish, Japanese, and Chinese. Emphasis is on medical and biological translation, including equipment, studies, and software. Prospective translators should possess at least one year of experience, have knowledge of the medical field, and have access to medical dictionaries. Their equipment should include a PC and modem or e-mail; software should include Word and WordPerfect. Resumes are reviewed by the recruiting department and responded to with a test translation, which is then evaluated. The company specializes exclusively in the medical field and its peripherals. Their services also include desktop publishing. Maintains a pool of 500+ translators.

Bizzy Box Translation Services, 16060 Ventura Boulevard, Suite 105, Encino, CA 91436
Phone: (818) 728-1288 Fax: (818) 728-1286
E-mail: mail@bizzy-box.com Website: www.bizzy-box.com
Contact: Nancy Afshar (Ponamarenko) / Member: ATA

Black Diamond Administrative Services, PO Box 23458, Fort Lauderdale, FL 33307-3458
Phone: (800) 685-4789 Fax: (866) 786-2276
E-mail: info@blackdiamond.org Website: www.blackdiamond.org
Contact: Maria Taiana / Member: ATA

Bloomberg L.P., 100 Business Park Drive, PO Box 888, Princeton, NJ 08542
Phone: (609) 279-4955 Contact: Elsa Shilling

Bowne Translation Services, 55 Water Street, New York, NY 10041
Phone: (212) 924-5500 Fax: (212) 229-3400

Bridge-Linguatec Language Services, 915 South Colorado Boulevard, Denver, CO 80246
Phone: (303) 777-7783 Fax: (303) 777-7246
E-mail: translations@bridgelinguatec.com Website: www.bridgelinguatec.com
Contact: Eric Clawson

Founded 1981. Translates mainly Spanish, French, German, Arabic, Dutch, Russian, and Portuguese. Emphasis on legal and medical. Prospective translators should, by preference, be native speakers. Resumes are filed by language and translators contacted by need. The company also provides ESL training for executives, foreign-language instruction, and interpretation services. Maintains a pool of 150 to 200 translators.

Bromberg & Associates, 3320 Caniff Street, Hamtramck, MI 48212
Phone: (313) 871-0080 Fax: (888) 225-1912
E-mail: jinny@brombergtranslations.com Website: www.brombergtranslations.com
Contact: Jinny Bromberg / Member: ALC, NAJIT, NCIHC, MiTIN

Bruce International Inc., 4800 SW Griffith Drive, Suite 100, Beaverton, OR 97005
Phone: (503) 643-8448 Fax: (503) 643-7174
E-mail: info@bruceinternational.com Website: www.bruceinternational.com
Contact: Jenny Bruce / Member: ATA

Burg Translation Bureau Inc., 29 South LaSalle, Suite 936, Chicago, IL 60603
Phone: (312) 263-3379 Fax: (312) 263-4325
E-mail: burg@burgtranslations.com Website: www.burgtranslations.com
Contact: Lodovico Passalacqua, President
Founded 1936. Member: ATA. Emphasis on technical translation. Translators carefully screened. Strong project management and QC with ISO 9001:2000 certified by TÜV Rheinland. Translation and typesetting. Sixty language pairs translated using both in-house staff and external translation professionals having minimum five years experience.

-C-

Carmazzi of Florida Inc., d/b/a Adriana Schaked Translations, 8698 Elk Grove Boulevard, Suite 3, Elk Grove, CA 95624
Phone: (305) 933-9595
Founded 1998. Member: ATA, RID. Provides interpretation (including sign language and over-the-phone interpretation) and translation services to many legal, health-care, corporate, government, education, and insurance-related companies.

Carolina Polyglot Inc., PO Box 36334, Charlotte, NC 28236
Phone: (704) 366-5781 Fax: (704) 364-2998
E-mail: wdepaula@carolinapolyglot.com Website: www.carolinapolyglot.com
Contact: Dr. William DePaula
Founded 1971. Member: ATA, CATI. Accepts unsolicited resumes. Resumes are filed by language pair. E-mail and fax filed electronically. Requirements for

applicants include academic degree, previous experience, professional affiliation/ accreditation, and references. Main languages (both ways) are French, Spanish, Italian, Portuguese, Romanian, German, Dutch, Arabic, Chinese, Vietnamese, and Japanese. Also translates Turkish, Farsi, Afrikaans, Hindi, Danish, Norwegian, Swedish, and Finnish. Main subjects are immigration, education, law, business, medicine, insurance, theology, ecology, literature, and computers. Uses over thirty translators.

Cascades Technologies Inc., 505 Huntmar Park Drive, Herndon Plaza, Suite 225, Herndon, VA 20170
Phone: (703) 793-7222 Fax: (703) 935-0061
E-mail: info@cascadestech.com Website: www.cascadestech.com

Caterpillar Inc., Dealer Capability Dept., Corp Translation, 501 SW Jefferson Avenue, Peoria, IL 61630
Phone: (309) 494-5216
E-mail: opherk_jorg@CAT.com
Contact: Dr. Jorg Opherk / Member: ATA

CC Scientific Ltd., 73920 Mountain View Avenue, Palm Desert, CA 92260
Phone: (760) 341-7544 Fax: (760) 341-7514
E-mail: ccsltd@aol.com
Contact: Dr. Jaime R. Carlo-Casellas / Member: ATA

Certified Languages International, 4724 SW Macadam Avenue, Suite #100, Portland, OR 97239
Phone: (800) 362-3241 Fax: (800) 362-2941
E-mail: kristin@certifedlanguages.com Website: www.certifiedlanguages.com
Contact: Kristin Quinlan / Member: ALC, ATA, CHIA, MMIA, NCIHC, NOTIS

Certified Translation Services, 1 Harbison Way, Suite 105, Columbia, SC 29212
Phone: (803) 781-7017 Fax: (803) 781-5052
Website: www.certifiedtranslationservices.com
Contact: Ed Crosby / Member: ATA

CETRA Inc., 7804 Montgomery Avenue, Suite 8, Elkins Park, PA 19027
Phone: (215) 635-7090 Fax: (215) 635-6610
E-mail: info@cetra.com Website: www.cetra.com
Contact: Dr. Jiri Stejskal, President
Founded 1994. Member: ALC, ATA. All languages and subjects. CETRA does use freelance, and they do accept resumes. The resumes are reviewed and filed together with information provided by the vendor via online form. You may fill out a form at http://www.cetra.com/Translator/join.htm.

CG Translations, 4012 Forest Knoll Lane, Las Vegas, NV 89129
Phone: (702) 395-1229 Fax: (702) 395-7068
E-mail: greenylv@gmx.net
Contact: Christiane Greenberg / Member: ATA

China Communications Consultants, PO Box 163, Bloomfield, CT 06002
Phone: (860) 614-1428 Fax: (860) 519-1238
E-mail: fzhou@chinacommunicationsconsultants.com
Website: www.chinacommunicationsconsultants.com
Contact: Feng Zhou, Interpreter/Translator / Member: ATA

Choice Translating Inc., 121 West Trade Street, Suite 2650, Charlotte, NC 28202
Phone: (704) 717-0043 Fax: (704) 717-0046
E-mail: translating@choicetranslating.com
Website: www.choicetranslating.com
Contact: Translating Project Manager / Member: ATA

CinciLingua Inc., 322 East 4th Street, Cincinnati, OH 45202
Phone: (513) 721-8782 Fax: (513) 721-8819
E-mail: inquire@cincilingua.com Website: www.cincilingua.com
Contact: Michael Sum
Founded 1972. Member: ATA, ASME. Translates to/from more than twenty-five languages including Spanish, French, German, Chinese, Japanese, Korean, Russian, and Portuguese. Prospective translators should have a college degree, professional experience in a specific area (e.g., technical, medical, legal, business), and references. Must have competency in Microsoft Word and Excel and should know PowerPoint and translation memory tools. Resumes are reviewed by the project manager and databased. Qualified candidates may be asked to translate a short sample for additional information.

Cititran.com, 11077 Biscayne Boulevard, Suite 211, Miami, FL 33161
Phone: (305) 892-0181 Fax: call first
E-mail: info@cititran.com Website: www.cititran.com

Clark Translations, 620 Quail Court, Exeter, CA 93221
Phone: (800) 519-3369 Fax: (866) 639-4771
E-mail: info@clarktranslations.com Website: www.clarktranslations.com
Contact: Bianca Clark / Member: ATA

CLS Communication Inc., 1500 Harbor Boulevard, Weehawken, NJ 07086
Phone: (877) 425-7266 Fax: (201) 223-0674
E-mail: info-ny@cls-communication.com
Website: www.cls-communication.com

Columbia Language Services, 11818 SE Mill Plain Boulevard, #307, Vancouver, WA 98684
Phone: (360) 896-3881 Fax: (360) 896-4074
E-mail: mail@columbia-language.com Website: www.columbia-language.com
Contact: Svetlana Linchuk / Member: ATA

CommGap International Language Services, 7069 South Highland Drive, Suite 201, Salt Lake City, Utah 84121
Phone: (801) 944-4049 Fax: (801) 944-4046
E-mail: info@commgap.com Website: www.commgap.com
Contact: Lelani P. Craig / Member: ATA, ALC, IMIA, NAJIT

Communicaid Inc., 1550 The Alameda, #155, San Jose, CA 95126
Phone: (408) 287-8853 Fax: (408) 516-5266
E-mail: info@communicaidinc.com Website: www.communicaidinc.com
Contact: Paula Madden / Member: ATA

Community Interpreter Services, Catholic Charities, 75 Kneeland Street, 8th Floor, Boston, MA 02111
Phone: (617) 350-4811 Fax: (617) 629-5768
E-mail: cis_request@ccab.com Website: www.cccis.org
Contact: Inna P. Gimelberg, Program Manager
Founded 1986. Member: ATA, MMIA, NETA. Accepts resumes for rare languages only for now. Translates Haitian Creole, Spanish, Cape Verdean Creole, Vietnamese, Russian, Portuguese, Cantonese/Mandarin Chinese, Vietnamese, Polish, Farsi, Bosnian, and Albanian. Also Somali, Swahili, Italian, French, Arabic, Khmer, and Laotian. They translate to/from a total of fifty languages. Emphasis on personal document translation. Prospective translators and interpreters should live in Massachusetts or a bordering state and possess at least a bachelor's degree, past translating experience, and fluency in at least two languages. Qualified resumes are responded to with an interview appointment. They are a nonprofit service operated by Catholic Charities. Maintains a pool of two hundred translators and interpreters.

ComNet International, 501-I South Reino Road, #358, Newbury Park, CA 91320
Phone: (818) 991-1277 Fax: (805) 498-9955
E-mail: agel@comnetint.com Website: www.translationstogo.com
Contact: Dr. Elias Agel
Founded 1989. Member: ATA. Translates all languages, in all subjects. Prospective translators should have extensive experience and should provide references. Resumes are reviewed and entered into a database. The company also provides desktop publishing, art production, and printing services. It also does voice-overs and dubbing. Specialties include Middle East consulting services,

electronic update filing, and interagency network cooperation. Maintains a pool of six hundred translators.

Compass Languages, 1666 Crofton Parkway, Crofton, MD 21114
Phone: (410) 451-4297 Fax: (410) 451-4298
E-mail: leo@compasslanguages.com Website: www.compasslanguages.com
Contact: Leo Brenninkmeyer
Founded 2001. Member: ATA. Uses freelance translators and accepts unsolicited resumes. Uses SMEs (subject matter experts) to match the project content with the translator. Specialists in legal, manufacturing, marketing, and telecom. All major languages. Has active pool of 250 translators.

Comprehensive Language Center, 2200 Wilson Boulevard, Suite 500, Arlington, VA 22201
Phone: (703) 247-0700 Fax: (703) 247-4292
Website: http://www.comlang.com
Contact: Carol Baran
Company founded 1980 as CACI. Member: ATA. Uses freelance translators and interpreters. Accepts unsolicited resumes, but not unsolicited phone calls. Qualified applicants are sent a database form which is processed and are called upon when needed in their area of expertise. Requirements include college degree, two years professional experience as a linguist, or appropriate certification/specialized degree. Over one hundred languages. Main areas are technical, legal, promotional, and business. Company also does training, transcription, software and web page localization, and video narration.

COMSYS, Global Enterprise Content Management, 1001 Fannin Street, Suite 600, Houston, TX 77002
Phone: (713) 386-1400
Website: gecm.comsys.com
Contact: Norman Newton Jr.
COMSYS was founded in 1973. Member: ATA, LISA, GALA, and STC. Full-service provider of globalization and localization services. Uses freelance translators and accepts unsolicited resumes. Translates in over one hundred languages with the vast majority of translation occurring in forty languages, which include German, Spanish, Italian, Japanese, Portuguese, Dutch, Russian, Chinese, and Swedish. Main industry sectors served include but are not limited to pharmaceutical, chemical, medical, engineering, oil and gas exploration and service, information technology, and electronics. Has active pool of two hundred translators throughout the world.

Comunicad Inc., 2818 North 72nd Court, Apt. 1, Elmwood Park, IL 60707
Phone: (708) 452-0288 Fax: (708) 575-0413
Contact: Megdalena Carreno Meza / Member: ATA

Connecting Cultures Inc., PO Box 262, Little Chute, WI 54140
Phone: (920) 687-0407 Fax: (920) 687-0371
info@connecting-cultures.com or rashelle@connecting-cultures.com
Contact: Rashelle Ludes LeCaptain, President / Member: ATA

Continental Book Company, 625 East 70th Avenue, #5, Denver, CO 80229
Phone: (303) 289-1761 Fax: (303) 289-1764
E-mail: cbc@continentalbook.com Website: www.continentalbook.com
Contact: Karen A. Manville / Member: ATA

Continental Communications Agency, 5105 East Los Angeles Avenue, #145,
Simi Valley, CA 93063
Phone: (805) 527-4446 Fax: (805) 527-4460
E-mail: cca1@roadrunner.com
Contact: Peter Charbonneau

Continental Interpreting Services Inc., 3111 North Tustin Avenue, Suite 235,
Orange, CA 92865
Phone: (800) 201-7121 Fax: (714) 283-9045
E-mail: veronica@wespeakyourlanguage.com
Website: www.wespeakyourlanguage.com
Contact: Veronica Amador / Member: ATA

Continental Language Services & Educational Consultants, 6600 Boulevard E,
Suite 12F, West New York, NJ 07093
Phone: (201) 861-2973 Fax: (201) 861-8617
E-mail: juan@continentallanguages.com Website: www.continentallanguages.com
Contact: Juan Jimenez, Director / Member: ATA

Conversa Language Center, 817 Main Street, 6th Floor, Cincinnati, Ohio 45202
Phone: (513) 651-5679 Fax: (513) 665-3792
E-mail: mail@conversatrans.com Website: www.conversatrans.com
Contact: Gerry Thiemann
   Founded 1989. Member: ATA. Uses in-house and freelance translators and
accepts unsolicited resumes. Translates mainly French, German, Spanish, Italian,
Japanese, Portuguese, Dutch, Russian, Chinese, Japanese, and Swedish. Main areas
are pharmaceutical, legal, commercial, chemical, medical, engineering, and elec-
tronics. Accepts unsolicited resumes. Has active pool of two hundred translators.

Cosmopolitan Translation Bureau, 53 West Jackson Boulevard, Suite 1260,
Chicago, IL 60604
Phone: (312) 726-2610 Fax: (312) 427-8591
Contact: Emanuel H. Steen / Member: ATA

Coto Interpreting, Translating & Graphics, 500 North Brand Boulevard, Suite 1700, Glendale, CA 91203
Phone: (818) 551-4545 Fax: (818) 551-1123
Website: www.languageline.com
Contact: Language Line Service located in Monterey, California / Member: ATA

Counterpoint Language Consultants Inc., PO Box 6184, Bridgewater, NJ 08807
Phone: (908) 231-0991 Fax: (908) 231-8266
E-mail: ctpt@ctpt.net Website: www.ctpt.net
Contact: Yellane Morize
Founded 1979. Member: ATA. Company uses freelance translators and interpreters. Accepts unsolicited resumes. Main languages (both ways) are French, German, Spanish, Chinese, Japanese, Portuguese, Italian, Russian, Greek, and Hindi. Also Thai, Gujarati, and Slovak. Main areas are pharmaceuticals, telecom, and legal. Provides worldwide language training.

C. P. Gauger Company Inc., 11300 West Theodore Trecker Way, West Allis, WI 53214
Phone: (414) 732-2000 Fax: (414) 732-2010
E-mail: margiet@cpgauger.com Website: www.cpgcanhelp.com
Contact: Margie Thoennes, Translation Services Manager / Member: ATA

C. P. Language Institute, 225 West 57th Street, Suite 404, New York, NY 10019
Phone: (212) 246-2054 Fax: (212) 247-2258
E-mail: info@cpli.com Website: www.cpli.com
Contact: Yuki Saito
Founded 1980. Member: ATA. Translates Chinese, Japanese, Korean, Spanish, Arabic, Russian, French, German, Hebrew, Hindi, Urdu, Vietnamese, Italian, Portuguese, Thai, Khmer, Tagalog, and Indonesian, both from and into English. Emphasis on advertising, technical, patent, financial, medical, legal, personal document, and textbook translation. Prospective translators should show proficiency in English and the target language and should be experienced. Resumes are responded to with a call-in or an e-mailed test translation in order to assess the candidate's ability. The company has two departments—programs and services. Programs is a language school providing small group and private language instruction. Services comprise translation, typesetting, formatting, interpretation, voice-overs, and subtitling. Maintains a pool of three hundred translators.

Cross Cultural Communications Systems Inc., PO Box 2308, Woburn, MA 01888
Phone: (781) 729-3736 ext. 110 Fax: (781) 729-1217
E-mail: vphillips@cccsorg.com
Contact: Vonessa Phillips / Member: ATA

Crossword Translation & Interpreting, 1530 Avenue C, Katy, TX 77493
Phone: (281) 391-3534 Fax: (281) 391-7043
E-mail: language@crosswordtranslation.com
Contact: Office Staff
    Founded 1997. Member: ATA. Accepts resumes. Translates and interprets most languages in all fields. Uses many translators and interpreters.

Cybertec USA Inc., 227 Dermody Street, Roselle, NJ 07203-2318
Phone: (908) 245-3305 Fax: (908) 245-5434
E-mail: mail@cybertecusa.com Website: www.cybertecusa.com
Contact: Joseph Nunes
    Technical Translation Bureau founded in 1990. Member: ATA, NYCT. Uses in-house and freelance professional translators. Accepts unsolicited resumes. Resumes are filed by language and specialty. Translators are required to be experienced, professional translators, preferably with language or other diploma and accreditation/certification. Translates mainly Portuguese (Euro, African, and Brazilian) and Western European and American languages. Specializes in technical and commercial subjects, including many industries, petroleum, medical devices, immunology, and biotech. Does over four million words per year. Over one hundred translators in company's pool. Offices in the United States and Portugal.

CyraCom International Inc., 7330 North Oracle Road, Tucson, AZ 85704
Phone: (520) 745-9447 Fax: (520) 745-9022
Website: www.cyracom.com
Contact: Paul Burns
    Founded 1997. Member: ATA. Provides telephonic interpretation services on demand twenty-four hours a day, seven days a week in about 150 languages. Has a secure system that provides rapid access to interpreters.

-D-

Detroit Translation Bureau, 30800 Telegraph Road, Suite 1930, Bingham Farms, MI 48025
Phone: (248) 593-6710 Fax: (248) 593-6720
E-mail: info@dtbonline.com Website: www.dtbonline.com
    Founded 1946. Member: ATA, LISA, SAW. Accepts resumes. Translates mainly Spanish (Mexico, Spain), Canadian French, German, Japanese, Italian, Norwegian, Dutch, Finnish, and Korean. Mainly automotive—technical, training, and marketing. Uses hundreds of translators.

DocuTrans Inc., 4712 South 2675 W, Roy, UT 84067
Phone: (801) 916-3924 Fax: (801) 776-4027
E-mail: translate@docutrans.com Website: www.docutrans.com
Contact: Gabriele H. Johnson / Member: ATA, BBB of Utah

DTS Language Services Inc., 7780 Brier Creek Parkway, Suite 335, Raleigh, NC 27617
Phone: (800) 524-0722 Fax: (919) 942-0686
E-mail: contact@dtstrans.com Website: www.dtstrans.com
Contact: Lucia Apollo Shaw
    Founded 1972. Member: ATA, DIA, STC. Accepts resumes only electronically. Requires five years minimum professional technical translation experience with related degree. Translates mainly Portuguese, French, Spanish, German, Italian, Czech, Vietnamese, Japanese, and Korean. Also Dutch, Finnish, Norwegian, Swedish. Mainly technical, medical, marketing, and patents.

Dynamic Language Center, 15215 52nd Avenue S, Suite 100, Seattle, WA 98188
Phone: (206) 244-6709 Fax: (206) 243-3795
E-mail: web@dynamiclanguage.com Website: www.dynamiclanguage.com

-E-

Echo International, Three Gateway Center, Floor 14 W, Pittsburgh, PA 15222
Phone: (412) 261-1101 Fax: (412) 261-1159
E-mail: ldutka@echointernational.com
Contact: Les Dutka, CEO

Eiber Translations Inc., 55 Northern Boulevard, Great Neck, NY 11021
Phone: (718) 463-2900 Fax: (718) 359-4073
E-mail: eibertrans@aol.com
Contact: Edna H. Eiber

eLocale Inc., PO Box 1806, Boulder, CO 80306
Phone: (877) 806-6060
E-mail: info@elocale.com Website: www.elocale.com

Eriksen Translations Inc., 32 Court Street, 20th Floor, Brooklyn, NY 11201
Phone: (718) 802-9010 Fax: (718) 802-0041
E-mail: info@erikseninc.com Website: www.erikseninc.com
Contact: Natasha Bonilla, Vendor Manager
    Founded 1986. Member: ASTD, ATA, GALA, NAJIT, NCIHC, NYCT, STC. Translates into and from all major languages. Emphasis on legal, financial,

advertising, education, pharmaceutical, and health care. Translators are encouraged to register on website. The company also provides typesetting services and website globalization. Maintains a pool of 6,000 translators.

Escalante Translations, 1930 Village Center Circle, #3-930, Las Vegas, Nevada
    89134
Phone: (888) 262-3468 (USA only) (702) 302-7676 Fax: (303) 388-2255
E-mail: info@escalante.com Website: www.escalante.com
Contact: Desiree Blum, Senior Vice President

Eurasia Translations Inc., 16530 Ventura Boulevard, Suite 206, Encino, CA 91436
Phone: (818) 907-9718 Fax: (818) 907-9763
E-mail: viola@eurasia-usa.com Website: www.eurasia-usa.com
Contact: Violetta Mordukhay
    Founded 1993. Member: ATA. Accepts resumes. Translates mainly Spanish, German, Hebrew, Russian, French, Arabic, Farsi, and Indonesian. Also Romanian, Slovak, Malay, Japanese, Polish, Czech, and Chinese. Mostly immigration, legal, and book publishing. Pool of over two hundred translators.

Eureka-Foreign College Evaluators & Translators, 6601-15 West Irving Park
    Road, Suite 204, Chicago, IL 60634
Phone: (773) 545-1700 Fax: (773) 545-1716
E-mail: eurekatranslator@aol.com Website: www.polishtranslations.com
Contact: Maria Beata Kapelski, Executive Director
    Founded 1992. Member: ATA, Translators and Interpreters Guild. Translates Polish, both from and into English, and German and Spanish into English. Emphasis on university admission documents, immigration and naturalization, labor department, business, technical, medical, and legal translation. Prospective translators should have an IBM-compatible PC, Word or WordPerfect, Windows, and a minimum of a bachelor's degree. Resumes are reviewed, and qualified persons contacted. The company specializes in credential evaluation and Polish-American consulting services for business cooperation, cultural, and marketing advisement and is currently looking for Polish translators and interpreters. Maintains a pool of ten translators.

Eurologos-San Jose (Costa Rica and California), 201 D Street, #8, San Rafael,
    CA 94901
Phone: (415) 259-6473 Fax: (415) 258-1607
E-mail: info@eurologos-sanjose.com Website: www.eurologos.com
Contact: Natalia Jimenez
    Founded 2003. Member: ATA. Offers translations in European, Asian, and Latin American languages with a special emphasis on English-to-Spanish

translations. Main areas of expertise: software, websites, telecommunications, legal, medical, tourism, education, real estate, and art and literature. Works with over five hundred translators, interpreters, editors, and linguistic specialists through the network of thirty-two worldwide locations.

EuroNet Language Services, 295 Madison Avenue, 45th Floor, New York, NY 10017
Phone: (212) 271-0401 Fax: (212) 271-0404
E-mail: euronet@mindspring.com
Contact: Anouk, HRM

Founded 1989. Member: NYCT, ATA. Uses freelance translators and interpreters. Accepts unsolicited resumes. Translates Spanish, French, Portuguese, Italian, Dutch, German, Swedish, and other European languages, both from and into English. Translates all subjects. Prospective translators must be native speakers with bilingual capacity in English and possess a university degree. Resumes are reviewed and added to a database. Maintains a pool of three hundred translators.

ExactLingua LLC, PO Box 5201, Williamsburg, VA 23188
Phone: (757) 564-3065 Fax: (757) 564-8666
E-mail: rromero@exactlingua.com Website: www.exactlingua.com
Contact: Dr. Ralph Romero

Member: ATA. ExactLingua specializes in technical, manufacturing, legal, medical, and financial translations in all language combinations. The company boasts a strong network of translators, editors, and desktop publishers located across the United States that guarantee the highest quality content and document delivery. ExactLingua also provides spoken-word interpretation in all languages, and language and cultural sensitivity training.

Excel Translations Inc., 114 Sansome Street, Suite 925, San Francisco, CA 94104
Phone: (415) 434-4224 Fax: (415) 434-4221
E-mail: info@xltrans.com Website: www.xltrans.com
Contact: Hervé Rodriguez

Founded 1995. Offices in California, Pennsylvania, and Spain. Member: ATA, NCTA, STC, HTML Guild. ISO 9001:2000 certified. Translates into and from all major European and Asian languages. Emphasis on software localization and life sciences. Prospective translators should have three years translation experience and a specialty field. They should be native speakers and have access to the Internet. Most translations done using TM tools. Applicants will need to take a test. Resumes are screened and entered into a database if test is successful. Applicants are notified by postcard. The company works with both freelancers and in-house translators and provides full DTP services. Maintains a pool of 1,000 translators.

Executive Linguist Agency Inc., 500 South Sepulveda Boulevard, Suite 300, Manhattan Beach, CA 90266
Phone: (310) 376-1409 Fax (310) 376-9285
E-mail: mail@executivelinguist.com Website: www.executivelinguist.com
Contact: Ronald R. Randolph

Expert Translators, 10621 North Kendall Drive, Suite 111, Miami, FL 33176
Phone: (305) 279-8353 Fax: (305) 273-4407
E-mail: info@experttranslators.com Website: www.experttranslators.com
Contact: Emily Correal or Angela Greiffenstein

-F-

Federal News Service, 1000 Vermont Avenue NW, Suite 500, Washington, DC 20005
Phone: (202) 347-1400 Fax: (202) 393-4733
E-mail: info@fednews.com Website: www.fednews.com
Contact: Marina Dovganych
  Founded 1987. Accepts resumes. Requires college degree. Translates/transcribes to and from over seventy languages. The company is a newswire that provides government transcripts, online news clipping, news monitoring services, and translations in almost any language.

FLS Inc., 3609 A-5 Memorial Parkway SW, Huntsville, AL 35801
Phone: (256) 881-1120 Fax: (256) 880-1112
E-mail: info@flstranslation.com Website: www.flstranslation.com
Contact: Judith H. Smith or Caroline S. Myers
  Founded 1979. Member: ATA. Uses freelance translators and interpreters. Unsolicited resumes accepted. Translates most languages. Over two hundred translators. Also places bilingual personnel for temporary or permanent positions, mostly Japanese.

Fluent Language Solutions, PO Box 563308, Charlotte, NC 28256-3308
Phone: (888) 225-6056 Fax: (704) 532-7429
E-mail: info@fluentls.com Website: www.fluentls.com
Contact: Daniel Roux

-G-

Garcia-Shilling International, 1402 Corinth, L.B. 139, Dallas, TX 75215
Phone: (214) 428-4428 Fax: (214) 428-4458

E-mail: acento@swbell.net
Contact: Luis A. Garcia Sr.

Garden & Associates Inc., 4301 Highway 7, Suite 140, St. Louis Park, MN 55416
Tel: (952) 920-6160 Fax: (952) 922-8150
E-mail: info@gardentranslation.com Website: www.gardentranslation.com
Contact: Tom Garden, CEO
   Garden & Associates Inc. specializes in medical, legal, and technical translation and interpretation services with eight hundred interpreters speaking over
115 languages, including "rare dialects." The ability to provide rare languages
and dialects puts them in a unique position to satisfy the growing global needs
of their clients.

Gazelle Globalization Group (g3), 451 Park Avenue South, New York, NY 10016
Phone: (212) 889-5077 Fax: (212) 686-5114
E-mail: info@g3translate.com Website: www.g3translate.com
Contact: Nancy Cearley/John Labati
   Member: ATA. Works with both freelance and in-house linguists and is open
to receiving resumes from translators. Gazelle Globalization Group handles projects in over one hundred languages and is specialized in the following fields: market research, medical/pharmaceutical/health care, financial services, government,
legal, and travel and tourism. In addition to translation, g3 provides cultural
consulting, website and software localization, foreign-language transcription,
interpreting, audio/video adaptation, subtitling, and typesetting services.

Gene Mayer Associates, 9 Depot Street, 2nd Floor, Milford, CT 06460
Phone: (203) 882-5990 Fax: (203) 882-5995
E-mail: info@design4language.com
   Founded 1985. Member: ATA, AIGA, Design Management Institute, National
Investor Relations Institute, CT Art Directors Club. Provides graphic design,
translation, and production of complex printed material used by global corporations. Emphasis on business (employee information, annual reports, marketing
brochures, corporate policy manuals). The firm handles translation, design, book
layout, and production in thirty languages. Prefers to work with agencies or with
translators with a qualified track record with large corporate clients.

Geneva Worldwide Inc., 261 West 35th Street, Suite 700, New York, NY 10001
Phone: (212) 255-8400 Fax: (212) 255-8409
E-mail: resumes@genevaworldwide.com Website: www.genevaworldwide.com
Contact: Craig Buckstein, COO
   Member: ATA, GSA, NAJIT, NYCT, OGS, RID. Geneva Worldwide was
founded in 1903. They translate Spanish, Creole, Chinese (traditional and simpli-
fied), Arabic, Polish, Korean, Bengali, Urdu, Russian, and Albanian. In addition

THE GLOBAL TRANSLATOR'S HANDBOOK

they also translate 180 more languages. Their main subjects are business, medical, legal, general, technical, and financial. They specialize in various types of translation. They do accept freelance along with resumes. The resumes are filed by language and coded by experience and SME. Requirements for applicants are professional resumes. Geneva Worldwide provides face-to-face interpretation and document translation in over 180 different languages. They provide multilingual services to many federal, state, city, and private agencies. They have several hundred translators in their pool.

The Geo Group, 6 Odana Court, Suite 205, Madison, WI 53719
Phone: (608) 230-1000 Fax: (608) 230-1010
E-mail: translation@thegeogroup.com Website: www.thegeogroup.com
Contact: Translation Manager
Founded 1991. Accepts resumes. Requires minimum three years translation/ interpreting experience. Main languages are Arabic, British English, Bulgarian, Chinese (simplified), Chinese (traditional), Czech, Danish, Dutch, Estonian, Finnish, Flemish, French, German, Greek, Hmong, Hungarian, Italian, Indonesian, Japanese, Korean, Latvian, Lithuanian, Maltese, Norwegian, Polish, Portuguese, Romanian, Russian, Serbian, Slovak, Slovene, Spanish, Swedish, Thai, Turkish, Ukrainian, and Vietnamese. Also other Asian and European languages. Main subjects are medical and medical equipment, automotive, marketing, computers, dairy equipment, legal, and audio/video. Uses a pool of over 650 translators.

Geotext Translations, 259 West 30th Street, 17th Floor, New York, NY 10001
Phone: (212) 631-7432 Fax: (212) 631-7778
E-mail: translations@geotext.com Website: www.geotext.com
Contact: Randon Burns

German Language Services, 4752 41st Avenue SW, Seattle, WA 98116
Phone: (206) 938-3600 Fax: (206) 938-8308
E-mail: maia@germanlanguageservices.com
Website: www.germanlanguageservices.com
Contact: Maia Costa
Founded 1979. Member: ATA, NOTIS, GACC. Accepts resumes only in electronic form. Requires formal training in translation or interpretation and five years experience. Only translates German.

GES Translation Services, 776A Manhattan Avenue, Room 105, Brooklyn, NY 11222
Phone: (718) 389-8453 Fax: (718) 389-4442
E-mail: ges@gests.us
Contact: Bozena Brzozowski

Global Institute of Languages and Culture Inc., 7301 NW 4th Street, Suite 110, Plantation, FL 33317
Phone: (954) 327-1662 Fax: (955) 327-8116
Website: www.theglobalinstitute.com
Contact: Antonieta Mercado
Member: ATA. Translates Spanish, Portuguese, Italian, French, German, and more, both from and into English. Emphasis on general, computer, medical, and legal translation. Prospective translators should have a college degree, experience, and should be native speakers of the target language. Resumes are responded to based on the applicant's qualifications and the company's needs. Maintains a pool of twenty translators.

Global Languages & Cultures Inc., 400 North May Street, Suite 101, Chicago, IL 60622
Phone: (312) 275-0465 Fax: (312) 275-0470
E-mail: edilia@e-translation.com Website: www.e-translation.com
Contact: Edilia Sotelo

Global Language Solutions Inc., 25 Enterprise, Suite 500, Aliso Viejo, CA 92656
Phone: (949) 798-1400 Fax: (949) 798-1410
E-mail: info@globallanguages.com Website: www.globallanguages.com
Contact: Inna Kassatkina

Global Translation Systems Inc., 910 Martin Luther King Jr. Boulevard, Chapel Hill, NC 27514
Phone: (919) 967-2010 Fax: (919) 929-1333
E-mail: mike@globaltranslation.com Website: www.globaltranslation.com
Contact: Michael Collins / Member: ATA

Global Visions, Foreign Language Consultants, 1620 Centerville Turnpike, Suite 102, Virginia Beach, VA 23464
Phone: (757) 479-1156 Fax: (757) 479-2555
E-mail: globalvisions48@msn.com
Contact: Kristi B. Emerson / Member: ATA

-H-

Health Outcomes Group, 445A Sutter Street, San Francisco, CA 94108
Phone: (415) 931-6161 Fax: (415) 931-6262
E-mail: david_himmelberger@healthoutcomesgroup.com
Website: www.healthoutcomesgroup.com
Contact: David Himmelberger

Heartland's Cross-Cultural Interpreting Services, 4753 North Broadway Avenue, Suite 400, Chicago, IL 60640
E-mail: ccists@heartlandalliance.org Website: www.heartlandalliance.org/ccis
Contact: Helder Weil
Founded in 1996, Cross-Cultural Interpreting Services is a program of Heartland Alliance, a highly regarded human rights organization in Chicago. They offer translation services in over seventy languages and evolve with the ever-changing needs in Chicago. Their primary fields are health care, education, law, and social service.

Hightech Passport Limited, 1590 Oakland Road, Suite B202, San Jose, CA 95131
Phone: (408) 453-6303 Fax: (408) 453-9434
E-mail: info@htpassport.com Website: www.htpassport.com
Contact: Anne-Marie Aubrespy, Marketing Manager
Founded 1992. Member: ATA, NCTA. Translates mostly from English into sixty languages. Emphasis on IT, web, medical, and scientific (UI, documentation, marketing localization). Complete range of internationalization, localization, linguistic, and functional services. The company also provides language engineering, multilingual desktop publishing, voice-over, and customized development. Maintains a pool of 1,500 linguists.

Honda R&D North America Inc., 21001 State Route 739, Raymond, OH 43067
Phone: (513) 645-6164 Fax: (513) 645-6341
E-mail: knason@oh.hra.com Contact: Kay T. Nason

-I-

IDEM Translation, 550 South California Avenue, Suite 310, Palo Alto, CA 94306
Phone: (650) 329-0170 Fax: (650) 858-4336
Contact: Mariam Nayiny / Member: ATA

Inaword, 1601 Cloverfield Boulevard, 2nd Floor, South Tower, Santa Monica, CA 90404
Phone: (310) 460-3200 Fax: (800) 805-7994
E-mail: info@inaword.net Website: www.inaword.net
Contact: Stella Fridman / Member: ATA

Inline Translation Services Inc., 100 West Broadway, Suite 520, Glendale, CA 91210
Tel: (818) 547-4995 Fax: (818) 547-4013
E-mail: info@inlinela.com Website: www.inlinela.com

Inlingua Inc., 171 East Ridgewood Avenue, Ridgewood, NJ 07450
Phone: (201) 444-9500 Fax: (201) 444-0116
E-mail: ridgewood@inlingua.com
Website: www.inlingua.com Second website: www.inlinguaMetroNY.com
Contact: Sandra Stern, Translation Services Coordinator
    Founded 1977. Member: ATA. Accepts resumes from translators and inter-preters. Requires ATA accreditation. Main languages are Spanish, French, Portuguese, German, Italian, Chinese, Japanese, Russian, and Arabic. Also Hindi, Hungarian, Polish, Romanian and Dutch Czech, Serbo-Croatian, Haitian-Creole, French Canadian. Mainly legal, pharmaceutical, and financial. Additional sub-jects that the company translates include websites, medical, cosmetics, electronics subjects, and tape transcriptions. Uses some 150 translators.

Inlingua Translation Service, 95 Summit Avenue, Summit, NJ 07901
Phone: (908) 522-0622 Fax: (908) 522-1433
E-mail: summit@inlingua.com
Contact: Erica Alicea
    Founded 1968. Uses freelance translators and interpreters. Accepts unsolic-ited resumes. Resumes are kept on file for future jobs. Applicants must have computer, fax, and modem. Ten top languages are Spanish, French, Italian, Portuguese, Russian, German, Chinese, Japanese, Danish, and Polish. Also translates Korean and Romanian. Main areas are licenses, birth certificates, and transcripts. Has pool of some thirty translators. Operates as language school with translation services.

Intermark Language Services Corporation, 2555 Cumberland Parkway, Suite
    295, Atlanta, GA 30339
Phone: (770) 444-3055 Fax: (770) 444-3002
E-mail: info@intermark-languages.com Website: www.intermark-languages.com
Contact: Tom West
    Founded 1995. Member: ATA. Accepts resumes. Interested in translators with a law or business degree. Translates mainly French, Spanish, German, Portuguese, and Swedish. Emphasis is on law and business translation. Prospective translators *must* provide a sample translation in every combination they wish to translate; ATA accreditation is preferred.

InterNation Inc., 299 Broadway, Suite 1400, New York, NY 10007
Phone: (212) 619-5545 Fax: (212) 619-5887
E-mail: info@internationinc.com Website: www.internationinc.com
    Founded 1990. Member: ATA, NYCT. Uses freelance translators and inter-preters. Accepts unsolicited resumes. Prospective translators are invited to regis-ter themselves in the online database at www.internationinc.com. All applicable database forms must be filled out completely. Translates from and into all major

languages, but predominantly works with Spanish, Portuguese, Italian, French, German, Japanese, Chinese, Russian, Korean, Arabic, Polish, Dutch, and the Scandinavian languages. InterNation specializes in foreign-language voice-overs and subtitling for corporate sales, image, training, safety, advertising videos, and infomercials as well as documentaries. Maintains a state-of-the-art digital recording studio in-house and has an online voice talent database with audio samples of four hundred native-language voice actors in over forty languages. Employs narrators and character actors mainly in the New York City area. Also translates commercial, financial, legal, technical, scientific, medical, pharmaceutical, PR material, and advertising copy. Maintains a pool of some 5,000 translators.

International Bureau of Translations Inc., PO Box 532189, Indianapolis, IN
    46253
Phone: (317) 679-4666 Phone (interpreters): (317) 590-3546 Fax: (317) 571-1509
E-mail: ibtinc@ibtworld.com Website: www.ibtworld.com
Contact: Demetria Gecewicz
Founded 1976. Indiana WBE status. Member: Indianapolis Chamber of Commerce. Provided sixty-seven languages last year. Emphasis on medical, technical, legal, business, and marketing translation. In addition to translation and desktop publishing, the company does foreign videos, court interpretation, cultural presentations, and conducts language classes. They research the cultural acceptability of company names, product names, and slogans, and are the official translators for the International Violin Competition. Prospective translators should be native speakers with access to a computer, modem, or fax. They should send a rate chart with their resume. Translators are contacted as the need arises. Maintains a pool of 150 translators.

International Communication by Design Inc., 1726 North 1st Street, Milwaukee,
    WI 53212
Phone: (414) 265-2171 Fax: (414) 265-2101
E-mail: info@icdtranslation.com Website: www.icdtranslation.com
Contact: Virginie Olier, Office Manager
Founded 1991. Member: ATA, Wisconsin World Trade Center, STC. Translates mainly Italian, Spanish, French, German, Portuguese, Dutch, Arabic, Greek, Japanese, and Chinese. Also Korean, Russian, and Swedish. Emphasis on technical manuals, medical, and legal translation. Also, substantial work with website localization. Prospective translators must be native speakers and ATA accredited, with a specific area of expertise. Resumes are filed and used as a resource for new translators, interpreters, and typesetters. They are a translation service company with a wide range of clients, from large corporations to smaller clientele. The company is actively involved within the translation community. Maintains a pool of over sixty translators.

International Contact Inc., 351 15th Street, Oakland, CA 94612
Phone: (510) 836-1180 Fax: (510) 835-1314
E-mail: info@intlcontact.com Website: www.intlcontact.com
Contact: Carla Itzkowich / Member: ATA

International Effectiveness Centers, 360 Pine Street, 3rd Floor, San Francisco, CA 94104
Phone: (415) 788-4149 Fax: (415) 788-4829
E-mail: iec@ie-center.com Website: www.ie-center.com
Contact: Taryk Rouchdy
Founded 1972. Member: ATA, NCTA. Translates Spanish, Chinese, Russian, and Portuguese both from and into English, French and Vietnamese from English, and Japanese into English. Emphasis on legal, technical, and children's book translation. Uses freelance translators and interpreters. Accepts unsolicited resumes. Prospective translators must have at least three years experience and be tested unless they hold current ATA accreditation. Resumes are screened for qualifications and appropriate equipment and, if qualified, entered into a database. The company also does desktop publishing in all languages, as well as voice-overs, dubbing, promotional work, cross-cultural and language training, and international business consulting. Maintains a pool of 7,000 translators in its database, 170 of whom are used regularly.

International Institute of Metro St. Louis, 3654 South Grand Boulevard, St. Louis, MO 63118
Phone: (314) 773-9090 Fax: (314) 773-2279
Website: www.iistl.org
Contact: Language Services Department
Founded 1919. Member: ATA, NAJIT, MICATA. Provides interpretation and translation services in 40+ languages.

International Institute of Wisconsin, 1110 North Old 3rd Street, Suite 420, Milwaukee, WI 53203
Phone: (414) 225-6220 Fax: (414) 225-6235
E-mail: info@iiwisconsin.org Website: www.iiwisconsin.org

International Language Center, 1416 South Big Bend Boulevard, St. Louis, MO 63117
Phone: (314) 647-8888 Fax: (314) 647-8889
E-mail: ilc@ilcworldwide.com Website: www.ilcworldwide.com
Contact: Dede S. Brunetti

International Language Services Inc., 5810 Baker Road, Suite 250, Minnetonka,
MN 55345
Phone: (952) 934-5678 Fax: (952) 934-4543
E-mail: bsichel@ilstranslations.com Website: www.ilstranslations.com
Contact: Barb Sichel, Director of Business Development
    Founded 1982. Translates Spanish, French, German, Italian, Portuguese,
Japanese, Swedish, Dutch, Danish, Chinese, and most other languages from
English. Emphasis on medical, technical, business, manufacturing, legal transla-
tion. Prospective translators should have ATA accreditation, references, a mini-
mum three to five years experience, and be native speakers of the target language.
Resumes are read and filed by language. Maintains a pool of over three hundred
translators.

International Language Source Inc., PO Box 338, Holland, OH 43528
Phone: (419) 865-4374 Fax: (419) 865-7725
E-mail: info@ilsource.com Website: www.ilsource.com
Contact: Ryan Stevens, Account Manager
    Founded 1981. Member: TAITA, ATA. Uses freelance translators and inter-
preters. Accepts unsolicited resumes. Prospective translators should have a specialty area and the appropriate resources for projects in that area. Resumes are
kept for six months in an active database. Contact may involve the paid translation of a short sample. Translates mainly French, Spanish, German, Italian, and
Chinese. Also Japanese, Portuguese, and Hebrew. Emphasis on glass manufacturing and retail, automotive OEM and aftermarket, furniture, legal, industrial, and
health-care translation. In addition to translation services, the company provides
video and interactive CD-ROM translation and voice-overs. The company is
willing to consider internships and cooperative projects with other translation
companies.

International Translating Bureau, 16125 West 12 Mile Road, Southfield, MI
48076-2912
Phone: (248) 559-1677 Fax: (248) 559-1679
E-mail: itbinc@itbtranslations.com Website: www.itbtranslations.com
Contact: Mariano Pallarés, President
    Founded 1977. Translates all language pairs. Emphasis on automotive, engi-
neering, machine tool, legal, medical, and public relations translation. Prospective
translators should be native speakers of the target language, have at least five years
residence in the source-language country, and have academic training or on-
job experience in a specialized field. Candidates must have computer, fax, and
current software, particularly WordPerfect and Word for Windows for PC or
Mac. Resumes are scanned for qualifications in which the company is interested
and filed for future use. The company offers accurate, nativelike translations.
Maintains a pool of 250 translators.

SOURCES OF TRANSLATION WORK

International Translating Company, 4144 North Central Expressway, Suite 600, Dallas, TX 75204
Phone: (214) 540-4991 Fax: (214) 540-4973
E-mail: language@itc4you.com Website: www.itc4you.com
Contact: Syed Rayees
Founded 1969. Member: Greater Dallas Chamber of Commerce. Translates Spanish, Chinese, French, German, Arabic, Russian, Japanese, Portuguese, Korean, Vietnamese, Bulgarian, Cambodian, Serbo-Croatian, Czech, Danish, Dutch, Farsi, Finnish, Greek, Gujarati, Hebrew, Hindi, Indonesian, Kurdish, Latin, Norwegian, Polish, Punjabi, Romanian, Hungarian, Swedish, Tagalog, Thai, Turkish, Ukrainian, and Urdu, both from and into English. Emphasis on petroleum, electronics, legal, business, advertising, food export, chemical, and civil engineering translations. Prospective translators must accept work *only* from translation companies, and *never directly from end users*. They must have either IBM or Macintosh computers, a modem, and a fax. Resumes are filed until a need arises. In addition to translation, the company also provides high-resolution typesetting in most languages. Maintains a pool of two hundred translators.

International Translation Service, PO Box 188331, Sacramento, CA 95818
Phone: (530) 753-7482 Fax: (530) 753-7482
E-mail: its_worldwide@yahoo.com
Contact: Garry Pratt
Founded 1970. Uses freelance translators and interpreters. Accepts unsolicited resumes. Prospective translators must be experienced in both their languages and specialty fields, and should possess a variety of means of communication, including phone, fax, and e-mail; they should have computers with the appropriate language fonts. Resumes are filed by language. Translates mainly Scandinavian, German, Spanish, and French, and also Estonian, Irish, Italian, Russian, Finnish, Portuguese, Polish, Dutch, and more. Translates mainly legal, scientific, commercial, and medical. Maintains a pool of some eighty translators.

Interpretations Inc., 8665 West 96th Street, Suite 201, Overland Park, KS 66212
Phone: (913) 782-9449 Fax: (913) 782-9559
E-mail: interp@exactwords.com Website: www.exactwords.com
Contact: Gloria J. Donohue
Founded 1991. Member: ATA, MICATA, International Trade Club, International Relations Council, Women's Resources Network. Translates mainly Spanish, French, German, Portuguese, Russian, Dutch, Swedish, and Italian. Also Danish, Finnish, and Korean. Emphasis on instructional and technical, legal, advertising, video script, and educational materials translation. Prospective translators must be native speakers and have five years experience; ATA accreditation is a must. They should be up to date on hardware and software. Resumes are reviewed and filed; a select number are asked to provide samples of their work

and/or translate short paragraphs. The company also provides interpreters for meetings, conferences, and telephone conferencing. Maintains a pool of about one hundred translators.

InterSol Inc., Three Point Drive, Suite 301, Brea, CA 92821
Phone: (714) 671-9180 Fax: (714) 671-9188
E-mail: solutions@intersolinc.com Website: www.intersolinc.com
Contact: Susana Turbitt
Founded 1996. Member: ATA. Accepts resumes. Translates mainly French, Italian, German, Spanish, Portuguese, Japanese, Chinese, Danish, Swedish, and Finnish. Mostly medical, electronics, computers, automotive, general business, travel, and sports. Also software localization. Uses some thirty translators.

Interspeak Translations Inc., 1133 Broadway, Suite 318, New York, NY 10010
Phone: (212) 679-4772 Fax: (212) 679-5084
E-mail: info@interspeaktrans.com Website: www.interspeaktrans.com
Contact: Silvia Zehn / Member: ATA

intransol.com (International Translation Solutions), 10 South 5th Street, Suite 990, Minneapolis, MN 55402
Phone: (612) 339-4660 Fax: (612) 339-3442
E-mail: translate@intransol.com Website: www.intransol.com
Contact: Jason Wood, President and CEO (jason@intransol.com)
Founded 1989. Member: ATA, GALA, STC. Intransol.com translates to/from all languages. Emphasis on technical, medical, legal, B2B, B2C, advertising, and marketing materials. Also provides multilingual typesetting and desktop publishing, multicultural marketing and design for global markets, simultaneous and consecutive interpreters, interpretation equipment, transcription services, and subtitling and voice-over services. Works with over 5,000 language professionals around the globe. Prospective freelancers should submit resumes to hr@intransol.com.

ION Translations LLC, 2980 College Avenue, Suite 8, Berkeley, CA 94705
Phone: (510) 841-5000 Fax: (510) 841-5003
E-mail: info@iontranslations.com Website: www.iontranslations.com
Contact: R. Blair Sly
Founded 2005. Member: ATA, NCTA. Uses freelance translators and interpreters. Accepts unsolicited resumes. Work samples and resumes submitted by e-mail are reviewed and graded. Translates all major Asian and European languages. Focuses on patents and other technical, scientific, pharma/biotech, and legal subjects.

IRU Language & Translation Services, 2909 Hillcroft Avenue, #538, Houston, TX 77057
Phone: (713) 266-0020 Fax: (713) 266-1716
E-mail: iru2000@aol.com Website: www.iru-services.com
Contact: Elke Krause

Founded 1989. Member: AATG, ATA, GACC, HITA, NACT, Houston-Leipzig Sister City Association. IRU specializes in the translation and interpretation of English, German, Spanish, French, Italian, Portuguese, Russian, Chinese, Korean, and Indonesian in addition to many other languages. The different fields/subjects of their expertise include, but are not limited to, legal, commercial, medical, technical, general, and personal. IRU does use freelance and they do accept resumes. Once a resume is received and the information is verified, it is then added to their freelance database. IRU requires that translators hold a translation degree or equivalent, and that interpreters be court certified and that teachers hold a degree for foreign-language education. The average workload is over 1,500 translations per year, with about forty translators in the database/pool. IRU is a well-established company, serving not only the greater Houston area, but also Baytown, Clear Lake, Orange, and Freeport, Texas. Other services include foreign-language and ESL classes, private language tutoring with an emphasis on German, cross-cultural seminars, and tour guiding/chaperone services for visitors. They offer prompt, accurate, and confidential services at competitive prices. IRU is also listed in the membership directory of the German American Chamber of Commerce, the Yellow Pages, and other directories.

ISI (Interpreting Services International Inc.), 6180 Laurel Canyon Boulevard, #245, North Hollywood, CA 91606
Phone: (818) 753-9181 Fax: (818) 753-9617
E-mail: info@isitrans.com
Contact: Cathi Rimalower

Italian Translations Company LLC, 5225 Pooks Hill Road, Suite 504-S, Bethesda, MD 20814
Phone: (301) 897-3728 Fax: (240) 465-1140
E-mail: italtranslations@cs.com
Contact: Mark L. Pisoni

Founded 1991. Member: ATA. Accepts resumes. Only translates Italian. Main subjects are economics and finance, legal, business, marketing, and medical. Uses fifteen translators.

ITW Interpreting Services Inc., PO Box 70040, Pasadena, CA 91117
Phone: (626) 303-5192 Fax: (626) 359-8053
E-mail: gordon@itwservices.com Website: www.itwservices.com
Contact: Gordon Lemke

Founded 1985. Member: ATA. Provides telephone interpreting with a focus on the insurance industry. Has an active pool of 130 interpreters speaking thirty-four languages.

Iverson Language Associates Inc., PO Box 511759, Milwaukee, WI 53203
Phone: (414) 271-1144 ext. 21 Fax: (414) 271-0144
E-mail: translators@iversonlang.com Website: www.iversonlang.com
Contact: Steven P. Iverson, President
Founded 1986. Member: ALC, ATA, STC, ASTD. Translates French, Spanish, Japanese, Italian, Arabic, Dutch, and Korean from English, and Portuguese, German, Polish, Chinese, and all other languages both from and into English. Emphasis on technical manuals (large machines), medical operators' manuals, spec sheets, financial, software, advertising packaging, and legal translations. Prospective translators should have computer, fax, current software, and e-mail. Must be native speakers in the target language, with a technical background and formal training in a specific field of concentration. Three years experience in the industry and good writing skills are preferred. Resumes are reviewed internally for the required criteria. Interested translators should complete the translator listing form at http://www.iversonlang.com/contact/translator.asp. The company provides translation, interpretation, typesetting, and video narration services in most major languages, as well as technical writing and illustration. Typesetting capabilities include Chinese and Japanese. Maintains a pool of six hundred translators. Iverson Language Associates is a long-standing member of the American Translators Association, and a founding member of the Association of Language Companies.

-J-

Japan-America Management Ltd., 2020 Hogback Road, Suite 17, Ann Arbor, MI 48105
Phone: (734) 973-6101 Fax: (734) 973-1847
E-mail: jamltdmi@ameritech.net
Contact: Landon Bartley / Member: ATA

Japan Communication Consultants, Empire State Building, 350 5th Avenue, Suite 3304, New York, NY 10118
Phone: (212) 759-2033 Fax: (212) 759-2149
E-mail: jcc@japancc.com Website: www.japancc.com
Contact: Mariko Numaguchi, Allan O'Hare / Member: ATA

Japan Pacific Publications Inc., 519 6th Avenue S, Suite 220, Seattle, WA 98104
Phone: (206) 622-7443 Fax: (206) 621-1786
E-mail: andrewt@japanpacific.com Website: www.japanpacific.com
Contact: Andrew Taylor, President
   Founded 1983. Member: ATA. Uses freelance translators and interpreters. Accepts unsolicited resumes. Resumes are entered into a database and evaluated for skills and experience. Main language is Japanese. Also translates Chinese and Korean. Main areas are agriculture, business, biomedical, tourism, marketing, software, and wood products. Translation, DTP, and pre-press. Also publishes biweekly Japanese-language newspaper and annual Japanese-language visitor guide to Seattle.

JLS Language Corporation, 135 Willow Road, Menlo Park, CA 94025
Phone: (650) 321-9832 Fax: (650) 329-9864
E-mail: info@jls.com Website: www.jls.com
Contact: Ms. Rikko Field, President
   Founded 1977. Member: ATA. Translates Japanese, Chinese, German, French, and Spanish, both from and into English, with other languages on request. Emphasis on high-tech translation. Prospective translators should have ATA accreditation, education, and industry experience. Resumes are screened and filed, and promising applicants are tested. In addition to high tech, the company also does agribusiness, biomedical, and patent translations and provides Chinese and Japanese desktop publishing. Maintains a pool of hundreds of translators.

John Benjamins Publishing Company, 763 North 24th Street, Philadelphia, PA
   19130
Phone: (215) 769-3444 Fax: (215) 769-3446
E-mail: paul@benjamins.com
Contact: Paul Peranteau
   Member: ATA. Publishes books and journals for translators. Employment for translators: none.

Josef Silny & Associates Inc., 7101 SW 102 Avenue, Miami, FL 33173
Phone: (305) 273-1616 Fax: (305) 273-1984
E-mail: translation@jsilny.com Website: www.jsilny.com
Contact: Marisa di Giovanni / Member: ATA

JTG Inc., 8245 Boone Boulevard, Suite 402, Vienna, VA 22182
Phone: (703) 548-7570 Fax: (703) 548-8223
E-mail: info@jtg-inc.com Website: www.jtg-inc.com
Contact: Muriel Jérôme-O'Keeffe / Member: ATA

-K-

Korean Consulting & Translation Service Inc., PO Box 154773, Irving, TX 75015
Phone: (972) 255-4808 Fax: (214) 853-5374
E-mail: sbammel@koreanconsulting.com Website: www.koreanconsulting.com
Contact: Steven S. Bammel, President
Founded 1999. Member: ATA. Only translates into and out of Korean, handling many different subjects. Korean-to-English freelance translators must be native English speakers. To apply, send resume with rates and be prepared to review brief training materials before doing a short translation test.

Kramer Translation, 893 Massasso Street, Merced, CA 95341
Phone: (209) 385-0425 Fax: (209) 385-3747
E-mail: keith@kramertranslations.com Website: www.kramertranslations.com
Contact: Keith & Marisa Ensminger / Member: ATA

-L-

LangTech International, 5625 SW 170th Avenue, Aloha, OR 97007
Phone: (503) 649-2478 (to fax, call first)
E-mail: langtech@oregonvos.net Website: www.dialoregon.net/~dforan
Contact: Douglas Foran, Owner
Founded 1994. Active member: ATA, NOTIS. Does not accept resumes. Translates French (European and Canadian), Spanish, Italian, and Portuguese (Brazilian and Lusitanian), both from and into English. Emphasis on scientific/technical, mechanical, electronics, automotive, agricultural, legal, health care/medical, and employee relations translation. Also interpretation and audio/visual narration.

Language Bank, The, 875 O'Farrell Street, San Francisco, CA 94109
Phone: (415) 885-0827 Fax: (415) 885-1304
Contact: Philip Nguyen, Manager
Founded 1987. Uses freelance translators and interpreters. Accepts unsolicited resumes. Resumes are screened for qualifications. Main languages are Spanish, Chinese, Vietnamese, Russian, Tagalog, Thai, Laotian, Cambodian, and French. Emphasis on social services. Pool of more than one hundred translators.

The Language Bank Inc., 729 Barnsdale Road, Unit E, LaGrange Park, IL 60526
Phone: (708) 352-2193 or (888) 852-1444 Fax: (708) 352-2347
E-mail: angela@language-bank.com Website: www.language-bank.com
Contact: Angela Merritt

SOURCES OF TRANSLATION WORK

Language Center, The, 25 Kennedy Boulevard, Suite 400, East Brunswick, NJ 08816-7077
Phone: (732) 613-4554 Fax: (732) 238-7659
E-mail: tlc@thelanguagectr.com Website: www.thelanguagectr.com
Contact: Mary Majkowski
Founded 1967. Member: ATA, TCD. Accepts resumes. Translates all languages. Main areas are health care, pharmaceutical, banking, and financial.

Language Center Inc., The, 7 Gilliam Lane, Riverside, CT 06878-0520
Phone: (203) 698-1907 Fax: (203) 698-2043
Contact: Siri Ostensen, President
Founded 1978. Translates (both ways) Spanish, French, German, Portuguese, all Scandinavian languages, Italian, Japanese, Chinese, and Russian. Emphasis on technical, commercial, and legal translation. Prospective translators should provide sample translations. Resumes are entered into a database. Maintains a pool of thirty translators.

Language Company Translations LLC, PO Box 721507, Norman, OK 73070
Phone: (405) 321-5380 Fax: (405) 366-7242
E-mail: nthtranslations@cox.net
Contact: Nancy T. Hancock, Director
Founded 1982. Member: ATA. Translates all languages in all disciplines. Potential translators should have experience and total fluency. They should be able to produce translations on disk and PDF if needed. Resumes are acknowledged and filed. Freelancers are contacted when appropriate work comes in. The company can take materials through final printing, working with commercial printers and supervising production. They also accept resumes from freelance interpreters. Maintains a pool of sixty translators.

Language Direct, 9801 Westheimer Road, Suite 302, Houston, TX 77042
Phone: (713) 917-6870 Fax: (713) 917-6806
E-mail: translation@langdirect.com Website: www.langdirect.com
Contact: Jylan Maloy / Member: ATA

Language Dynamics, 931 Howe Avenue, #107, Sacramento, CA 95825
Phone: (916) 920-4062 Fax: (916) 920-3594
E-mail: juanvallej@aol.com
Contact: Rhody Vallejo
Founded 1979. Translates Spanish, French, Italian, Russian, Chinese, and Hmong. All subject areas are translated. Prospective translators should be of high quality. Resumes are read and kept on file for contact on an as-needed basis.

Language Exchange Inc., The, PO Box 750, Burlington, WA 98233
Phone: (360) 755-9910 Fax: (360) 755-9919
E-mail: langex@langex.com Website: www.langex.com
Contact: Jaye Stover / Member: ATA

Language Group, The, PO Box 68425, Virginia Beach, VA 23471
Phone: (757) 431-9004 Fax: (757) 431-0447
E-mail: info@thelanguagegroup.com Website: www.thelanguagegroup.com
Contact: Giovanni Donatelli
Founded 1999. Member: ALC. Accepts resumes via e-mail. Translates mainly Chinese, Croatian, Czech, French, German, Italian, Japanese, Norwegian, Polish, and Spanish. Mostly technical, engineering, finance, and marketing. Uses some 150 translators.

Language Innovations LLC, 1725 I Street NW, Suite 300, Washington, DC 20006
Phone: (202) 349-4180 Fax: (202) 349-4182
E-mail: info@languageinnovations.com Website: www.languageinnovations.com
Contact: Brian S. Friedman / Member: ATA

Language Intelligence Ltd., 16 North Goodman Street, Rochester, NY 14607
Phone: (585) 244-5578 Website: www.languageintelligence.com

Language Line Services, 1 Lower Ragsdale Drive, Building 2, Monterey, CA 93940
Phone: (831) 648-7436 Fax: (831) 648-7436
E-mail: dhansman@languageline.com Website: www.languageline.com
Contact: Dale Hansman

Language Matters, 1445 Pearl Street, Suite 215, Boulder, CO 80302
Phone: (303) 442-3471 Fax: (303) 442-5805
E-mail: info@languagematters.com Website: www.languagematters.com
Contact: Nicole Cee
Founded 1992. Member: ATA, TCA, CTA (Colorado Translators Association). Translates medical, technical, legal documents, patents, and marketing material in all languages. Has a pool of over eight hundred translators.

Language Network Inc., The, 14902 Preston Road, Suite 404-731, Dallas, TX 75254
Phone: (972) 960-9955
E-mail: sinckchristine@yahoo.com
Contact: Christine J. Sinck / Member: ATA

LanguageOne, 2305 Calvert Street NW, Washington, DC 20008
Phone: (202) 328-0099 Fax: (202) 328-1610
E-mail: translations@languageone.com Website: www.languageone.com
Contact: Lorraine B. Smith / Member: ATA

Language Plus, 4110 Rio Bravo, Suite 202, El Paso, TX 79902
Phone: (915) 544-8600 Fax: (915) 544-8640
E-mail: speak@languageplus.com Website: www.languageplus.com
Contact: Connie Gyenis / Member: ATA

Language Services Associates Inc., 607 North Easton Road, Building C, Willow
   Grove, PA 19090
Phone: (215) 657-6571 Fax: (215) 659-7210
E-mail: lschriver@lsaweb.com Website: www.lsaweb.com
Contact: Laura T. Schriver
Founded 1991. Member: ATA, DVTA, NAJIT, CHICATA, NOTA. Uses
freelance translators and interpreters. Accepts unsolicited resumes. Resumes
are acknowledged, kept, and used when needed. Applicants should have ATA
accreditation. Main languages (both ways) are Spanish, German, French,
Chinese, Japanese, Korean, Vietnamese, Russian, Hindi, Italian, and Tamil.
Also Cambodian, Arabic, Farsi, Hebrew, Dutch, and more. Emphasis on legal
and medical translation. Maintains a pool of 745 translators. They have 4,000
subcontractors.

Language Services Consultants Inc., PO Box 412, Ardmore, PA 19003
Phone: (610) 617-8962 Fax: (610) 617-9108
E-mail: ruth.karpeles@verizon.net or lsctranslations@msn.com
Website: www.lsctranslations.com
Contact: Ruth S. Karpeles
Founded 1992. Member: ATA, DVTA. Accepts resumes. Translates 80+
languages and Braille. Mostly medical, health, business, education, and social
services. Uses some 200+ translators.

Language Source, PO Box 13114, Wauwatosa, WI 53213
Phone: (414) 607-8766 Fax: (414) 201-0014
E-mail: langsource@langsource.com Website: www.langsource.com
Contact: Elizabeth Brudele-Baran

Language Training Center Inc., 5750 Castle Creek Parkway, Suite 387,
   Indianapolis, IN 46250
Phone: (317) 578-4577 Fax: (317) 578-1673
E-mail: mgeorge@languagetrainingcenter.com Website: www.languagetraining
   center.com
Contact: Martin George, Director
Founded 1993. Member: ATA, TESOL, IFLTA, INTESOL. The Language
Training Center translates English to Spanish, Spanish to English, English to
German, German to English, French to English, English to French, Chinese to
English, English to Chinese, Japanese to English, and English to Japanese. The

THE GLOBAL TRANSLATOR'S HANDBOOK

main subjects that they translate are handbooks and legal contracts. They specialize in corporate documents. They do use freelance and they also accept resumes. Once they receive them, they file them by language and special area. They require that you have experience. They are a full-service language center that teaches, translates, and acclimates clients in the languages of the world. A leader in the translation field for over twenty years. They have forty translators in their pool.

Languages Translation Services, 34726 31st Court SW, Federal Way, WA 98023
Phone: (253) 835-0107 Fax: (775) 993-7988
E-mail: info@advancedtranslationservices.com
Website: www.advancedtranslationservices.com
Contact: Daniel Shamebo Sabore
   Translation, interpretation, editing, proofreading, voice-over, transcription, localization, film subtitling, instruction, and consulting in a timely and reliable manner in more than two hundred languages globally. Recruits qualified linguists and accepts unsolicited mail. A sampling of the languages provided: Acehness, Adarigna, Afarigna.

LanguageWorks Inc., The, 1123 Broadway, Suite 201, New York, NY 10010
Phone: (212) 447-6060 Fax: (212) 447-6257
E-mail: resources@languageworks.com Website: www.languageworks.com
Contact: Resources / Member: ATA

Larisa Zlatic Language Services, 11411 Toledo Drive, Austin, TX 78759
Phone: (512) 626-3854 Fax: (512) 338-9384
E-mail: larisaz@serbiantranslator.com Website: www.lztranslation.com
Contact: Larisa Zlatic, Ph.D.
   Founded 1991. Provides Slavic languages to meet the demands of globalization and outsourcing in emerging East and Central European markets. In addition to translation and software localization, it offers other language services, such as interpretation, voice-over, editing and proofreading, international marketing and branding evaluation, computational linguistics consulting, Serbian language teaching, and more.

Lazar & Associates, 1516 South Bundy Drive, Suite 311, Los Angeles, CA 90025
Phone: (310) 453-3302 Fax: (310) 453-6002
E-mail: languages@lazar.com Website: www.lazar.com
Contact: Elaine Lazar
   Founded 1995. Member: corporate members of ATA and Association of Language Companies. General Services Administration certified. Accepts resumes for all languages. Mostly government, medical, pharmaceutical, IT, business, legal, and technical equipment manuals. Has a pool of over 3,000 translators, interpreters, and transcribers.

Legal Interpreting Services Inc., 26 Court Street, Suite 2003, Brooklyn, NY 11242
E-mail: agerenburd@lis-translations.com Website: www.lis-translations.com
Phone: (718) 786-7890
Contact: Alexandra Gerenburd

Leggett & Platt Inc., PO Box 757, Number 1 Leggett Road, Carthage, MO 64836
Phone: (417) 358-8131 Fax: (417) 359-5767
E-mail: rociohosken@leggett.com Website: www.leggett.com
Contact: Rocio Hosken, International and Translation Services Manager /
   Member: ATA

LetSpeak Inc., Phone: (239) 274-5700 Fax: (239) 274-9709
E-mail: info@letspeak.com Website: www.letspeak.com
Contact: Allendy Doxy / Member: ATA

Lexiteria Corporation, The, 2459 Smoketown Road, Lewisburg, PA 17837
Phone: (570) 522-0122 Fax: (570) 522-5053
E-mail: translation@lexiteria.com Website: www.lexiteria.com
Contact: Robert Beard
   Founded 2000. Member: ATA since 2002. Uses native-speaking freelance
translators in the target-language country and translates from virtually any language to any language in any format. Accepts unsolicited resumes. They match
translators to the customer and refer all jobs from matched clients to their regular
translator(s). Much experience in automotive, financial, medical, insurance, children's literature, and marketing fields.

Liaison Language Center, 2730 North Stemmons Freeway, Suite 508, Dallas, TX
   75207
Phone: (214) 528-2731 Fax: (214) 634-7775
E-mail: info@liaisonlanguage.com Website: www.liaisonlanguage.com
Contact: Gerda Stendell
   Founded 1978. Member: ATA. Uses freelance translators and interpret-
ers. Translates mainly Spanish, Portuguese, German, French, Italian, Korean,
Japanese, Chinese (Mandarin and Cantonese), and Vietnamese. Mostly legal,
oil, and insurance. Has a pool of around one hundred active translators and
interpreters.

Lingo Systems, 15115 SW Sequoia Parkway, #200, Portland, OR 97224
Phone: (503) 419-4856 Fax: (503) 419-4873
E-mail: info@lingosys.com Website: www.lingosys.com
Contact: Jeff Williams
Translates into 100+ languages.

Lingotek Inc., 15 West Scenic Point Drive, Suite 325, Draper, Utah 84020
Phone: (801) 705-9310 Fax: (801) 705-9311
E-mail: services@lingotek.com Website: www.lingotek.com
Contact: Jeff Labrum, Silvia Carvalho
 Member: ATA, GALA, LISA, TAUS. Lingotek was founded in January of 2001. Lingotek offers translation work to and from any language in the world. Lingotek uses freelance professional translators and is always accepting new resumes from translators. Please provide your resume to services@lingotek.com and list your qualifications and rates or go to www.lingotek.com for more information. Lingotek has also developed proprietary software enabling collaborative translation and the ability to capture, grow, and reuse linguistic assets.

Lingua Communications Translation Services, 9321 Lavergne Avenue, Suite 101, Skokie, IL 60077
Phone: (847) 673-1607 Fax: (847) 673-1669
Contact: Alex Babich, General Partner
E-mail: lingua@cifmet.com
 Founded 1989. Member: ATA, MASA. Uses 285 language combinations. Prospective translators should possess experience, speed, and quality at market-level pricing. Resumes are filed against need; translators are then contacted. Lingua maintains a pool of over five hundred translators.

Linguistic Systems Inc., 201 Broadway, Cambridge, MA 02139
Phone: (877) 654-5006 Fax: (617) 528-7491
E-mail: info@linguist.com Website: www.linguist.com
Contact: Martin Roberts, President
 Founded 1967. Member: ATA. Uses freelance translators and interpreters. Applicants should have relevant education and experience. Translates all languages, all subjects. The company provides translation, interpretation, voice-over, and post-editing of machine translation. Maintains a pool of about 4,000 translators.

LLE Language Services, 1627 K Street NW, Suite 610, Washington, DC 20006
Phone: (888) 464-8553 ext. 224 Fax: (202) 785-5584
E-mail: hlacy@lle-inc.com Website: www.lle-inc.com
Contact: Heidi G. Lacy
 Founded 1979. Resumes are carefully screened; prospective translators and interpreters are then interviewed over the phone, references are checked, and then applicant is tried out on a small project first. LLE requires a minimum of two years experience. Translates all languages "from Arabic to Zulu," both from and into English. Emphasis in all technical areas. The company is the creator of LLE-Link, a 24-hour-a-day, 365-day-a-year telephone interpretation service using conference calling. Maintains a pool of forty-two full-time people with

2,000+ linguists in its database. With its rapidly growing client base, LLE has opportunities for highly qualified linguists in each of its business units: instruction, assessment, face-to-face interpretation, translation, and telephonic interpretation. If you are interested in working with LLE on a freelance basis, please go to their website at www.lle-inc.com for information on positions and languages they are currently recruiting for. Resumes may be submitted under the Jobs/Contract Positions tab.

LRA Interpreters Inc., 5455 Wilshire Boulevard, #1015, Los Angeles, CA 90036
Phone: (323) 933-1006 Fax: (323) 933-1153
E-mail: LA@Lrausa.com Website: www.Lrausa.com
Contact: Abel Plockier / Member: ATA

Lucent Technologies Global Translation, 2400 Reynolds Road, Winston-Salem, NC 27106
Phone: (336) 727-6218 Fax: (336) 727-3221
Contact: Marta C. Rhodes / Member: ATA

LUZ, 1160 Battery Street, Suite 375, San Francisco, CA 94111
Phone: (415) 981-5890 Fax: (415) 981-5898
Website: www.luz.com
Contact: Sanford Wright / Member: ATA

-M-

M^2 Limited, 9210 Wightman Road, Montgomery Village, MD 20886
Phone: (301) 977-4281 Fax: (301) 926-5046
E-mail: info@m2ltd.com Website: www.m2ltd.com
Contact: Audrey Moyer
   Founded 1979. Member: ATA, STC, World Trade Center. Accepts unsolicited resumes. Applicants should be native speakers of the target language, with two to five years minimum experience. Translates mainly Spanish, French, Italian, German, Portuguese, Chinese, Japanese, Korean, Dutch, and Russian. Emphasis on computer software, technical documentation, web pages, and localization. The company does not provide interpreting services. The company has become a specialist in the localization of computer-based equipment and software and is heavily involved in software development, training, and adaptation of English-language materials for use in other cultures and languages. In addition to translators, the company is interested in proofreaders and editors in all languages. Maintains a pool of 2,000 translators.

MAGNUS International Trade Services Corporation, 1313 North Grand Avenue, #280, Walnut, CA 91789
Phone: (909) 595-8488 Fax: (909) 598-5852 or (800) 730-3080
Website: www.manuscorp.com
Contact: Richard Antoine
   Member: ATA, PCLA, HPRMA, LA-FTA, NOTA. Translates Spanish, Chinese, Vietnamese, Tagalog, Korean, Portuguese, French, German, and Russian from English, as well as Hindi, Farsi, Armenian, Hmong, Lao, and Arabic. Emphasis on health care, medical, pharmaceutical, engineering, legal, technical, and general business translation. Prospective translators should have certification (if possible), appropriate education, and field experience. Resumes are responded to with a standard contract, and contractors called as needed.

Marion J. Rosley Secretarial, Transcription & Translation Services, 41 Topland Road, Hartsdale, NY 10530
Phone: (914) 682-9718 Fax: (914) 761-1384
E-mail: mrosley@rosley.com Website: www.rosley.com
Contact: Marion J. Rosley, President
   Founded 1977. Member: NYCT, World Trade Council of Westchester, Westchester County Association, Westconn. Translates all languages. Emphasis on legal, medical, technical, and business correspondence translation. The company provides interpreting services in all languages. Prospective translators should have excellent skills and reasonable prices. Resumes are filed for future use. Maintains a pool of hundreds of translators. The company provides secretarial, transcription, and translation services, including cassette transcription of conferences.

MasterWord Services Inc., 303 Stafford, Suite 204, Houston, TX 77079
Phone: (713) 589-0810 Fax: (713) 589-1104
Contact: Mila Green
   Founded 1993. Member: ATA, Azeri Translators Association. Translates Russian, Spanish, Azeri, Brazilian Portuguese, and Chinese, both from and into English. Emphasis on oil and gas, drilling, legal, and medical translations. Prospective translators should have significant translation experience, especially in the oil/gas or legal areas, and show quality performance on the company's certification exam. All resumes are acknowledged, and after prescreening, approximately 10 percent are sent an in-house certification exam, primarily in Russian or Spanish. They are then phoned for an in-person interview. The company also has offices in Baku, Azerbaijan, and is involved in ongoing projects in Europe, South America, and Asia. They also have affiliates in Washington, DC, New York, London, and Moscow. Maintains a pool of thirty-five to fifty translators.

M/C International, PO Box 506, Chagrin Falls, Ohio 44022
Phone: (440) 543-5652 Fax: (216) 820-4329
E-mail: mcinternational@stratos.net Website: www.translationHQ.com
Contact: Mrs. E. Marchbank
    Founded 1969. Accepts resumes. Translates Spanish, French, German, Italian, Portuguese, and Russian. Translates mainly French, German, Dutch, Italian, Portuguese, Spanish, Arabic, Chinese, and Japanese, but covers most languages of the world through their affiliates in the UK, Canada, South America, Europe, Africa, Asia, the Orient, Russia, Ukraine, and others. Emphasis on technical, legal, and commercial translation. The company is a full-service translation bureau. It also provides in-house technical manual preparation in English and all foreign languages, including on-the-premises technical illustration, graphic design, DTP, photo retouching, and digital photography.

McNeil Multilingual, 2821 15th Avenue S, St. Cloud, MN 56301
Tel: (800) 259-2774 Fax: (202) 330-5776
E-mail: contact@mcneilmultilingual.com Website: www.mcneilmultilingual.com

M. E. Sharpe Inc., 80 Business Park Drive, Armonk, NY 10504
Phone: (914) 273-1800 Fax: (914) 273-2106
E-mail: journals@mesharpe.com Website: www.mesharpe.com
Contact: C. P. Chetti / Member: ATA

Mena's International Corporation, 2517 Nicollet Avenue S, Minneapolis, MN 55404
Phone: (612) 872-8392 Fax: (612) 872-7861
Contact: Maximo Mena / Member: ATA

Mercury Marine, W6250 West Pioneer Road, Fond du Lac, WI 54936
Phone: (414) 929-5299 Fax: (414) 231-8916
Contact: Gary Fenrich / Member: ATA

Merrill Translations, 225 Verick Street, New York, NY 10014
Phone: (212) 367-5970 Fax: (212) 367-5969
E-mail: translations@merrillcorp.com Website: www.merrillcorp.com
Resumes: resumestrans@merrillcorp.com
Contact: Thomas Alwood
    Founded 1998. Member: ATA, ITI. Translates mainly English to Spanish, French, German, Italian, Portuguese, Japanese, Chinese, Korean, Swedish, and Russian. They work in sixty-four different languages. Subjects translated are legal, financial, advertising, medical, and technical. They primarily focus on document translation. They also do some interpreting. Merrill Translations does use freelance and they do accept resumes. The resumes are all reviewed, and qualified

candidates are contacted to continue the registration process. They are mainly interested in applicants with a college education and experience in legal and financial work. Merrill Translations is the foreign-language services division of Merrill Corporation, a diversified document services company. They have offices in over fifty locations in the United States and Europe. Merrill Translations production offices, located in New York and London, offer a full range of foreign-language services, focused on the financial, life sciences, advertising, and legal industries as well as general corporate clients. In addition to translation, localization, interpreting, and foreign-language typesetting services, they also coordinate services with Merrill Corporation's other document management solutions, including printing and distribution anywhere in the world. They have more than 2,000 translators in their pool.

Metropolitan Interpreters and Translators Worldwide Inc., 110 East 42nd Street, Suite 802, New York, NY 10017
Phone: (212) 986-5050 Fax: (212) 983-5998
E-mail: dgrote@metlang.com Website: www.metlang.com
Contact: Daniel Grote, Vice President of Sales
Founded 1990. Member: ATA, NYCT, NAJIT, IAFL, RID. Uses freelance translators and interpreters. Accepts unsolicited resumes. Resumes are entered in a database. Translates all languages. Emphasis on legal and law enforcement. About five hundred in translator pool.

MGE Lingual Services, 136 36th Street Drive SE, Suite A-4, Cedar Rapids, IA 52403
Phone: (319) 366-1038 Fax: (319) 366-1047
E-mail: mike@mge-lingual.com Website: www.mge-lingual.com
Contact: Michael G. Elliff / Member: ATA

Monti Interpreting & Translation Services Inc., 1535 North Maitland Avenue, Maitland, FL 327511
Phone: (888) 686-6007 Fax: (407) 830-1860
E-mail: caroline@montitrans.com Website: www.montitrans.com
Contact: Caroline Montalvo
Founded 1997. Member: ATA. Accepts resumes. Translates mainly Spanish, Creole, Vietnamese, French, Chinese, Arabic, Bosnian, Croatian, Cambodian, Portuguese, and Turkish. Mostly medical, legal, and corporate literature. Maintains a pool of fifty translators and five hundred interpreters.

Morales Dimmick Translation Service Inc., 1409 West South Slope, Emmett, ID 83617
Phone: (208) 365-2622
E-mail: projects@mdtranslation.com Website: www.mdtranslation.com
Contact: Chris

Founded 1989. Member: ATA, IMA. Accepts resumes. Main languages are Spanish, Bosnian, Laotian, Vietnamese, and Arabic. Mostly business, medical, legal, and insurance. Maintains a pool of sixty-five translators.

MTS Multinational Translating Service, 928 Connetquot Avenue, Central Islip, NY 11722
Phone: (631) 581-8956 Toll Free: (800) 864-5069 Fax: (631) 224-9435
E-mail: info@mtsinc.us Website: www.mtsinc.us
Contact: Lisa Alesci / Member: ATA

MultiLing International Inc., 86 North University Avenue, 3rd Floor, Provo, UT 84601
Phone: (801) 377-2000 Fax: (801) 377-7085
E-mail: request@multiling.com Website: www.multiling.com
Contact: Michael V. Sneddon
Founded 1988. Member: ATA, STC, Utah Information Technology Association, Software Publishers Association. Translates Spanish, French, Dutch, German, Italian, Japanese, Chinese, Swedish, Danish, Russian, and all other languages, both from and into English. Emphasis on high-tech product localization and the translation of related documents. Prospective translators must be native speakers of the target language, with an undergraduate and preferably a master's degree, and an area of special expertise. They should have a good software and desktop publishing background and several years of experience and accreditation. The company works in all areas of translation, including working with translation software and aiding in its further development. Maintains a pool of 1,400 translators.

The Multi-Lingual Group, 8 Faneuil Hall Marketplace, 3rd Floor, Boston, MA 02109
Phone: (617) 973-5077 Fax: (617) 787-3124
Contact: Felice Bezri
Founded 1994. Member: NAJIT. Translates Spanish, French, Italian, and Portuguese, both from and into English, German, Swedish, Arabic, and Cantonese into English, and Japanese and Mandarin from English. Emphasis on medical studies, computer, legal, and military translation. Prospective translators should be ATA members with extensive experience in written translation and specialization in one or more fields. Resumes are reviewed on a regular basis with a particular eye to the experience of the candidate. The company also provides simultaneous interpreting in over fifty languages and offers cross-cultural consulting. Maintains a pool of approximately 320 translators.

Multilingual Communications Corporation, PO Box 7164, Pittsburgh, PA 15213
Phone: (412) 621-7450 Fax: (412) 621-0522

E-mail: mktg@mccworld.com Website: www.mccworld.com
Contact: Cathy Rosenthal
Founded 1977. Member: ATA. Translates Spanish, French, German, Chinese, Japanese, Russian, Italian, Korean, Portuguese, Arabic, and Korean, both from and into English. Emphasis on technical, legal, and medical software translation. Prospective translators should possess native proficiency and background in a specialized field. Resumes are evaluated on receipt, then contacted and tested. Their services include software localization. Maintains a pool of five hundred translators.

Multilingual Solutions, 22 West Jefferson Street, Suite 402, Rockville, MD 20850
Phone: (301) 424-7444 Fax: (301) 424-7331
E-mail: mlsinc@mlsolutions.com Website: www.mlsolutions.com

Multilingual Translations Inc., 1510 Front Street, Suite 200, San Diego, CA 92101
Phone: (619) 295-2682 Fax: (619) 295-2984
E-mail: mcardenas@multitrans.com Website: www.multitrans.com
Contact: Michael Ramírez Cardénas / Member: ATA

Multilingual Word Inc., 1431 West 32nd Street, Minneapolis, MN 55408
Phone: (612) 929-4203
E-mail: multilingualword@aol.com Website: www.multilingualword.com
Contact: Michelle Livon / Member: ATA

-N-

Narragansett Translations & Interpreting Inc., 37 Chaffee Street, Providence, RI 02909
Phone: (401) 274-4077
E-mail: narragansett@usa.net Website: www.narragansetttranslations.com

NCS Enterprises LLC, 1222 Hope Hollow Road, 2nd Floor, Carnegie, PA 15106
Phone: (412) 278-4590 Fax: (412) 278-4595
E-mail: eflosnik@ncs-pubs.com Website: www.ncs-pubs.com
Contact: Eileen Flosnik
Founded 1992. Member: ATA. Uses freelance translators and interpreters. Accepts unsolicited resumes. All resumes are reviewed and entered into a database.

Nelles Translations, 20 North Wacker Drive, Chicago, IL 60606
Phone: (312) 236-2788 Fax: (866) 615-8606
Contact: Don Hanley

Founded 1956. Member: ATA, Chicagoland Chamber of Commerce, Chicago Convention & Tourism Bureau. Translates Spanish, French, German, Italian, Portuguese, Polish, Russian, Japanese, Chinese, Korean, and numerous other languages, both from and into English. Emphasis on patent, print advertising, legal, brochures and manuals, and personal document translation. Prospective translators should be experienced and have references. They may be tested at the discretion of the company. Resumes are acknowledged, and promising applicants are contacted. The company provides interpreting and voice-over services in addition to translation.

NetworkOmni Multilingual Communications, 4353 Park Terrace Drive, Westlake Village, CA 91361
Phone: (818) 706-7890 Fax: (818) 735-6305
E-mail: support@networkomni.com Website: www.networkomni.com
Founded 1978. Member: ATA. Translates French, Italian, German, Spanish, Chinese, Korean, and Japanese, both from and into English. Handles a variety of subjects. Excellence is the primary requirement for prospective translators. Resumes are followed up with a call and a registration skills packet. The company has five separate divisions: interpretations, translations, tele-interpretations, transcriptions, and video interpretations, and all are supported by Omni's quality control staff. Maintains a pool of eight hundred translators.

New England Translations, 185 Devonshire Street, Suite 900, Boston, MA 02110
Phone: (617) 426-1299 Fax: (617) 426-2283
E-mail: info@newenglandtranslations.com Website: www.newenglandtranslations .com
Contact: Ken Krall, Director
Founded 1986. Member: ATA. Uses freelance translators and interpreters. Accepts unsolicited resumes. Resumes are entered into a database by language and specialty. Requires experience. Translates Spanish, Portuguese, French, German, Italian, Chinese, Vietnamese, Korean, and Japanese from English, and Spanish into English. Emphasis on finance, legal, marketing, industrial, and medical translation, with specialties in financial and medical. Prospective translators should have PC or Mac, fax, and modem. A small sample translation should be sent with the resume. Resumes are entered into a database by language pair and technical specialty after qualifications are reviewed. The company is dedicated to the translation of all major languages. It also provides instruction in Spanish only. Maintains a pool of eight hundred translators.

Newtype Inc., 447 Route 10 East, Suite 14, Randolph, NJ 07869
Phone: (973) 361-6000 Fax: (973) 361-6005
E-mail: mporto@newtypeinc.com Website: www.newtypeinc.com
Contact: Mark Porto / Member: ATA

Foreign-language translations and complete graphic arts services in over 130 languages.

Northern Virginia Area Health Education Center (NVAHEC), 3131-A Mt. Vernon Avenue, Alexandria, VA 22305
Phone: (703) 549-7060 Fax: (703) 549-7002
E-mail: info@nvahec.org Website: www.nvahec.org
Contact: Dallice Joyner, Executive Director
Founded 1996. Member: ATA. Provides interpretation and translation services for a wide array of assignments, including health, mental health, human/ social services, educational, business, legal, and conferences. It also offers training classes for future interpreters, as well as continuing education sessions. Services are offered in the metropolitan area and in Montgomery County (MD) in more than thirty different languages, including Spanish, Vietnamese, Korean, Amharic, Farsi, and Arabic.

Northwest Interpreters Inc., PO Box 65024, Vancouver, WA 98665
Tel: (360) 566-0492 Fax: (360) 566-0453
E-mail: info@nwiservices.com Website: www.nwiservices.com
Contact: Vic Marcus
Over 1,000 interpreters and translators available in over one hundred languages.

NovaTrans Enterprises Inc., PO Box 3903, Boca Raton, FL 33427
Phone: (561) 368-0865 Fax: (954) 255-5161
Contact: Janet T. Aliaga / Member: ATA

N.O.W. Translations, 23054 Covello Street, West Hills, CA 91307
Phone: (818) 716-9112 Fax: (818) 888-6962
E-mail: thomasc@nowtranslations.com Website: www.nowtranslations.com
Contact: Thomas Clement / Member: ATA

-O-

Omega Translation Services, PO Box 745, Iowa City, IA 52244
Website: www.omegatranslationservices.com
Contact: Timothy C. Parrott, M.A.

OmniLingua Inc., 600 Boyson Road NE, Suite 300 Cedar Rapids, IA 52402
Phone: (800) 395-6664 Fax: (319) 365-7893
E-mail: info@omnilingua.com Website: http://oesede1.oettli.com

SOURCES OF TRANSLATION WORK

1-800-Translate, 865 United Nations Plaza, New York, NY 10017
Phone: (800) 872-6752 Fax: (212) 818-1265
E-mail: info@1-800-translate.com Website: www.1-800-translate.com
Contact: Ken Clark

1-Stop Translation USA LLC, 3700 Wilshire Boulevard, #630, Los Angeles, CA 90010
Phone: (213) 480-0011 Fax: (213) 232-3223
E-mail: info@1stoptr.com Website: www.1stoptr.com
Contact: Francesca Riggio
Founded 1994. Member: ATA, ALC, GALA. Offices in the United States, China, and Korea. Asian languages specialist, providing clients a direct link to Asia. Primary languages include Chinese (traditional and simplified), Japanese, Korean, Vietnamese, Thai, Malay, Indonesian, and Tagalog. Only employs translators who are experienced in providing the highest levels of quality and reliability to their list of over four hundred clients. Areas of specialty are wide ranging, and resumes for qualified translators will be accepted.

OneWorld Language Solutions, 2909 Cole Avenue, Suite 120, Dallas, TX 75204
Phone: (214) 871-2909 Fax: (214) 871-2907
E-mail: ghayes@oneworldlanguage.com Website: www.oneworldlanguage.com
Contact: Gabriele Hayes, Director
Founded 1990. Member: ATA, META. Uses freelance translators and interpreters. Accepts unsolicited resumes. Requires experience, prefers ATA members. Resumes are entered in a database, and applicants are contacted when the need arises. Translates (both ways) mainly Spanish, French, German, Italian, and Russian. Also Japanese, Dutch, and Chinese. Provides interpretation and language training. Maintains a pool of over four hundred translators.

-P-

Pacific Dreams Inc., 25260 SW Parkway Avenue, Suite D, Wilsonville, OR 97070
Phone: (503) 783-1390 Fax: (503) 783-1391
E-mail: info@pacificdreams.org Website: www.pacificdreams.org
Contact: Ken Sakai / Member: ALC, ATA

Pacific Interpreters Inc., 707 SW Washington, Suite 200, Portland, OR 97205
Phone: (877) 272-2434 Fax: (503) 445-5501
E-mail: recruitment@pacificinterpreters.com Website: www.pacificinterpreters.com
Contact: Jennifer Ruden
Founded 1992. Member: ATA, SOMI, NOTIS, NAJIT, ASTM

Pacific Ring Services Inc., 1143 Christina Mill Drive, Newark, DE 19711
Phone: (302) 369-1518 Fax: (302) 369-1618
E-mail: pacific@dca.net Website: www.pacificring.com
Contact: Motoko Yuasa, Registered U.S. Patent Agent
  Member: ATA. Pacific Ring Services Inc. specializes in patents and patent litigation support.

Pangea Lingua Translations & Communications, 3620 North Washington
  Boulevard, Indianapolis, IN 46250
Toll Free: (877) 726-1605 Phone: (317) 920-1600 Fax: (317) 920-1601
Contact: Liddy Romero
  Founded 1990. Member: ATA. Accepts resumes. Translates in over 140 languages. Since 1990, has provided linguistic consulting services to small businesses, Fortune 500 companies, and government agencies. Maintains pool of over 1,000 translators.

Paragon Language Services, 5657 Wilshire Boulevard, Suite 310, Los Angeles,
  CA 90036
Toll Free: (800) 499-0299 Phone: (323) 966-4655 Fax: (323) 651-1867
E-mail: info@paragonls.com Website: www.paragonls.com
Contact: Hanne R. Mintz / Member: ATA, ALC

Peritus Precision Translations Inc., 460 Seaport Court, Suite 10, Redwood City,
  CA 94063-5548
Phone: (650) 421-2500 Fax: (650) 421-2501
E-mail: info@peritustranslations.com Website: www.peritustranslations.com
Contact: Dagmar Dolatschko / Member: ATA

Phoenix Translations, 2110 Suite E, White Horse Trail, Austin, TX 78757
Phone (512) 343-8389 Toll Free (877) 452-1348 Fax (512) 343-6721
E-mail: service@phoenixtranslations.com Website: www.phoenixtranslations.com
Contact: Sharon Quincy

Precision Translating Services, 150 West Flagler Street, Museum Tower
  Penthouse II, Miami, FL 33130
Phone: (305) 373-7874 Fax: (305) 381-7874
E-mail: info@pretran.com Website: www.pretran.com
Contact: Vicente J. de la Vega / Member: ATA

Premier Translation Services Ltd., 62 Stonicker Drive, Lawrenceville, NJ 08648
Phone: (609) 538-9333 Fax: (609) 530-0079
Contact: Renée Zarelli Esq. President

Founded 1994. Member: ATA. Accepts resumes. The language pairs they translate are French into English, Italian into English, and Spanish into English. Only translates legal and business documents. They do not accept CVs and only handle F/E legal translations for corporations/law firms. Prospective translators should be ATA members, accredited if applicable. Minimum three years full-time experience, college education or higher. Equipment should include WordPerfect or Word and modem. Resumes are reviewed on a monthly basis. The company specializes in using lawyers and individuals with a strong legal background, in both the United States and other legal systems, for translation and editing. Freelance translators do not have to be members of ATA, or accredited by ATA, for consideration. Maintains a pool of fifty translators.

Princeton Technical Translation Center, 333 Bolton Road, East Windsor, NJ 08520
Phone: (609) 443-6770
Contact: Charles Teubner, Director
Website: http://www.princetontranslations.com.
Founded 1982. Member: ATA, STC. Translates French, German, Spanish, Italian, Portuguese, Chinese, Japanese, Russian, and Scandinavian languages, both from and into English. Prospective translators should have advanced technical degrees and be proficient in Word/WordPerfect and related software.

Professional Translating Services Inc., Courthouse Tower Building, 44 West Flagler Street, 18th Floor, Miami, FL 33130
Phone: (305) 371-7887 Fax: (305) 371-8366
E-mail: info@protranslating.com Website: www.protranslating.com
Contact: Luis A. de la Vega
Founded 1973. Member: ATA. Accepts resumes. Translates mainly Spanish, Portuguese, French, Italian, German, Japanese, Russian, Chinese, Arabic, and Hebrew. Translations are in legal, technical, financial, and advertising. Has a pool of over 350 translators.

-Q-

Quantum Inc., 240 South 9th Street, Philadelphia, PA 19107
Phone: (215) 627-2251 Fax: (215) 627-5570
Website: http://quantumtranslations.com

-R-

R. R. Donnelley Financial Translation Services, 75 Park Place, New York, NY 10007
Phone: (212) 341-7877 Fax: (212) 341-7506
Contact: Aouck F. Le Fur / Member: ATA

Ralph McElroy Translation Company, 910 West Avenue, Austin, TX 78701
Phone: (512) 472-6753 Fax: (512) 472-4591
E-mail: customerservice@mcelroytranslation.com
Website: www.mcelroytranslation.com
Contact: Patricia Bown
Founded 1968. Member: ATA, STC. Accepts resumes. Translates mainly German, Japanese, French, Spanish, Italian, Portuguese, Russian, Chinese, Dutch, and Korean. Mostly engineering, technical, medical, legal, pharmaceutical, chemical, patents, localization, and high tech. Several hundred active translators.

Rancho Park Publishing Inc., 8601 Little Creek Farm Road, Chapel Hill, NC 27516
Phone: (919) 942-9493 Fax: (919) 942-9396
E-mail: ranchopark@gmail.com Website: www.ranchopark.com
Contact: Stan Cheren
Founded 1988. Specializes in multilingual typesetting for translation agencies and their clients. All major languages, all major applications, Mac and PC.

Rapport International, 93 Moore Road, Sudbury, MA 01776
Phone: (978) 443-2540 Fax: (206) 339-7160
E-mail: rapport@rapportintl.com Website: www.rapportintl.com
Contact: Wendy Pease / Member: ATA

Rennert Bilingual Translations, 216 East 45th Street, 17th Floor, New York, NY 10025
Phone: (212) 867-8700 Fax: (212) 867-7666
E-mail: translations@rennert.com Website: www.rennert.com
Contact: Chad Orr, Director
Founded 1973. Member: ATA, New York Circle of Translators. Translates all languages. Emphasis on all aspects of patent law, marketing, public relations, business and finance, videos and educational material translation, and website localization. Prospective translators should possess training and experience in the specific fields. Resumes are reviewed for education and experience, and a Rennert application is sent to the translator for completion. Maintains a pool of 3,000 translators.

Rescribe, PO Box 503981, San Diego, CA 92150-3981
Phone: (800) 870-6639 Fax: (858) 487-5292
E-mail: erin@rescribe.com Website: www.rescribe.com
Contact: Erin Berzins
Founded 2001. Member: ATA. Accepts resumes. Translates into Spanish, French, Chinese, Vietnamese, Japanese, Italian, Dutch, German, Korean, Russian, and Tagalog, as well as other languages. Wide variety of subject areas.

SOURCES OF TRANSLATION WORK

RIC International Inc., 1035 Cambridge Street, Suite 11, Cambridge, MA 02141
Phone: (800) 240-0246 Phone 2: (617) 621-0940 Fax: (617) 621-2552
E-mail: info@ricintl.com Website: www.ricintl.com
Member: ATA

Richard Schneider Enterprises Inc., 27875 Berwick Drive, Suite A, Carmel,
California 93923
Telephone: (800) 500-5808 Fax: (408) 904-5199
E-mail: service@idioms.com Website: www.idioms.com
Contact: Richard A. Schneider / Member: ATA

RussTech, 1338 Vickers Road, Tallahassee, FL 32303
Phone: (850) 562-9811 Fax: (850) 562-9815

-S-

Sajan Inc., 625 Whitetail Boulevard, River Falls, WI 54022
Phone: (715) 426-9505 Fax: (715) 426-0105
E-mail: info@sajan.com Website: www.sajan.com
Contact: Angel Zimmerman, Director of Operations
Founded 1997. Member: ATA. They translate English into most languages.
Accepts freelance resumes (contact language@sajan.com for details on how to
submit resumes). They require five or more years translating experience and
translating in particular fields. Also ATA accreditation or equivalent in target lan-
guage country. Their annual workload is about 20 million words per year. They
have 1,200 active translators and about 7,000 translators in their pool.

Sarjam Communications Ltd., 1008 NE 122nd Avenue, Portland, OR 97230
Phone: (503) 287-9277 Fax: (503) 252-9220
E-mail: sarjam@sarjam.com
Contact: Seth A. Reames
Sarjam Communications provides Japanese-English and English-Japanese
translation, interpretation, and consultation to the entertainment media and
media technology industries. Highly experienced translators, interpreters, and
specialized consultants (Japanese/English only) are encouraged to provide their
CV for consideration for participation in translation projects, interpreting assign-
ments, and consultative business.

S.B.F. TRANSLATIONS INC., 5601 Collins Avenue, #1021, Miami Beach, FL 33140
Phone: (305) 866-6079 Fax: (305) 866-6162
E-mail: sbftrans@aol.com
Contact: Silvia B. Fernandez

Founded 1994. Member: ATA. Accepts resumes. Translates Spanish, Portuguese, and Creole. Mostly legal, medical, immigration, and Christian books. Has three translators.

Schreiber Translations Inc., 51 Monroe Street, Suite 101, Rockville, MD 20850
Phone: (301) 424-7737 Fax: (301) 424-2336
E-mail: translation@schreibernet.com Website: www.schreibernet.com
Contact: Milton Shattuck, COO
Founded 1984. Member: ALC, ATA. Uses freelance translators and interpreters. Accepts unsolicited resumes only on website. Translates (both ways) mainly Japanese, Russian, German, French, Spanish, Chinese, Italian, Arabic, Korean, Vietnamese, Hebrew, Polish, and Dutch, and close to ninety additional languages and dialects. Emphasis on patents, aerospace, law, medicine, communications, computers, engineering, public relations, military and maritime subjects, chemical subjects, and business and finance. In addition to translation and interpretation, the company produces multilingual brochures and advertisements, prints manuals and business literature in a variety of multinational fonts, and does voice-overs for video and films. Maintains a pool of over 1,300 translators—350 active, and 200 of those very active.

SH3 Inc., 7101 College Boulevard, Suite 500, Overland Park, KS 66210
Phone: (913) 747-0410 Fax: (913) 747-0417
E-mail: chubbard@sh3.com Website: www.sh3.com
Contact: Cathy Hubbard, Owner/General Manager
Founded 1980. Member: ALC, ATA, GALA, STC. Translates all major languages. Emphasis on agricultural and industrial equipment, and consumer equipment translation. Prospective translators should have SDL/Trados tools, advanced TagEditor proficiency, and experience in engineering, electronic, and industrial areas. Resumes are reviewed by subject specialty, experience, language, and tools, and are flagged for a future contact. Does around 30 million words a year. The company deals in high-volume, highly technical manuals. Maintains an active pool of 150 translators.

Speak Easy Languages, 757 South Main Street, Plymouth, MI 48170
Phone: (734) 459-5556 Fax: (734) 459-1460
Contact: Cristina Clark
Founded 1980. Member: ATA. Translates all major language pairs. Emphasis on automotive business, brochures, advertising, and legal translation. Prospective translators should be ATA accredited and possess fax and modem capabilities. Resumes are filed and the applicant called upon as the circumstance arises. The company also provides talent for voice-over work. Maintains a pool of one hundred translators.

STG Inc., 12330 Pinecrest Road, Reston, VA 20191
Phone: (703) 716-5000 Fax: (703) 716-5005
Contact: John Sapienza

Superior Translations, 1924 Minnesota Avenue, Duluth, MN 55802
Phone: (218) 727-2572 Fax: (218) 727-2653
E-mail: info@superiortranslations.com Website: www.superiortranslations.com
Contact: Elisa A. Troiani
Founded 1993. Member: ATA. Uses freelance translators and interpreters. Accepts unsolicited resumes. Resumes for translation and interpretation should be e-mailed. Applicants are carefully screened and required to submit samples, references, and tests. Requirements are honesty, accuracy, editing/proofing skills, reasonable rates, punctuality, and an eye for detail. Translates mainly Spanish, French, German, Japanese, Chinese, Russian, Portuguese, Italian, Polish, and Hmong. Emphasis on all subject areas. Has five hundred to six hundred translators in its pool.

Suzuki, Myers & Associates Ltd., PO Box 852, Novi, MI 48376
Phone: (248) 344-0909 Fax: (248) 344-0092
E-mail: office@suzukimyers.com Website: www.suzukimyers.com
Contact: Kumiko Oh
Founded 1984. Member: ATA, MITN, Japan-America Society. Translates Japanese and Korean only, both from and into English. Emphasis on manufacturing-related translation (autos, engineering, quality design, robotics, plastics, assembly, electronics, paint, contracts, product liability). Prospective translators should be competent and diligent. Resumes are responded to with a phone call. The company provides translation, interpretation, and consultation services in North American–Japanese relations. They also provide DTP services. Maintains a pool of about forty translators.

-T-

Techno-Graphics and Translations Inc., 1451 East 168th Street, South Holland, IL 60473
Phone: (708) 331-3333 Fax: (708) 331-0003
E-mail: techno@wetrans4u.com Website: www.wetrans4u.com
Contact: Dave Bond or Pinay Gaffney
Founded 1972. Member: ATA. Uses freelance translators and interpreters. Accepts unsolicited resumes. Resumes are entered in a database. Requires native ability and technical background. Translates (both ways) mainly European, Asian, Scandinavian, and Middle Eastern languages. Main areas are industrial, agriculture, automotive, medical, and telecommunications. Worldwide pool of two hundred translators.

TechTrans International Inc., 2200 Space Park Drive, Suite 410, Houston, TX 77058
Phone: (281) 335-8000 Fax: (281) 333-4396
E-mail: info@tti-corp.com Website: www.tti-corp.com
Contact: Beth Williams / Member: ATA

Techworld Language Solutions, 1250 West 14 Mile Road, Suite 102, Clawson, MI 48017
Phone: (248) 288-5900 Fax: (248) 288-7900
Contact: Fred Meinberg / Member: ATA

Telelanguage Inc., 421 SW 6th Avenue Suite 1150, Portland, OR 97204
Phone: (888) 877-8353 Fax: (503) 246-6002
E-mail: info@telelanguage.com Website: www.telelanguage.com
Contact: Andre Lupenko / Member: ATA

Telelingua International, 2 Madison Avenue, Larchmont, NY 10538
Phone: (914) 833-3305 OR (800) 930-0232
E-mail: lmellet@telelingua.com or hbaraona@telelingua.com
Website: www.telelingua.com
Contact: Hector E. Baraona, Director of Operations
hbaraona@telelingua.com
Member: GALA, LISA. Telelingua is a private holding company whose aim is to invest in its subsidiaries and develop their activities in the multilingual translation market. Based in Brussels, Paris, and in the university towns of Louvain-la-Neuve in Belgium, Princeton in New Jersey, Berkeley in California, as well as Manila, Philippines, its subsidiaries, operating in the fields of technical translation, software localization, the globalization of Internet sites, and the development of software translation aids, make the Telelingua group one of the global leaders in this expanding market. It also has strategic alliances in Latin America, central Europe, and Asia, thus providing its customers with a global solution to its GILT requirements. They translate into over sixty-five languages including the traditional English to F.I.G.S. and all Asian languages. The main areas of subject matter expertise are ERP software, medical/medical devices, pharmacology, finance, legal, and manufacturing. They use both in-house and freelance translators, which are prescreened and qualified by a strict quality assurance (QA) process. They do accept resumes, though you must be a certified professional with a minimum five years working experience to be considered. Telelingua is also recognized for its leadership in developing and integrating some cutting edge translation technologies. T-Portal is a collaborative web-based environment that brings customers, projects, language resources, and technologies together in real time to manage and build measurable efficiencies into the localization process. They have approximately 2,500 translators in their pool of professionals.

Total Benefit Communications Inc., 1117 Perimeter Center West, Suite 212, Atlanta, GA 30338
Phone: (678) 579-9600 Fax: (678) 579-9595
E-mail: tbc@benefitproject.com
Contact: Representative / Member: ATA

Trans Global Translation & Immigration Services, 175 Fontainbleau Boulevard, Suite 2G 8, Miami, FL 33172
Phone: (305) 552-9793 Fax: (305) 223-4080
Member: ATA

TransACT Communications Inc., 5105 200th Street SW, Suite 200, Lynnwood, WA 98036
Phone: (425) 977-2100 Fax: (425) 776-3377
E-mail: support@transact.com Website: www.transact.com
Contact: Ms. Kelsye Nelson
TransACT is the premier provider of multilingual parent notification documents to school districts nationwide. TransACT solutions combine expert content with innovative RoadMap technology, personal training, and support so you can achieve compliance with confidence.

Trans-Caribe Communications Inc., 9109 Queen Elizabeth Court, Orlando, FL 32818
Phone: (407) 532-9039 Fax: (407) 260-6349
Contact: Sherry E. Allen-Diaz / Member: ATA

Transemantics Inc., 1337 Connecticut Avenue, 4th Floor, Washington, DC 20036
Phone: (202) 686-5600 Fax: (202) 686-5603
E-mail: translation@transemantics.com
Contact: M-L Wax Cooperman, Director / Member: ATA
Translation, interpreting, and related services.

Transfirex Translation Services Inc., 20423 Waters Point Lane, Germantown, MD 20874
Phone: (301) 528-1695 Fax: (301) 542-0185
E-mail: info@transfirex.com Website: www.transfirex.com
Contact: Margaret Johnson
Founded 2001. Member: ATA. Accepts resumes. All languages, all subjects. Has a pool of twenty-five translators.

Transimpex Translations, 8301 East 166th Street, Belton, MO 64012
Phone: (816) 561-3777 Fax: (816) 561-5515

Website: www.transimpex.com
Contact: Ingrid Pelger, Doris Ganser, or Brian White
   Founded 1974. Member: ATA, board member of International Trade Club of Greater Kansas City. Uses freelance translators and interpreters. Accepts unsolicited resumes. Resumes are put in database until needed. Requires degree in linguistics or translation. Main languages translated are German, French, Spanish, Portuguese, Italian, Japanese, Russian, and Arabic. Translates all subjects, with long experience in localization. Has overall pool of some 5,000 translators, with about 150 active ones.

Translate4me Inc., 9720 Wilshire Boulevard, Suite 205, Beverly Hills, CA 90212
Phone: (310) 274-9771 Fax: (310) 274-9431
E-mail: translation@translate4me.com Website: www.translate4me.com
Contact: Heidi Fulford
   Member: ATA, ITI, BBB, NAWBO. The main languages that they translate are English to French, German, Spanish, and Italian. They also translate into over one hundred languages. They translate into all subjects. Translate4me Inc. does use freelance, and they do accept resumes. You may send your resume to usa@translate4me.com. Suitable applicants are sent an application form, terms of business, and are reference checked. They require that applicants have graduated and have at least five years translation experience. They should also have professional translator's qualifications. They have about 3,000 translators in their pool.

Translation Aces Inc., 29 Broadway, Suite 2301, New York, NY 10006
Phone: (212) 269-4660 Fax: (212) 269-4662
Contact: Serge Nedeltscheff
   Founded 1952. Member: NY Circle, NY Chamber of Commerce. Translates Spanish, French, German, Japanese, Italian, Portuguese, Russian, and Greek, both from and into English, as well as *all* other language pairs. Emphasis on legal, patent, medical, financial, scientific, advertising, engineering, and almost all other areas of translation. Prospective translators should have "experience, experience, experience." Resumes are responded to with the company's application form. The company has forty-five years experience in providing the legal, financial, advertising, medical, and governmental communities with translation, interpreting, voice-over, and consulting services. Maintains a pool of about four hundred translators.

Translation Company of New York LLC, 8 South Maple Avenue, Marlton, NJ 08053
Phone: (856) 983-4733 Fax: (856) 983-4595
E-mail: tcny2000@cs.com Website: www.tcny2000.com
Contact: Jennifer C. Thompson or Liliana Stevcic

Founded 1983. Uses freelance translators and accepts unsolicited resumes. Translates mainly French, German, Spanish, Italian, Japanese, Portuguese, Dutch, Russian, Chinese, and Swedish. Main areas are pharmaceutical, chemical, medical, engineering, electronics, and tourism. Has active pool of two hundred translators.

Translation Source, 8582 Katy Freeway, Suite 240, Houston, TX 77024
Phone: (713) 465-0225 Fax: (281) 966-1869
E-mail: maria.quintero@translation-source.com
Website: www.translation-source.com
Contact: Maria Quintero
Founded 2001. Member: ATA and ALC. Uses freelance translators and accepts unsolicited resumes.

Translations Unlimited, 1455 Forest Hill SE, Grand Rapids, MI 49546
Phone: (616) 550-7057 Fax: (616) 526-8583
E-mail: translationsu@gmail.com
Contact: Leslie Mathews, Director
Founded 1980. Member: ATA. Accepts resumes. Main languages are French, Spanish, German, Japanese, Portuguese, Italian, Chinese, and Korean. Main areas are patents, sales literature, contracts, employee handbooks, medical and legal documents, and technical specifications. Translator pool of twenty-five to thirty.

Translations.com, 3 Park Avenue, 40th Floor, New York, NY 10016
Phone: (212) 689-1616 Fax: (212) 685-9797
E-mail: info@translations.com Website: www.translations.com
Contact: Pamela Kraljevich
Founded 1999. Member: ATA. Accepts resumes. Translates mainly Spanish, French, German, Chinese, Japanese, Portuguese, Italian, Korean, Norwegian, and Swedish. Mostly software, IT-telecom, finance, travel, and medical. Provides full suite of globalization services. Pool of five hundred translators.

Translation3, 49 Union Park, #2, Boston, MA 02118
Phone: (617) 482-2223 Fax: (617) 482-2121
E-mail: jjtranslation3@translation3.com Website: www.translation3.com
Contact: Jacqueline M. Jacquiot / Member: ATA

The Translators Inc., PO Box 303, Topsfield, MA 01983
Phone: (978) 887-9234 Fax: (978) 887-6657
E-mail: info@thetranslatorsinc.com Website: www.thetranslatorsinc.com
Contact: Jim Swift, Personnel Manager
Founded 1980. Accepts resumes. Translates all languages, mostly medical, patents, human resources, computer, sci-tech, legal, electronic, and engineering. Unlimited translator pool.

Transperfect Translations International Inc., 3 Park Avenue, 39th Floor,
New York, NY 10016
Phone: (212) 689-5555 Fax: (212) 251-0981
E-mail: info@transperfect.com Website: www.transperfect.com
Contact: Information / Member: ATA, GALA

Transtek Associates Inc., 599 North Avenue, Door 9, Wakefield, MA 01888
Phone: (781) 245-7980 Fax: (781) 245-7993
Website: www.transtekusa.com
    Founded 1964. Member: ATA. Uses freelance translators and interpreters.
Accepts unsolicited resumes.

Trustforte Language Services, 271 Madison Avenue, 3rd Floor, New York, NY
10016
Phone: (212) 481-4980 Fax: (212) 481-4972
E-mail: info@trustfortelanguages.com Website: www.trustfortelanguages.com
Contact: Jackie Cordero
    Founded 1992. Member: ATA. Accepts resumes. Works in most languages.
Provides translators and interpreters to a variety of fields, from business to
entertainment.

-U-

United Nations Translators & Interpreters Inc., 1906 East Robinson Street,
Orlando, FL 32803
Phone: (407) 894-6020 Fax: (407) 894-6693
E-mail: unti@unti.com Website: www.unti.com
Contact: Fiona Como
    Founded 1991. Member: ATA. Accepts resumes. Translates mainly Spanish,
Creole, French, German, Arabic, Farsi, Italian, Portuguese, and Vietnamese.
Mostly legal, medical, technical, and INS documents. Uses about fifty translators.

University Language Center Inc., 1313 5th Street SE, Suite 201, Minneapolis,
MN 55414
Phone: (612) 379-3823 Fax: (612) 379-3832
E-mail: info@ulanguage.com Website: www.ulanguage.com
Contact: Therese Shafranski, Translation Department Manager
    Founded 1986. Member: ATA. Accepts resumes. Translates Spanish, French,
German, Italian, Portuguese, Russian, Chinese, Japanese, and Hmong, as well as
Turkish, Indonesian, Arabic, and all Southeast Asian languages. Emphasis in all
technical areas. The company handles all phases of production from translation
to camera-ready art, including cultural assessment of the source documents.
Maintains a pool of 250 translators.

University Translators Services LLC, 220 North 5th Avenue, Ann Arbor, MI
48104
Phone: (734) 655-7295 Fax: (734) 655-1345
E-mail: lfinch@univtrans.com Website: www.univtrans.com
Contact: Laurie Finch, Owner
Founded 1987. Member: ATA. They do accept resumes. They prefer that you
have experience as well as certification. Having work experience or a degree in a
specialty area is a plus. They work with all languages. Subjects include automotive and manufacturing of all types, patents, legal documents, consumer surveys,
promotional brochures, court interpreting, subtitling/voice-over, website HTML
pages, and software localization. Their workload is about 50 percent written
translation and 50 percent interpretation. University Translators Services is a
woman-owned agency operating in the capacity of an LLC partnership.

U.S. Translation Company, 1893 East Skyline Drive, Suite 203, South Ogden,
UT 84403
Phone: (801) 393-5300 Fax: (801) 393-5500
E-mail: info@ustranslation.com Website: www.ustranslation.com
Contact: David Utrilla / Member: ATA

-V-

Vital International Programs Inc., 34514 Dequindre, Suite C, Sterling Heights,
MI 48310
Phone: (586) 795-2500 Fax: (586) 795-5763
E-mail: lnespolo@protranslating.com website: www.vitalinternational.com
Contact: Lil Néspolo

Voices for Health Inc., 2851 Michigan NE, Suite 104, Grand Rapids, MI 49506
Phone: (616) 233-6505 Fax: (616) 233-6522
E-mail: info@voicesforhealth.com Website: www.voicesforhealth.com
Contact: Scott Van Til, Translations; Van Nguyen, Interpretation Coordinator
Founded 1997. Member: ATA. Accepts resumes. Translates mainly Spanish,
Vietnamese, Chinese, and Arabic. Mostly health care and social services. Uses
hundreds of linguists.

-W-

Welocalize Inc., 241 East 4th Street, Suite 207, Frederick, MD 21701
Phone: (301) 668-0330 Fax: (301) 668-0335
E-mail: info@welocalize.com Website: www.welocalize.com
Contact: E. Smith Yewell / Member: ATA

Word for Word Inc., 325 West Chickasaw Road, Virginia Beach, VA 23462
Phone: (757) 557-0131 Fax: (757) 557-0186
E-mail: wrd4wrd@exis.net
Contact: Curtis Hovey / Member: ATA

Word Magic Software Inc., c/o Translation Technologies Corporation—U.S.
Distributor, PO Box 689, Alief, TX 77411-0689
Phone: (281) 564-3022 Fax: (713) 559-8370
E-mail: info@wordmagicsoft.com Website: www.wordmagicsoft.com
Contact: Ricardo Arguello Jr.
Founded 1989. Word Magic Software only translates English into Spanish.
They translate any subject. They do not use freelance and they do not accept
resumes. They have English-Spanish translation software, dictionary, thesaurus,
spell checker, and verb conjugator. They also offer translation services in both
languages, English and Spanish.

Worldwide Translations Inc., 2994 Marble Cliff Court, Henderson, NV 89052
Phone: (800) 293-0412 Fax: (800) 536-6995
E-mail: wwtranslate@cs.com Website: www.wwtranslations.com
Contact: Robert Sansing, President
Founded 1994. Member: ATA, RAPS, FDLI, DIA, NAJIT. Accepts resumes.
Translates mainly French, Italian, German, Spanish, Dutch, Portuguese, Greek,
Swedish, Japanese, and Chinese. Emphasis on medical, machinery manufacture,
and computer products translation. Prospective translators should be native-
speaking ATA members with five or more years technical translation experience
and references. Resumes are responded to by telephone when work becomes
available. The company is expert in the CE mark and medical device areas and
specializes in the translation of instructional manuals. They hold their translators to a high standard of accuracy. Maintains a pool of over one hundred
translators.

Wudang Research Association, 801 International Parkway, 5th Floor, Lake
Mary, FL 32746
Phone: (407) 562-1993
E-mail: info@wudang.com Website: www.wudang.com
Contact: Theresa M. Morgan

U.S. TRANSLATION COMPANIES BY LOCATION

ALABAMA
Huntsville Alamex Translation Service, FLS

SOURCES OF TRANSLATION WORK

ARIZONA
Mesa A Foreign Language Service
Oro Valley CyraCom
Phoenix Choice Hotels International
Tucson CyraCom International

CALIFORNIA
Alhambra Asian Link
Berkeley Accent on Languages, Avantext, Berkeley Scientific Translation, Okada & Sellin Translations, OSTrans LLC
Beverly Hills ABC Worldwide Translations & Interpretations, Translate4me Inc.
Brea InterSol Inc.
Carmel Richard Schneider Enterprises
Davis Avantpage
Encino Bizzy Box, Eurasia International
Exeter Clark Translations
Glendale Atlas, Coto, Inline, Omega
Hollywood ISI
Huntington Beach ATS
Irvine Global Language Solutions/The Russian Word, Tru Lingua
Laguna Beach The Language Connection
Los Angeles Better Communications, Inaword, Lazar & Associates, LRA Interpreters, 1-Stop Translation USA, Paragon Language Services, Rancho Park Publishing
Manhattan Beach Executive Linguist Agency
Menlo Park JLS
Merced Kramer Translation
Monterey Language Line Services
Newbury Park ComNet International
Oakland International Contact
Orange Continental Interpreting Services
Palm Desert CC Scientific
Palo Alto BioMedical Translators, Health Outcomes Group, IDEM Translation
Pasadena ITW Interpreting
Redondo Beach Corporate Translations
Sacramento International Translation Service, Language Dynamics
San Carlos Peritus Precision Translations
San Diego Certified Interpreters & Translators, Interpreters' Index.com, Multilingual Translations, Rescribe
San Francisco Amelise Inc., Auerbach International, Excel Translations, Health Outcomes Group, International Effectiveness Centers, The Language Bank, LUZ, Rosetta

San Jose Comunicaid, Hightech Passport Limited
San Mateo Avid Translations
San Rafael Eurologos-San Jose
Santa Clarita America Translating Services
Santa Monica Lazar & Associates
Simi Valley Continental Communications Agency
Studio City Always Ready Translation Services
Thousand Oaks NetworkOmni Multilingual Communications
Walnut MAGNUS International Trade Services
West Covina American Education Research Corp.
West Hills N.O.W. Translations
Westlake Village Agnew Tech-II, ComNet International

COLORADO
Aurora Asian Pacific
Boulder Language Matters
Denver Bridge-Linguatec, Continental Book Company
Englewood Liaison Multilingual Services, Syntes

CONNECTICUT
Farmington China Communications Consultants
Millford Gene Mayer Associates
Riverside The Language Center

DELAWARE
Newark Pacific Ring Services
Wilmington Back to Basics

DISTRICT OF COLUMBIA
Washington ADA Inc., Federal News Service, Language Innovations, LLE
  Language Services, LanguageOne, Transemantics

FLORIDA
Altamonte Springs Monti Interpreting & Translation Services
Aventura Carmazzi
Bay Harbor Islands CITI Translation Center Inc.
Boca Raton NovaTrans Enterprises
Coral Springs Semantics Translations & Publishing
Fort Lauderdale Allslavic Translation Services, Artra International, Babel Tower
Lantana All Global Solutions International
Mary Lake AccessOnTime, Wudang Research Association
Miami Albors and Associates, American International Business Counsel,
  Expert Translators, Josef Sliny & Associates, Precision Translating Services,
  Professional Translating Services, Traducciones LinguaCorp, Trans Global

Miami Beach American Evaluation and Translation Service, SBF Translation Services

Orlando The Language Bank, Trans-Caribe, United Nations Translators & Interpreters

Plantation The Global Institute of Languages and Culture

Tallahassee RussTech

Winter Park Albors & Associates

GEORGIA

Atlanta ALTA Language Services, Atlantic International Translators, Intermark Language Services, Total Benefit Communications

Columbus Total System Services

Loganville 3DWord

HAWAII

Honolulu Babel Corporation

Makawao Origin—The Language Agency

IDAHO

Boise eLocale Inc.

Eagle Northwest Translations

Emmett Morales Dimmick Translation Service

ILLINOIS

Chicago Accuworld, Advance Language Studios, Atlas Language Services, Burg Translation Bureau, China Beacon, Cosmopolitan Translation Bureau, Eureka-Foreign College Evaluators & Translators, Global Languages & Cultures, Heartland Cross-Cultural Interpreting Services, Nelles Translations, Quintana Multi-Lingual Services

Darien Arabic Dialects

Elmwood Park Comunicad

Glenview Argo Translation

Palatine Square D/Schneider

Peoria Caterpillar Inc.

Skokie Lingua Communications Translation Services

South Holland Techno-Graphics

INDIANA

Indianapolis International Bureau of Translations, Language Training Center Inc., Pangea Lingua

IOWA

Cedar Rapids MGE Lingual Services, OmniLingua

KANSAS
Kansas City JLR Global Communications
Overland Park Interpretations Inc.
Shawnee Around the World

KENTUCKY
Louisville Languages Unlimited

LOUISIANA
Metairie Alpha Tech Communications
New Orleans McDermott International

MARYLAND
Bethesda Advanced Communication and Translation, Italian Translations Company
Columbia Translingua
Crofton Compass Languages
Frederick Welocalize.com
Germantown Transfirex Translation Services
Montgomery Village M² Limited
Rockville ALC Inc., Allworld Language Consultants, Multilingual Solutions, Schreiber Translations, Transfirex

MASSACHUSETTS
Acton Wordnet
Andover ArchiText Inc.
Boston American Translation Partners, Brigham and Women's Hospital, Community Interpreter Services, The Multi-Lingual Group, New England Translations, Translation3
Cambridge Linguistic Systems, RIC International
Lowell Agencia Internacional
Middleboro Rapport International
Randolph American ESL
Somerville Affordable Business Services
Sudbury Rapport International
Topsfield The Translators
Wakefield Transtek
Waltham COMSYS Services, Venturi Technology Partners
Winchester Cross Cultural Comm Systems
Woburn Cross Cultural Communications
Worcester Baystate Interpreters

MICHIGAN
Ada Alticor Inc.

Ann Arbor Japan-America Management, University Translators Services LLC
Bingham Farms Detroit Translation Bureau
Clawson Techworld
Grand Rapids Translations Unlimited, Voices for Health
Novi Suzuki, Myers
Plymouth Speak Easy Languages
Southfield Bromberg & Associates, International Translating Bureau
Sterling Heights Vital International Programs Inc.

MINNESOTA
Brooklyn Park A–Z Friendly Languages
Duluth Superior Translations, Toward
Minneapolis Accu Trans, APS International, Arthur International, Betmar
   Languages, Garden & Associates, International Translation Solutions, Mena's
   International Corp., Multilingual Word, University Language Center
Minnetonka International Language Services
Wayzata Inlingua Language & Intercultural Services

MISSOURI
Belton Transimpex
Carthage Leggett & Platt
Kansas City Language Link Corporation, SH3 Inc.
St. Louis Calvin International Communications, International Institute of Metro
   St. Louis, International Language Center

NEVADA
Henderson Worldwide Translations Inc.
Las Vegas CG Translations, Escalante Translations, eTranslations

NEW HAMPSHIRE
Bedford ABLE International
Nashua Eurotext Translations, TEXTnology

NEW JERSEY
Bedminster Ambassador Translating
Bridgewater Counterpoint Language Consultants
Carlstadt O'Sullivan Menu Corporation
Clinton aiaTranslations, Atkins International
East Brunswick The Language Center
East Windsor Princeton Technical Translation Center
Lawrenceville Premier Translation Services
Marlton Translation Company of New York
Morristown Allen Translation Service

Parsippany Newtype Inc.
Pennsauken A2Z Global Language Solutions
Princeton Bloomberg L.P., Telelingua International
Princeton Junction Telelingua
Randolph Newtype Inc.
Ridgewood Inlingua
Roselle Park Cybertec USA
South Orange Auracom
Summit Inlingua
Weehawken CLS Communications
West New York Continental Communications
Windsor Princeton Technical Translation Center

NEW YORK
Armonk M. E. Sharpe Inc.
Brooklyn Bilingual Professional Agency, Eriksen Translations, GES Translation
  Services
Central Islip MTS Multinational Translating Service
Fresh Meadows Eiber Translations
Gansevoort Copper Translation Services
Great Neck Eiber Translations
Hartsdale Marion J. Rosley
Long Island City Legal Interpreting Services
Marlton Translation Company of New York
Medford Angora Business Services
New York City Alanguage Bank, Audio to Go, Bowne Translation Services, C. P.
  Language Institute, EuroNet Language Services, Gazelle Localization Group,
  Geneva Worldwide Inc., Geotext Translations, InterNation Inc., Interspeak
  Translations, Japan Communication Consultants, The Languageworks,
  Merrill Translations, Metropolitan Interpreters and Translators Worldwide,
  1-800-Translate, R. R. Donnelley, Rennert, Translation Aces, Translations
  .com, Transperfect, Trustforte, WKI
Niskayuna All Language Translations
Poughkeepsie Accurapid Translation Services, The Language Service
Rochester Advanced Language Translation, Language Intelligence
Schenectady All Language Translations, Copper Translation Service

NORTH CAROLINA
Chapel Hill DTS Language Services, Global Translation Systems
Charlotte Avantgarde Translations, Carolina Polyglot, Choice Translating &
  Interpreting
Salem Lucent Technologies Global Translation

SOURCES OF TRANSLATION WORK

OHIO
Chagrin Falls M/C International
Cincinnati CinciLingua Inc., Conversa Language Center
Columbus Access Interpreters, ALTCO Translations, ASIST
Holland International Language Source
Pickerington World Inc.
Raymond Honda R&D North America

OKLAHOMA
Norman Language Company Translations

OREGON
Aloha LangTech International
Beaverton Bruce International
Portland Certified Languages International, Lingo Systems, Pacific Interpreters, Sarjam Communications, Telelanguage
Wilsonville Pacific Dreams

PENNSYLVANIA
Abington ABS Translation & Interpreting Service
Ardmor Language Services Consultants
Carnegie NCS Enterprises
Elkins Park CETRA
Lewisburg Lexiteria
Melrose Park CETRA Inc.
Philadelphia ISI, John Benjamins Publishing, Quantum Inc.
Pittsburgh Echo International, Multilingual Communications Corporation
Wayne Americlic
Willow Grove Language Services Associates
Wind Gap Affinity Language Services

RHODE ISLAND
Pawtucket Narragansett Translations & Interpreting

SOUTH CAROLINA
Columbia Certified Translation Services

TENNESSEE
Memphis Transglobal
Old Hickory NiS International Services

TEXAS
Alief Word Magic Software

Austin Adams Globalization, Larisa Zlatic Language Services, Phoenix Translations, Ralph McElroy
Dallas Accento, Accurate Spanish Translations, Garcia-Shilling International, International Translating & Typesetting, The Language Network, Liaison Language Center, OneWorld Language Solutions
El Paso Language Plus
Houston AE Inc. Translations, Airspeed, American Bureau, Crossword, IRU Language & Translation Services, Language Direct, MasterWord, TechTrans International, Translation Source, Word Magic Software
Irving Korean Consulting & Translation Service
Katy Crossword Translation & Interpreting
Plano American Language Technologies
San Antonio Barinas Translation Consultants

UTAH
Centerville TermSeek
Midvale Asian Translation Service
Ogden U.S. Translation Company
Provo MultiLing International
Roy DocuTrans Inc.
Salt Lake City CommGap International Language Services

VIRGINIA
Alexandria Alexandria Translations, JTG, Northern Virginia Area Health Education Center, Trados
Arlington ASET, Comprehensive Language Center, Inlingua
Harrisonburg Linguistic Services
Herndon Cascades Technologies
McLean BBC Multilingual Translations
Reston Antiquariat Literary Services, PSC Inc.
Triangle Albanian Translation Services
Virginia Beach Global Visions, The Language Group, Word for Word
Williamsburg ExactLingua

WASHINGTON
Burlington The Language Exchange
Federal Way Languages Translation Services
Lynnwood SinoMetrics International
Mukilteo TransACT
Seattle Academy of Languages, Dynamic Language Center, German Language Services, Japan Pacific Publications, Openworld, Sinometrics
Vancouver Columbia Language Services

WISCONSIN
Fond du Lac Mercury Marine
Little Chute Connecting Cultures
Madison Allegro Translations, Geo Group
Milwaukee Argo Translation, International Communication by Design, International Institute of Wisconsin, Iverson Language Associates
River Falls Sajan
Wauwatosa Language Source
West Allis C. P. Gauger

U.S. GOVERNMENT AGENCIES

All U.S. government agencies need translation from time to time. The question is when and where. There is no simple way to find out, but persistence does pay off, and if you keep exploring by reading the *Commerce Business Daily* (http://www.cbd-net.com), and by following leads, you will find translation work with the government.

Another way to find out about translation in the government is by locating the companies that have translation contracts with federal agencies. The government can provide this kind of information, and you can contact those companies and offer your services.

A word of warning: most government agencies do not accept unsolicited resumes. However, they do post available positions, which are usually accessible through the voice mail menu when you call them. In addition, you may now find websites for all the major agencies, as well as useful sites listing job opportunities throughout the entire government (see below).

Visit www.jobapplicationsearch.org to check information on availability of jobs in the entire federal government and to guide you through the federal job application process.

The following is a list of federal agencies and some comments about the translation needs of each agency.

Agency for International Development (AID), The Ronald Reagan Building, 1300 Pennsylvania Avenue NW, Washington, DC 20523
Phone: (202) 712-5043 Website: www.usaid.gov
AID is in charge of the U.S. Foreign Aid program. As such, it works in practically every language. Much of the work is done either in-house or in the target country, but from time to time AID needs translation services and is worth contacting.

Agriculture, U.S. Department of, 1400 Independence Avenue SW, Washington, DC 20250
Phone: (202) 720-4623 Website: www.usda.gov

This department, oddly enough, actually offers translation courses. We don't know much about its translation needs, except that there must be some, so feel free to find out for yourself.

Air Force, Department of the, The Pentagon, Washington, DC 20330
Phone: (703) 545-6700 Website: www.af.mil
This is a huge organization. Over the years it has done an enormous volume of translation, and was a pioneer in machine translation. The present status is not clear. You can try them, but there is no telling whether you'll find out anything specific. Ask them to send you literature about their language and translation needs.

Army, Department of the, Personnel & Employment Service, 6800 Army
Pentagon, Washington, DC 20310-6800
Phone: (703) 545-6700 Website: www.army.mil
Like the Air Force, the Army too has done and still does a very large volume of translation. The problem is how to get to the sources, which are spread all over creation. Knowing someone at the Pentagon or at any of the bases helps. You'll need to talk to the procurement people either locally or at the above number.

Central Intelligence Agency (CIA), Office of Public Affairs, Washington, DC
20505
Phone: (703) 482-0623 Website: www.cia.gov
The CIA hires a good number of translators in a great variety of languages. If interested in a CIA language career, call to inquire about employment. General descriptions of various jobs for language specialists are available on its website.

Citizenship and Immigration Service, U.S. (USCIS), 425 I Street NW,
Washington, DC 20536
Phone: (202) 205-2000 Website: www.uscis.gov
The CIS uses the services of interpreters in many languages in all of its court locations in the United States. Call to inquire about participating in this program.

Commerce, Department of, 1401 Constitution Avenue NW, Washington, DC
20230
Phone: (202) 482-2000 Website: www.commerce.gov
They have an interesting Japanese program which you may want to inquire about. Otherwise, they translate when they have to. Some Commerce agencies that engage in translation are the Patent and Trademark Office, the International Trade Administration, and the National Technical Information Service.

Congress, Library of (LOC), 101 Independence Avenue SE, Washington, DC 20540
Phone: (202) 707-5000 Website: www.loc.gov
The LOC employs full-time translators.

Defense, Department of (DoD), Washington Headquarters Services, 1155 Defense Pentagon, Washington, DC 20301-1155
Phone: (703) 604-6219 Website: www.defenselink.mil
Inquire about translation work with DoD agencies at the Defense Supply Office at the Pentagon. You may want to stop over there to look at their records. DoD does a great deal of translation.

Drug Enforcement Administration (DEA), Office of Personnel, 2401 Jefferson Davis Highway, Alexandria, VA 22301
Phone: (800) 882-9539 Website: www.dea.gov
Ask them about Spanish translation and/or interpreting. They do a great deal of this kind of work.

Education, Department of, 400 Maryland Avenue SW, Washington, DC 20202
Phone: (800) 872-5327 (general inquiries) Website: www.ed.gov

Energy, Department of (DOE), 1000 Independence Avenue SW, Washington, DC 20585
Phone: (202) 586-9534 (the Energy Library) Website: www.energy.gov
The technical library of the DOE needs translation from time to time and usually contracts out translation work. Call to inquire.

Environmental Protection Agency (EPA), Ariel Rios Building, 1200 Pennsylvania Avenue NW, Washington, DC 20460
Phone: (202) 564-0300 Website: www.epa.gov
The EPA usually contracts out translation work.

Federal Bureau of Investigations (FBI), J. Edgar Hoover Building, 935 Pennsylvania Avenue NW, Washington, DC 20535-0001
Phone: (202) 324-3000 (main number) Website: www.fbijobs.gov
The FBI employs full-time translators both at its Washington headquarters and in its field offices. All FBI language employees must be U.S. citizens. (Some exceptions are made for rare or unusual languages; linguists must then be legal resident aliens). Call to inquire (ask for the applicant coordinator).

Federal Trade Commission (FTC), Human Resources Management Office, Room 723, 600 Pennsylvania Avenue NW, Washington, DC 20580
Phone: (202) 326-2222 Website: www.ftc.gov
The FTC is involved in trade with the newly independent nations of Europe. You may want to find out if they need any translation work in this area.

Foreign Broadcast Information Service (FBIS), PO Box 2604, Washington, DC 20013
Phone: (703) 521-5638

Traditionally, FBIS, operating also as JPRS (Joint Publications and Research Service), has provided employment for translators in many languages and has farmed out translation to hundreds of freelancers. The volume is not what it used to be, but it is still worth inquiring, particularly if you work in languages like Arabic, Farsi, French, German, Russian, and many less common languages.

Health and Human Services, Department of (HHS), 200 Independence Avenue SW, Washington, DC 20201
Phone: (202) 619-0257 Toll Free: (877) 696-6775 Website: www.hhs.gov

Housing and Urban Development, Department of (HUD), 451 7th Street SW, Washington, DC 20410
Phone: (202) 708-1112 Website: www.hud.gov
HUD maintains a division of Immigrant Services, which involves both print and oral media and utilizes both translators and interpreters.

Inter-American Foundation, Personnel Department, 901 North Stuart Street, 10th Floor, Arlington, VA 22203
Phone: (703) 306-4301 Website: www.iaf.gov
May have a need for Spanish translation.

Interior, Department of the (DOI), 1849 C Street NW, Washington, DC 20240
Phone: (202) 208-3100 Website: www.doi.gov

Joint Publications and Research Service, PO Box 2604, Washington, DC 20013
See Foreign Broadcast Information Service.

Justice, Department of (DOJ), 950 Pennsylvania Avenue NW, Washington, DC 20530-0001
Phone: (202) 514-2000 Website: www.usdoj.gov
The DOJ is a major source of translation and interpreting. If you are interested in working for this department, you may want to do some research first and find out which agencies of the DOJ have been doing translation lately, and in what languages, and then find out who is doing the work (mostly farmed out) and contact those sources.

Labor, Department of (DOL), 200 Constitution Avenue NW, Washington, DC 20210
Phone: (202) 219-6677 (job openings) Website: www.dol.gov
Two DOL agencies, namely OSHA (Occupational Safety and Health Agency) and BLS (Bureau of Labor Statistics) have need for translation and interpretation in Spanish and other languages.

SOURCES OF TRANSLATION WORK

National Aeronautics and Space Administration (NASA), 300 E Street SW, Washington, DC 20546-0001

Phone: 1-877-NSSC123 (NASA Shared Services Center) Website: www.nasa.gov

NASA does a very large volume of translating and interpreting, but mostly through its major contractors, like Hewlett Packard, Lockheed, IBM, and others. You can contact NASA for information on those companies and then contact them and ask to talk to their small business office for more information.

National Institutes of Health (NIH), 9000 Rockville Pike, Bethesda, MD 20892

Phone: (301) 496-4000 Website: www.nih.gov

The NIH translates medical materials in a variety of languages, mostly through contractors.

National Security Agency (NSA), Fort George G. Meade, MD 20755

Phone: (866) 672-4473 (recruitment and staffing) Website: www.nsa.gov

NSA employs a large number of language specialists, mainly in the area of cryptography. They have an active recruitment program. Call to inquire.

National Virtual Translation Center, 935 Pennsylvania Avenue NW, Washington, DC 20535

Website: www.nvtc.gov

This organization provides translation services to many different government agencies. Applicants must be U.S. citizens. Applications may only be submitted online; see website for more information.

Navy, Department of the, Chief of Information, ATTN: Department of the Navy, 1200 Navy Pentagon, Room 4B463, Washington, DC 20350-1200

Phone: (703) 545-6700 Website: www.navy.mil

The Navy as a whole does a large volume of translation. It is difficult, though, to locate the specific sources. If you are a Navy veteran, you have a better chance of getting assignments.

Nuclear Regulatory Commission (NRC), 11555 Rockville Pike, Rockville, MD 20852-2738

Phone: (301) 415-7000 Website: www.nrc.gov

The NRC contracts out its translation needs. If interested, find out who their present contractor is and get in touch with them.

Peace Corps, 1111 20th Street NW, Washington, DC 20526

Phone: (800) 424-8580 Website: www.peacecorps.gov

The Peace Corps teaches a great many languages, and if you want to get involved in their language program, call to inquire.

State, Department of, 2201 C Street NW, Washington, DC 20520
Phone: (202) 647-4000 Website: www.state.gov
The State Department employs translators and interpreters, and farms out a great deal of translation and interpreting work. To find out more about it, call the Language Services office and ask for information.

Transportation, Department of (DOT), 1200 New Jersey Avenue SE, Washington, DC 20590
Phone: (202) 366-4000 Website: www.dot.gov
DOT does not have ongoing translation needs, but they do a translation project from time to time.

Veterans' Affairs, Department of (VA), 810 Vermont Avenue NW, Washington, DC 20420
Phone: (202) 273-5400 Website: www.va.gov
The VA may need translation occasionally, especially in Spanish. If you are a veteran, you may have a better chance to get assignments.

Voice of America, Language Services, 330 Independence Avenue SW, Washington, DC 20237
Phone: (202) 619-0909 (job hotline) Website: www.voa.gov

MAJOR ORGANIZATIONS

Inter-American Development Bank, 1300 New York Avenue NW, Washington, DC 20577
Phone: (202) 623-1000 Website: www.iadb.org
The bank hires French, Spanish, and Portuguese translators, mostly translating *into* English, and farms out a great deal of work in these languages.

International Monetary Fund (IMF), 700 19th Street NW, Washington, DC 20431
Phone: (202) 623-7000 Website: www.imf.org
The IMF employs translators and farms out translation work on such topics as finance, economic development, economic affairs in Third World countries, banking, and insurance.

Organization of American States (OAS), 17th Street & Constitution Avenue NW, Washington, DC 20006
Phone: (202) 458-6824 Website: www.oas.org
The OAS translates a good volume of Spanish and Portuguese and some French from and into English.

SOURCES OF TRANSLATION WORK

United Nations, 1st Avenue at 46th Street, New York, NY 10017
Phone: (212) 326-7000 Website: www.un.org
The UN employs a large number of translators and interpreters. If you are interested in a UN career, call their employment office and ask for the job application form, which contains detailed information on their requirements for employment.

The World Bank Group, 1818 H Street NW, Washington, DC 20433
Phone: (202) 473-1000 Website: www.worldbank.org
The World Bank employs translators and farms out translation work on such topics as finance, economic development, economic affairs in Third World countries, banking, and insurance.

World Health Organization (WHO), Avenue Appia 20, 1211 Geneva 27, Switzerland
Phone: (+41 22) 791 21 11 Website: www.who.org
Compiles and translates medical data in different languages.

MAJOR COMPANIES

The following is a listing of major companies that conduct business on an international scale. They represent opportunities for translators with the right languages and technical specialties to market their skills.

Alcatel-Lucent Inc., 600–700 Mountain Avenue, Murray Hill, NJ 07974
Phone: (908) 508-8080 Fax: (908) 508-2576 Website: www.alcatel-lucent.com
AT&T spinoff Lucent Technologies manufactures telecommunications equipment, operating in more than ninety countries.

Alcoa Company, 201 Isabella Street, Pittsburgh, PA 15212-5858
Phone: (412) 553-4545 Fax: (412) 553-4498 Website: www.alcoa.com
Alcoa is the world's top producer of aluminum products and packaging plastics, with operations in twenty-three countries, and exploring new markets in Asia, and Central and South America.

Allergan Incorporated, PO Box 19534, Irvine, CA 92623
Phone: (714) 246-4500 Fax: (714) 246-6987 Website: www.allergan.com
Allergan is the second largest maker of contact lenses (after Bausch & Lomb) as well as other eye-care products. They also produce skin-care products. Outside the United States, the company operates in China, India, Latin America, and Southeast Asia.

Allied Waste (used to be **Browning-Ferris Industries**), 15880 North Greenway-Hayden Loop, Suite 100, Scottsdale, AZ 85260
Phone: (480) 627-2700 Website: http://investor.alliedwaste.com
Allied Waste is a rapidly expanding waste disposal firm operating in 770 locations including Asia, Europe, the Middle East, and North America.

American Express, American Express Tower, World Financial Center, 200 Vesey Street, New York, NY 10285
Phone: (212) 640-2000 Fax: (212) 619-9802 Website: www.americanexpress.com
AmEx operates in the United States and more than 160 other countries worldwide, providing travel related services (credit cards and traveler's checks). A second arm of the company provides financial advisor services in thirty-six countries.

Amerisource Bergen, 1300 Morris Drive, Suite 100, Chesterbrook, PA 19087
Phone: (610) 727-7000 Website: www.amerisourcebergen.com
AmerisourceBergen began operations in August of 2001 following the merger of AmeriSource Health Corporation and Bergen Brunswig. Bergen Brunswig is a pharmaceutical distributor with most of its sales going to hospitals and managed care facilities. They operate primarily in the United States, but do business in Mexico as well.

Amgen Inc., 1 Amgen Center Drive, Thousand Oaks, CA 91320
Phone: (805) 447-1000 Fax: (805) 447-1010 Website: www.amgen.com
Amgen is one of the world's largest biotechnology companies. It operates worldwide, with offices in the United States, Canada, China, Japan, and several European countries.

Amoco/BP, 28100 Torch Parkway, Warrenville, IL 60555
Phone: (630) 836-5000 Website: www.bp.com
Amoco is North America's largest natural gas producer and one of the world's largest chemical and oil companies, with offices in forty countries, including the Middle East, South America, Eastern Europe, the North Sea region, and China.

AMR Corporation, PO Box 619616, DFW Airport, TX 75261
Phone: (817) 963-1234 Website: www.aa.com
American Airlines is the top U.S. airline, serving more than 170 destinations worldwide. Hub offices include locations in the continental United States and San Juan, Puerto Rico. In addition, American has inaugurated a new route to Paris. AMR bought out Trans World Airlines in 2001.

Anheuser-Busch Companies Inc., 1 Busch Place, St. Louis, MO 63118
Phone: (800) 342-5283 Website: www.anheuser-busch.com

Anheuser-Busch is the world's largest beer brewer, selling its products in over seventy countries.

AOLTimeWarner, 1 Time Warner Center, New York, NY 10019
Phone: (212) 484-8000 Fax: (212) 956-2847
Website: www.timewarner.com
Time Warner, the huge multimedia company, has sales in the United States, Europe, the Pacific Rim, and elsewhere, and is currently investing in Japan's cable TV industry.
Time Warner and AOL merged in 2000 to make AOLTimeWarner.

Apple Computer Inc., 1 Infinite Loop, Cupertino, CA 95014
Phone: (408) 996-1010 Fax: (408) 974-2113 Website: www.apple.com
Apple is the world's number-two computer manufacturer. It has manufacturing facilities outside the United States in Ireland and Singapore, and conducts business worldwide.

Aramark Corporation, 1101 Market Street, Philadelphia, PA 19107
Phone: (215) 923-2853 Website: www.aramark.com
Aramark is a diversified service company, with dozens of businesses under its corporate aegis. Although most of its operations are in the United States, it also operates in Canada, Belgium, Germany, the Czech Republic, Hungary, Spain, Mexico, Japan, and Korea.

Archer-Daniels-Midland Company, 4666 Fairies Parkway, Decatur, IL 62526
Phone: (217) 424-5200 Fax: (217) 424-6196 www.admworld.com
ADM is a processor of grain, seed, and vegetable products, with two hundred plants and worldwide marketing and operations.

Armstrong World Industries, 2500 Columbia Avenue (17603), PO Box 3001, Lancaster, PA 17604
Phone: (717) 397-0611 Fax: (717) 396-2787 www.armstrong.com
Armstrong manufactures floor coverings, furniture, and building products, producing and marketing its products worldwide. Twenty-three of its facilities are in eleven countries outside the United States, mostly in Europe, but in other regions as well.

Asarco, 5285 East Williams Circle, Suite 2000, Tucson, AZ 85711
Phone: (520) 798-7500 Fax: (520) 798-7780 Website: www.asarco.com
Asarco is one of the world's leading producers of copper, lead, zinc, silver, and gold. Outside the United States, the company maintains mines in Mexico and Peru.

Ashland Inc., 50 East Rivercenter Boulevard, PO Box 391, Covington, KY 41012
Phone: (859) 815-3333 Website: www.ashland.com
Ashland is one of the United States' largest refiners of petroleum and works in nonpetroleum energy and chemical production as well. In addition to its U.S. refineries, the company does resource exploration in Australia, Nigeria, and Morocco and has facilities in sixteen foreign countries. It markets its products and services in more than 140 countries.

AT&T Corporation, 32 Avenue of the Americas, New York, NY 10013-2412
Phone: (212) 387-5400 Fax: (212) 226-4935 Website: www.att.com
AT&T provides communications, computer, and network services worldwide and has ninety-two manufacturing facilities around the globe.

Atlantic Richfield Company, 515 South Flower Street, Los Angeles, CA 90071
Phone: (213) 486-3511 Fax: (213) 486-2063 Website: www.arco.com
Atlantic Richfield is the sixth largest U.S. oil company. It drills for oil and gas in China, Dubai, and Indonesia and is developing projects in the former Soviet Union.

Automatic Data Processing Inc., 1 ADP Boulevard, Roseland, NJ 07068-1728
Phone: (201) 994-5000 Fax: (201) 994-5387 Website: www.adp.com
ADP is the number-one payroll and tax filing processor in the United States, with fifty-three processing centers in the U.S., one in Canada, and two in Europe, and is continuing to expand internationally.

Avery Dennison, 150 North Orange Grove Boulevard, Pasadena, CA 91103
Phone: (626) 304-2000 Fax: (626) 792-7312 Website: www.averydennison.com
Avery Dennison is the leading U.S. producer of labels, as well as forty software support programs. The company has two hundred manufacturing facilities and sales offices in thirty-three countries worldwide, with Asian regional headquarters in Hong Kong.

Avis, 6 Sylvan Way, Parsippany, NJ 07054
Phone: (973) 496-3500 Fax: (516) 222-6677 Website: www.avis.com
Avis is the United States' second-largest car rental and leasing company, with 4,800 locations in 140 countries worldwide.

Avon Products Inc., 1345 Avenue of the Americas, New York, NY 10020
Phone: (212) 282-5000 Fax: (212) 282-6049 Website: www.avon.com
Avon is the world's leading direct seller of beauty products, manufacturing its products in eighteen countries, with subsidiaries in forty-five countries. Its operations extend from the Americas (with a large Brazilian market) to Europe and the Pacific region.

Baker Hughes, 2929 Allen Parkway, Suite 2100, Houston, TX 77019
Phone: (713) 439-8600 Fax: (713) 439-8699 Website: www.bakerhughes.com
   Baker Hughes produces equipment and materials for the oil drilling and mining industries, operating sixty-three manufacturing plants, thirty-six of which are outside the United States, both in Europe and the Western Hemisphere.

Ball Corporation, 10 Longs Peak Drive, Broomfield, CO 80021
Phone: (303) 469-3131 Fax: (303) 460-2127 Website: www.ball.com
   Originally known for its glass jars, Ball is expanding into aluminum can and PET plastic manufacture. It has joint ventures operating in Brazil, China, the Philippines, and Thailand.

Bank of America Corporation, Bank of America Corporate Center, 100 North Tryon Street, Charlotte, NC 28255
Phone: (800) 432-1000 Fax: (415) 622-8467 Website: www. bankofamerica.com
BankAmerica does business in thirty-six countries in all regions of the world.

The Bank of New York Mellon, 1 Wall Street, New York, NY 10286
Phone: (212) 495-1784 Fax: (212) 495-2546 Website: www.bnymellon.com
   The Bank of New York operates businesses throughout the United States and in twenty-nine other countries, primarily in Europe and Asia.

Bausch & Lomb, 1 Bausch and Lomb Place, Rochester, NY 14004
Phone: (585) 338-6000 Fax: (585) 330-6007 Website: www.bausch.com
   Bausch & Lomb is the largest manufacturer of contact lenses and their peripheral products. The company's other products include skin care, sunglasses, and hearing aids. B&L products are sold in over seventy countries worldwide.

Baxter Healthcare Corporation, 1 Baxter Parkway, Deerfield, IL 60015
Phone: (847) 948-2000 Fax: (847) 948-3642 Website: www.baxter.com
   Baxter is a producer of medical specialty products and medical/laboratory products and distribution, with 71 manufacturing plants in twenty-one countries, 149 distribution centers, and 25 research facilities worldwide.

Bechtel Group, 50 Beale Street, San Francisco, CA 94105
Phone: (415) 768-1234 Fax: (415) 768-9038 Website: www.bechtel.com
   Bechtel is a designer and builder of facilities for the power, petroleum, chemical, and mining and metals industries, and other major industries. They conduct business in more than fifty countries in Asia, Europe, the Middle East, Latin America, and Africa, as well as the United States and Canada.

Becton, Dickinson, and Company, 1 Becton Drive, Franklin Lakes, NJ 07417
Phone: (201) 847-6800 Fax: (201) 847-6475 Website: www.bd.com

Becton, Dickinson manufactures and sells medical supplies and devices and diagnostic systems, primarily in the United States and Europe, but also throughout the rest of the world. It has offices in Brazil, France, Japan, Mexico, Singapore, and Canada.

Black & Decker Corporation, 701 East Joppa Road, Towson, MD 21286
Phone: (410) 716-3900 Fax: (410) 716-2933 Website: www.blackanddecker.com
Black & Decker is the world's largest producer of power tools and accessories, and electric lawn and garden tools, as well as other products, all of which are marketed in over one hundred countries. The market is primarily the United States and Europe, but they also reach other regions.

The Boeing Company, 100 North Riverside, Chicago, IL 60606
Phone: (312) 544-2000 Website: www.boeing.com
Boeing has been the world's number-one commercial aircraft maker for more than thirty years and one of America's largest exporters, serving all areas of the world, with recent contracts in Malaysia.

Borden Inc., 180 East Broad Street, Columbus, OH 43215
Phone: (614) 225-4000 Fax: (614) 225-3410 Website: www.bordenchem.com
Borden is a producer of dairy products, pasta, and chemicals, operating manufacturing and processing facilities in the United States and Puerto Rico, as well as Canada, Brazil and Latin America, the Far East, and Western Europe.

Bristol-Myers Squibb Company, 345 Park Avenue, New York, NY 10154-0037
Phone: (212) 546-4000 Fax: (212) 546-4020 Website: www.bms.com
Bristol-Myers Squibb is one of the largest pharmaceutical companies in the United States, with business in Europe, the Middle East, Africa, the Pacific region, and other countries in the Western Hemisphere. Its largest markets are in the United States, France, and Japan.

Browning-Ferris Industries Inc., 757 North Eldridge, Houston, TX 77079
Phone: (713) 870-8100 Fax: (713) 870-7844 Website: www.bfi.com
Browning-Ferris is a rapidly expanding waste disposal firm operating in 770 locations including Asia, Europe, the Middle East, and North America.

Brunswick Corporation, 1 North Field Court, Lake Forest, IL 60045
Phone: (847) 735-4700 Fax: (847) 735-4765 Website: www.brunswick.com
Brunswick is a leisure services and manufacturing company, making sports equipment and operating bowling alleys and pizza restaurants. Outside the United States, it maintains five facilities in Germany and Austria.

SOURCES OF TRANSLATION WORK

Burlington Industries Inc., 3330 West Friendly Avenue, Greensboro, NC 27410
Phone: (336) 379-2855 Fax: (901) 379-4504 Website: www.burlington-ind.com
   Burlington Industries manufactures fabrics for the apparel and home furnishings industries, operating primarily in the United States, but with three plants in Mexico.

Caltex Petroleum Corporation, 125 East John Carpenter Parkway, Irving, TX 75602-2750
Phone: (972) 830-1000 Fax: (972) 830-1081 Website: www.caltex.com
   Caltex Petroleum, a joint venture between Texaco and Chevron, has operations in sixty-one countries, primarily in Africa, Australasia, Asia, and the Middle East.

Campbell Soup Company, 1 Campbell Place, Camden, NJ 08103-1701
Phone: (856) 342-4800 ext. 2225 Website: www.campbellsoups.com
   Campbell, a leading producer and distributor of brand-name food products, does its primary non-U.S. business in Europe, although it now has joint ventures with several producers in Japan and recently acquired a German soup manufacturer.

Cargill Incorporated, PO Box 9300, Minneapolis, MN 55440-9300
Phone: (800) 227-4455 Website: www.cargill.com
   Cargill, primarily a food company, also has its hand in finished steel and financial services, with 1,000 foreign offices in sixty-five countries, including Mexico, the Philippines, and South Africa.

Case Corporation, 700 State Street, Racine, WI 53404
Phone: (414) 636-6011 Fax: (414) 636-5043 Website: www.casecorp.com
   Case is North America's second-largest manufacturer of farm equipment, with retail stores in the United States and 150 countries, as well as plants in Brazil, Canada, France, Germany, and the UK.

Caterpillar Inc., 100 North East Adams Street, Peoria, IL 61629
Phone: (309) 675-1000 Fax: (309) 675-5800 www.caterpillar.com
   Caterpillar is the world's number-one manufacturer of machinery for construction, mining, and agriculture, with 38 plants in 12 countries and 187 dealerships in 128 countries in all parts of the world. It has set up a holding company in China.

Chevron Corporation, 6001 Bollinger Canyon Road, San Ramon, CA 94583
Phone: (925) 842-1000 Fax: (415) 894-0348 Website: www.chevron.com
   Chevron is a fully integrated oil and gas company with operations in the United States and about one hundred other countries worldwide, and is involved in a joint venture in Saudi Arabia.

Chiquita Brands International Inc., 250 East 5th Street, Cincinnati, OH 45202
Phone: (513) 784-8000 Fax: (513) 784-8030 Website: www.chiquita.com
Chiquita distributes its fruit and vegetable products worldwide.

Chrysler Corporation, 1000 Chrysler Drive, Auburn Hills, MI 48326-2766
Phone: (248) 576-5741 Fax: (248) 512-2912 Website: www.chryslercorp.com
   Chrysler Corporation not only produces motor vehicles, but also operates two
car rental companies and a variety of financial, leasing, and insurance services
related to its products. In addition to its U.S. manufacturing plants, it has facilities in Austria and Venezuela, and sells many of its products in over one hundred
countries throughout the world.

The Chubb Corporation, 15 Mountain View Road, PO Box 1615, Warren, NJ
   07059
Phone: (908) 903-2000 Fax: (908) 903-2027 Website: www.chubb.com
   Chubb Corporation is a large property/casualty company operating through-
out the United States and in twenty-five other countries in Europe, Asia, and
Latin America.

Cigna Corporation, 2 Liberty Place, 1601 Chestnut Street, Philadelphia, PA 19192
Phone: (215) 761-1000 Fax: (215) 761-5515 Website: www.cigna.com
   Cigna is one of America's top insurance companies, operating in the United
States, Europe, Latin America, and Asia.

Citicorp, 399 Park Avenue, New York, NY 10043
Phone: (212) 559-1000 Fax: (212) 559-5138 Website: www.citibank.com
   Citicorp is the largest banking company in the United States and the only
global full-service consumer bank, with more than 3,400 locations in ninety-five
countries worldwide, primarily in Western Europe, the Asia/Pacific region, Latin
America, Canada, and Japan.

The Clorox Company, 1221 Broadway, Oakland, CA 94612-1888
Phone: (510) 271-7000 Fax: (510) 832-1463 Website: www.clorox.com
   Clorox produces, in addition to cleaning products, Kingsford products (char-
coal, insecticides, chemicals) and food products. Its products are sold in more
than ninety countries and are produced in more than thirty-five plants in Latin
America (but not Brazil), South Korea, Canada, and the United States.

The Coastal Corporation, Coastal Tower, 9 Greenway Plaza, Houston, TX 77046
Phone: (713) 877-1400 Fax: (713) 877-6754 Website: www.thecoastalcorporation.com
   Coastal Corporation is an energy company involved in oil and gas exploration,
petroleum refining, coal mining, and the like, with marketing and distribution
operations around the world.

The Coca-Cola Company, PO Box 1734, Atlanta, GA 30301
Phone: (404) 676-2121 Fax: (404) 676-6792 Website: www.coca-cola.com
   Coca-Cola, the world's largest soft-drink and beverage company, is a presence in nearly every region of the world.

Colgate-Palmolive Company, 300 Park Avenue, New York, NY 10022
Phone: (212) 310-2000 Fax: (212) 310-3405 Website: www.colgate.com
   Colgate-Palmolive, a giant in the oral, personal, and household care and pet food markets, operates 66 facilities in the United States and 235 in over 60 other countries throughout the world.

Compaq Computer Corporation (see Hewlett Packard)

Computer Associates, 1 Computer Associates Plaza, Islandia, NY 11749
Phone: (631) 342-6000 Fax: (631) 342-6800 Website: www.ca.com
   Computer Associates integrates systems management software for small computers with mainframe software, offering over three hundred software products. The company has over one hundred offices in thirty countries.

ConAgra, 1 Conagra Drive, Omaha, NE 68102
Phone: (402) 595-4000 Fax: (402) 595-4707 Website: www.conagra.com
   ConAgra is a diversified food company with products ranging from agricultural supplies to production to marketing brand-name food products, with international offices in twenty-seven countries.

ConocoPhillips, 600 North Dairy Ashford, Houston, TX 77079-1175
Phone: (281) 293-1000 Website: www.conocophillips.com
   A fully integrated energy company, ConocoPhillips conducts exploration and production operations in the United States, the UK, Nigeria, and Norway, with most of its sales in those regions.

Consolidated Freightways Inc., 805 Broadway, Suite 205, Vancouver, WA 98660
Phone: (360) 448-4000 Website: www.cfwy.com
   Consolidated Freightways is a freight and delivery company with operations in North America and eighty-nine countries elsewhere in the world.

Continental Airlines Inc., 1600 Smith Street, Houston, TX 77002
Phone: (713) 834-5000 Fax: (713) 834-2087 Website: www.continental.com
   In addition to locations in the United States, Continental flies to fifty-eight destinations in Australasia, Europe, and Latin America.

Continental Grain Company, 277 Park Avenue, New York, NY 10172-0002
Phone: (212) 207-5100 Fax: (212) 207-2910 Website: www.contigroup.com

Continental Grain is one of the world's largest commodities traders, with offices and facilities in about sixty countries, including Switzerland and Hong Kong.

Cooper Industries Inc., 600 Travis Street, Suite 5600, Houston, TX 77002
Phone: (713) 209-8400 Fax: (713) 739-8995 Website: www.cooperindustries.com
Cooper Industries manufactures and sells automotive and electrical products, hardware, and tools throughout the world, primarily in Europe and the Americas, including Brazil and the North Sea region.

Corning Incorporated, One Riverfront Plaza, Corning, NY 14831
Phone: (607) 974-9000 Fax: (607) 974-8091 Website: www.corning.com
Corning is a major producer of glass products, including computer screens and optical fiber, with forty-one plants in eight countries and lab services in ten countries, particularly in the United States and Europe.

Crown Cork & Seal Company, 1 Crown Way, Philadelphia, PA 19154
Phone: (215) 698-5100 Fax: (215) 676-7245 Website: www.crowncork.com
Crown Cork & Seal is a worldwide producer of caps and seals for glass, metal, and plastic jars, bottles, and other containers, operating seventy plants in the United States and sixty-eight plants in other countries, primarily in Europe and the Americas.

Cummins Engine Company Inc., Box 3005, Columbus, IN 47202
Phone: (812) 377-5000 Fax: (812) 377-4937 Website: www.cummins.com
Cummins manufactures diesel engines, with manufacturing operations in fourteen countries and markets in all parts of the world.

Cyprus Amax Minerals Company, 9100 East Mineral Circle, Englewood, CO 80112
Phone: (303) 643-5000 Fax: (303) 643-5049 Website: www.cyprusamax.com
Cyprus Amax is America's largest mining company, operating in the United States and the UK, Australia, Sweden, the Netherlands, Russia, Chile, and Peru.

Dana Corporation, 4500 Dorr Street, Toledo, OH 43615
Phone: (419) 535-4500 Fax: (419) 535-4643 Website: www.dana.com
Dana Corporation specializes in under-the-hood equipment for motor vehicles (axles, drive shafts, filters, valves, etc.), with 550 manufacturing, assembly, and distribution facilities in thirty-three countries, including Mexico, China, and Brazil.

Deere & Company, 1 John Deere Road, Moline, IL 61265
Phone: (309) 765-8000 Fax: (309) 765-5772 Website: www.deere.com

Deere & Company is the world's largest manufacturer of farm equipment and a leading producer of industrial and lawn care equipment, selling its products in more than 160 countries worldwide, including Europe and China. It has a new factory in Mexico.

Dell Computer Corporation, 1 Dell Way, Round Rock, TX 78682
Phone: (512) 338-4400 Fax: (512) 728-3653 Website: www.dell.com
Dell sells sixty-four computer systems in seven product families as well as software and peripherals in more than 130 countries, mostly in the Americas and Europe.

Deloitte, 1633 Broadway, New York, NY 10019
Phone: (212) 489-1600 Fax: (212) 489-1687 Website: www.deloitte.com
Deloitte operates accounting offices in more than 126 countries worldwide.

Delta Air Lines Inc., 1030 Delta Boulevard, Atlanta, GA 30320-6001
Phone: (404) 715-2600 Fax: (404) 715-2100 Website: www.delta-air.com
Delta serves the United States and thirty other countries, including a hub in Germany.

DHL Worldwide Express, 1200 South Pine Island Road, Suite 600, Plantation, FL 33324
Phone: (415) 593-7474 Fax: (415) 593-1689 Website: www.dhl.com
DHL is an international shipper operating out of separate headquarters in California and Brussels, with 19 hubs and 1,900 offices in 224 countries. It has developed a new minihub in Panama.

Dole Food Company Inc., PO Box 5132, Westlake Village, CA 91359-5132
Phone: (818) 879-6600 Fax: (818) 879-6615 Website: www.dole.com
Dole is one of the world's largest distributors of fresh and processed fruits, vegetables, and nuts, with operations in the Americas, Asia, Africa, and Europe, and markets worldwide.

Domino's Pizza Inc., 30 Frank Lloyd Wright Drive, Ann Arbor, MI 48106-0997
Phone: (734) 930-3030 Fax: (303) 668-4614 Website: www.dominos.com
Domino's, the pizza delivery company, has stores in the United States and Canada as well as Latin America (including Brazil), the Middle East, Western Europe, and the Far East.

The Dow Chemical Company, 2030 Dow Center, Midland, MI 48674
Phone: (517) 636-1000 Fax: (517) 636-1830 Website: www.dow.com
Dow Chemical makes and supplies more than 2,500 product families, with ninety-four plants in the United States and thirty foreign countries worldwide. It sells its products in 164 countries.

Dow Jones & Company Inc., 200 Liberty Street, New York, NY 10281
Phone: (212) 416-2000 Fax: (212) 416-4348 Website: www.dowjones.com
Dow Jones, a media company specializing in business news and information, reaches markets in all parts of the world in print, online, and by satellite, radio, TV, pager, and fax. It has new services in Latin America and Italy.

Dresser Inc., 15455 Dallas Parkway, Addison, TX 75001
Phone: (972) 361-9800 Fax: (972) 361-9903 Website: www.dresser.com
Dresser is one of the largest energy service companies in the world, with more than one hundred manufacturing plants in fifty countries and facilities serving more than eighty countries, particularly in Asia, the Middle East, Latin America, and Africa.

The Dun & Bradstreet Corporation, 103 JFK Parkway, Shorthills, NJ 07078
Phone: (973) 921-5500 Website: www.dnb.com
Dun & Bradstreet is the world's largest marketer of information, software, and services for business decision making, with a worldwide clientele, primarily in the United States and Europe.

E.I. DuPont de Nemours, 1007 Market Street, Wilmington, DE 19898
Phone: (302) 774-1000 Fax: (302) 774-7321 Website: www.dupont.com
DuPont is the United States' largest chemical company and operates in about seventy countries worldwide, primarily in the United States and Europe, and is currently working on joint ventures with China.

Eastman Kodak Company, 343 State Street, Rochester, NY 14650
Phone: (585) 724-4000 Fax: (716) 724-1089 Website: www.kodak.com
Eastman Kodak does business worldwide, currently focusing on emerging markets in Brazil, China, India, and Russia.

Eaton Corporation, 1111 Superior Avenue, Cleveland, OH 44114
Phone: (216) 523-5000 Fax: (216) 523-4787 Website: www.eaton.com
Eaton is a manufacturer of highly engineered products from basic automotive components to electrical power grids, with 150 facilities in eighteen countries, primarily in the United States, Europe, Latin America, and Canada. It has recently acquired companies in the Netherlands, Thailand, and Brazil.

Electronic Data Systems Corporation (EDS), 5400 Legacy Drive, Plano, TX 75024
Phone: (972) 604-6000 Fax: (972) 605-2643 Website: www.eds.com
EDS provides systems and management consulting in thirty-seven countries, primarily in the United States and Europe.

SOURCES OF TRANSLATION WORK

Eli Lilly and Company, Lilly Corporate Center, Indianapolis, IN 46285
Phone: (317) 276-2000 Fax: (317) 277-6579 Website: www.lilly.com
Lilly researches, produces, and markets pharmaceuticals with operations in 27 countries and markets in 117, especially in the United States, Japan, the Middle East, and Europe.

Emerson Electric Co., 8000 West Florissant Avenue, St. Louis, MO 63136
Phone: (314) 553-2000 Fax: (314) 553-3527 Website: www. emerson.com
Emerson produces both commercial and industrial machinery, systems, and appliances in 360 facilities worldwide, including new ventures in China, India, and Eastern Europe.

Equifax Inc., 1600 Peachtree Street NW, Atlanta, GA 30309
Phone: (404) 885-8000 Fax: (404) 885-8055 Website: www.equifax.com
Equifax is a credit reporting agency with operations in the United States, Australia, Canada, the Caribbean, Europe, and Latin America.

The Equitable Companies Inc., 1290 Avenue of the Americas, New York, NY 10014
Phone: (212) 554-1234 Fax: (212) 707-1755 Website: www.equitable.com
Equitable is an insurance company with a brokerage and investment banking subsidiary and commercial real estate development and management services which, although it operates solely in the United States, is partnered with French insurance giant Axa.

Ernst & Young International, 5 Times Square, New York, NY 10036
Phone: (212) 773-3000 Fax: (212) 773-6350 Website: www.ey.com
Ernst & Young, one of the big six accounting firms, maintains more than 670 offices in over 130 countries around the world.

ExxonMobil Corporation, 5959 Las Colinas Boulevard, Irving, TX 75039-2298
Phone: (972) 444-1000 Fax: (972) 444-1882 Website: www.exxonmobil.com
Exxon, the world's largest publicly owned integrated oil company, operates in the United States and in over one hundred other countries, with new drilling operations in Eastern Russia and other former Soviet states, China, and West Africa.

FedEx Corporation, 942 South Shady Grove Road, Memphis, TN 38120
Phone: (901) 369-3600 Fax: (901) 395-2000 Website: www.fedex.com
FedEx offers package delivery services throughout the United States and in 192 foreign countries, with recent expansions into Guyana, Marshall Islands, Bhutan, Brunei, French Guiana, Micronesia, Palau, and Suriname.

Fluor Corporation, 6700 Las Colinas Boulevard, Irving, TX 75039
Phone: (469) 398-7000 Fax: (469) 398-7255 Website: www.fluor.com
   Fluor is the world's largest engineering and construction firm, with operations in more than eighty countries, especially in North America, Europe, and the Asia/Pacific region, with a new facility in Indonesia.

FMC Corporation, 1735 Market Street, Philadelphia, PA 19103
Phone: (215) 299-6000 Fax: (215) 299-6140 Website: www.fmc.com
   FMC manufactures chemicals for the agriculture, food, and pharmaceutical markets, and makes machinery for the defense, food processing, and transportation industries. It operates one hundred facilities and mines in the United States and twenty other countries, principally in Europe and the Americas.

Ford Motor Company, PO Box 6248, Dearborn, MI 48126
Phone: (313) 322-3000 Fax: (313) 323-2959 Website: www.ford.com
   Ford, the world's number-two automaker, has operations in thirty countries, including a joint project with Volkswagen in Portugal.

Freeport-McMoRan Copper & Gold Inc., 1 North Central Avenue, Phoenix, AZ 85004
Phone: (602) 366-8100 Fax: (602) 234-8337 Website: www.fcx.com
   Freeport-McMoRan is the number-one international mining company, with facilities in twenty-five countries and sales primarily in the Americas. A large portion of their operations is in South America.

Fruit of the Loom, 1 Fruit of the Loom Drive, Bowling Green, KY 42102
Phone: (270) 781-6400 Fax: (270) 781-1754 Website: www.fruit.com
   Fruit of the Loom, maker of underwear and activewear, has sixty-one manufacturing facilities in the United States, the UK, Ireland, Canada, Jamaica, and Honduras and El Salvador, with plans to move more of its production outside the United States.

Gannett Co. Inc., 7950 Jones Branch Drive, McLean, VA 22107
Phone: (703) 854-6000 Fax: (703) 558-3506 Website: www.gannett.com
   Gannett is the United States' largest newspaper publisher, with facilities in the United States, the UK, Canada, Germany, Hong Kong, and Switzerland.

The Gap Inc., 2 Folsom Street, San Francisco, CA 94105
Phone: (650) 952-4400 Fax: (650) 427-2795 Website: www.gapinc.com
   The Gap, operator of 1,508 casual clothing stores, does business in the United States and Puerto Rico, the UK, Canada, and France, and most recently in Japan and Germany.

Gateway Inc., 7565 Irvine Center Drive, Irvine, CA 92618
Phone: (949) 471-7000 Fax: (949) 471-7041 Website: www.gateway.com
   Gateway manufactures and is a direct marketer of computers, with facilities in the United States, Australia, Canada, China, Europe, Japan, and Mexico.

Genentech Inc., 1 DNA Way, South San Francisco, CA 94080
Phone: (650) 225-1000 Fax: (650) 225-6000 Website: www.gene.com
   Genentech markets biotechnology products in North America, Europe, and Japan, and licenses products worldwide.

General Electric Company, 3135 Easton Turnpike, Fairfield, CT 06828
Phone: (203) 373-2211 Fax: (203) 373-3497 Website: www.ge.com
   General Electric, the giant company that makes everything from lightbulbs to jet engines, operates in the United States and Puerto Rico, with 113 plants in twenty-five other countries. Its market is worldwide with locations in 160 countries.

General Motors Corporation, 100 Renaissance Center, Detroit, MI 48243
Phone: (313) 556-5000 Fax: (313) 556-5108 Website: www.gm.com
   General Motors extends its manufacturing and assembly operations beyond the United States and Canada into the UK, Austria, Germany, Belgium, Brazil, Mexico, and Spain.

General Re Corporation, 695 East Main Street, Stamford, CT 06904-2351
Phone: (203) 328-5000 Fax: (203) 328-6423 Website: www.genre.com
   General Re is the largest property/casualty reinsurer in the United States, with operations in the United States and in over twenty-three other countries worldwide, primarily Germany.

The Gillette Company, 800 Boylston Street, Boston, MA 02199
Phone: (617) 421-7000 Fax: (617) 421-7123 Website: www.gillette.com
   Gillette, manufacturer of shaving products and other toiletries, as well as personal and household appliances, sells its products in more than two hundred countries and manufactures them in twenty-four, primarily in Europe and Latin America, with newer markets in Japan.

The Goldman Sachs Group L.P., 85 Broad Street, New York, NY 10004
Phone: (212) 902-1000 Fax: (212) 902-3000 Website: www.gs.com
   Goldman Sachs is an equities and fixed income broker and underwriter, investment banker, asset manager, and commodities trader in Asia, Australia, Europe, and North America.

The Goodyear Tire & Rubber Company, 1144 East Market Street, Akron, OH 44316
Phone: (330) 796-2121 Fax: (330) 796-2222 Website: www.goodyear.com
Goodyear is the world's largest rubber manufacturer, with plants in the United States and twenty-six other countries in Europe, the Americas, and Asia. It has recently become involved in joint ventures in India and China, with planned expansion into Brazil, Indonesia, Malaysia, and Thailand.

Great A&P Tea Co., 2 Paragon Drive, Montvale, NJ 07645
Phone: (201) 573-9700 Fax: (201) 930-8144 Website: www.aptea.com
Although A&P operates in the United States and Canada, most of the company is owned by the German firm Tengelmann, which also plans to take the A&P name to the Netherlands.

Halliburton Company, Suite 2400, 1401 McKinney Street, Houston, TX 77010
Phone: (713) 759-2600 Website: www.halliburton.com
Halliburton, an energy, engineering, and construction services company, conducts business in the United States and in more than one hundred other countries around the world, including Japan, China, Germany, and Vietnam. It conducts drilling operations in the Middle East and North Sea regions.

Hallmark Cards Inc., 2501 McGee Trafficway, Kansas City, MO 64108
Phone: (816) 452-6672 Fax: (816) 274-5061 Website: www.hallmark.com
Hallmark distributes its products in more than one hundred countries.

H&R Block Inc., 4400 Main Street, Kansas City, MO 64111
Phone: (816) 753-6900 Fax: (816) 753-5346 Website: www.hrblock.com
H&R Block operates 9,577 offices in the United States, Canada, Australia, and Europe.

Harris Corporation, 1025 West NASA Boulevard, Melbourne, FL 32919
Phone: (407) 727-9100 Fax: (407) 727-9344 Website: www.harris.com
Harris is a defense electronics manufacturer that has branched out into semiconductors, telecommunications systems, and radio and TV broadcasting equipment. It has twenty-nine plants and about four hundred offices worldwide, including Russia, Malaysia, and Singapore.

Hasbro Inc., 1027 Newport Avenue, Pawtucket, RI 02861
Phone: (401) 431-8697 Fax: (401) 431-8535 Website: www.hasbro.com
Hasbro, the number-two toy company in the United States, designs, manufactures, and markets its products throughout the world with operations in twenty-five foreign countries.

SOURCES OF TRANSLATION WORK

HCA Healthcare, 1 Park Plaza, Nashville, TN 37203
Phone: (615) 344-9551 Fax: (615) 320-2266 Website: www.hcahealthcare.com
  Columbia/HCA is the operator of 320 hospitals in the United States, the UK, and Switzerland.

The Hearst Corporation, 250 West 55th Street, New York, NY 10019
Phone: (212) 649-2000 Fax: (212) 765-3528 Website: www.hearstcorp.com
  Hearst, one of the world's largest diversified media companies, markets its products throughout the United States and in more than eighty countries, with a newspaper in Russia and interest in a French Canadian cable television company.

Hercules Incorporated, 1313 North Market Street, Wilmington, DE 19894
Phone: (302) 594-5000 Fax: (302) 594-5400 Website: www.herc.com
  Hercules is in the large-scale chemical business, with subsidiaries and affiliates in twenty-four countries, primarily in Europe, but also including Mexico (serving customers in Central and South America). It has a new plant in Shanghai.

Hershey Foods Corporation, 100 Crystal A Drive, Hershey, PA 17033
Phone: (717) 534-6799 Fax: (717) 534-6760 Website: www.hersheys.com
  Hershey operates outside the United States in Italy, Germany, Belgium, Japan, and the Netherlands, with successful newer ventures in Russia and plans to expand into the Latin American and Chinese markets.

Hewlett-Packard Company, 3000 Hanover Street, Palo Alto, CA 94304
Phone: (650) 857-1501 Fax: (650) 857-5518 Website: www.hp.com
  Hewlett-Packard, producer of computers and printers for home and office, operates facilities in the United States and 16 other countries, with 600 sales and support offices in more than 120 countries.

Hilton Hotels Corporation, 9336 Civic Center Drive, Beverly Hills, CA 90210
Phone: (310) 278-4321 Fax: (310) 205-4599 Website: www.hilton.com
  Hilton owns, manages, or franchises hotels in the United States, the UK, Australia, Hong Kong, Ireland, Belgium, and Turkey.

H. J. Heinz Company, 600 Grant Street, Pittsburgh, PA 15219
Phone: (412) 456-5700 Fax: (412) 237-6128 Website: www.heinz.com
  Heinz operates eighty-eight food-processing plants in twenty-one countries and has markets internationally, especially in Europe and the Asia/Pacific region.

Honeywell Inc., 101 Columbia Road, Morristown, NJ 07962
Phone: (973) 455-2000 Fax: (973) 455-4807 Website: www.honeywell.com
  Honeywell is one of the world's top manufacturers of control systems and components, operating in ninety-five countries, primarily in the United States, Europe, and the Pacific Rim.

Hormel Foods Corporation, 1 Hormel Place, Austin, MN 55912-3680
Phone: (507) 437-5611 Fax: (507) 437-5489 Website: www.hormel.com
Hormel markets its products in more than forty countries, such as Australia, the UK, Hong Kong, Japan, Korea, Mexico, Panama, and the Philippines.

Hughes Network Systems LLC, 11717 Exploration Lane, Germantown, MD 20876
Phone: (301) 428-5500 Fax: (301) 428-1868 Website: www.hughes.com
Hughes Electronics has worldwide operations on all continents and maintains a network of eighteen communications satellites orbiting the earth.

Hyatt Hotels Corporation, Hyatt Center, 71 S. Wacker Drive, Chicago, IL 60606
Phone: (312) 750-1234 Fax: (312) 750-8550 Website: www.hyatt.com
Hyatt's international division is responsible for the company's worldwide network of hotels, with its most recent units in Saudi Arabia and Azerbaijan.

IBM Corporation, 1 New Orchard Road, Armonk, NY 10504
Phone: (914) 765-1900 Fax: (914) 765-7382 Website: www.ibm.com
IBM, the world's top computer company (hardware and software), sells its products worldwide.

Illinois Tool Works Inc., 3600 West Lake Avenue, Glenview, IL 60025-5811
Phone: (847) 724-7500 Fax: (847) 657-4261 Website: www.itwinc.com
Illinois Tool Works makes a large range of equipment for the automotive, construction, food and beverage, and general industrial markets, with major non-U.S. plants and offices in the UK, Australia, Canada, Ireland, Belgium, Germany, Sweden, Switzerland, France, Italy, Spain, Japan, and Malaysia.

Ingersoll-Rand Company, 155 Chestnut Ridge Road, Montvale, NJ 07645
Phone: (201) 573-0123 Fax: (201) 573-3172 Website: www.ingersoll-rand.com
Ingersoll-Rand is a leading manufacturer of nonelectrical industrial machinery, with plants in the United States, Canada, Europe, Asia, Latin America, and Africa, and worldwide sales, especially in Europe.

Intel Corporation, 2200 Mission College Boulevard, Santa Clara, CA 95054
Phone: (408) 765-8080 Fax: (408) 765-6284 Website: www.intel.com
Intel, the number-one maker of integrated circuits, including the Pentium chip, has plants in the United States and Puerto Rico, Ireland, Israel, Malaysia, and the Philippines, with sales in the United States, Europe, and the Asia/Pacific region.

International Paper Company, 6400 Poplar Avenue, Memphis, TN 38197
Phone: (901) 419-9000 Website: www.ipaper.com
International Paper has production facilities in 27 countries and distribution in 130, primarily in the United States and Europe, and is hoping to increase its access to markets in South America and the Pacific Rim.

SOURCES OF TRANSLATION WORK

ITT Industries Inc., 1133 Westchester Avenue, White Plains, NY 10604
Phone: (914) 641-2000 Fax: (914) 696-2950 Website: www.ittind.com
ITT Industries, another spinoff from the ITT split, supplies automotive components and systems, high-tech electronics for commercial and defense markets, and pumps, valves, and the like for fluid handling. The company operates worldwide, primarily in the United States, Canada, Western Europe, and the Asia/Pacific region. The fluid technology division has joint manufacturing ventures in Brazil and China.

John Hancock Insurance Company, 601 Congress Street, Boston, MA 02210
Phone: (617) 572-6000 Fax: (617) 572-6451 Website: www. johnhancock.com
John Hancock has added financial services to its base insurance business, licensed throughout the United States and Canada, with subsidiaries and affiliates in the UK, Belgium, Indonesia, Malaysia, and Thailand, and doing business in forty-six countries worldwide, including opening a new office in Beijing.

Johnson and Johnson, 1 Johnson and Johnson Plaza, New Brunswick, NJ 08933
Phone: (732) 524-0400 Fax: (732) 524-3300 Website: www.jnj.com
Johnson and Johnson manufactures and markets a complete range of healthcare products, with operations in 50 countries and sales in more than 175, including joint ventures in China and Japan, and recent entry into the Eastern European market.

Johnson Controls Inc., 5757 North Green Bay Avenue, Milwaukee, WI 53201
Phone: (414) 524-1200 Fax: (414) 228-2302 Website: www.jci.com
Johnson Controls' main markets are batteries, commercial facilities management, plastic containers, and vehicle seating, operating in more than five hundred locations worldwide, primarily in the United States and Europe, with the recent acquisitions of Czech and French companies.

J.P. Morgan & Co., Incorporated, 60 Wall Street, New York, NY 10250-0060
Phone: (212) 483-2323 Fax: (212) 648-5193 Website: www.jpmorgan.com
J.P. Morgan, an international banking company, conducts banking and investment operations in the United States and thirty countries worldwide, with new offices in China, Poland, the Czech Republic, and Mexico.

Kellogg Company, 1 Kellogg Square, Battle Creek, MI 49016-3599
Phone: (616) 961-2000 Fax: (616) 961-2871 Website: www.kelloggscompany.com
Kellogg's food business has manufacturing facilities in 20 countries and distribution in 160, mostly in the United States and Europe, and includes facilities in Russia, India, Argentina, and China.

Kelly Services Inc., 999 West Big Beaver Road, Troy, MI 48084
Phone: (248) 362-4444 Fax: (248) 244-4154 Website: www.kellyservices.com
Kelly provides temporary workers in clerical, technical, light industry, and personal care from over 1,000 offices in the United States, the UK, Ireland, Australia and New Zealand, Canada, Denmark, Norway, France, the Netherlands, and Switzerland.

Kimberly-Clark Corporation, 351 Phelps Drive, Irving, TX 75038
Phone: (972) 281-1200 Fax: (978) 281-1435 Website: www.kimberly-clark.com
Kimberly-Clark, recently merged with Scott, is a paper products giant, with plants in the United States and 25 foreign countries and sales in 150, primarily in Europe, Asia, and Latin America.

Kmart Corporation, 3100 West Big Beaver Road, Troy, MI 48084
Phone: (810) 643-1000 Fax: (810) 643-5636 Website: www.kmart.com
Kmart has retail stores in the United States and Canada, as well as in Puerto Rico, Mexico, and Singapore.

Koch Industries Inc., 4111 East 37th Street N, Wichita, KS 67220
Phone: (316) 828-5500 Fax: (316) 828-5739 Website: www.kochind.com
Koch is in the energy business, with refineries, pipelines, chemical technology, and even cattle ranches and financial services. The company has operations in the United States, the UK, Canada, and Singapore.

KPMG Peat Marwick LLP, 3 Chestnut Ridge Road, Montvale, NJ 07645
Phone: (201) 307-7000 Fax: (201) 930-8617 Website: www.kpmg.com
KPMG, one of the big six accounting firms, does much of its business outside the United States, with offices in 142 countries, including the former Soviet Union. The company's main headquarters is in the Netherlands.

Lands' End Inc., 1 Lands' End Lane, Dodgeville, WI 53595
Phone: (608) 935-9341 Fax: (608) 935-4260 Website: www.landsend.com
Lands' End catalog sales of apparel and soft goods recently launched a catalog business in Japan, as well as small mailings (through its UK distribution center) of native language, native currency catalogs in France, Germany, and the Netherlands. The company has plans to continue to expand internationally.

Lear Corporation, 21557 Telegraph Road, Southfield, MI 48086
Phone: (248) 447-1500 Fax: (248) 447-1722 Website: www.lear.com
Formerly Lear Seating, the company makes auto seats and other interior components. It operates joint ventures in China and Thailand and recently acquired a component manufacturer in Sweden.

SOURCES OF TRANSLATION WORK

Levi Strauss Associates Inc., 1155 Battery Street, San Francisco, CA 94111-1230
Phone: (415) 544-6000 Fax: (415) 544-3939 Website: www.levistrauss.com
   Levi Strauss is the world's largest clothing maker with production/warehouse
and distribution facilities around the world, and operations in seventy-two countries, primarily in the Americas, Europe, and the Asia/Pacific region.

Lexmark International Group Inc., 740 New Circle Road NW, Lexington, KY
   40550
Phone: (606) 232-2000 Fax: (606) 232-2403 Website: www.lexmark.com
   Formerly part of IBM, Lexmark is a manufacturer of computer printers and
supplies, as well as typewriters. Its products sell in over one hundred countries
worldwide.

Liz Claiborne Inc., 5901 West Side Avenue, North Bergen, NJ 07047
Phone: (201) 682-6000 Website: www.lizclaiborne.com
   Liz Claiborne apparel is produced in more than fifty countries, mainly in the
United States, China, Hong Kong, Indonesia, South Korea, and Sri Lanka, with
sales in Asia (excluding Myanmar), Latin America (including Brazil), and the
Middle East.

Lockheed Martin Corporation, 6801 Rockledge Drive, Bethesda, MD 20817
Phone: (301) 897-6000 Fax: (301) 897-6704 Website: www.lockheedmartin.com
   Lockheed Martin is the nation's largest defense contractor with products such
as missiles, navigational systems, spacecraft, and satellite communication systems. The company has contracts in the Netherlands and China.

LSI Logic Corporation, 1621 Barber Lane, Milpitas, CA 95035
Phone: (866) 574-5741 Fax: (408) 954-3108 Website: www.lsi.com
   LSI manufactures integrated circuits and owns Nihon Semiconductor (now
LSI Logic Japan Semiconductor). Its products are sold in North America, Europe,
Japan, and the Pacific Rim.

Manpower Inc., 100 Manpower Place, Milwaukee, WI 53212
Phone: (414) 961-1000 Fax: (414) 961-7081 Website: www.manpower.com
   Manpower is the world's largest temporary employment company, with 2,400
offices in the United States and Canada, the UK, Australia, Europe, Israel, Latin
America, and Japan.

Marriott International Inc., Marriott Drive, Washington, DC 20058
Phone: (301) 380-3000 Fax: (301) 380-3969 Website: www.marriott.com
   Marriott is in the hospitality business, owning hotels, restaurants, cruise ships,
and so forth, with units in twenty-five countries worldwide.

Mars Inc., 6885 Elm Street, McLean, VA 22101
Phone: (703) 821-4900 Fax: (703) 448-9678 Website: www.mars.com
Mars not only produces candy items, but also produces and markets pet food, rice, and ice cream bars. It has over sixty operating plants in thirty-one countries worldwide, including Russia and other former Soviet states, Africa, the Middle East, India, and China.

Marsh & McLennan Companies Inc., 1166 Avenue of the Americas, New York, NY 10036-2774
Phone: (212) 345-5000 Fax: (212) 345-4808
Website: www.marshmac.com
Marsh & McLennan is a top insurance brokerage service, with operations in more than eighty countries, primarily in the United States, Canada, and Europe.

Masco Corporation, 21001 Van Born Road, Taylor, MI 48180
Phone: (313) 274-7400 Fax: (313) 792-6135 Website: www.masco.com
Masco is a major manufacturer of home furnishings, kitchen, and bathroom products, with plants in the United States and twelve other countries, and sales primarily in the United States and Europe. The company has acquired a firm in Germany and has expanded its distribution and business facilities into the Philippines.

Mattel Inc., 333 Continental Boulevard, El Segundo, CA 90245-5012
Phone: (310) 252-2000 Fax: (310) 252-2179 Website: www.mattel.com
Mattel has offices and facilities in thirty-seven countries worldwide, with manufacturing plants in China, Indonesia, Malaysia, Italy, and Mexico, and markets its toys in 140 countries.

McDermott International Inc., 777 North Eldridge Parkway, Houston, TX 77079
Phone: (281) 870-5901 Website: www.mcdermott.com
McDermott is in the marine construction business, producing power generating facilities and equipment, offshore pipelines, nuclear submarine services, and shipbuilding, with worldwide markets, including a joint venture with a former competitor in France. It is also part of a consortium developing oil and gas fields off Sakhalin.

McDonald's Corporation, 2111 McDonald's Drive, Oak Brook, IL 60523
Phone: (603) 623-3000 Fax: (603) 623-5004 Website: www.mcdonalds.com
McDonald's has restaurants in eighty-nine countries, mostly in the Americas, Japan, and Europe, but in all other parts of the world as well, with its most recent venture in India.

SOURCES OF TRANSLATION WORK

McGraw-Hill Companies Inc., 1221 Avenue of the Americas, New York, NY 10020-1095
Phone: (212) 512-2000 Fax: (212) 512-4871 Website: www.mcgraw-hill.com
McGraw-Hill produces educational and professional publications, information and media services, and financial services worldwide, including new branches in Hong Kong and Singapore.

McKesson Corporation, 1 Post Street, San Francisco, CA 94104
Phone: (415) 983-8300 Fax: (415) 983-7160 Website: www.mckesson.com
McKesson is the largest wholesale drug distributor in the United States and Canada, with additional operations in Mexico.

McKinsey & Company, 55 East 52nd Street, 21st Floor, New York, NY 10022
Phone: (212) 446-7000 Fax: (212) 446-8575 Website: www.mckinskey.com
McKinsey is a business consulting firm with sixty-nine offices in thirty-five countries.

Mead Corporation, 8821 Washington Colony Drive, Dayton, OH 45458
Phone: (937) 438-1817 Fax: (937) 461-2424 Website: www.mead.com
Mead Corporation is a paper and packaging producer with plants and offices in the United States, the UK, Canada, Mexico, Western Europe, and Japan.

Medtronic, 710 Medtronic Parkway, Minneapolis, MN 55432-5604
Phone: (763) 514-4000 Fax: (763) 514-4879 Website: www.medtronic.com
Medtronic manufactures medical devices and is the number-one manufacturer of pacemakers. It is building a new plant in China.

Merck & Co. Inc., 1 Merck Drive, Whitehouse Station, NJ 08889-0100
Phone: (908) 423-1000 Fax: (908) 423-2592 Website: www.merck.com
Merck is the largest pharmaceutical company in the world, with global operations, primarily in North America, Europe (including Cyprus), and the Asia/Pacific region. There is a subsidiary in Peru and a joint venture in China.

Merisel Inc., 127 West 30th Street, 5th Floor, New York, NY 10001
Phone: (212) 594-4808 Website: www.merisel.com
Merisel is the world's number-one wholesale computer hardware and software distributor, with offices in the Americas, Europe, and Australia.

Merrill Lynch & Co. Inc., see Bank of America.

Metropolitan Life, 1 Madison Avenue, New York, NY 10010-3690
Phone: (212) 578-2211 Fax: (212) 578-3320 Website: www.metlife.com
MetLife and its affiliates operate in the United States, the UK, Canada, Mexico, Argentina, Portugal, Spain, Hong Kong, South Korea, and Taiwan.

Micro Warehouse Inc., 535 Connecticut Avenue, Norwalk, CT 06854
Phone: (203) 899-4000 Fax: (203) 899-4203 Website: www.microwarehouse.com
Micro Warehouse is a catalog seller of computer products with distribution in fifteen countries worldwide.

Microsoft Corporation, 1 Microsoft Way, Redmond, WA 98052
Phone: (425) 882-8080 Fax: (425) 936-7329 Website: www.microsoft.com
Microsoft is active in all phases of the computer systems and software industry, most recently in the Internet area, with support subsidiaries and marketing in nearly fifty countries and worldwide sales, mostly in the United States and Europe.

Monsanto Company, 800 North Lindbergh Boulevard, St. Louis, MO 63167
Phone: (314) 694-1000 Fax: (314) 694-6572 Website: www.monsanto.com
Monsanto, an American chemical giant, has sales throughout the world. They also deal with agricultural technologies on a worldwide basis.

Morgan Stanley Dean Witter, 1585 Broadway, New York, NY 10036
Phone: (212) 761-4000 Fax: (212) 761-0086 Website: www.msdw.com
Morgan Stanley is an investment banking and brokerage firm which operates in the United States and throughout Western Europe and Asia.

Morton International Inc., 123 North Wacker Drive, Chicago, IL 60606
Phone: (312) 807-2000 Fax: (312) 807-2241 Website: www.mortonsalt.com
In addition to salt, Morton International produces packaging adhesives, liquid plastic coating materials, electronic materials, and dyes. The company operates in the United States, the UK, the Bahamas, Canada, Mexico, France, Germany, the Netherlands, Italy, and Japan. It is merging its airbag manufacturing operations with those of a company in Sweden.

Motorola Inc., 1303 East Algonquin Road, Schaumburg, IL 60196
Phone: (847) 576-5000 Fax: (847) 538-5191 Website: www.motorola.com
Motorola makes both communications equipment items and the components inside them, with manufacturing facilities in the United States and eighteen foreign countries, and sales around the world. Recent joint ventures involve Japan and China.

Nabisco Holding Corporation, 7 Campus Drive, Parsippany, NJ 07054
Phone: (973) 682-5000 Fax: (973) 503-2153 Website: www.nabisco.com
The leading international producer of cookies and crackers, Nabisco sells its products in more than eighty-five countries worldwide.

National Semiconductor, 2900 Semiconductor Drive, Santa Clara, CA 95052
Phone: (408) 721-5000 Fax: (408) 739-9803 Website: www.national.com
National Semiconductor's products include integrated circuits, mixed-signal control systems, and chip designs, produced in plants in the United States, the UK, the Philippines, Singapore, and Malaysia, and sold throughout the Americas, Asia, and Europe.

Navistar International Corporation, 455 North Cityfront Plaza Drive, Chicago, IL 60611
Phone: (312) 836-2000 Fax: (312) 836-3982 Website: www.navistar.com
Navistar is the United States' largest manufacturer of heavy- and medium-sized trucks, and the leading supplier of school bus chassis, with sales throughout North America and exports to more than seventy-seven countries worldwide, including recent expansions into Mexico and South America.

NCR Corporation, 1700 South Patterson Boulevard, Dayton, OH 45479
Phone: (937) 445-1936 Fax: (937) 445-1682 Website: www.ncr.com
NCR manufactures point-of-sale terminals and barcode scanners, ATMs, and other similar equipment. It operates 1,000 offices and 50 development and manufacturing facilities in more than 130 countries.

New York Life Insurance, 51 Madison Avenue, New York, NY 10010
Phone: (212) 576-7000 Fax: (212) 576-8145 Website: www.newyorklife.com
New York Life operates in the United States, the UK, Bermuda, Mexico, Argentina, Indonesia, South Korea, Hong Kong, Taiwan, and China.

Newell Rubbermaid Inc., 10 B. Glenlake Parkway, Suite 300, Atlanta, GA 30328
Phone: (770) 407-3800 Fax: (770) 407-3970 Website: www.newellrubbermaid.com
Rubbermaid, manufacturer of gardening accessories, housewares, furniture, decorations, toys, office products, and leisure items, operates facilities in the United States and nine foreign countries, including Mexico and Japan, and sells its products worldwide, including Eastern Europe.

Newmont Mining Corporation, 1700 Lincoln Street, Denver, CO 80203
Phone: (303) 863-7414 Fax: (303) 837-5837 Website: www.newmont.com
Newmont mines gold in Indonesia, Mexico, Peru, and Uzbekistan and operates a joint venture with Japan in Indonesia.

Nike Inc., 1 Bowerman Drive, Beaverton, OR 97005
Phone: (503) 671-6453 Fax: (503) 671-6300 Website: www.nike.com
Nike, manufacturer and purveyor of athletic shoes, apparel, and accessories, sells its products in 110 countries and maintains administrative offices in the United States, Canada, Hong Kong, Austria, and the Netherlands.

Northwest Airlines Corporation, 2700 Lone Oak Parkway, Eagan, MN 55112-3034
Phone: (612) 726-2111 Fax: (612) 727-7617 Website: www.nwa.com
Northwest serves eighty countries worldwide, with hubs in the United States and Japan, and recently entered a code-sharing agreement in Korea, as well as doubling its service to China.

Novell Inc., 404 Wyman Street, Waltham, MA 02451
Phone: (800) 529-3400 Website: www.novell.com
Novell's software is marketed worldwide through offices in the United States and fifty-six foreign countries.

Nucor Corporation, 1915 Rexford Road, Charlotte, NC 28211
Phone: (704) 366-7000 Fax: (704) 362-4208 Website: www.nucor.com
Nucor is a steelmaker with operations in the United States and in the Republic of Trinidad and Tobago.

Occidental Petroleum, 10889 Wilshire Boulevard, Los Angeles, CA 90024
Phone: (310) 208-8800 Fax: (310) 443-6690 Website: www.oxy.com
Occidental Petroleum operates worldwide, with a recently established subsidiary in Japan, and drilling sites in the Middle East.

Olsten Corporation, 175 Broad Hollow Road, Melville, NY 11747-8905
Phone: (516) 844-7800 Fax: (516) 844-7011 Website: www.olsten.com
Olsten is the third-largest temporary staffing agency and the leader in home health-care services in the United States, the UK, Mexico, Argentina, Denmark, Germany, and Sweden.

Omnicom Group Inc., 437 Madison Avenue, New York, NY 10022
Phone: (212) 415-3600 Fax: (212) 415-3530 Website: www.omnicomgroup.com
Omnicom is the number-one advertising agency in the world, operating in more than sixty countries.

Oracle Corporation, 500 Oracle Parkway, Redwood Shores, CA 94065
Phone: (415) 506-7000 Fax: (415) 506-7200 Website: www.oracle.com
Oracle is a leading vendor of software and a developer of database management systems, with operations in ninety countries worldwide, mostly in the United States and Europe.

PACCAR Inc., 777 106th Avenue NE, Bellevue, WA 98004
Phone: (425) 468-7400 Fax: (425) 468-8216 Website: www.paccar.com
PACCAR is the world's third-largest heavy-duty truck manufacturer, with plants in the United States, the UK, Canada, Australia, and Mexico, and has added sales in Central and South America.

Packard Bell NEC Inc., 10850 Gold Center Dr, #200, Rancho Cordova, CA 95670
Phone: (916) 388-0101 Fax: (916) 388-1109 Website: www.packardbell.com
Packard Bell is the number-one seller of PCs in retail mass markets, with manufacturing and distributing centers in Brazil, France, Israel, Japan, Hong Kong, and Singapore.

Parker-Hannifin Corporation, 6035 Parkland Boulevard, Cleveland, OH 44124
Phone: (216) 896-3000 Fax: (216) 896-4000 Website: www.parker.com
Parker-Hannifin makes fluid power systems and components, with 158 plants and 102 offices, stores, and warehouses worldwide.

Pennzoil Company, 700 Milam Street, Houston, TX 77002
Phone: (713) 546-4100 Website: www.pennzoil.com
Pennzoil has drilling operations in the United States, Canada, Indonesia, and Qatar, and sells its products in sixty countries. It owns and operates a sulfur terminal in Belgium and has signed contracts for projects in Egypt. It has undeveloped acreage in Azerbaijan, Qatar, and Venezuela.

PepsiAmericas Inc., 60 South 6th Street, Minneapolis, MN 55402
Phone: (612) 661-4000 Fax: (612) 661-3737 Website: www.whitmancorp.com
Whitman's business consists of Pepsi bottling, muffler manufacture, and walk-in refrigerators, with the last items being produced in the United States, the UK, Canada, and Mexico, and joint ventures in Asia and Europe.

Pepsico Inc., 700 Anderson Hill Road, Purchase, NY 10577-1444
Phone: (914) 253-2000 Fax: (914) 253-2070 Website: www.pepsico.com
Pepsico's food and beverage products are sold worldwide, especially in North America and Europe.

Pfizer Inc., 235 East 42nd Street, New York, NY 10017-5755
Phone: (212) 733-2323 Fax: (212) 733-7851 Website: www.pfizer.com
Pfizer's pharmaceutical products are manufactured in 30 countries and sold in more than 150 worldwide, including joint ventures in Hungary and Japan.

Philip Morris Companies Inc., 6601 West Broad Street, Richmond, VA 23230
Phone: (804) 274-2000 Website: www.philipmorrisusa.com
In addition to tobacco products, Philip Morris is in the food and beer production business, with worldwide distribution of its products, primarily in the United States and Europe.

Pitney Bowes Inc., 1 Elmcroft Road, Stamford, CT 06926-0700
Phone: (203) 356-5000 Fax: (203) 351-6835 Website: www.pitneybowes.com
Pitney Bowes mailing equipment is sold worldwide, primarily in the United States and Europe, with recent ventures in France, Germany, Mexico, and China.

Polaroid Corporation, 300 Baker Avenue, Concord, MA 01742-2131
Phone: (781) 386-2000 Fax: (617) 386-3924 Website: www.polaroid.com
Polaroid not only makes cameras, lenses, and film, but has also expanded into the electronic imaging market. Its products are sold worldwide, mostly in the United States and Europe, and are manufactured in the United States, the UK, Mexico, and the Netherlands.

PPG Industries Inc., 1 PPG Place, Pittsburgh, PA 15272
Phone: (412) 434-3131 Fax: (412) 434-2448 Website: www.ppg.com
PPG is the United States' leading glass manufacturer, with plants in the United States, the UK, Canada, Mexico, Spain, France, Germany, the Netherlands, Italy, and Taiwan.

Premark International Inc., 1717 Deerfield Road, Deerfield, IL 60015
Phone: (847) 405-6000 Fax: (708) 405-6013 Website: www.primarkintl.com
Premark markets food storage containers, professional food products, small appliances, and fitness equipment, manufacturing in fifteen countries and selling in over one hundred throughout the world, with plans to expand into India in the near future.

PricewaterhouseCoopers, 300 Madison Avenue, New York, NY 10017
Phone: (646) 471-4000 Fax: (646) 471-4444 Website: www.pwcglobal.com
One of the big six accounting firms, PricewaterhouseCoopers maintains offices in 119 countries, including Vietnam.

Procter & Gamble Company, 1 Procter & Gamble Plaza, Cincinnati, OH 45201
Phone: (513) 983-1100 Fax: (513) 983-9369 Website: www.pg.com
Procter & Gamble is a household products company with international markets around the world.

The Prudential Insurance Company, 751 Broad Street, Newark, NJ 07102-3777
Phone: (973) 802-6000 Fax: (973) 367-8204 Website: www.prudential.com
Prudential operates in the United States, Italy, Spain, Taiwan, Japan, and Korea.

Quaker Oats Company (a unit of **Pepsico**), PO Box 049003, Chicago, IL 60604
Phone: (312) 821-1000 Fax: (312) 222-8323 Website: www.quakeroats.com
Quaker products are mostly grain-based foods and noncarbonated beverages, with operations worldwide, and sales around the world, primarily in North America and Europe.

Quantum Corporation, 1650 Technology Drive, Suite 700, San Jose, CA 95110
Phone: (408) 944-4000 Fax: (408) 894-4152 Website: www.quantum.com
Quantum is the world's leading supplier of hard disks, with manufacturing facilities in the United States and Indonesia. Its affiliate, Matsushita-Kotobuki

Electronics, has plants in Ireland, Japan, and Singapore. The company's products are sold internationally, primarily in the United States and Europe.

Qwest, 180 California Street, Denver, CO 80202
Phone: (800) 899-7780 Fax: (303) 992-1724 Website: www.qwest.com
Qwest provides combined cable TV/telephone services, with interests in Europe, South America, and Asia.

Radio Shack Corporation, 300 RadioShack Circle, Fort Worth, TX 76102-1964
Phone: (817) 415-3700 Fax: (805) 415-2647 Website: www.radioshack.com
Radio Shack is one of the world's leading electronics retailers, with stores in the United States, Canada, and Europe and a manufacturing plant in China.

Ralston Purina Group, Checkerboard Square, St. Louis, MO 63164
Phone: (314) 982-1000 Fax: (314) 982-2134 Website: www.purina.com
RPG's main lines are pet foods and soy protein technologies. The company also owns Eveready, the battery producer. RPG has 125 plants worldwide, and markets its products around the world.

Raytheon Company, 870 Winter Street, Waltham, MA 02451
Phone: (781) 522-3000 Website: www.raytheon.com
Raytheon's operations fall into four categories: aircraft, appliances, electronics, and engineering and construction, with principle operations in the Americas, Europe, the Middle East, and the Pacific Rim.

The Reader's Digest Association Inc., Reader's Digest Road, Pleasantville, NY 10570
Phone: (914) 238-1000 Fax: (914) 238-4559 Website: www.rd.com
The Reader's Digest is a global publishing and entertainment empire, and is moving into CD-ROM and online technologies. Its sales are international, with emphasis on Europe and the United States.

Reebok International Ltd., 1895 JW Foster Boulevard, Canton, MA 02021
Phone: (781) 401-5000 Fax: (781) 401-7402 Website: www.reebok.com
Reebok manufactures athletic shoes, apparel, and equipment, selling its products in 140 countries, primarily in the United States, the UK, and the rest of Europe, and with a new joint venture in China.

Reynolds American Inc., 401 North Main Street, Winston-Salem, NC 27101-2990
Phone: (336) 741-2000 Fax: (336) 741-4238 Website: www.reynoldsamerican.com
RJR is divided into a food products division and a tobacco products division, and sells its products in more than 160 countries worldwide. Its tobacco processing plants include locations in Poland and Turkey.

Rockwell Automation, 1201 South 2nd Street, Milwaukee, WI 53204-2496
Phone: (414) 382-2000 Fax: (414) 382-4444 Website: www.rockwellautomation.com
Rockwell is involved in all areas of technological support, manufacturing automation systems, chips, modems, and so forth around the world, and with a recent joint venture agreement with China.

Rohm and Haas Company, 100 Independence Mall West, Philadelphia, PA 19106
Phone: (215) 592-3000 Fax: (215) 592-3377 Website: www.rohmhaas.com
Rohm and Haas manufactures specialty chemical products, and is best known as the maker of Plexiglas. It has worldwide operations and a joint venture in Germany.

Ryder System Inc., 11690 NW 105th Street, Miami, FL 33178
Phone: (305) 500-3726 Fax: (305) 500-4129 Website: www.ryder.com
Ryder provides both full-service leasing and short-term rental of trucks, tractors, and trailers in the United States, the UK, Canada, Germany, Mexico, Argentina, Brazil, and Poland.

Sanmina-SCI Corporation, 2700 North 1st Street, San Jose, CA 95134
Phone: (408) 964-3555 Fax: (408) 964-3636 Website: www.sanmina.com
SCI manufactures electronics in the Americas, Europe, and Asia.

Sara Lee Corporation, 3500 Lacey Road, Downers Grove, IL 60515
Phone: (312) 726-2600 Fax: (312) 726-3712 Website: www.saralee.com
In addition to food products, Sara Lee's business includes personal and household items, with plants in the United States and thirty-five other countries, and sales worldwide, primarily in the Americas, Europe, and Asia.

S. C. Johnson & Son Inc., 1525 Howe Street, Racine, WI 53403-2236
Phone: (414) 260-2000 Fax: (414) 260-2133 Website: www.scjohnsonwax.com
S. C. Johnson is one of the world's largest makers of consumer chemical specialty products, operating in all global regions, including Africa and Ukraine.

Schering-Plough Corporation, 2000 Galloping Hill Roada, Kenilworth, NJ 07033
Phone: (908) 298-4000 Website: www.sch-plough.com
Schering-Plough produces pharmaceuticals, with sales throughout the world, and new plants starting in China, Mexico, and Singapore.

Schlumberger Limited, 5599 San Felipe, 17th Floor, Houston, TX 77056
Phone: (713) 513-2000 Website: www.slb.com
Schlumberger combines oil field services and exploration with an electronics and technology business, operating in one hundred countries, and with international sales areas including France.

Seagate Technology Inc., 920 Disc Drive, Scotts Valley, CA 95066
Phone: (408) 438-6550 Fax: (408) 438-7205 Website: www.seagate.com
 Seagate manufactures hard drives and is moving into software. It has sales offices in fourteen countries, with most sales in the United States and the Far East. It manufactures its products in the United States, the UK, China, Malaysia, Singapore, and Thailand.

Sears Holdings Corporation, 3333 Beverly Road, Hoffman Estates, IL 60179
Phone: (847) 286-2500 Fax: (847) 286-7829 Website: www.sears.com
Sears has stores in the United States, Canada, and Mexico.

Sherwin-Williams Company, 101 Prospect Avenue, NW, Cleveland, OH 44115
Phone: (216) 566-2000 Fax: (216) 566-2947 Website: www.sherwin-williams.com
 Sherwin-Williams paints, chemicals, and automotive coatings are licensed in thirty-six foreign countries, with subsidiaries in Canada, Argentina, Brazil, the Caribbean, and Mexico.

Silicon Graphics Inc., 1140 East Arques Avenue, Sunnyvale, CA 94085
Phone: (650) 960-1980 Fax: (650) 961-0595 Website: www.sgi.com
 Silicon Graphics makes graphics computers and software for both the professional and consumer markets, with 130 offices in the Americas, Europe, and the Pacific region.

Smurfit-Stone Container Corporation, 150 North Michigan Avenue, Chicago, IL 60601
Phone: (312) 346-6600 Fax: (312) 580-2272 Website: www.stonecontainer.com
 Stone produces paperboard and paper packaging, with plants in the United States, the UK, Canada, Australia, Germany, the Netherlands, Belgium, France, Costa Rica, Mexico, and Venezuela, with sales in the United States, Canada, and Europe.

Snap-on Incorporated, 2801 80th Street, Kenosha, WI 53143
Phone: (262) 656-5200 Fax: (414) 656-5577 Website: www.snapon.com
 Snap-on is the top manufacturer of mechanics' hand tools, produced in the United States and nine other countries. The company has sales in Canada, Mexico, Japan, Germany, the Netherlands, and Spain.

Spiegel Brands Inc., 711 3rd Avenue, New York, NY 10017
Phone: (212) 986-2585 Fax: (212) 916-8281 Website: www.spiegel.com
 Spiegel operates both catalog sales and retail outlets in the United States, Canada, Germany, and Japan.

Sprint Corporation, 6391 Sprint Parkway, Overland Park, KS 66251-4300
Phone: (913) 624-6000 Fax: (913) 624-3088 Website: www.sprint.com
Sprint's telecommunications services have expanded to Mexico and China, as well as France and Germany.

Stanley Works, 1000 Stanley Drive, New Britain, CT 06053
Phone: (860) 225-5111 Fax: (860) 827-3895 Website: www.stanleyworks.com
Stanley tools are manufactured and distributed throughout the United States and in seventeen other countries, with recent expansions into China, India, Eastern Europe, and Latin America.

Steelcase Inc., 901 44th Street SE, Grand Rapids, MI 49508
Phone: (616) 247-2710 Fax: (616) 246-4041 Website: www.steelcase.com
Steelcase is the world's largest manufacturer of office furniture, with plants in the United States, the UK, Canada, France, Morocco, the Ivory Coast, Belgium, Germany, Spain, Portugal, and Japan. Its products are sold worldwide, with a recent joint venture in India.

Sun Microsystems, 4150 Network Circle, Santa Clara, CA 95054
Phone: (650) 960-1300 Fax: (650) 969-9131 Website: www.sun.com
Sun Microsystems provides Internet solutions, distributing its products in more than 125 countries worldwide, most recently in South Africa.

Sunoco Inc., 1735 Market Street, Suite LL, Philadelphia, PA 19103-7583
Phone: (215) 977-3000 Fax: (215) 977-3409 Website: www.sunocoinc.com
Sun is an oil company with operations in the United States, the UK, and the North Sea region.

Tenet HealthSystem Medical Inc., 13737 Noel Road, Dallas, TX 75240
Phone: (469) 892-2200 Fax: (469) 893-8600 Website: www.tenethealthcare.com
Tenet is a health-care provider with facilities in the United States and Spain.

Texas Instruments Incorporated, 12500 TI Boulevard, Dallas, TX 75243
Phone: (972) 995-2011 Fax: (972) 995-4360 Website: www.ti.com
TI manufactures computer chips, computers, defense electronics, calculators, and printers, with operations in seventeen countries, and sales primarily in the United States, East Asia, and Europe.

Textron Inc., 40 Westminster Street, Providence, RI 02903
Phone: (401) 421-2800 Fax: (401) 421-2878 Website: www.textron.com
Textron, a major defense contractor, makes such varied products as helicopters, windshield washers, and watchbands, as well as providing financial services and insurance. It operates in the United States and abroad, with sales in the United States, Canada, Europe, the Asia/Pacific region, and Mexico.

SOURCES OF TRANSLATION WORK

Time Warner Inc., 1 Time Warner Center, New York, NY 10019-8016
Phone: (212) 484-8000 Fax: (212) 956-2847 Website: www.timewarner.com
Time Warner, the huge multimedia company, has sales in the United States, Europe, the Pacific Rim, and elsewhere, and is currently investing in Japan's cable TV industry.

Transamerica Corporation, 600 Montgomery Street, 23rd Floor, San Francisco, CA 94111
Phone: (415) 983-4000 Fax: (415) 983-4400 Website: www.transamerica.com
Transamerica's insurance business operates in the United States and Canada, but its leasing business has branches in forty-seven countries (including Japan), and its commercial finance business is in six countries.

TRW Inc., 1900 Richmond Road, Cleveland, OH 44124
Phone: (216) 291-7000 Fax: (216) 291-7629 Website: www.trw.com
TRW provides advanced technology products and services, with manufacturing, R&D, and other facilities in the United States and twenty-two other countries, and sales primarily in the United States and Europe. The company has recently begun joint ventures in China, India, and Turkey.

Tyco International Ltd., 9 Roszel Road, Princeton, NJ 08540
Phone: (609) 720-4200 Website: www.tyco.com
Tyco International produces fire protection systems, operating 250 offices on five continents, with sales in North America, Europe, and the Asia/Pacific region.

Tyson Foods Inc., 2210 West Oaklawn Drive, Springdale, AR 72764-6999
Phone: (501) 290-4000 Fax: (501) 290-4061 Website: www.tyson.com
Tyson operates production and distribution facilities in the United States and twelve other countries, participating in joint ventures in China and Mexico. Its products are sold in Canada, Hong Kong, Japan, and several other Asian countries and in the Caribbean.

UAL Corporation, 77 West Wacker Drive, Chicago, IL 60601
Phone: (312) 997-8000 Website: www.ual.com
United Airlines serves 144 airports in 31 countries, with new cargo services to Japan and other Asian destinations.

UBS Financial Services, 1285 Avenue of the Americas, New York, NY 10019
Phone: (212) 713-2000 Fax: (212) 713-4889 Website: www.ubs.com
They offer a variety of banking, financial, and real estate services at 310 offices in the United States and Puerto Rico, the UK, Switzerland, Hong Kong, Singapore, and Japan.

Union Carbide Corporation (subsidiary of the **Dow Chemical Company**), PO Box 4393, Houston, TX 77210
Phone: (713) 978-2016 Fax: (713) 978-2394 Website: www.unioncarbide.com
Union Carbide produces petrochemical products, operating in fourteen countries around the world with a new complex in Kuwait, and a joint venture in China.

Unisys Corporation, Unisys Way, Blue Bell, PA 19424
Phone: (215) 986-4011 Fax: (215) 986-2312 Website: www.unisys.com
Unisys is one of the world's largest computer companies, producing computer systems, software, and services to commercial and government clients. The company has clients in one hundred countries worldwide.

United Health Group, 9900 Bren Road E, Minnetonka, MN 55343
Phone: (952) 936-1300 Fax: (952) 936-1819 Website: www.uhc.com
A managed care provider, operating in all fifty states and in Puerto Rico. It also has operations in Germany, Hong Kong, and South Africa.

United Parcel Service, 55 Glenlake Parkway NE, Atlanta, GA 30328
Phone: (770) 828-6000 Fax: (770) 828-6593 Website: www.ups.com
UPS is the world's number-one package delivery company, operating in more than two hundred countries worldwide, with hubs in North America, Germany, Hong Kong, and Singapore.

United Technologies, United Technologies Building, Hartford, CT 06101
Phone: (860) 728-7000 Fax: (860) 728-7979 Website: www.utc.com
United Technologies is a conglomerate producing such diverse items as air-conditioning systems, elevators and escalators, aircraft engines, and helicopters, with operations on all continents, and sales worldwide.

Universal Corporation, 1501 North Hamilton Street, Richmond, VA 23230
Phone: (804) 359-9311 Fax: (804) 254-3584 Website: www.universalcorp.com
Universal buys and processes leaf tobacco, with operations in thirty-three countries and sales primarily in the United States, Europe, and Latin America. It has a presence in Africa, Eastern Europe, and China.

US Airways Inc., 111 West Rio Salado Parkway, Tempe, AZ 85281
Phone: (480) 693-0800 Fax: (480) 693-5546 Website: www.usairways.com
USAir serves cities in the United States, Canada, the Caribbean, France, Spain, Italy, and Germany.

USAA, 9800 Fredericksburg Road, San Antonio, TX 78288
Phone: (210) 498-2211 Fax: (210) 498-9940 Website: www.usaa.com

USAA provides insurance and financial services worldwide, with regional offices in the United States, the UK, and Germany.

USG Corporation, 550 West Adams Street, Chicago, IL 60661-3676
Phone: (312) 436-4000 Fax: (312) 436-4093 Website: www.usg.com
USG's wall and ceiling products are produced in thirteen countries, including a joint venture in Saudi Arabia.

USX-Marathon Oil Corporation, 5555 San Felipe Road, Houston, TX 77056-2723
Phone: (713) 629-6600 Fax: (713) 296-2952 Website: www.marathon.com
Marathon conducts exploration and development activities in fifteen countries and sells its petroleum products primarily in the United States and Europe. It recently signed an agreement with the Russian government.

Verizon Communications Inc., 140 West Street, New York, NY 10007
Phone: (212) 395-1000 Fax: (212) 571-1897 Website: www.verizon.com
As the number-two telecommunications provider, they provide land and wireless services to both global and domestic customers.

VF Corporation, 105 Corporate Center Boulevard, Greensboro, NC 27408
Phone: (336) 424-6000 Fax: (336) 424-7631 Website: www.vfc.com
VF manufactures apparel under a variety of brand names, and sells its products around the world.

Visa International Inc., 900 Metro Center Boulevard, Foster City, CA 94404
Phone: (650) 432-3200 Fax: (650) 432-7436 Website: www.visa.com
Visa, the largest consumer payment system, operates in 247 countries worldwide.

Walt Disney Company, The, 500 South Buena Vista Street, Burbank, CA 91521
Phone: (818) 560-1000 Fax: (818) 560-1930 Website: www.disney.com
Disney is the biggest entertainment company in the world, with theme parks, studios, retail stores, and other ventures in the United States, Europe, and Japan.

Whirlpool Corporation, 2000 North M-63, Benton Harbor, MI 49022-2692
Phone: (269) 923-5000 Fax: (269) 923-3722 Website: www.whirlpoolcorp.com
Whirlpool makes major household appliances in the United States, South America (including Brazil), Mexico, France, Italy, Germany, Sweden, Slovakia, India, and China.

William Wrigley Jr. Company, 410 North Michigan Avenue, Chicago, IL 60611
Phone: (312) 644-2121 Fax: (312) 644-0097 Website: www.wrigley.com
Wrigley is the world's number-one maker of chewing gum, with operations in twenty-nine countries, including factories in Hungary, Slovenia, the Czech Republic, and China. Its newest factory is under construction in Russia.

W. R. Grace & Co., 7500 Grace Drive, Columbia, MD 21044-4098
Phone: (410) 531-4000 Fax: (410) 531-4367 Website: www.grace.com
Grace is the world's largest specialty chemicals company with operations around the world.

Xerox Corporation, 45 Glover Avenue, Norwalk, CT 06856-4505
Phone: (203) 968-3000 Fax: (203) 968-3430 Website: www.xerox.com
Xerox operates offices, manufacturing plants, and other facilities and sells its products worldwide, and is currently forming a joint production venture with Japan and China.

Yellow Corporation, 10990 Roe Avenue, Overland Park, KS 66211
Phone: (913) 696-6100 Fax: (913) 696-6116 Website: www.yellowcorp.com
Yellow Freight operates freight terminals and owns trucks, tractors, and trailers throughout North America.

Zenith Electronics, 2000 Millbrook Drive, Lincolnshire, IL 60069
Phone: (847) 391-8183 Fax: (847) 391-7291 Website: www.zenith.com
Zenith has locations in the United States, Canada, Mexico, and a purchasing office in Taiwan.

APPENDIX 5

Translation Courses and Programs

Academic programs for those interested in translation and interpretation are in a state of flux. There is a growing recognition of the fact that the most critical need for the practicing translator is hands-on experience, although some of the policy makers in academia continue to cling to theory rather than practice. Programs are growing and expanding to include many new areas. If interested in an academic program, contact one or more of the following schools and find out more about their latest offerings.

As with the translation agency listings in appendix 4, detailed information in the following entries is the result of responses to an information questionnaire sent to the various schools. The quantity of such information is based on those responses and does not reflect any value judgment on the part of the editors.

A new development in American education is "distance learning," or learning at home through the Internet. This can become a real blessing for translators, many of whom are well past their school years. The translation program at New York University (see below) is in the process of setting up distance learning for translation. Check their website for details.

UNITED STATES

ARIZONA

Arizona State University, Languages and Literatures, PO Box 870202, Tempe, AZ 85287
Phone: (602) 496-0611 Fax: (480) 965-0135 Website: www.asu.edu
E-mail: maria.teresa.martinez@asu.edu Contact: Maria Teresa Martinez
Spanish Translation Certificate Program, now in its seventeenth year. Covers literary, legal, medical, sci-tech, business, and financial translation. Prerequisites include an introductory course in linguistics.

ARKANSAS

University of Arkansas, Department of English, 333 Kimpel Hall, Fayetteville, AR 72701 Phone: (479) 575-4301 Fax: (479) 575-5919 Website: www.uark.edu
E-mail: mfa@uark.edu Contact: Davis McCombs

Offers literary translation program (MFA). This certificate program is for people bilingual in Spanish and English who wish to work in the courts as an interpreter and translator, or who desire to work as a state or federally certified interpreter and translator in other areas of the public or private sector, or who want to sharpen their bilingual skills for translation and interpretation.

CALIFORNIA

California State University, Long Beach, 1250 Bellflower Boulevard, Long Beach, CA 90840
Phone: (916) 278-6011 Website: www.csulb.edu
Offers BA in Spanish translation.

California State University, Los Angeles, 5151 State University Drive, Los Angeles, CA 90032-8619
Phone: (323) 343-5964 Website: www.calstatela.edu
Certificate program in legal interpretation and translation: Spanish/English

California State University, Sacramento, 6000 J Street, Sacramento, CA 95819
Phone: (916) 278-6011 Website: www.csus.edu
Offers courses in translation and interpretation.

Fuller Theological Seminary, 135 North Oakland Avenue, Pasadena, CA 91182
Phone: (626) 584-5400 Website: www.fuller.edu
Offers graduate degrees in Bible translation.

Monterey Institute of International Studies, Graduate School of Translation and Interpretation Studies, 460 Pierce Street, Monterey, CA 93940
Phone: (831) 647-4170 Fax: (831) 647-3560 Website: www.miis.edu
E-mail: ddeterra@miis.edu Contact: Diane de Terra
Now in its thirty-fourth year, the school offers an M.A. degree in Chinese, French, German, Japanese, Korean, Spanish, Russian, and English translation. All major technical areas of translation are taught, including computer-assisted translation, software localization, terminology, and the business of translation. The school also offers an M.A. in Interpreting—Simultaneous, Consecutive, and Conference. Students must have a B.A. with a 3.0 GPA and a TOEFL of 600+, as well as study abroad and GRE. The graduate school is an independent entity within the Monterey Institute. The school also offers certificates to students lacking a B.A. but who demonstrate the necessary level of language proficiency.

San Diego State University, Department of Spanish and Portuguese Languages and Literature, 5402 College Avenue, San Diego, CA 92182
Phone: (619) 594-6588 Fax: (619) 594-5293 Website: sdsu.edu
E-mail: cdegueld@mail.sdsu.edu Contact: Christian DeGuelde

SDSU's translation program has been in place eighteen years. The university offers certificates in translation studies and in court interpreting in Spanish-English. Translation covers all major technical areas; interpreting is legal only. Students must have advanced Spanish grammar or equivalent courses, and must pass a proficiency examination in English. There are five courses in translation and six in court interpreting, including an internship. The university also provides training for state and federal accreditation examinations in court interpreting.

San Jose State University, Department of Foreign Languages, 1 Washington Square, San Jose, CA 95192-0091
Phone: (408) 924-4602 Fax: (408) 924-4607 Website: www.sjsu.edu
E-mail: msigler@jsuvm.sjsu.edu Contact: Dr. M. del Carmen Sigler, Chair

Although SJSU offers courses in Chinese, French, German, Greek, Hebrew, Italian, Japanese, Latin, Portuguese, Russian, and Spanish, its translation offerings are limited to one introductory course—"Translation: Theory and Practice"—in Spanish only. The course has been offered for several years. It is considered an elective in the bachelor's degree in Spanish program. The prerequisite for the course is the attainment of an advanced level in the study of Spanish. The course deals with texts from most major technical areas. SJSU plans to offer more courses in translation in the future, at least one of which will be at the M.A. level.

Stanford University, Stanford, CA 94305
Phone: (415) 497-1068 Website: www.stanford.edu

Offers certificate program in translation and interpretation done in tandem with the Monterey Institute of International Studies.

University of California, Los Angeles, 10995 Le Conte Avenue, Los Angeles, CA 90024
Website: www.ucla.edu

Offers certificate in interpretation and translation in Spanish.

CONNECTICUT
Wesleyan University, Middleton, CT 06457
Website: www.wesleyan.edu
Offers Interpreters for the Deaf Workshop.

DISTRICT OF COLUMBIA
American University, Department of Language and Foreign Studies, 4400 Massachusetts Avenue NW, Washington, DC 20016
Phone: (202) 885-2381 Fax: (202) 885-1076 Website: www.american.edu/lfs
E-mail: lfs@american.edu Contact: Consuelo Galls

American University's translation program has been operating for thirteen years. It teaches French, Spanish, Russian, and German translation, with an emphasis on translation into English. Students are required to have completed the third-year level of their language. Courses cover general translation, covering a variety of areas including business, literature, journalism, and so forth. Students are awarded a certificate on completion of the course. Study materials vary with the language. There is no interpreter training.

Gallaudet College, Department of ASL, Linguistics and Interpretation, 800 Florida Avenue NE, Washington, DC 20002
Phone: (202) 651-5450 Fax: (202) 651-5741 Website: www.gallaudet.edu
E-mail: interpretation@gallaudet.edu Contact: Valerie L. Dively
Only liberal arts college exclusively for the deaf. Offers master's degree in ASL.

Georgetown University, 1221 36th Street NW, Washington, DC 20057
Website: www.georgetown.edu
E-mail: interp1@guvax.georgetown.edu
Offers certificate of proficiency as conference interpreter, and certificate in translation in French, Spanish, German, Italian, and Portuguese.

FLORIDA
Florida A&M University, Office of International Services and Summer Sessions, Translation and Critical Languages Center, 304 Perry Paige N, Tallahassee, FL 32307
Phone: (904) 561-2482 Website: www.famu.edu
Contact: Dr. Eva C. Wanton, Associate Vice President for Academic Affairs
Florida A&M's translation program has been operating for ten years and offers a B.A. in Spanish and French and a minor in these degree programs. Instruction in German, Chinese, Japanese, and other languages on request is also available. Prerequisites for the program include successful completion of a written entrance exam and an oral proficiency interview. The program teaches courses in legal, medical, business, scientific, and educational translation. Training materials include journals, newspapers, magazines, and textbooks. Successful completion of the program requires eighteen semester hours of translations and an internship at an overseas translation institute, as well as written and oral exit examinations.

Florida International University, Department of Modern Languages University Park Campus, Miami, FL 33199
Phone: (305) 348-2851 Fax: (305) 348-1085 Voice Mail: (305) 348-2049 Website: www.fiu.edu
Contact: Dr. Leonel A. de la Cuesta, Director Translation-Interpretation Program
FIU's Translation-Interpretation Program has been in operation since 1980. It teaches translation primarily in Spanish-English, with some French as well. The program awards certificates in translation studies and legal translation. The university also offers simultaneous and consecutive (but not conference) interpreter

training in English-Spanish and awards a certificate in court interpreting. Students are required to have at least two years of college education and must be bilingual. Studies cover most major areas of technical translation (legal, medical, business, technological-scientific, literary, journalism, publishing, etc.).The university also provides support training for practicing translators and interpreters who want to strengthen their skills in the field.

Miami-Dade College/Inter-American Campus, 627 SW 27th Avenue, Room 1336, Miami, FL 33135
Phone: (305) 237-6073 Website: www.mdc.edu
Contact: Humberto Cerna
Offers courses and concentration in translation and interpretation for medical, legal, and business.

University of Florida, Translation Studies, 319 Grinter Hall, Gainesville, FL 32611
Phone: (352) 392-0375 ext. 809 Website: translationstudies.ufl.edu/program.shtml
E-mail: elowe@latam.ufl.edu Contact: Elizabeth Lowe
Offers graduate and undergraduate certificates in translation studies.

GEORGIA

Georgia State University, Modern and Classical Languages, PO Box 3970, Atlanta, GA 30302
Phone: (404) 651-2747 or (404) 651-2265 Fax: (404) 651-1785 Website: www.gsu.edu/~wwwmcl
E-mail: acash@gsu.edu Contact: Dr. Annette G. Cash
The graduate-level certificate programs in translation and interpretation were introduced in 1979 in the Department of Modern and Classical Languages. It provides professional training for bilingual students interested in a career in translation and/or interpretation. They have translation programs in French, German, and Spanish. They are designed to develop advanced translation skills for students interested in acquiring a high level of proficiency in a specific language combination. The program provides professional training in medical and legal interpretation for students who wish to become interpreters. The program is currently offered in Spanish.

HAWAII

University of Hawaii at Manoa, Center for Interpretation and Translation Studies, 1859 East-West Road, #104, Honolulu, HI 96822
Phone: (808) 956-6233 Fax: (808) 956-2078 Website: http://cits.hawaii.edu
E-mail: cits@hawaii.edu Contact: David Ashworth, Director
The Center for Interpretation and Translation Studies (CITS) was established in 1988 at the University of Hawaii at Manoa within the College of Languages, Linguistics and Literature. The center's primary goal is to provide, through

theoretically based academic programs, basic training in interpretation and non-fiction translation. The center currently offers a certificate training program in the summer in translation and interpretation (SIIT) in English in combination with Japanese, Mandarin, and Korean and will offer certificate programs for other languages when demand is sufficient and qualified instructors are available. Currently, CITS does not offer a degree at the graduate or undergraduate level, except as a liberal studies major. Additional objectives of the center are the development of a research-based training methodology, a teacher-training program, and interdisciplinary research through links with university-wide resources. CITS also serves the community by acting as a clearinghouse of information on professional resources and practices. It provides the community at large with a broad range of educational opportunities by sponsoring lectures, seminars, and workshops.

IDAHO
College of Southern Idaho, PO Box 1238, Twin Falls, ID 83303
Phone: (208) 733-9554 Website: www.csi.edu
Offers courses with translation component.

IOWA
University of Iowa, 425 English Philosophy Building, Iowa City, IA 52242
Website: http://uiowa.edu
Phone: (319) 335-0330 Fax: (319) 335-2535 Contact: Daniel Weissbort
  Offers MFA in comparative literature with translation component. Also: graduate-level apprenticeship. Contact: Gertrud G. Champe, Translation Laboratory, 123 North Linn Street, Iowa City, IA 52246. Also: B.A., major in languages with translation component (French and Italian). Contact: Jacques Bourgeacq/Michel Laronde.

ILLINOIS
Northern Illinois University, Department of Foreign Languages and Translation, Watson Hall 111, DeKalb, IL 60115
Phone: (815) 753-1259 Website: www.forlangs.net
E-mail: annie@niu.edu Contact: Annie Birberick, Chair
  Offers programs of study in fifteen languages. Language majors may choose either a language and literature emphasis or a business and translation emphasis for their program.

University of Illinois at Urbana-Champaign, 707 South Mathews Street, Urbana, IL 61801 Website: www.uiuc.edu E-mail: emartin@uiuc.edu
Offers courses in Russian and French literary translation.

TRANSLATION COURSES AND PROGRAMS

INDIANA

Indiana University, University Budget Office, Bryan Hall 115, Bloomington, IN 47405

Phone: (812) 855-6818 Fax: (812) 855-8990

www.indiana.edu/complit/trans.html Contact: Mariam Ehteshamis

Indiana U. has been offering a literary translation program for about twenty years. The school teaches about twenty-six languages, from Arabic to Zulu. Courses include the theory and practice of literary translation, which have resulted in some highly regarded translations from Chinese, French, German, Greek, Italian, Japanese, Romanian, and Spanish, among others.

KANSAS

Johnson County Community College, College Boulevard at Quivira Road, Overland Pass, KS 66210

Website: www.jccc.net

Kansas State University, Department of Modern Languages, 104 Eisenhower Hall, Manhattan, KS 66506-1003

Phone: (785) 532-1988 Fax: (785) 532-7004 Website: www.k-state.edu

E-mail: bradshaw@ksu.edu Contact: Dr. Bradley A. Shaw, Associate Professor

Kansas State teaches Spanish, French, German, Japanese, Russian, Italian, Arabic, and Latin. Although there is no translation program, KSU offers an Introduction to Spanish Translation course, designed for upper-level undergraduates and graduate students. It features bidirectional exercises, a variety of texts, and a discussion of professional issues.

MARYLAND

University of Maryland, French and Italian Department, 3106 Jimenez Hall, College Park, MD 20742

Phone: (301) 405-4024 Fax: (301) 314-9928 Website: www.umd.edu

Offers translation courses in French and Italian. Subjects covered are literary, journalistic, commercial, and political. There are about four courses in French at the undergraduate level that deal with translation. Two of these focus on business French. There is also a French translation course at the graduate level. One undergraduate course in Italian deals with literary translation. Most other languages taught by the university offer courses in translation or with a translation component.

MASSACHUSETTS

Elms College, Chicopee, MA 01013

Website: www.elms.edu

Offers French and Spanish translation courses.

University of Massachusetts, Amherst, Translation Center, 442 Herter Hall, Amherst, MA 01003
Phone: (413) 545-2203 Fax: (413) 577-3400 Website: www.umass.edu/transcen
E-mail: gentzler@complit.umass.edu Contact: Shawn Lindholm. Program Director: Edwin Gentzler
The program is now in its twelfth year. Offers M.A. in translation studies. Also a court interpretation program. Program consists mainly of literary and cultural studies, but also business and technical translation. Also teaches interpretation which leads to a certificate.

MICHIGAN
Marygrove College, 8425 West McNichols Road, Detroit, MI 48221-2599
Phone: (313) 862-8000 ext. 374 Fax: (313) 864-6670 Website: www.marygrove .edu Contact: Dr. Karen Davis
Marygrove's translation program has been in operation since 1974. It teaches literary, legal, medical, scientific, and commercial translation in Arabic, French, and Spanish. The program awards a certificate of achievement for the completion of three separate workshops. The college also offers training in consecutive interpretation in Arabic, French, and Spanish. Students are required to have four semesters of college-level work in French or Spanish, and Arabic requires three semesters of college-level Arabic. The third workshop features an independent project chosen by the student, following guidelines set by the ATA and the MLA (Modern Language Association).

Western Michigan University, Kalamazoo, MI 49008
Website: www.wmich.edu
Offers technical translation courses.

MINNESOTA
St. Olaf College, 1520 St. Olaf Avenue, Northfield, MN 55057
Website: www.stolaf.edu
Offers courses in Spanish and Russian translation.

NEBRASKA
University of Nebraska at Kearney, Department of Modern Languages, Thomas Hall 215, Kearney, NE 68849
Phone: (308) 865-8536 Fax: (308) 865-8806 Website: www.nebraska.edu
E-mail: gonzaleze1@unk.edu Contact: Dr. Eduardo Gonzalez, Translation/ Interpretation Program
U-Nebraska at Kearney's Translation/Interpretation Program has been in operation for twenty-one years. Under the aegis of modern languages, the program offers both B.A.s and certificates in French, German, and Spanish translation and interpretation. Students are required to demonstrate proficiency or

successfully accomplish senior-level language studies. Both literary and nonliterary translation are taught. Students who complete the program are ready for graduate studies, and in some cases professional employment as translators and/or interpreters.

NEVADA
University of Nevada, Reno, NV 89557
Website: www.unr.edu
Offers court interpreter seminar/workshops and courses in Spanish translation.

NEW JERSEY
Montclair State University, Department of Modern Languages and Literatures, Dickson Hall, Upper Montclair, NJ 07043
Phone: (973) 655-4283 Website: http://chss2.montclair.edu/French
E-mail: oppenheim@mail.montclair.edu Contact: Dr. Lois Oppenheim
Montclair State's translation program has been in operation for twenty-six years. It concentrates in French, but the university also offers courses in German, Hebrew, Arabic, and Russian. The university offers both certificates and B.A.s. It teaches scientific, economic, legal, and literary translation. Specific areas vary from semester to semester. There is also one course in interpreting (simultaneous, consecutive, and conference) for French-language students. Students must be at least juniors majoring in their language. They are required to do an individual long translation in their senior year. The program prepares students for career opportunities in the New York/New Jersey metropolitan area, in industry and commerce, advertising and tourism, and governmental services. Students are encouraged to double-major in a technical specialty.

Rutgers, the State University, Department of Spanish and Portuguese, 105 George Street, New Brunswick, NJ 08901
Phone: (732) 932-9412 ext. 25 Fax: (732) 932-9837 Website: www.rutgers.edu
E-mail: zatlin@rci.rutgers.edu Contact: Phyllis Zatlin
Rutgers has been offering a Spanish translation program for many years. In 1987, an M.A. option was added, along with a certificate in translation. Requirements include proficiency at native or near-native level in Spanish and English. Areas covered are legal, technical, literary, and other subjects. There is also simultaneous and consecutive interpreter training in Spanish. The program also offers an internship in translation and interpretation.

NEW YORK
Binghamton University (SUNY), Translation Research and Instruction Program, PO Box 6000, Binghamton, NY 13902
Phone: (607) 777-6555 Fax: (607) 777-2280 Website: http://trip.binghamton.edu

E-mail: trip@binghamton.edu or rarrojo@binghamton.edu Contact: Rosemary
Arrojo
SUNY-Binghamton's Translation Research and Instruction Program is an
autonomous graduate teaching unit, not affiliated with any department in the
university. The program has been operating since January 1971. Languages
offered are Arabic, Chinese, Spanish, French, German, Japanese, Korean,
Portuguese, Italian, Russian, and Modern Greek. The university offers graduate
certificates incorporated into a master's or doctoral degree. Students must have
high fluency in their source language and effective expression in their target language. Emphasis is on literary and scholarly translation, with generalist studies
scheduled for January 1998. Management of terminology databases is also taught.
Study materials include *Beyond the Western Tradition*. There is no interpreter
training. Computer-assisted translation is offered.

Brooklyn College, 2900 Bedford Avenue, Brooklyn, NY 11210
Website: www.brooklyn.edu
Offers translation courses.

City University of New York, 33 West 42nd Street, New York, NY 10036
Phone: (212) 817-8480 Fax: (212) 642-2205 Website: www.cuny.edu
Contact: Rachel M. Brownstein
Offers M.A. in liberal studies: specialization in translation, with an emphasis
on business, legal, medical, and science/technology translation.

Columbia University, Barnard College, 3009 Broadway, New York, NY 10027
Website: www.barnard.edu
Offers a B.A. in French with a concentration in translation and literature.

Fordham University, Fordham Road, Bronx, NY 10458
Website: www.fordham.edu
Offers courses in translation through individual language departments.

Hofstra University, Hempstead, NY 11550
Website: www.hofstra.edu
Offers literary translation courses in several languages and a "practical transla-
tion" course (French only).

New York University, School of Continuing Education and Professional Studies,
Foreign Languages Translation Studies, 10 Astor Place, Suite 504E, New York,
NY 10003
Phone: (212) 998-7028 Fax: (212) 995-4139 Website: www.nyu.edu
E-mail: milena.savova@nyu.edu Contact: Milena Savova, Translation Studies
Coordinator

NYU's translation program has been in operation for seventeen years. It offers translation certificates in English-Spanish, English-Portuguese, Spanish-English, French-English, Arabic-English, and German-English on site, and English-Spanish online, as well as English-Spanish court interpreting. The Arabic-English program is a military documents class, unlike the other languages. The program emphasizes legal, commercial, medical, and technical translation with elective courses available in marketing, literary, and terminology/database management, among others. Since it is a hands-on, intensive translator and interpreter-training program, students translate "real-life" texts in the translation program and use language labs in the court interpreting program. In addition, a wide variety of internships are available. Students must pass an entrance exam to prove proficiency in both target and source languages. They must maintain a B or better average and complete the program within four years. NYU has recently added many online classes in their translation department.

State University of New York at Albany, 1400 Washington Avenue, Albany, NY
    12222 Website: www.albany.edu
Offers post-master's degree certificate in Russian translation.

NORTH CAROLINA
University of North Carolina at Charlotte, Charlotte, NC 28223
Phone: (704) 687-4227 Website: www.uncc.edu
E-mail: msdoyle@email.uncc.edu Contact: Dr. Michael Scott Doyle
    Offers a translation certificate program for undergraduates in French, Spanish, and German. They also offer a graduate certificate in translating and translation studies with a focus on English-Spanish.

Wake Forest University, 1834 Wake Forest Road, Winston-Salem, NC 27106
Phone: (336) 758-5255 Website: www.wfu.edu
E-mail: furmano@wfu.edu
Offers graduate certificate in Spanish Translation/Localization.

NORTH DAKOTA
North Dakota State University, Fargo, ND 58105
Website: www.ndsu.nodak.edu
Offers translation courses in French and Spanish.

OHIO
Antioch College, Japan Program, Yellow Springs, OH 45387
Phone: (513) 767-7331 Fax: (513) 767-6469 Website: www.antioch-college.edu
Contact: Harold Wright, Professor of Japanese
    Antioch offers courses in Japanese, Spanish, German, and French translation into English. Although there is no specific translation program, the college does

offer a workshop in poetry translation. Students are required to know the source and target languages in order to take this course.

Baldwin-Wallace College, Berea, OH 44017
Website: www.bw.edu
Offers translation courses in French, German, and Spanish.

Bowling Green State University, Bowling Green, OH 43403
Website: www.bgsu.edu
Offers translation courses.

Kent State University, Institute for Applied Linguistics, Kent, OH 44242
Phone: (330) 672-1814 Fax: (330) 673-0735 Website: http://appling.kent.edu/
    IAL-BSProgram.htm
E-mail: gkoby@kent.edu (for B.S. program), bbauer@kent.edu (for M.A. program) Contact: Geoffrey Koby
Offers M.A. in French, German, and Spanish translation with an emphasis on computer-assisted translation and interpreting; literary and cultural translation; commercial, legal, diplomatic, medical, technical, and scientific. Also offers B.S. in French, German, Russian, and Spanish translation.

Ohio State University, 1841 Millikin Road, Columbus, OH 43210
Website: www.osu.edu
Offers B.A. in Russian translation.

Wright State University, Colonel Glenn Highway, Dayton, OH 45435
Website: www.wright.edu
Offers translation courses.

OKLAHOMA

Tulsa Community College, International Language Center, 909 South Boston, MC-423, Tulsa, OK 74135
Phone: (918) 595-7851 Fax: (918) 595-7910 Website: www.tulsacc.edu
E-mail: tpena@tulsaacc.edu Contact: Tina Pena
Tulsa Community College requires four semesters within the target language before accepting undergraduate students into its specialized translation program, which offers both Spanish and French. Students are introduced to the basic concepts and responsibilities related to translating. Instructor handouts and specialized documents provide practice with various types of materials. The result is an associate's degree. The college offers Spanish, French, Arabic, Chinese, Japanese, Greek, Hebrew, Italian, Latin, and Russian.

PENNSYLVANIA

Carnegie-Mellon University, Department of Modern Languages, Baker Hall 160, Schenley Park, Pittsburgh, PA 15213-3890

Phone: (412) 268-2934 Fax: (412) 268-1328 Website: www.carnegiemellon.edu

E-mail: grtucker@andrew.cmu.edu Contact: Professor G. Richard Tucker, Head, Department of Modern Languages

Carnegie-Mellon teaches French, German, Japanese, Russian, Spanish, Mandarin Chinese, and Italian, but does not offer a specialized translation program. Online courses in Spanish and French are also offered.

Immaculata University, Office #4, Faculty Center, Immaculata, PA 19345

Website: www.immaculata.edu

E-mail: kclark@immaculata.edu Contact: Kathleen M. Clark

Offers an associate's degree in professional Spanish and a B.A. program in international business French.

La Salle University, 1900 West Olney Avenue, Philadelphia, PA 19141

Phone: (215) 951-1209 Website: www.lasalle.edu

E-mail: gomez@lasalle.edu

La Salle offers a graduate certificate in translation for Spanish-English through the department of bilingual/bicultural graduate studies. The curriculum for the CIT (Certificate in Translation) is designed to address three of the principal environments in which translations (English/Spanish-Spanish/English) are currently, and more intensely in the future, needed: that is, legal, medical, and business environments. In addition, governing translation principles are also studied for application to language environments not covered by the program.

Mt. Aloysius College, 7373 Admiral Peary Highway, Cresson, PA 16630-1999

Website: www.mtaloy.edu

The Sign Language/Interpreter Education Department at Mount Aloysius offers an associate of arts degree and a bachelor of arts degree intended to prepare students for entry-level positions primarily in educational settings.

Pennsylvania State University, 311 Burrowes Building, University Park, PA 16802

Phone: (814) 863-0589 Fax: (814) 863-8882 Website: www.psu.edu

Contact: Earl E. Fitz/Tom Beebee (Comparative Literature)

Offers a Ph.D. in comparative literature, translation option. Also: courses in French-American business translation, commercial and technical translation, international conference terminology, and Russian translation.

University of Pittsburgh, Language Learning Resource Center, Pittsburgh, PA 15260

Phone: (412) 624-5900 Fax: (412) 624-6793 Website: www.pitt.edu

E-mail: ptoth@pitt.edu or lctl@pitt.edu Contact: Dr. Paul D. Toth

The University of Pittsburgh offers translation courses through each individual language department. There is also a certificate in American Sign Language program.

PUERTO RICO
Universidad de Puerto Rico, Translation Program, Rio Piedras, PR 00931
Phone: (787) 764-0000 ext. 2047 Fax: (787) 764-4065 Website: www.upr.edu
Contact: Yvette Torres

Offers an M.A. in translation and a postgraduate certificate of specialization in translation

RHODE ISLAND
University of Rhode Island, Kingston, RI 02881
Website: www.uri.edu

Offers translation courses. Languages taught: Spanish, French, Hebrew, Modern Greek, Arabic, Chinese, Japanese, Portuguese, Russian, Italian, and German.

SOUTH CAROLINA
Lander University, 320 Stanley Avenue, Greenwood, SC 29649
Phone: (864) 388-8265 Fax: (864) 388-8090 Website: www.lander.edu
Contact: Warren Westcott
Offers translation courses in Spanish.

University of Charleston, 66 George Street, Charleston, SC 29407
Phone: (803) 953-5718 Fax: (803) 953-6342 Website: www.cofc.edu
E-mail: benmaman@cofc.edu Contact: Virginia Benmaman

Offers a certificate program in legal interpreting (Spanish) and medical and health care interpreting (Spanish).

TEXAS
Texas Tech University, Lubbock, TX 79409
Website: www.ttu.edu E-mail: cmll@ttu.edu
Offers French translation courses.

University of Texas at Arlington, Department of Modern Languages, Box 19557, 701 Planetarium Place (formerly 701 College Street), Arlington, TX 76019-0557
Website: www.uta.edu
E-mail: rosenboom@uta.edu Contact: Becky Rosenboom

Offers courses in translation within individual language departments, and a certificate in translation studies for Spanish-English.

University of Texas at Austin, Spanish and Portuguese Department, Austin, TX 78712 Phone: (512) 471-4936 Fax: (512) 471-8073 Website: www.utexas.edu E-mail: fhensey@utexas.edu Contact: Professor Fritz Hensey or Madeline Sutherland-Meier (Department Head)

Austin's translation program started in fall 1996. The university offers selected courses as part of an interdepartmental M.A. in translation under the aegis of Foreign Language Education. Program emphasis is mostly on literary translation. There is also a general introductory course in consecutive Spanish-English interpreting.

University of Texas at El Paso, El Paso, TX 79968
Website: www.utep.edu
Offers undergraduate certificate in Spanish-English translation as a minor.

UTAH

Brigham Young University, 3190 JFSB, Provo, UT 84602-6705
Phone: (801) 422-2837 Website: www.byu.edu
E-mail: cherilee_devore@byu.edu
Offers a B.A. in Spanish translation.

VIRGINIA

George Mason University, Fairfax, VA 22030
Phone: (703) 993-1220 Fax: (703) 993-1245 Website: www.gmu.edu
E-mail: dgerdes@gmu.edu Contact: Dick Gerdes

Offers graduate certificate program in translation. The certificate program in translation provides professional training for students who wish to acquire proficiency in a specific language combination, either English-French or English-Spanish.

WASHINGTON

Translation and Interpretation Institute at Bellevue Community College, World Language Program, Continuing Education, 3000 Landerholm Circle SE, Seattle, WA 98007
Phone: (206) 938-3600 Website: www.conted.bcc.ctc.edu
E-mail: rsiegent@bcc.ct.edu Contact: Rene Siegenthaler

T&I Institute has been in operation since 1994, with translation programs in various languages according to demand. The program awards a certificate, with college credit also available. The course covers basic translation skills. Students must show a high proficiency in their working languages. T&I also awards a certificate in simultaneous and consecutive interpreting in Spanish, French, and Japanese. Courses at T&I include advanced workshops, training in ethics and business practices, and courses dealing with technology and terminology management.

University of Washington, 5001 25th Avenue NE, Seattle, WA 98195
Website: www.washington.edu
Offers translation courses.

WISCONSIN
NorthCentral Technical College, 1000 Schonfield Avenue, Wausau, WI 54401
Website: www.ntc.edu
Offers program for interpreters.

University of Wisconsin–Milwaukee, PO Box 413, Milwaukee, WI 53201
Phone: (414) 964-6931 Fax: (414) 229-2939 Website: www.uwm.edu
E-mail: srascon@uwm.edu or kscholz@uwm.edu Contact: Susan Rascon
    M.A. in foreign languages and literature—translation track and a graduate certificate program for translation. Offers translation of Spanish, French, and German.

CANADA

ALBERTA
University of Alberta, Modern Languages & Cultural Studies, 200 Arts, Edmonton, AB T6G 2E6, Canada
Phone: (780) 492-1187 Fax: (780) 492-9106 Website: www.ualberta.ca
E-mail: amalena@ualberta.ca Contact: Dr. Anne Malena
    Offers M.A. and Ph.D. in translation studies. MLCS Certificate in Translation Studies: academic certificate in French, German, and Spanish available as part of B.A. Prepares students to further their education and training in translation and translation studies.

BRITISH COLUMBIA
Langara College, Department of Modern Languages, 100 West 49th Avenue, Vancouver, BC V5Y 2Z6, Canada
Phone: (604) 323-5282 Fax: (604) 323-5555 Website: www.langara.ca
E-mail: dyada@langara.bc.ca Contact: Dorothy Yada, Department Chair
    Langara offers courses in French, Spanish, German, Japanese, and Chinese, but does not have a translation program.

NEW BRUNSWICK
Université de Moncton, Moncton, Nouveau Brunswick E1A 3E9, Canada
Phone: (506) 858-4214 Fax: (506) 858-4166 Website: www.umoncton.ca
E-mail: grognig@umoncton.ca
Offers B.A. in translation for English-French.

TRANSLATION COURSES AND PROGRAMS

ONTARIO

Laurentian University, Department of French Studies and Translation, 935 Ramsey Lake Road, Sudbury, Ontario P3E 2C6, Canada
Phone: (705) 675-1151 Fax: (705) 675-4885 Website: www.laurentian.ca/www .francais
E-mail: bdubeprevost@nickel.laurentian.ca Contact: Ronald Henry, Chairman
The English-French translation program is thirty-one years old. Degree offered is bachelor of science in languages (B.S.L.). Applicants must have solid background in English and French, and take a writing competence test in both languages. The program covers general, business-commercial, scientific, and technical translation. Simultaneous and consecutive interpretation are also taught.

University of Ottawa School of Translation and Interpretation, PO Box 540, Station A, Ottawa, Ontario K1N 6N5
Website: www.uottawa.ca Contact: Dr. Annie Brisset
Offers B.A. in French-English and French-Spanish-English translation. It also has programs for M.A. in translation and a Ph.D. in translation studies.

QUEBEC

Université de Montréal, C.P. 6128, Succ. "Centre-Ville," Montréal, QC H3C 317, Canada
Phone: (514) 343-6024 Fax: (514) 343-2284 Website: www.umontreal.ca
E-mail: gilles.belanger@umontreal.ca Contact: Gilles Belanger
B.A. and M.A. in English-French translation. Areas covered are technical, commercial, legal, medical, and literary.

Université Laval, 2289 Pavillon De Koninck, Cité Universitaire, Québec, QC G1K 7P4, Canada
Phone: (418) 656-2131 ext. 700 Fax: (418) 656-2622 Website: www.ulaval.ca
E-mail: alan.manning@lli.ulaval.ca Contact: Dr. Alan Manning
Offers B.A., M.A., and graduate diploma in translation studies for French-English-Spanish. Covers literary, legal, medical, sci-tech, economic, sociological, and administrative translation.

Translator Organizations

AMERICAN TRANSLATORS ASSOCIATION (ATA) CHAPTERS AND OTHER GROUPS
The ATA is the main organization of American translators.

ATA Chapters
Atlanta Association of Interpreters and Translators (AAIT)
RosaBurkard@aait.org http://www.aait.org
Carolina Association of Translators and Interpreters (CATI)
catiadmin@catiweb.org http://www.catiweb.org
Delaware Valley Translators Association (DVTA)
contactDVTA@cs.com http://www.dvta.org
Michigan Translators/Interpreters Network (MiTiN)
info@mitinweb.org http://www.mitinweb.org
Mid-America Chapter of ATA (MICATA)
translate@kc.rr.com http://www.ata-micata.org
Midwest Association of Translators and Interpreters (MATI)
MATIemail@matiata.org http://www.matiata.org
National Capital Area Chapter of ATA (NCATA)
president@ncaa.org http://www.ncata.org
New York Circle of Translators (NYCT)
president@nyctranslators.org http://www.nyctranslators.org
Northeast Ohio Translators Association (NOTA)
pres@ohiotranslators.org http://www.notatranslators.org
Northern California Translators Association (NCTA)
ncta@ncta.org http://www.ncta.org
Northwest Translators and Interpreters Society (NOTIS)
info@notisnet.org http://www.notisnet.org
Upper Midwest Translators and Interpreters Association (UMTIA)
tara@visi.com http://www.umtia.com

ATA Affiliated Groups
Austin Area Translators and Interpreters Association (AATIA)
president@aatia.org http://www.aatia.org

Houston Interpreters and Translators Association (HITA)
steven@techlanguage.com http://www.hitagroup.org
Iowa Interpreters and Translators Association (IITA)
info@iitanet.org http://www.iitanet.org
New Mexico Translators and Interpreters Association (NMTIA)
lopezfam@cybermesa.com http://www.cybermesa.com/~nmtia
Tennessee Association of Professional Interpreters and Translators (TAPIT)
info@tapit.org http://www.tapit.org
Utah Translators and Interpreters Association (UTIA)
katyab@xmission.com

Other Groups
American Literary Translators Association (ALTA)
lindy.jolly@utdallas.org http://www.literarytranslators.org
American Medical Writers Association (AMWA)
amwa@amwa.org http://www.amwa.org
Arizona Court Interpreters Association (ACIA)
quantum45@juno.com http://www.aciaonline.org
Association of Language Companies (ALC)
info@alcus.org http://www.alcus.org
Association of Translators and Interpreters in the San Diego Area (ATISDA)
abenzo@ucsd.edu http://www.atisda.org
California Court Interpreters Association (CCIA)
ccia2006@aol.com http://www.ccia.org
Chicago Area Translators and Interpreters Association (CHICATA) info@
chicata.org http://www.chicata.org
Colorado Translators Association (CTA)
t.young@nitaonline.org
Delaware Translators' Network (DTN)
levinx@cs.com
El Paso Interpreters and Translators Association (EPITA)
margaritamijo@gmail.com http://www.metroplexepita.org
Fédération internationale des traducteurs/International Federation of Translators (FIT) (ATA is affiliated with FIT)
secretariat@fit-ift.org http://www.fit-ift.org
International Medical Interpreters Association (IMIA)
imiaweb@gmail.com http://www.imiaweb.org
Medical Interpreters Network of Georgia (MING)
michael@mingweb.org http://www.mingweb.org
Metroplex Interpreters and Translators Association (MITA)
http://www.dfw-mita.com
National Association of Judiciary Interpreters and Translators (NAJIT) head-
quarters@najit.org http://www.najit.org

National Council on Interpreting in Health Care (NCIHC)
info@ncihc.org http://www.ncihc.org
Nevada Interpreters and Translators Association (NITA)
http://www.nitaonline.org
New England Translators Association (NETA)
info@netaweb.org http://www.netaweb.org
Society for Technical Communication (STC)
stc@stc.org http://www.stc.org
The Translators and Interpreters Guild (TTIG)
info@ttig.org http://www.ttig.org
Washington State Court Interpreters and Translators Society (WITS)
http://www.witsnet.org

INTERNATIONAL FEDERATION OF TRANSLATORS (FIT)

FIT (Fédération internationale des traducteurs) is the worldwide federation of translator associations.

Member associations:

EUROPE

Austria

Osterreichischer Ubersetzer-und Dolmetscherverband "Universitas," Gymnasiumstrasse 50, A-1190 Wien
Phone: +43 1-368 60 60 Fax: +43 1-368 60 08 Website: www.universitas.org
Osterreichischer Verband der Gerichtsdolmetscher, Postfach 14, A-1016 Wien
Phone: +43 1 479 65 81 Fax: +43 1 478 37 23 Website: www.gerichtsdolmetscher.at
Ubersetzergemeinschaft im Literaturhaus, Interessengemeinschaft von Ubersetzern literarischer und wissenschaftlicher Werke, Literaturhaus, Seidengasse 13, A-1070 Wien
Phone: +43 1-526 20 44 18 Fax: +43 1-526 20 44 30 Website: www.translators.at

Belgium

Chambre belge des traducteurs, interprètes et philologues [Belgische Kamer van Vertalers, Tolken en Filologen], Secrétariat: rue Montoyer, 24, bte 12, B-1000 Bruxelles
Phone: +32 2-513 09 15 Fax: +32 2-513 09 15 Website: www.translators.be

Croatia

Hrvatsko Drustvo Znanstvenih i Tehnickih Prevoditelja (HDZTP) [Croatian Association of Scientific and Technical Translators], Amruševa 19/II, 10000 Zagreb
Phone: +385 1-49 22 730 Fax: +385 1-48 17 658

Cyprus
Pancyprian Union of Graduate Translators and Interpreters, 51A Riga Fereou
Street, CY-3091 Limassol
Phone: +357 5-35 90 51 Fax: +357 5-37 87 81

Czech Republic
**Jednota tlumočniku a prekladatelu (JTP) [Union des interpretes et tra-
ducteurs],** Senovazne namestR 23 CZ-110 00 Praha 1
Phone: +420 2-24 14 25 17 Fax: +420 2-24 14 23 12 Website: www.jtpunion.org

Denmark
**Dansk Translatørforbund [Danish Association of State-Authorized
Translators and Interpreters],** Nørre Farimagsgade 35, DK-1364 København
K Website: www.dtfb.dk
**Forbundet Kommunikation og Sprog [The Union of Communication and
Language Professionals],** Skindergade 45-47, Postboks 2246, DK-1019
København K
Phone: +45-33 91 98 00 Fax: +45-33 91 68 18 Website: www.kommunikationog
sprog.dk
Translatørforeningen-The Association of Danish Authorized Translators,
Skindergade 45-47 3. Sal, DK-1159 København K
Phone: +45-33 11 84 14 Fax: +45-33 11 84 15 Website: www.translatorforeningen.dk

Finland
**Suomen kaantajien tulkkien liitto (SKTL) [Finnish Association of Translators
and Interpreters],** Meritullinkatu 33 A, FI-00170 Helsinki
Phone: +358 9-44 59 27 Fax: +358 9-44 59 37 Website: www.sktl.net

France
Société française des traducteurs (SFT) a/s Certex, 22, rue de la Pépinière,
F-75008 Paris
Phone: +33-01 42 93 99 96 Fax: +33-01 45 22 33 55 Website: www.sft.fr
**Union nationale des experts traducteurs-interpretes pres les cours d'appel
(UNETICA),** att.: María Lebret-Sánchez 12, rue de Volembert, F-95100 Argenteuil
Phone: +33 1 39 80 97 66 Fax: +33 1 39 98 72 18 Website: www.unetica.fr

Germany
Assoziierte Dolmetscher und Ubersetzer in Norddeutschland e.V. (ADU),
Wendenstrasse 435, D-20537 Hamburg
Phone: +49 40-219 10 01 Fax: +49 40-219 10 03 Website: www.adue-nord.de
Contact: Terence Oliver
**ATICOM e.V., Fachverband der Berufsubersetzer und Berufsdolmetscher
e.V.,** Geschäftsstelle: Winzermarkstr. 89, D-45529 Hattingen

Phone +49 23-24 59 35 99 Fax +49 23-24 68 10 03 Website: www.aticom.de
Contact: Reiner Heard
Bundesverband der Dolmetscher und Übersetzer e. V. (BDÜ), Bundesge-
schäftsstelle, Kurfurstendamn 170, D-10707 Berlin
Phone: +49 30-88 71 28 30 Fax: +49 30-88 71 28 40 Website: www.bdue.de
Contact: Peter Krakenwitzer
Verband der Übersetzer und Dolmetscher Berlin e.V. (VÜD), Weydingerstrasse
14-16, Raum 316, 10178 Berlin
Phone: +49 30 28096722 Fax: +49 30 28096723 Website: www.vued.de
Contact: Natália Rózsa

Greece
Panhellenic Association of Translators, Komninon 8 Street, GR-54624
Thessaloniki
Phone: +30 2310 266 308 or +30 2310 268 542 Fax: +30 2310 266 010 Website:
www.pem.gr
Societe hellenique des traducteurs de littérature (EEML), Tsakona 7, Paleo
Psychiko, GR-15452 Athens
Phone: +30 1-671 74 66 Fax: +30 1-671 74 66

Ireland
Irish Translators' and Interpreters' Association, Irish Writers' Centre, 19
Parnell Square, Dublin 1
Phone: +353 1-872 13 02 Fax: +353 1-872 62 82 Website: www.translatorsassocia
tion.ie
Contact: Miriam Lee

Italy
Associazione Italiana Traduttori ed Interpreti (AITI), Viale delle Milizie 9,
I-00192 Roma
Phone: +39 347 24 04 45 31 Fax: +39 06 233 295 502 Website: www.aiti.org

Netherlands
Dutch Court Interpretes and Legal Translators Association, Parijslaan 69,
Nl-5627 TW Eindhoven
Phone: +31 412 646 694 Fax: +31 412 646 694 Website: www.sigv-vereniging.nl
Nederlands Genootschap van Tolken en Vertalers (NGTV), Postbus 77, 2300
AB Leiden
Phone: 0031 71 524 9360 Fax: 0031 71 524 9360 Website: www.ngtv.nl

Norway
Norsk Faglitteraer Forfatter- og Oversetterforening, Uranienborgvn 2, N-0258
Oslo

Phone: +47-22 12 11 40 Fax: +47-22 12 11 50 Website: www.nffo.no
Norsk Oversetterforening (NO), Postboks 579, Sentrum, N-0105 Oslo 1
Phone: +47-22 47 80 90 Fax: +47-22 42 03 56 Website: www.oversetterforeninen.no
Statsautoriserte Translatorers Forening (STF), Springarstien 17, N-4021
Stavanger
Phone: +47-51 54 21 90 Fax: +47-51 54 14 27 Website: www.statsaut-translator.no

Poland
Polish Society of Sworn and Specialised Translators PO Box 23, PL-00967
Warszawa 86
Phone: +48 22 839 4952 Fax: +48 22 839 4952 Website: www.tepis.org.pl

Russia
Union of Translators of Russia (UTR), 101B, b.1, Pr. Mira, RU-129085, Moscow
MIL
Phone: 7-495-616-3980 Fax: 7-495-958-1076

Serbia
Association of Literary Translators of Serbia, Francuska 7, 11000 Belgrade
Phone: +381 011 626 081 Fax: +381 011 626 278

Slovakia
APTOS—Slovenská Spolo nost Prekladateľov Odbornej Literatury, Laurinská
2, SK-80508 Bratislava
Phone/Fax: +421 7-54 43 12 94 Website: www.sspol.sk

Slovenia
Association of Scientific and Technical Translators of Slovenia (DZTPS),
Petkovskovo nabrezje 57, SLO-1000 Ljubljana
Phone: +386 1-231 78 62 Fax: +386 1-232 01 31 Website: www.dztps.si

Spain
Asociación Colegial de Escritores de Cataluña (ACEC), Carrer Canuda no. 6,
6e, 08002 Barcelona
Phone: +34 93 318 87 48 Fax: +34 93 302 78 18
Website: www.acec-web.org
Asociación Espanola de Traductores, Correctores e Intérpretes (ASETRAD),
Gran Via, 71-2 planta, 28013 Madrid
Website: www.asetrad.org
**Asociación Profesional de Traductores, Correctores e Intérpretes de Lengua
Vasca [Euskal Itzultzaile, Zuzentzaile eta Interpretarien Elkartea (EIZIE)],**
Zemoria 25, E-20013 Donostia—San Sebastián
Phone: +34 943 277 111 Fax: +34 943 277 288 Website: www.eizie.org

Traductors i Interprets Associats Pro-Col.legi (TRIAC), Diputacio 239, 1r 2a C, E-08007 Barcelona
Phone: +34 93-487 70 33 Website: www.traductors.com

Sweden
Federation of Authorized Translators in Sweden (FAT), c/o Mr. Jan Runesten, Tegelbruksvägan 6, Se-17830 Ekero
Phone: +46 8 560 359 17 Website: www.eurofat.se
Contact: Jan Runesten
Swedish Association of Professional Translators (SFÖÖ), Secretariat: Box 1091, SE-269 21 Båstad
Phone: +46 4 31 755 00 Fax: +46 4 31 769 90 Website: www.sfoe.se
Contact: Anne Verbeke

Switzerland
Association suisse des traducteurs, terminologues et interprètes (ASTTI), Secretariat: Postgasse 17, CH-3011 Bern
Phone: +41 31 313 88 10 Fax: +41 31 313 88 99 Website: www.astti.ch
Contact: João Esteves Ferreira

Turkey
Çeviri Dernegi Association of Translators, Büyükdere cad. 93 Kat 5, TR-34387 Mecidiyekoy Şişli, Istanbul
Phone: +90 0212 212 02 40 Fax: +90 0212 211 08 15 Website: www.ceviridernegi.org

United Kingdom
Cymdeithas Cyfieithwyr Cymru—Association of Welsh Translators and Interpreters, Bryn Menai, Ffordd Caergybi, GB-Bangor, Gwynedd, LL57 2AJ
Phone: +44 1248 371 839 Fax: +44 1248 371 850 Website: ww.welshtranslator.org.uk
Institute of Translation and Interpreting, Fortuna House, South Fifth Street, GB-Milton Keynes, MK9 2EU
Phone: +44 1908 325 250 Fax: +44 1908 325 259 Website: www.iti.org.uk
The Translators' Association, 84 Drayton Gardens London SW10 9SB
Phone: +44 171-373 66 42 Fax: +44 171-373 57 68 Website: www.societyofauthors.net

NORTH AMERICA

Canada
Canadian Translators, Terminologists and Interpreters Council (CTTIC), 1 Nicholas Street, Suite 1402, Ottawa, ON K1N 7B7

Phone: (613) 562-0379 Fax: (613) 241-4098 Website: www.cttic.org
Literary Translators' Association of Canada (LTAC), SB 335 Concordia
University, 1455, boul. de Maisonneuve ouest Montréal, QC H3G 1M8
Phone: (514) 848-8702 Fax: (514) 848-4514 Website: www.attlc-ltac.org

Cuba
Cuban Association of Translators and Interpreters, Linea No. 507 esq.a D,
Vedado, C. de La Habana, Cuba

Guatemala
Asociación Guatemalteca de Intérpretes y Tradutores (AGIT), Att: Alcira
García-Vassaux 6a Avenida 14-21, Zona 9, Guatemala City, Guatemala
Central America
Phone: +502 2254-1114, +502 2289-5800 Fax: +502 2254-1114
Website: www.agitguatemala.org

Mexico
Organización Mexicana de Traductores Capítulo Occidente, Av. Vallarta 1525-
304, Col. Americana, Guadalajara, Jalisco 44100
Phone: (52-33) 3124 0236 Fax: (52-33) 3124 0237 Website: www.omt.org.mx

Panama
Asociación Panamena de Traductores e Intérpretes, Apartado 6-9006, El
Dorado, Republic of Panama

United States
American Literary Translators Association (ALTA), University of Texas at
Dallas, Box 830 688 Mail Station MC35, Richardson, TX 75083-0688
Phone: (972) 883-2093 Fax: (972) 883-6303 Website: www.literarytranslators.org
American Translators' Association (ATA), 225 Reinekers Lane, Suite 590
Alexandria, VA 22314
Phone: (703) 683-6100 Fax: (703) 683-6122 Website: www.atanet.org

SOUTH AMERICA

Argentina
Asociación Argentina de Traductores e Intérpretes, Malabia 2379, 14th Floor,
Apt. "A," CP1425EZG, Buenos Aires, Argentina
Website: www.aati.org.ar
Contact: María Cristina Pinto
Colegio de Traductores Publicos de la Ciudad de Buenos Aires (CTPBA),
Callao 289—4 Piso, 1022 Buenos Aires

Phone/fax: +54 1-371 86 16 or: +54 1-372 79 61 Website: www.traductores.org.ar
Contact: Graciela Steinberg

Brazil

Sindicato Nacional dos Tradutores (SINTRA), Rua da Quitanda 194 / Salas 1206/1207, Centro—Rio de Janeiro—RJ CEP: 20.091-000
Phone: +55 21-22 53 16 16 Fax: +55 21-22 63 60 89 Website: www.sintra.ong.org

Chile

Colegio de Traductores e Intérpretes de Chile AG (COTICH), Luis Thayer Ojeda 95, Of. 207, Providencia, Santiago 9
Phone: +56 2-251 2887 Website: www.cotich.cl

Costa Rica

Asociación Costarricense de Traductores e Intérpretes Profesionales (ACOTIP), Apdo. 225-2050, San Pedro, San José

Peru

Asociación de Traductores Profesionales del Peru (ATPP), Casilla Postal 18-0251, Lima 18
Website: www.atpp.org.pe
Colegio de Traductores del Peru, Boulevard Tarata 269, Of. 207, Miraflores, Lima 18
Phone: (51-1) 444-9084 Fax: (51-1) 444-9084
Website: www.colegiodetraductores.org.pe

Uruguay

Colegio de Traductores Públicos del Uruguay, Colonia 892, Piso 6 esc. 604, 11.100 Montevideo
Phone/Fax: +598 2-903 31 30 Website: www.colegiotraductores.org.uy

Venezuela

Colegio Nacional de Traductores e Intérpretes, Apartado Postal 52108, Sabana Grande, Colinas de Bello Monte, VE-Caracas 1050A
Website: www.conalti.org

AFRICA

Congo

Association de traducteurs et intérpretes professionels du Congo (ATIPCO)
Phone: 243 990111107, 243 815014540, 243 998003647

Egypt
Egyptian Translators Association (EGYTA), Cairo
Phone: 202 26742627 Fax: 202 26742628

Ethiopia
National Association of Translators and Interpreters of Ethiopia (NATIE),
PO Box 1542, Addis Ababa
Phone: 251 111 220760

Morocco
École supérieure ROI FAHD de traduction, Université Abdelmalek Essâdi,
Route du Charf, B.P. 410, Tanger

South Africa
South African Translators' Institute (SATI), PO Box 1710, Rivona, 2128
Phone: +27 11-803 26 81 Fax: +27 11-803 26 81 Website: www.translators.org.za

ASIA

China
**Science and Technology Translators' Association of the Chinese Academy of
Sciences,** Bureau of International Cooperation, 52 Sanlihe Road, Beijing 100864
Phone: +86-10-821 33 44, poste 2422 Fax: +86-10-851 10 95 Website: www
.sttacas.org
Contact: Juliang Qiu
Translators' Association of China, Wai Wen Building, 24 Baiwanzhuang Street,
Beijing 10037
Phone: +86-10-6899 5897 Fax: +86-10-6832 6681
Contact: Youyi Huang Website: www.tac-online.org.cn

Hong Kong
Hong Kong Translation Society Ltd., PO Box 20186, Hennessy Road Post Office
Phone: +852-816 82 18 Fax: +852-855 71 09 Website: www.hkts.org.hk

India
Indian Translators Association, K-5/B, Lower Ground Floor, Kalkaji, New
Delhi-110019
Phone: +91-11-26291676 Fax: +91-11-41675530 Website: www.itaindia.org

Indonesia
Association of Indonesian Translators Himpunan Penerjemah Indonesia, c/o
Pusat Penerjemahan FIB UI, Jalan Salemba Raya 4, Jakarta 10430
Phone: +62 21 319 021 12 Fax: +62 21 315 59 41 Website: www.wartahpi.org

Iran

Association of Iranian Translators and Interpreters, PO Box 17665-315, Tehran, Iran

Iraq

Iraqi Translators' Association, Al-Joboory Sons Building, 2nd Floor, Opposite rear gate of Al-Mustansiriya University, Palestine Street, Baghdad
Phone: 07902375609

Israel

Israel Translators' Association POB 16173, Tel Aviv 61161
Website: www.ita.org.il

Japan

Japan Society of Translators (JST), Surugadai-Yagi-Bldg. 4F, Kanda Ogawamachi 3-8-5, Chiyodaku, Tokyo 101-0052
Phone: Fax: +81 3 5317 0578 Website: www.japan-s-translators.org

Jordan

Jordanian Translators' Association, c/o Dr. Abdulla Shunnaq, PO Box 4990, Yarmouk University, 211—63 Irbid Fax: +962-2-727 78 00

Lebanon

École de traducteurs et d'interprétes de Beyrouth (ETIB), Rue de Damas, B.P. 17-5208, Mar Mikkael, Beyrouth 1104 2020
Phone: +961 1 421 000 ext. 5512
Website: www.etib.usj.edu.lb
Université de Balamand, Deir El Balamand, El Koura, B.P. 100, Tripoli
Phone: +961-6-83 02 50 Fax: +961-6-93 02 78 Website: www.balamand.edu.lb
Contact: Georges Nahas

South Korea

Korean Society of Translators (KST), 2F. Shinmunro Building, 238 Shinmunro 1-ga, Jongro-gu, Seoul 110-061
Phone: +82-2-725 0506 Fax: +82-2-725 1266 Website: www.kstinc.or.kr
Contact: Il-Jun Cho

Turkey

Çeviri Dernegi Translation Association, Sehit muhtar cad. Tekyaz Apt. No: 2/2, Taksim-Istanbul
Phone: 0212 250 85 78 Fax: 0212 253 98 52 Website: www.ceviridernegi.org

United Arab Emirates
Faculty of Foreign Language, Translation and Mass Communication, Ajman
University of Science and Technology, PO Box 346, Ajman
Phone: +971-6-746 66 66 ext. 442 Website: www.ajman.ac.ae
Contact: Tarwat Al-Sakran

OCEANIA

Australia
Australian Institute of Interpreters and Translators (AUSIT), PO Box 1070,
Blackburn North, VIC 3130
Phone/Fax: +61 3-98 77 43 69 Website: www.ausit.org

New Zealand
New Zealand Society of Translators and Interpreters (NZSTI) [Te Ropu
Kaiwhakamaori a-waha, a-tuhi o Aotearoa], PO Box 109-677, Newmarket,
Auckland
Phone: +64 9 529 11 38 Fax: +64 9 529 11 38 Website: www.nzsti.org

Translator Accreditation

The American Translators Association (ATA) offers accreditation in twenty-three language pairs: from English into Dutch, Finnish, French, German, Hungarian, Italian, Japanese, Polish, Portuguese, Russian, and Spanish, and from those languages (plus Arabic) into English. Once you have started to translate in any of these languages, I strongly urge you to look into ATA accreditation. While it is not a must, it is certainly prestigious and adds professional credibility to your work.

The ATA is the main organization of translators in the United States. During my twenty years of association with this organization, I have seen it double and triple its membership to some 10,000 translators. Its annual conference and its local chapter meetings provide a wonderful opportunity for meeting colleagues and learning more about the world of translation. Its publications are very valuable tools for translators, and its monthly magazine, *The ATA Chronicle*, is a superb professional publication.

For more information about ATA accreditation, call or write to:
ATA Headquarters
225 Reinekers Lane, Suite 590
Alexandria, VA 22314
Phone: (703) 683-6100
Fax: (703) 683-6122
This information is also accessible at their website: www.atanet.org.

Professional Periodicals for Translators

For a field as rich and varied as translation, the number of professional periodicals for translators available is extremely sparse. The following is a list of such publications.

Available from the American Translators Association (ATA)
225 Reinekers Lane, Suite 590, Alexandria, VA 22314
Phone: (703) 683-6100 Fax: (703) 683-6122 E-mail: ata@atanet.org

ATA Chronicle
The best periodical publication for translators in the United States. Monthly, with one issue for November–December.
ATA members: free. Nonmembers: U.S. $50; Canada and Mexico $75; other $95.

ATA Proceedings
A yearly publication containing papers presented at the annual ATA conference. A rich source of information in many fields of translation.
ATA members: free at the ATA conference. Nonmembers: $50.

ATA Source
Newsletter of the literary division of the ATA.
25 Frederick Street, Montclair, NJ 07042

Sci-Tech Translation Journal
Publication of the Science and Technology Division of the ATA.
c/o A-B Typesetting, 806 Main Street, Poughkeepsie, NY 12603

From the ATA Chapters
Apuntes
Leticia Molinero, 237 Lafayette Street, #2W, New York, NY 10012; E-mail: 1053.14462@compuserve.com
Published by the Spanish Group of the New York Circle of Translators.

CATI Quarterly
PO Box 482, Cary, NC 27512-0482; Phone: (919) 851-1901
Published by the Carolina Association of Translators and Interpreters.

Gotham Translator
PO Box 4051, Grand Central Station, New York, NY 10163; Phone: (212) 912-9070
Published by the New York Circle of Translators.

NCTA Translorial
PO Box 14015, Berkeley, CA 94712-5015; Phone: (510) 845-8712.
Published by the Northern California Translators Association.

NOTIS Newsletter
PO Box 25301, Seattle, WA 98125-2201; Phone: (206) 382-5642
Published by the Northwest Translators and Interpreters Society.

Additional Publications
Translation Review
ALTA (American Literary Translators Association)
University of Texas, PO Box 830688, Richardson, TX 75083
Quarterly.

MT News International
AMTA (Association for Machine Translation in the Americas), 655 15th Street
NW, Suite 310, Washington, DC 20005

Polyglot
Newsletter of CCIA (California Court Interpreters Association), 1722 J Street,
Suite 20, Sacramento, CA 95814

Babel
John Benjamins Publishing Company, PO Box 27519, Philadelphia, PA 19118-
0519
International journal of translation.

Language Today
Language Publications Limited, 128 Derby Road, Long Eaton, Nottingham NG10
4ER, UK
Internet magazine accessible at www.logos.it/language_today. Also available in
hardcopy print version.

PROFESSIONAL PERIODICALS FOR TRANSLATORS

Proteus
Quarterly newsletter of NAJIT (National Association of Judiciary Interpreters and Translators), c/o D. Orrantia, John Jay College, 445 West 59th Street, New York, NY 10019

Multilingual Communications and Computing
Multilingual Computing Inc., 319 North First Avenue, Sandpoint, ID 83864; Phone: (208) 263-8178
A journal on the latest foreign-language technology.

Target
John Benjamins Publishing Company, PO Box 27519, Philadelphia, PA 19118-0519
International Journal of Translation Studies.

Language International
John Benjamins Publishing Company, PO Box 27519, Philadelphia, PA 19118-0519
Magazine for language professionals.

Terminology
John Benjamins Publishing Company, PO Box 27519, Philadelphia, PA 19118-0519
International journal of theoretical and applied issues in specialized communication.

Bibliography

ATA Proceedings. Published annually by the American Translators Association, Alexandria, VA.

ATA Scholarly Monographs

Bowen, David, and Margareta Bowen, eds. *Interpreting: Yesterday, Today and Tomorrow.* Binghamton: SUNY, 1990.

Gaddis Rose, Marilyn, ed. *Translation Excellence.* Philadelphia: John Benjamins, 2008.

Hammond, Deanna L., ed. *Professional Issues in Translation and Interpretation.* Philadelphia: John Benjamins, 1994.

Krawutschke, Peter, ed. *Translator and Interpreter Training and Foreign Language Pedagogy.* Binghamton: SUNY, 1989.

Larson, Mildred, ed. *Translation: Theory and Practice, Tension and Interdependence.* Philadelphia: John Benjamins, 2008.

Vasconcellos, Muriel, ed. *Technology as Translation Strategy.* Philadelphia: John Benjamins, 1995.

Books

Baker, Mona. *In Other Words: A Coursebook in Translation.* New York: Routledge, 1992.

Bassnett, Susan. *Translation Studies.* New York: Routledge, 1991.

Bell, Roger T. *Translation and Translating: Theory and Practice.* Burnt Mill, Harlow: Longman, 1991.

Bierman, Bernard. *A Translator-Warrior Speaks: A Personal History of the ATA.* Nyack, NY: IRM Corp., 1987.

Biguenet, John, and Rainer Schulte, eds. *The Craft of Translation.* Chicago: University of Chicago Press, 1989.

Child, Jack. *An Introduction to Spanish Translation*. Lanham, MD: University Press of America, 1992.

De Jongh, Elena M. *An Introduction to Court Interpreting: Theory and Practice*. Lanham, MD: University Press of America, 1992.

Delisle, Jean, and Judith Woodsworth, eds. *Translators through History*. Philadelphia: John Benjamins, 1995.

Gambier, Yves, Daniel Gile, and Christopher Taylor, eds. *Conference Interpreting: Current Trends in Research*. Amsterdam/Philadelphia: John Benjamins, 1997.

Gile, David. *Basic Concepts and Models for Interpreter and Translator Training*. Amsterdam: John Benjamins, 1995.

Glenn, John. *Glenn's Guide to Translation Agencies*. San Francisco, CA: John Glenn, 1997.

Gonzalez, Victoria Vasquez, and Holly Mikkelson. *Fundamentals of Court Interpretation: Theory, Policy and Practice*. Durham, NC: Carolina Academic Press, 1991.

Hammond, Deanna, ed. *Professional Issues for Translators and Interpreters*. Philadelphia: John Benjamins, 1995.

Lambert, Sylvie, and Barbara Moser-Mercer. *Bridging the Gap (Empirical Research in Simultaneous Interpretation)*. Philadelphia: John Benjamins, 1994.

Larson, Mildred. *Meaning-Based Translation*. Lanham, MD: University Press of America, 1984.

Newmark, Peter. *Approaches to Translation*. Bristol, PA: Multilingual Matters, 1993.

———. *Paragraphs on Translation*. Bristol, PA: Multilingual Matters, 1993.

Phillips, Michael, and Salli Raspberry. *Marketing without Advertising*. Berkeley, CA: Nolo Press, 1990.

Rubinstein, Marv. *21st Century American English Compendium*. Rockville, MD: Schreiber Publishing, 2000.

Samuelsson-Brown, Geoffrey. *A Practical Guide for Translators*. Bristol, PA: Multilingual Matters, 1993.

Seleskovitch, Danica. *Interpreting for International Conferences*. Washington, DC: Pen and Booth, 1978.

Snell-Hornby, Mary. *Translation Studies: An Integrated Approach*. Amsterdam/Philadelphia: John Benjamins, 1988.

Sofer, Morry. *Guide for Translators*. Rockville, MD: Schreiber Publishing, 1995.

Toury, Gideon. *Descriptive Translation Studies—and Beyond*. Philadelphia: John Benjamins, 1995.

Whitmeyer, Claude, Salli Raspberry, and Michael Phillips. *Running a One-Person Business*. Berkeley, CA: Ten Speed Press, 1989.

Wright, Sue Ellen, and Leland Wright. *Scientific and Technical Translation*. Philadelphia: John Benjamins, 1993.

Index

Adelard of Bath, 13
Alfred the Great, 10
American Translators Association
(ATA): accreditation, 329; chapters,
cooperating, local groups, 317; liability
insurance through, 84; networking via,
90; periodicals, 331
Arabic: demand for translation in,
39; dictionaries, 114; in history of
translation, 11; problems in translating,
39; software in, 175
Ataturk, Kemal, 41

Bhagavad Gita, 12
Bible: in history of translation, 8–11

Charlemagne, 10
Chinese: demand for translation in,
37; dictionaries, 120; problems in
translating, 37; software in, 175
Columbus, 13
Commerce Business Daily: as source of
translation work, 179, 257
computers: basic software for translators,
53; the Internet, 57; language software
sources, 175; in machine translation, 54;
and terminology management, 64; as
translation area, 71

dictation: as translation aid, 19, 49
Dosho, 12

Ebla, 7
embassies: as source of translation work, 85

French: ATA accreditation in, 329; demand
for translation in, 33; dictionaries, 129;
problems in translating, 33; software
in, 175

Gallaudet, 100
Gandhi, Mahatma, 12
Gerard of Cremona, 13
German: ATA accreditation in, 329;
demand for translation in, 32;
dictionaries, 133; in history of
translation, 10, 13; problems in
translating, 32; software in, 175
government agencies: addresses for
individual agencies, 257; as source of
translation work, 88
Gujarati, 12

Hebrew: ATA accreditation in, 329;
dictionaries, 140; in history of
translation, 7; problems in translating,
40; software in, 175; twentieth-century
revival of, 40
Hemingway, Ernest, 11
Herman the German, 13
Hsuan-tsang, 12
Hunayn ibn Ishaq, 12

Ibn Tibbon, 13
interpretation, oral: confusion with
translation, 100; consecutive, 98; escort,
98; general categories of, 97; over-the-
phone, 98; pros and cons of, 100; sight